The Optina Elders Series

ELDER SEBASTIAN OF OPTINA

ELDER SEBASTIAN OF OPTINA AND KARAGANDA

ELDER SEBASTIAN
of Optina

by
TATIANA V. TORSTENSEN

Translated by David Koubek

ST. HERMAN OF ALASKA BROTHERHOOD
1999

Front cover: Portrait of St. Sebastian, preserved in the parish church founded by him, which is dedicated to the Nativity of the Most Holy Theotokos.

FIRST ENGLISH EDITION

Translated from the Russian edition: *Karagandinski Starets Prepodobny Sevastian [The Karaganda Elder, St. Sebastian],* compiled by Vera Koroleva and published by Pravoslavny Palomnik [Orthodox Pilgrim], Moscow, 1997, as well as from various original Russian sources.

Library of Congress Cataloging in Publication Data:

Tatiana V. Torstensen
        Elder Sebastian of Optina.
        Translated from the Russian.

Library of Congress Catalogue Card Number: 98-87947
ISBN: 0-938635-62-X

Dedicated to the memory of
a distant disciple of Optina,

ARCHIMANDRITE MITROPHAN
(MANUILOV †1986)

on the eve of the 100th anniversary
of his birth.

Optina Monastery, rising from the ashes of communist persecution.
Photograph taken in the late 1980s.

CONTENTS

Archimandrite Mitrophan (Manuilov).
Photo taken at the St. Tikhon Orphanage in San
Francisco, founded by St. John (Maximovitch).

INTRODUCTION

A Distant Disciple

> *...You bear within your heart the Cross of the*
> *Lord and co-suffer with Him in His love for*
> *sinners. Now this sanctity, which is within*
> *your loving heart, will be visible to all....*
> —Basil Kireyevsky, on
> Elder Macarius of Optina

1. FATHER MITROPHAN

WE DEDICATE this volume of the *Optina Elders Series* on St. Sebastian of Optina and Karaganda to the memory of a humble, distant Optina disciple, Father Archimandrite Mitrophan Manuilov (1900-1986), who knew Fr. Sebastian at the time of the shameful liquidation of Optina by the God-hating communists. Fr. Mitrophan had known many saints and confessors in much-suffering Russia under communist rule, which made him a significant witness of twentieth-century saints.

In his native Voronezh he had been in close contact with living saints who raised him in traditional old Orthodoxy, alien to many foreign tendencies. He was the son of a priest-martyr and the spiritual son of an outstanding holy pastor, Fr. Mitrophan Buchnev, who in turn was a disciple of Optina Elders Anatole II and Nektary. Fr. Mitrophan Buchnev's daughter Nadezhda became his loving wife. Elder Nektary liked to call her his "favorite spiritual daughter." It was just after her repose that Fr. Mitrophan met Archbishop John Maximovitch, and our Fr. Mitrophan at once recognized in him the power of a blessed man, a Saint in the spirit of genuine foolishness-for-Christ's-sake. In Voronezh there had lived another Fool-for-Christ's-sake, Blessed Theoktista Mikhailovna. Fr. Mitrophan was close to her, and she saved his life several times through her gift of clairvoyance. Thanks to her prayers he was spared exile and death in the soviet labor camps.

After World War II and his emigration to the West where he, still a layman, worked in refugee camps, he met Blessed Archbishop John, who found in him a man close to his own heart. Archbishop John offered to ordain him, that he might serve God. Fr. Mitrophan became his cleric and his defender when some clergymen having no experience with holy people persecuted Blessed Archbishop John, seeing him merely as an oddity. Fr. Mitrophan related many incidents to us, from which it is obvious how genuine Archbishop John was in his behavior as a saint in the full tradition of Holy Russia.

We saw Fr. Mitrophan's fervency, and we were inspired by his burning love for the truth. This was what we wanted, for it made us closer to Optina. Fr. Mitrophan knew that Optina spirit well and knew its people. When Optina had already been closed he walked many miles to see Elder Nektary, whose cell-attendant, the future Elder Sebastian, lived close by.

Fr. Mitrophan in turn became close to us. He willed us all his vestments left from St. John, his complete set of service books, his rare patristic books which he was gathering from the Holy Land and relics of saints for our monastery.

After the repose of St. John Fr. Mitrophan's health failed rapidly, and he eventually retired to a monastery in New York, where he wanted to be tonsured into the great schema, for which he had long been ready and for which he had prepared the necessary schema robes. But he was denied his last request and died in a hospital bed, beside his beloved icon of the Theotokos

"Unexpected Joy." Before this icon, during his last years, a Moleben with an Akathist was daily served. He died on January 1/14, the Feast of Christ's Circumcision, in 1986.

We remember him vividly as a fervent soul, abhorring insensitivity, keeping constant vigil and battling the passions. But first of all he was a loving pastor, molded in the Optina spirit from his younger days by his father-in-law, Archpriest Mitrophan, who died in 1938 as a martyr, exiled to cold Siberia, and whose biography he authored under an assumed name.

In introducing this full biography of St. Sebastian of Optina and Karaganda, it is good to remember humble, now-forgotten carriers of the Optina spirit such as Fr. Mitrophan. Being far away in distant lands, facing new, spiritually ignorant generations while weeping and lamenting over the loss of the Paradise of Optina, they nevertheless, through stubborn love of sanctity, managed to transmit the immortal values of genuine monasticism and cause an interest in Orthodoxy that "discovers" and turns to Elders such as St. Sebastian and glorifies their eternal memory.

2. BISHOP NEKTARY

While in San Francisco, Fr. Mitrophan was in close contact with another Optina disciple, Bishop Nektary (Kontzevitch), who also knew Fr. Sebastian.

In remembering his days in Optina Monastery, Bishop Nektary would often describe the Optina brethren in a very warm, often humorous fashion, lovingly accentuating peculiarites and relating descriptive anecdotes from the lives of these monks on the eve of Optina's closure and soon thereafter. His monastic impressions were vivid and endearing, and would often evoke contrition of heart both in him and in his listeners.

St. Nektary of Optina had two cell-attendants, Peter and Sebastian. The first was a simpleton, zealous yet clumsy. He was a man of absolute obedience, to the point that he did not think for himself, and the recollection of his bumbling devotedness would bring a smile to Bishop Nektary's face and evoke endearing comments.

The other disciple, Sebastian, was also zealous and not yet fully matured then. But being of the "intellectual" type, he was clumsy in a different way than Peter—he still had some spiritual pretensions and would occasionally make ungainly "spiritual comments." Bishop Nektary recalled how once Elder Nektary was, for some reason, blessing the room with holy water. As he proceeded to bless the corners of the room, a black cat was dozing on the windowsill. The Elder did not fail to sprinkle holy water on the cat, at which the cat awoke, jumped down from the windowsill and ran away. The young Fr. Sebastian then ventured to make a "spiritual comment" to the nearby women: "See, there was a devil in that cat—and the Elder chased the devil out of it!" Hearing this, the Elder turned around and humbled Fr. Sebastian down with a loving smile, as if to say, "Where did you get *that* idea from?" The simple folk there chuckled.

After the closure of Optina, Fr. Sebastian rapidly matured into a very compassionate pastor, and was remembered as a worthy successor of the dying Elder Nektary. Bishop Nektary, being very young at that time, did not stay in contact with Fr. Sebastian; but his mother, the nun Nektaria, treasured a holy memory of Fr. Sebastian up to her death. In the words of Bishop Nektary, the spiritual image of Fr. Sebastian was that of a longsuffering, quiet bearer of the deep Optina monastic vision—a vision which Bishop Nektary kept before him to the end of his days.

3. SAINT SEBASTIAN

In the present volume of the *Optina Elders Series,* the greater portion of Elder Sebastian's biographical materials was collected and written by one of his personal physicians, Tatiana Vladimirovna Torstensen, a talented writer. An abridged version of her manuscript was published in Russian in the journal *Nadezhda*. After reading it we wanted very much to obtain the complete version of this *prima vita* of Fr. Sebastian. God crowned our desire in 1990, when we were handed, in one of Russia's holy monasteries, a complete manuscript for publication, along with a portrait of the Elder. The translation was begun and serialized in the St. Herman Brotherhood's magazine, *The Orthodox Word*. Then, in 1992, the late author's brother met us in Moscow and handed us another version of his sister's manuscript, containing material not in the previous version. In addition, having made contact with the Elder's spiritual children in Karaganda, we were sent a variety of additional material over the years. Finally, in 1998, to commemorate the official canonization of Elder Sebastian, which took place on September 29, 1997 (o. s.), a volume, lovingly compiled by Vera Koroleva, was published in Russia containing, in addition to the previously mentioned material, the recollections of the Elder's spiritual children. This English edition is a compilation of all the above-mentioned texts, and is therefore the most complete text available on Elder Sebastian.

Optina Monastery is now open again, filled with monks of good intention. Spiritual life is alive there, as in olden times touching the lives of the lay people who come to visit. To restore the holy tradition of Optina eldership in these days would be a miracle, beyond human power. Yet with God nothing is impossible, and we may perhaps see this come to pass some day, as a glorious sign of victory before the end of time. May our All-Merciful God grant it! Amen.

Abbot Herman
Sunday of All Saints of Russia,
May 31/June 13, 1999

Icon of the Synaxis of the Holy Elders of Optina.

FOREWORD
to the Russian Edition

Angels are a light for monks," says St. John Climacus, "and monastic life is a light for all humanity." But the height of heights of Christianity, the best expression of monasticism, is eldership.

Being the direct continuation of prophetic service, eldership arose in the time of early Christianity along with the rise of monasticism, as its guiding principle. It combined within itself the eremitic *podvig* of inward activity and service to the world in all its fullness, in its spiritual as well as its temporal needs.

In Russia, a special exponent of this spiritual podvig was the Optina Monastery of the Entrance of the Theotokos into the Temple in Kozelsk. The heart of Optina, the place where the pulse of its life beat, from which proceeded that grace-filled power that sanctified the inhabitants of the Monastery, was the famous Optina Skete—the abode of the holy Optina Elders.

The idea for its creation belonged to a protector of monasticism and eldership, Bishop Philaret, the future Metropolitan of Kiev. He persuaded the ascetic-disciples and followers of St. Paisius Velichkovsky, who were then dwelling in the Roslavl Forests, to establish a skete at Optina Monastery. Thus there arrived at Optina Fr. Moses (Putilov) and his brother Anthony. When Fr. Moses, after his founding of the Optina Skete (in 1821), was made Superior of the whole Monastery (1826), there arrived (in 1829) from the St. Alexander of Svir Monastery the divinely wise man of prayer, Fr. Leonid (Leo in schema), who placed a beginning to eldership here. It was through him that the impulse was given that inspired the subsequent generations of elders over the course of an entire hundred years, up to the very end of the life and flourishing of Optina Monastery. The subsequent Elders, Fr. Macarius and Fr. Ambrose, likewise great Elders, were his true disciples.

From the time of Elder Macarius, who attracted a series of persons belonging to the educated class of society to the translation of patristic literature, Optina Monastery became well known in the circle of contemporary writers. From that time on the cream of intellectual Russia began to visit Optina Monastery and its Skete. The many grace-filled gifts of the Elders and, what is no less important, the uninterrupted successive link between the Optina ascetics established the glory of Optina throughout all of Russia. During the time of Elder Ambrose who, when still a novice, was given over "from one hand to another" by Fr. Leo before his repose to Fr. Macarius, Optina reached its prime. The glory of the Elder thundered throughout all of Russia, and people from all corners of the country made their way to him. The Elders that followed—Fr. Anatole (Zertsalov), Elder Ambose's disciple Fr. Joseph, Elder Barsanuphius—were like unto their teachers in the grace of enlightenment.

Many renowned names of religious figures, philosophers and writers are connected with Optina Monastery. Here would visit Gogol, Dostoyevsky, Vladimir Solovyev, the secret Optina monk Constantine Leontiev, and the Kireyevsky brothers, who are buried within the walls of Optina, beside the Elders. The last impulse of the dying Tolstoy was deeply symbolic—it was towards Optina, and for him this meant towards the Church of Christ. "More essential than any book or any thought," wrote

Ivan Vasilievich Kireyevsky, "is to find a holy Orthodox elder, who might be your guide, to whom you might impart your every thought; and to hear about it, not his opinion, more or less intelligent, but the judgment of the Holy Fathers."

The last Elders—Theodosius the wise (†1920), Anatole (Potapov) the consoler (†1922) and the wondrous Nektary (†1928)—continued that same tradition. It fell to their lot to survive until the time when the age-old edifice of Russian government came crashing down, and a party of godless atheists took power over the country. The Lord decreed that Elders Theodosius and Anatole depart unto eternity before the time of the closure of Optina (1923) and be buried within the walls of the holy Monastery.

Elder Nektary, being in exile under strict observation in the village of Kholmishche, bound by the prohibition against receiving anyone, recalled the words of the Gospel: *Him that cometh to me I will in no wise cast out* (John 6:37), and continued to assuage the spiritual thirst of the people who, at the height of the revolutionary godlessness, rushed to the Elder for spiritual support.

Gradually weakening, Elder Nektary quietly departed this temporal, sorrowful life unto eternal life on April 29, 1928 and was buried in the isolated cemetery of the village of Kholmishche, 37 miles from Kozelsk.*

One of the last All-night Vigils in Optina was celebrated by Hieromonk Nikon (Belyaev) on June 15, 1924 on the eve of the day of the commemoration of St. Tikhon of Kaluga. Fr. Nikon, the beloved disciple and co-mystic of Elder Barsanuphius, was young in years, but in spiritual wisdom he surpassed other elders

---

*On July 3/16, 1989 the translation of the relics of Elder Nektary from the Kholmishche cemetery to the Optina Monastery Catholicon of the Entrance of the Theotokos took place. See I. M. Kontzevitch, *Elder Nektary of Optina*, (Platina, California: St. Herman of Alaska Brotherhood, 1998).

adorned with gray hairs. By the will of God's Providence it was precisely he who was to be the last to leave the dear Monastery, to which believers had formerly rushed, hoping for spiritual consolation and counsel. And Fr. Nikon took upon himself not only the duty of confessor, but also of elder. The Vigil took place, not in the monastery church, but in the infirmary kitchen. Further, in expectation of the coming calamities, there began for Fr. Nikon a sorrowful, unaccustomed, very difficult life in Kozelsk, together with the Optina brethren who had settled there, and the nuns of the ravaged Shamordino Convent. How the Optina monks lived, the Lord alone knows.

The first Optina Elder, Hieroschema-monk Leo, once said that "the time will come when our Skete will fall into neglect, and only cats will live in it." And before his blessed repose (†1841) he made the following prayer: "'I thank Thee, O Lord, my merciful Creator, that I have escaped those misfortunes and sorrows which await the coming times.' But I don't know if you will escape them." (The last words referred to the Elder's cell-attendant.)

Long before the revolution Elder Barsanuphius, like a father to his son, said to his disciple Fr. Nikon (then Nicholas), "Here I look at you, a green youth, and I think: I won't live until those terrible days, but you will.... The monasteries will be in a state of great persecution and oppression.... The time will come when it will be hard in Optina.... True Christians will huddle in tiny churches.... Perhaps you will live to those days when Christians will again be tortured. I'm speaking of tortures like those of ancient times.... The persecution and torture of the ancient Christians will, perhaps, be repeated. You will live until those times. Remember my words. Then you'll say, 'Yes, I remember—Batiushka Barsanuphius said all this to me.... How many years have gone by!' Remember my words, that you'll see 'the evil day.' And again I repeat—you have nothing to fear. The grace of God will cover you."

The body of Fr. Nikon lies in far-off Pinega, in the Archangelsk province, where he was banished by the bolsheviks in the "diseased exile" of 1930. There he died from tuberculosis of the lungs on June 25 (o.s.), 1931.

One of the last Elders* who grew up from the root of pre-revolutionary Optina is Schema-archimandrite Sebastian (Fomin, †1966)—a disciple of Elder Joseph and, after his death, of Elder Nektary. Having absorbed within himself the traditions and the grace-filled patristic spirit of Optina Monastery and having been tried, like iron, in the furnace of fiery trials, enduring banishment and imprisonment in the soviet camps, he, by the ineffable judgments of God, bore his service of eldership in the sultry steppe of Central Kazakhstan, in much-suffering and blessed Karaganda where, during the period from the 1930s to the 1950s, one of the most tragic acts of the God-fighting drama of our century unfolded. The unbounded steppe of Kazakhstan stretches out like a massive antimension, filled with the blood of the martyrs and sanctified by their prayers, over which the Optina Elder, Schema-archimandrite Sebastian of blessed memory, extended his powerful wings.

—Vera Koroleva
1998

---

*Also considered as being among the last Optina Elders are: Hieroschema-monk Macarius (Inozemtsev, †May 4, 1970), in the city of Belev, Tula province; Schema-monk Ioasaph (Moiseyev, †March 25, 1975), in the city of Gryaz, Lipets province; Schema-archimandrite Ambrose (Ivanov, †October 2, 1978), in the village of Balabanovo, Kaluga province; and Schema-abbot Paul (Drachev, †March 16, 1981), in the village of Cherkassa, Tula province.

Chronology

1884   October 28. Stephen Vasilievich Fomin is born to Basil and Matrona Fomin in the village of Kosmodamianskoye in the Orel province.

1888   Brought for the first time to Optina and meets Elder Ambrose.

1909   January 3. Enters the Skete of St. John the Forerunner in Optina Monastery as cell-attendant to Elder Joseph.

1912   Tonsured as a riassaphore monk. Becomes cell-attendant to Elder Nektary.

1917   Tonsured into the mantia with the name Sebastian.

1923   Ordained hierodeacon. Closure of Optina Monastery.

1927   Ordained hieromonk.

1928   April 29. Repose of Elder Nektary. Assigned as parish priest in the village of Kozlov.

1933   February 25. Arrested. Sentenced to 7 years in labor camps.

1934   May 26. Arrival at Karlag labor camp in Kazakhstan.

1939   April 29. Released from Karlag and settles in Mikhailovka.

1952   Permission granted by authorities for "prayer-house."

1955   Church of the Nativity of the Theotokos officially established.

1957   December 9/22. Elevated to rank of archimandrite.

1964   December 18/31. Awarded mitre and archpastoral staff.

1966   April 6/19. Repose in Mikhailovka.

1997   September 29/October 12. Local canonization in Alma-Ata. October 9/22. Uncovering of holy relics and their translation to the Mikhailovka church.

1998   April 19/May 2. Translation of holy relics to newly built cathedral in Karaganda and consecration of left side-altar to St. Sebastian.

PART I

The PRIMA VITA of Elder Sebastian of Optina and Karaganda

By Tatiana Vladimirovna Torstensen

Follow after charity, and desire spiritual gifts, but rather that ye may prophesy....
He that prophesieth speaketh unto men to edification, and exhortation, and comfort (I Cor. 14:1, 3).

Icon of St. Sebastian, painted for his canonization in 1997.

I

Youth and Life in Optina

THE BLESSED ELDER Schema-archimandrite Sebastian (Stephen Vasilievich Fomin in holy baptism) was born on the 28th of October, 1884, to a poor peasant family in the village of Kosmodamianskoye in the Orel Province. His father Basil and mother Matrona had three sons. The eldest, Hilarion, was born in 1872; the middle son, Romanus, in 1877; and the youngest, Stephen, in 1884. Stephen was named in honor of St. Stephen the Sabbaite, the writer of canons, on whose day he was born.

In 1888 his parents brought their children to Optina Monastery, to Elder Ambrose. Stephen was then four years old, but he remembered this visit well, and the kind eyes of the grace-filled Elder. Throughout his entire life he had a portrait of the Elder in his cell at the head of his bed.

Stephen's father and mother were in poor health, and suffered from pulmonary disease. They were religious people. They both died during the same year, 1889, while still young (evidently of cholera). The eldest brother, Hilarion, recalled, "When my parents died I was seventeen years old. We had over twenty-four acres of land, and we had to work it with our own hands. The housekeeping wasn't extensive, but who was going to manage it? There were three of us brothers, and we bickered and fought amongst ourselves—who would separate us and rec-oncile us?" In order to strengthen the family, Hilarion got mar-ried a year after the death of their parents. The younger brothers were weaker in health than he. He married right away, since oth-erwise he would not have been able to set his life and farm aright.

Stephen, at that time five years old, grew up in the young family of his brother. He was attached to his middle brother Ro-manus because of the latter's kind, gentle soul and soft heart.

The eldest brother, Hilarion, was of a character totally dif-ferent than that of his younger brothers. He was demanding, not gentle, and often abused the youngsters. Stephen discovered the burden of orphanhood early. Recalling his childhood, Elder Se-bastian would say, "If only there had been someone left of the fe-male sex—either a grandmother, or a sister, or an aunt—who could have taken care of me at such an age. It was hard without my mother, and even with my brother's wife it wasn't easy. I re-member how when I was eight years old I asked my brother's wife for some milk, but she said to me, 'Wait.' I got angry and took the hemp canvas that she had bleached and was drying in the sun, and threw it on the ground and poured mud all over it. She complained to my brother. My brother yelled at me and beat me. There was someone to beat me and yell at me, but there was no one to feel sorry for me."

Romanus, from his earliest years, had a strong inclination toward prayer and he yearned for the monastic life. He had re-ceived a blessing from Elder Ambrose of Optina to enter the Monastery, and in accordance with Romanus' request, Hilarion took him to Optina in 1892, three years after the death of their parents. He was received into the Skete of the Forerunner.

Stephen dearly missed his brother and dreamed, as soon as he grew up, of entering the Monastery and joining him. He studied diligently and finished the three-year parish school in his village. He had a great thirst for reading. Stephen's health had been poor since his birth. Helping his eldest brother in his tasks, Stephen worked at field labor a little; but mostly he worked with the flocks, as a shepherd. This work was in harmony with his soul and strength. He was a good shepherd—he loved the livestock and had rapport with them; the peasants valued him, but more importantly, he had time for the reading of books and for prayer. The parish priest and village teacher gave him books; in this way his self-education continued. All the conditions of his life strengthened him in his unwavering striving for the monastic life. Those his own age were not overly fond of him, because he was humble and meek. They laughed at him and teased him, calling him "monk." Sometimes it was even worse: knowing that he was compassionate not only towards people, but towards animals as well, they once took a cat and threw it to a pack of dogs, and they tore it to pieces. Elder Sebastian would later relate this with sorrow.

It was a great joy and consolation for Stephen during the winter when, freed from work in the village, he could visit his brother in Optina Monastery. The latter would give him spiritual books to read. These visits had a great spiritual influence on Stephen, and when he grew up he began to ask his eldest brother to allow him to go and stay with Romanus in the Monastery; but the former would not permit him, saying, "What kind of a monk would you be? You aren't of any use at all, and who on earth is going to help me with the farming?" And so, Stephen remained to help his brother.

In 1908 Romanus, after an illness, received the monastic tonsure in his cell and was named Raphael. On December 16, 1908, in the monastery church dedicated to St. Mary of Egypt, he was clothed in the mantia by the Superior, Archimandrite Xenophont.

By this time Hilarion's young family had become stronger, and Stephen, confirmed in his desire for monastic life, arranged his domestic passport in the provincial government office and went to the Skete of Optina Monastery, to his brother Raphael. He was received there on January 3, 1909, and assigned as a cell-attendant to Elder Joseph.

Optina Monastery is located in the Kaluga Province, two miles from the town of Kozelsk, on the opposite bank of the Zhizdra River (a tributary of the Oka). A raft would ferry the monks across. The Skete was located about half a mile from the Monastery. The path to the Skete led at first through the monastery orchard. Upon exiting the confines of the orchard, up to the very gates of the Skete, the little path led through a pine forest, between majestic pine trees two to three arm-spans in circumference. The gate was beneath the bell-tower, upon which were depicted the faces of the Prophets: John the Baptist, Elijah with the black raven, Elisha, etc. To the right and left of the gate, as one entered through it, there stood two identical little houses with glassed-in balconies. It was in these that the great Optina Elders lived. These were their cells. Adjoining the small houses, outside the fence, two huts with porches had been added on, in which the Elders were able to receive lay people, especially women, whose entrance into the Skete itself was forbidden by the rule. Outside the Skete enclosure, behind the right cell of the Elders stood another little house— this was the cell of the skete Superior. Throughout the interior of the Skete were the cells of the monks. Alongside the large church were the refectory, kitchen and bathhouse.

Living with Elder Joseph, Stephen found in him a great spiritual instructor. He later often recalled this time: "We (he and the other cell-attendant) lived with the Elder as with our own father. We prayed with him, ate with him, read with him, and listened to his instruction."

Elder Joseph, who lived in the cell on the right, was a deeply revered Optina Elder. He was born on November 2, 1837. In

ОПТИНА ПУСТЫНЬ. Видъ Предтечева скита

The holy gates of the St. John the Forerunner Skete of Optina
Monastery. At right is the "hut" in which Elders Ambrose,
Joseph and Nektary lived.

his early youth he had come to Optina with the blessing of Elder Ambrose. He was Elder Ambrose's closest disciple, and in 1860 became his cell-attendant and moved into this cell on the right side, where the Elder was living. He was in truth the "beloved child" of Fr. Ambrose, who gave spiritual birth to him and nourished him within the walls of the humble, lowly "hut," which was permeated by the precepts of the great Elders Leonid and Macarius. Here, in this narrow cell, which became for Fr. Joseph a school of piety, he undertook the work of the very highest of sciences—monasticism—and in due time became himself an instructor of monks.

He lived with Elder Ambrose in this cell until the latter's death (1891). For twelve years after that he fulfilled the duty of skete Superior and Elder of the Skete and Monastery. In 1905, due to an illness, he laid aside his responsibility. He was now in his declining years, and his strength had noticeably left him. This luminary of monasticism was quietly dying out, but although he was weakening physically, he was vigorous and clear in spirit. In 1905, by decree of the Holy Synod, Abbot Barsanuphius was assigned to the post of skete Superior.

In April of 1911, on the third day of Pascha, Elder Joseph was stricken with his fatal illness. On May 9 he peacefully parted from his much-suffering body, and at 1:30 in the morning on May 10 three strokes of the skete bell, followed by the monastery bell, announced the Elder's repose. On May 12 the coffin with his body was lowered by the brothers into his grave, beside the grave of Elder Ambrose. The meek disciple, who had spent thirty years with the great Elder, was laid to eternal rest at the feet of his instructor.

Great was Stephen's grief at the Elder's repose, but the Lord did not leave him unconsoled. Into Fr. Joseph's cell moved Elder Nektary, the spiritual son of Fr. Anatole (Zertsalov) and Fr. Ambrose. Elder Nektary had an unusually humble disposition

Elder Joseph of Optina.

and was the most "mystical" of all the Optina Elders. Stephen remained in the cell as his cell-attendant and became his spiritual son. He lived with Elder Nektary until the Monastery was closed in the spring of 1923—for a total of twelve years.

In all, Fr. Sebastian lived with Elder Joseph and Elder Nektary for seventeen years. Under the guidance of these two Elders, he developed the spiritual gifts which he had had since birth and acquired many new, lofty ones—the gifts of meekness, discernment, exalted prayer, clairvoyance, mercifulness and compassion. Later, great love was to lead him to take upon himself the podvig of eldership in an exceptionally difficult and grievous time.

In 1912 Stephen was tonsured as a riassaphore monk. In April of that same year, as a result of intrigues and slanders, Elder Barsanuphius was transferred from Optina Monastery to be the Superior of the Golutvin Monastery. Leaving the Skete after the Moleben for travellers, Elder Barsanuphius said the following to comfort the grieving brothers: "Abbot Mark, who reposed recently in the Monastery, told me that when Fr. Macarius was dying, he foretold that after him there would be, as elders, Fr. Ambrose, Fr. Hilarion and Fr. Anatole (Potapov), and that eldership would not be lacking in the Skete. Among the last elders would be people even higher in their spiritual gifts than the great Elders—Fathers Leonid, Macarius, Ambrose and Anatole (Zertsalov)." With Elder Barsanuphius' transfer from Optina, a council of the senior brethren assigned Fr. Nektary to be the confessor and Elder for the brethren.

As Fr. Sebastian's spiritual father for so many years, Elder Nektary defined his entire spiritual path and all his great spiritual achievements. Elder Nektary did not resemble any of the other Optina Elders, either his contemporaries or his predecessors, not only because he was the most mystical, but also due to his whole inner as well as outer character....

Elder Nektary had two cell-attendants. Fr. Stephen was the older of the two, and the Elder called him "Summer," because of his soft-heartedness and compassion. The younger one, Fr. Peter,* he called "Winter." He was coarser and stricter. When the people in the Elder's "hut" began to despair and murmur due to the long time they had to wait for the Elder, he would send Fr. Stephen out to console them. But when those who were waiting began to make a fuss, then Fr. Peter would come out and with strictness would make peace and calm the people down.

Some incidents occurred which were related by his spiritual children (who themselves witnessed this). It would happen that Fr. Stephen would come out holding in one hand spiritual postcards and in the other "Trinity Leaflets,"** and he would begin to present them to those who were there. When they would look at the postcards or read the Leaflets it would turn out that in these were the answers to the questions which they were waiting to ask Elder Nektary.... Later the Elder would come out of his cell to see the people and would say, jokingly, "Fr. Stephen's already taken my piece of bread away." He thus gave everyone to understand that Fr. Stephen was already capable of taking his place when this was needed.

Fr. Sebastian himself related that Elder Nektary would usually come out of his cell late, at 2:00 or 3:00 in the afternoon. The people would keep sending Fr. Sebastian to tell the Elder that they were waiting for him, that many of them needed to go home.

---

*Ryassaphore-monk Peter (Shviryev) was a former sailor, who had been to Mount Athos before the revolution. He was sincerely devoted to Elder Nektary, who loved him in return. He was simple-hearted and rustic. He was tonsured into the mantia just prior to the Elder's death in 1928, at the latter's orders. He later labored in the mines and died in an accident.

**Popular spiritual pamphlets printed by the Holy Trinity-St. Sergius Lavra.—Ed.

Monk Sebastian in the St. John the Forerunner Skete.
Photograph taken before the closure of Optina in 1923.

Fr. Stephen would go into the cell to inform the Elder, who would say, "Right away, I'm getting ready; I'll get dressed and go." But he wouldn't come out. And when he did come out, he would turn to Fr. Stephen in front of everyone: "How is it that up to now you haven't told me even once that so many people are waiting impatiently for me?" And Fr. Stephen would beg forgiveness and bow low before him.

On Great Saturday, April 13, 1913, at the time of the bringing out of the Winding Sheet,* Fr. Stephen's brother, Fr. Raphael, reposed in the infirmary from tuberculosis. He had been ill for about three weeks. During his last days he received the Holy Mysteries daily, and on the day before his death was tonsured into the great schema. As the *Skete Chronicle* informs us, Fr. Raphael had the obedience of senior flower gardener, and occasionally replaced the choir director on the right cliros. He was distinguished by his taciturn and gentle nature.

Fr. Stephen was tonsured into the mantia with the name Sebastian (in honor of the holy Martyr Sebastian, who is commemorated on December 18/31) in the fateful year of 1917. The revolution was thundering. The age-old edifice of the Russian state was crashing down. The time of the persecution of the Church of Christ had begun.

In expectation of the inescapably approaching changes, the Optina monks quietly and unnoticeably continued to live in the Monastery. News had already reached them of the closure of churches and monasteries and of the confiscation of their possessions. And in Optina as well, on the monastery wall, there had already appeared an ominous, insolent inscription threatening the pillage of the Monastery. They heard similar statements by word of mouth.

---

* An iconographic representation of Christ's burial, carried into church from the altar by the priest, and which is venerated by the faithful during the services of Saturday of Passion Week.

On January 10/23, 1918, Optina Monastery was closed by the soviets, but the Monastery continued to exist under the guise of an agricultural commune. Many, especially the young novices, left the Monastery, being dissatisfied with work in the commune, where strict demands were made of them. Those who remained, the majority of whom were aged monks, firmly resolved not to leave the Monastery until the last moment, until they were expelled. All lived in fear, each day and each hour expecting banishment, arrest, prison and death.

A museum called "Optina Hermitage" was set up on the monastery territory. The Skete no longer existed, but Elder Nektary remained living in the elder's "hut" with his cell-attendants and, exhausted under his burden of sorrows, continued receiving people.

In 1923, at the end of the fifth week of Great Lent, a liquidation committee began its work in the Monastery. Church services were discontinued. The monks were gradually moved out. The Monastery came under the authority of the Glavnauki (Ministry of Science). The monastery buildings were occupied by a children's home, the museum office, and private apartments. A large portion of the brothers' quarters was turned into part of the museum or occupied as apartments for summer visitors. The majority of the Optina brothers moved to Kozelsk and villages close by. Some bought small houses and dwelt together in small groups. To them were added the nuns of Shamordino and other already closed convents, who had formerly been guided by the Optina Elders. For the monks that were left without a roof over their heads, without a crust of bread, who had no prospects for the future, their sole consolation was prayer. In the Skete the cells of the Elders were restored by order of Fr. Sebastian to their original appearance, both inside and out.

In 1923, two months before the closure of the Monastery, Fr. Sebastian was ordained to the rank of hierodeacon.

Elder Nektary of Optina during his younger days.

When the Monastery was closed Elder Nektary was arrested and exiled beyond the bounds of the province. It is said that at the time of his arrest, when the authorities demanded that he refuse to receive visitors, all the Optina Elders appeared to him and said, "If you wish to be with us, do not turn away from your spiritual children."And he did not refuse them.

Initially the Elder lived in the village of Plokhino (27 miles from Kozelsk). Then he moved to the village of Kholmishche in the Briansk province (30 miles from Kozelsk). After the Elder's arrest Fr. Sebastian lived in Kozelsk together with the Optina brethren and often visited the Elder in his place of exile.

At one point Fr. Sebastian rented a room in the village of Kholmishche not far from Fr. Nektary. He frequently travelled from the village on errands, with the blessing of Elder Nektary, to Kozelsk, Kaluga and the surrounding villages.

In 1927 Fr. Sebastian was ordained a hieromonk by the bishop of Kaluga. Elder Nektary blessed Fr. Sebastian to serve in a parish after his death.The repose of Elder Nektary followed on April 29, 1928. He surrendered his holy soul to God under the epitrachelion of his spiritual son, Fr. Adrian Rymarenko (later Archbishop Andrew of New Diveyevo in New York, †1978). Fr. Adrian had come from Kiev in response to an urgent telegram. At the funeral, priests from Kozelsk and Kaluga and many spiritual children of Elder Nektary gathered. Elder Nektary was buried in the village cemetery, located on a little hillock along the road through the forest. Fr. Sebastian wept inconsolably at the burial and then again at the Elder's grave. He cried so hard that from that time on his head began to shake somewhat, and this tremor remained with him right up to his death.

After the funeral Fr. Sebastian departed at first to Kozelsk, then to Kaluga, and then to Tambov. There he received an assignment at a parish in the village of Kozlov, now Michurinsk, in the St. Elias Church, at the invitation of the rector, Archpriest Fr. Vladimir Andreyevich Nechayev.* He received the assignment from Bishop Vassian (Pyatnitsky) of Tambov and Kozlov. Fr. Sebastian served in the St. Elias Church in Kozlov for five years, from 1928 until 1933, right up to the time of his arrest, and enjoyed great popularity and love there. During this period he waged a tireless battle against the renovationists.**

Fr. Sebastian maintained his connection with the Optina brethren who were living in dispersal. Thus, in 1929 he gave the Holy Mysteries to the dying Hierodeacon Cyril (Zlenko, †July 19, 1932), the former secretary of Elder Barsanuphius, who had returned from exile in Kzyl-Ordinsk.

Soon Archpriest Vladimir Nechayev was arrested, and Fr. Sebastian took upon himself the care of his family—Matushka Olga and the children.

Services in the parish church, with regard to their order of prayer, noticeably differed from the reverent services of the Optina Skete, to which Fr. Sebastian was accustomed. It would happen that on some feast he would return from the church in an upset state. He did not like the unprayerful, overly ornate singing, and wanted the cliros to sing the way it had been done in the Skete. But the choir director liked the singing to be louder and more cheerful, and wasn't even against tapping his feet. Fr. Sebastian instructed the choir director to take a blessing before services, for what and how to sing. He would say, "You have to sing in such a way that people will want to pray and weep." But the choir director would object: "The altar is his, and the cliros is

---

*The father of the present Metropolitan of Volokolamsk and Yuriev, Pitirim (Nechayev).

**That is, members of the so-called "Living Church," a schismatic organization approved of and supported by the communist regime, which radically changed the age-old traditions of the Church in an attempt to compromise with and "sell out" to the spirit of this world. The believers of Russia rejected this movement decisively.—Ed.

mine." But Fr. Sebastian did not allow him this liberty, and they sang the way he blessed them to, monastically.

It would also happen that the male singers would, on great feast days, demand money for wine. But Fr. Sebastian would never comply with these requests. If he did permit them to have some wine, it would be with water. At dinner he would feed them to satiety and would buy them shirts, and would console them as much as possible—but not with vodka. And for this "lack of love" he endured unpleasantness from men during his whole life.

There began to gather in Kozlov with Fr. Sebastian sisters of the same spirit. The first to arrive was Mother Agrippina from Shamordino, whom the Elder assigned to sing on the cliros. Then Mother Febronia arrived from the same Convent, and he assigned her to do the housekeeping. Once, after dealing with the housework, she went out into the courtyard of the house for a rest. Thoughts began to weary her: "What have I come here for? Batiushka is just like all batiushkas; the work is the same as it is at home." Suddenly the Elder came out of the house, sat beside her and said, "What have you come to me for? I'm just like all batiushkas." She understood that he saw all her thoughts and fell at his feet, begging forgiveness. Now she understood that Fr. Sebastian was not at all like everyone else. Mother Febronia remained with the Elder permanently; she was near him during his years of imprisonment in the camps and lived in Karaganda until her death.

Soon two girls from a merchant family came to the Elder. One of them, Nun Barbara, had been given by her parents to Shamordino at the age of twelve. They came to the Elder dressed in civilian clothes—in slippers, fine dresses and scarves. The Elder took a look at them and told Mother Febronia, "Bring these girls some boots, jackets and simple kerchiefs. Let them put them on and go to church." They obeyed unquestioningly and went to church in the clothing that was brought to them. There they stood, right at the threshold behind the stove, so that no one would see them or be carried away by the sight of the young ladies. That is how the Elder sometimes humbled people.

Nun Barbara was endowed with a good voice—an alto—and an excellent memory. She was even made the ecclesiarch. In addition, she was called the "peacekeeper," since she reconciled those who quarrelled. The Elder said about her, "If Barbara had been a monk, she would have been a hieromonk."

At that time other monks and nuns from ravaged monasteries were living in Kozlov, as well as laymen who had formerly visited Optina. And the hearts of those who were sincerely seeking salvation were drawn, by the creative power of the spirit of God, to Fr. Sebastian. This could not help but attract the attention of the local authorities.

Hieromonk Sebastian in the village of Kozlov, 1928.

2

Arrest and Exile

On February 25, 1933, Fr. Sebastian was arrested together with nuns Barbara, Agrippina and Febronia and taken to the city of Tambov to the GPU for investigation. At the inter-rogations Fr. Sebastian's contacts with people one in spirit with him and his attitude towards the soviet authorities were brought to light. Concerning this the Elder gave a direct answer: "I look upon all the measures of the soviet authority as the anger of God; this authority is a punishment for the people. I have expressed such views among those close to me, as well as among the rest of the citizens with whom I have had occasion to speak on this topic. At these times I have said that one must pray, pray to God, and also live in love. Then only can we be delivered from this. I have been little pleased with the soviet authorities because of the closing of churches and monasteries, since by this the Orthodox Faith is being destroyed."*

Parcels from unauthorized persons were not accepted at the GPU, so the Elder's spiritual children who were left in freedom summoned a distant relative of his to Tambov by telegram. They accompanied her to the prison and she gave him a parcel

---

*From the soviet files of the U.F.S.B. of the Tambov province. File no. P-12791, vol. 1.

and spoke with him. At dinner time, when the prisoners were led out of the prison through the courtyard to the dining hall, the sisters would stand at the gate and look through the cracks. The Elder, passing by the gate, would bless them.

At the June 2, 1933 session of the GPU, the extrajudicial examination decreed: "Stephen Vasilievich Fomin, found guilty in accordance with statute 58-10 of the criminal law code, is sentenced to be imprisoned in a corrective labor camp for seven years, counting the term from February 2, 1933."

The Elder had his head and beard shaved. When he passed by the gate for the last time, he could not even lift his head out of sorrow.

The medical commission acknowledged that, due to the limited movement of his left elbow (the Elder had hurt his left arm as a child), he was not fit for heavy physical labor. Despite the conclusion of the commission, Fr. Sebastian was sent to the Tambov province for the felling of a forest, which was beyond his strength. His spiritual children learned of the location of the tree-cutting, and in spite of the great distance, found it possible to bring him parcels, and to console and support him as much as each one could. On Sundays the convicts were released to go home. It was too far for Fr. Sebastian to go home to Kozlov, but on the side of the forest where he was, in a small village, were his spiritual children, who awaited him on Saturday evenings. All arrangements were made there—he could wash, change his clothes, eat, pray and rest. He passed his Sundays in prayer and conversation, about which the Elder himself would say, "It was just like Pascha! Like visiting Paradise!" And on Monday he again had to go to the forest to work. But this too passed. A year later Fr. Sebastian was transferred to the Karaganda camp (Karlag*) in the settlement of Dolinka, where he arrived on May 26, 1934.

---

*For historical information concerning this camp see Appendix, p. 437.

And so, Hieromonk Sebastian of Optina was brought by transport to the torrid steppes of Central Kazakhstan, to one of the departments of the Karlag.

Concerning his time in the camp the Elder recalled that they beat him, tortured him, and demanded one thing—that he renounce God. He replied, "Never." Then they sent him to the criminals' barracks. "There," they said, "they'll quickly re-educate you." One can imagine what the criminals did to the weak, middle-aged priest.

Due to his poor health the Elder was assigned to work as a bread cutter and then as a guard of the storehouses in the camp zone. During his nightly guard shifts he never allowed himself to sleep—he labored at prayer. The authorities, coming to check on him, always found him awake. Fr. Sebastian related that movies were sometimes shown in the zone,* and all the prisoners were rounded up in the "club." "I didn't go to the movies," he recalled. "Everyone would go, but I would say to my fellow-worker, 'You go to the movie in my place, and I'll stand guard for you.'" But if he had to go, then the Elder would come to the club ahead of time and would lie down in a secluded corner or under a bench. Sometimes he would nap and take a rest, and sometimes he would pray.

During the last years of his imprisonment the Elder's guard was relaxed somewhat, and he lived in the supply depot of the third department of the camp, located near Dolinka. He carried water using bullocks to the residents of the Central Industrial Gardens. It would happen in the winter that he would bring the water and then go up to the bullock and warm his stiffened hands on him. The people would bring out mittens and give them to him. The next day he would again come without mittens (he would either give them to someone or they would be

---

*These were generally propaganda movies, aimed at the "re-education" of the prisoners.—ED.

taken away), and he would again warm his hands on the bullock. His clothing was old and ragged. When the Elder was freezing at night he would climb into the stable and warm himself among the warm animals. The residents of the Gardens would give him food—pirog and lard. He ate what he could, but brought the lard to the prisoners in the department. "I was in prison," the Elder recalled, "but I never broke the fast. If they would give me some kind of swill with a piece of meat in it, I would not eat it, but would trade it for someone's bread ration."

Mothers Barbara and Febronia, who had been arrested with the Elder, were not given a sentence. Mother Agrippina was sent to the Far East, where she was freed a year later. She wrote to Fr. Sebastian about her intention to go to her home village, but he blessed her to come immediately to Karaganda. She came in 1936 and was able to meet with the Elder. He proposed that she buy a small house in the settlement of Greater Mikhailovka, close to Karaganda, and settle in it; she was to come to see him every Sunday, "if only there is some vehicle going in that direction." Two years later Mothers Febronia and Barbara came to Karaganda. A house was bought on Lower Street—a small, old storehouse with a caved-in ceiling. In it they fixed up two rooms, plus a kitchen and a vestibule. There was also a garden with a well. Mothers Agrippina and Barbara found work in the hospital in the New City while Febronia, being poorly educated, worked on a collective farm. Other nuns as well came to Karaganda—Kira, Martha and Maria. They settled in nearby Tikhonovka. The nuns became acquainted with believers and began secretly to gather for common prayer. When they learned that Fr. Sebastian was in Dolinka, the believers began to help him. On Sundays the nuns would come to see the Elder. In addition to groceries and clean linens they brought him the Holy Gifts, cuffs and an epitrachelion. They would go out to a small grove, where the Elder would receive

Communion and the sisters would confess and commune also. The prisoners and the camp authorities came to love the Elder. The love and faith in his heart had conquered malice and enmity. He led many in the camp to faith in God—and not only to faith, but to *real* faith. When Fr. Sebastian was released, he had spiritual children in the zone who, after their terms, went to him in Mikhailovka. Many years later, when the church was opened in Mikhailovka, the residents of the Dolinka Central Industrial Gardens went there and recognized in the noble-looking Elder-priest their former water-bearer.

The author, Tatiana Vladimirovna Torstensen, in 1953, a year after she met Elder Sebastian and became his spiritiual daughter.

3

Life in Karaganda

His term of imprisonment came to an end. Fr. Sebastian was released from the camp on April 29, 1939, on the eve of the Feast of the Ascension of the Lord. He came to his novices in the tiny house, where the floor was stained with yellow clay, and his bed was in the kitchen behind a screen, on a large trunk. And there they lived—Mother Fyosha, Mother Varya, Mother Grusha,* Mother Catherine (who came to him from prison later), and the Elder. They arose early in the morning and read the prescribed prayer rule; then the sisters went to work and the Elder remained at home. He went for water, made lunch, and repaired and cleaned shoes. The sisters were embarrassed by this, but the older nuns who were living in Tikhonovka told them, "You don't understand what he's doing, so keep silent." They served Liturgy in secret, and the Elder read the daily cycle of services every day.

Before the war he travelled to the Tambov Province. His spiritual children, who had waited many years for his return from the camp, hoped that he would remain with them in Russia. But Fr. Sebastian, not seeking to do his own will, but giving himself over to the will of God, after living for a week in the village

---

*Diminutives for the names Febronia, Barbara and Agrippina, respectively.—TRANS.

of Sukhotinka, returned again to Karaganda, to that lot that had been appointed him by God's Providence.

The inhabitants of Karaganda in those years consisted of those very same repressed peasants who had been attached to the the coal mines "permanently," as well as the freed former prisoners of the Karlag, who had been sentenced to "perpetual exile in Karaganda." More than two thirds of the inhabitants of the city did not have passports. The exiles lived in dark storerooms, earthen huts and sheds, and were obliged every ten days to register at the commandant's office.

Karaganda was a hungry city, and bread was especially hard to come by during the war and the years afterwards. The Elder himself would go to the store to receive bread by ration card. He would dress as a simple old man, in a very modest, drab suit. He would go there and stand in line. The line would reach the store and he would be shoved aside. He would again stand at the end of the line. This happened more than once. People noticed this, and seeing his mildness and meekness, began to let him in ahead of the line and give him bread.

In 1944 a larger house was bought for Fr. Sebastian and the sisters on West Street. I was in the other house for the first time in 1952. After the Elder's arrival they had finished remodeling the house, and by the time I came it had already been comfortably laid out. Fr. Sebastian had a room sufficient for his needs. There was also a long, narrow refectory with a table as long as the room. The table had benches on either side; after the Elder's arrival, many people could always be found sitting around it. This refectory separated his quarters from the nun's rooms. (There were two other rooms in the house.) A door from the hallway led into the kitchen.

At the end of 1943 they had gone to the Elder to ascertain how things would go with him, and at the beginning of 1944 they brought him to his new home. He entered the house just like a landlord, looking here and there and stating what needed to be rearranged.

"But what on earth for, Batiushka?" they objected. "We won't be in Kazakhstan forever; the war is coming to an end and we can go back with you to our native land." "And who will be there waiting for us?" asked the Elder. "Who's going to arrange your livelihood? Living conditions will be more difficult for us there; we'll live here. Here all our living conditions will be easier. Here everything in life is different and the people here are different. The people here are hospitable, they're conscientious, they've known much sorrow; and so, my dear ones, we'll live here. We'll bring more good here. This is our second homeland—after all, we've already spent ten years here and have gotten used to it."

Thus they remained permanently. They remained in Karaganda until their deaths and gave up on their dream of returning home. In the Mikhailovka Cemetery they are all buried alongside the Elder. He buried three of the nuns himself—Agrippina, Barbara and Catherine—although all of them were considerably younger than he.*

---

* They all fell ill with heart ailments after bandits fell upon the little house on Lower St. They were frightened half to death, and this shock undermined their health. Mother Fyosha was not at home on that night nor on the day before, and she survived the other three. Fr. Sebastian, foreseeing the danger, insisted on moving his novices to "Melkombinat," that is, to the area of a [grain-milling] factory, where many of his spiritual children lived. This was far from Mikhailovka. But the nuns in no way wanted to travel so far from the church; the daily labor of travelling such a distance frightened them, and they did not obey the Elder. For this they suffered—none of them lived long after the bandits' assault; they died, one after the other, of heart attacks. Soon after this attack, he bought them a home next to the church. He convinced the owners to make the sale. But the strength of the three nuns had already been undermined. Their names in monasticism were: Alexandra, Vera, and Elena. Mother Fyosha was tonsured after the Elder's death with the name Thecla. The last of the three who had followed him from Michurinsk, Alexandra, the Elder buried on January 16, 1966, three months before his own death. Only Mother Febronia (Fyosha) survived Fr. Sebastian: she lived ten years more and died on March 17, 1976.

Some of the remaining adobe huts in Mikhailovka, like the ones
Elder Sebastian and his nuns first settled in.

The first thing was to find a place to settle temporarily, and
then, when possible, to buy a small house, or half of one or a
third of one, where there would be only one room, a kitchen and
a little terrace, or just a room and an unheated vestibule as a
summer kitchen.

Small houses were at that time available and inexpensive in
Karaganda. They were being sold by those who had been sent
there in the 1930s. When they had established themselves finan-
cially, working in the pits and mines and earning money there,
and as their families began to grow, they built for themselves
newer, more spacious, quality homes with beautifully carved,
enormous gates, like those they had once had in their homeland;
and they sold the old adobe huts. The finer, higher quality
homes were being sold by those who were able to return to European Russia after the war.

Fr. Sebastian helped everyone who came to him and those
who wished to stay. He would give money for the purchase of a
cottage to those who had none, or would offer some money to

those who did not have enough. The money they would eventually pay back to him he would give away to others, and so on.

In the meantime in Karaganda, new pit mines were opened. Around Karaganda the mines and shafts multiplied like mushrooms. People were in great demand; it was easy to find work, and people were freely allowed to build homes. Soon the "Batiushka-ites" in Mikhailovka became quite numerous and continued to grow in number, but the Elder was always bright and loving, and kind and approachable to all.

In November of 1946, with the blessing of the Elder, the Orthodox residents of Mikhailovka handed in to the appropriate local authorities an application for the registration of a religious community. Not obtaining an affirmative answer there, the believers addressed their petition to Alma-Ata, to the plenipotentiary of religious affairs in Kazakhstan. In November of 1947, in reply to this petition, a directive arrived at the executive committee of the province of Kazakhstan, "to forbid Priest Sebastian Fomin to serve in the church he has opened without authorization." The application was submitted to Alma-Ata again in 1947 and in 1948. Believers travelled to Moscow to petition, promising to support the Alma-Ata diocesan administration. The parents of soldiers who had died during the Second World War wrote to the military commander of the Karaganda Province that their sole consolation was to pray for their sons who had died in the war. "But," one letter said, "they deprive us even of this possibility."

Then the nun and eldress Agnia* came—a very wonderful, talented artist. At twelve years of age she had left the girls' gymnasium and asked her family to take her to the Sukhotin Convent of the Theotokos of the Sign, where at that time there was a renowned icon-painting school, in which the best and most famous painters taught the nuns iconographic skills. Next to the

---

*See Part V, Chapter 1, p. 387.

Convent was a large orphanage and school. The instructors in the school also taught the nun-artists a curriculum of general education with, of course, a spiritual orientation.

Mother Agnia had been a spiritual daughter of Elder Barsanuphius. Each year, receiving leave [from the Convent], she had travelled to Optina Monastery. She had come to know Fr. Sebastian well through the Optina Skete and had also seen him every year prior to the closure of Optina. She was seven or eight years younger than Fr. Sebastian. She said that in his youth he had been very handsome, with an especially radiant face; he had been very friendly and gentle with visitors, and had tried to do all he could for them. Elder Barsanuphius called him "the grace-filled one." Elder Joseph loved him dearly and said of him, "He is a tender soul." And indeed, Fr. Sebastian often wept upon hearing an account of someone's grief.

She related to me that she was once conversing with Fr. Sebastian on the balcony of Elder Barsanuphius' cell while waiting to be received by the Elder, and put her hand on the banister. Fr. Sebastian, explaining something to her, put his hand on her hand. She abruptly withdrew her hand. In great perplexity he looked at her and said, "What's the matter, sister?" She understood her emotional error and forever remembered the incident.

Mother Agnia once drew an artistically executed portrait of Fr. Barsanuphius, which was later requested by the Tretyakov Gallery. Not long before his death, Fr. Barsanuphius gave her this portrait, which he so highly prized. It always hung in her cell in Karaganda. She would say, "I didn't paint the portrait; Fr. Barsanuphius painted it through my hand." She was well-read, and wrote in a refined manner, with calligraphic quality. Inwardly she was quite intelligent and deep.

There also came to Karaganda the nun and eldress Anastasia.* By the blessing of Elder Nektary she had taken upon herself

_____
*See Part V, Chapter 2, p. 405.

the podvig of foolishness-for-Christ's-sake. She often committed acts that went against common sense, the meaning of which would be revealed later. She endeavored to conceal her care for everyone and the angelic kindness of her soul behind outward severity, at times making harsh remarks to those close to her and exposing their sins and failings. But the only people who feared Mother Anastasia were those who had not yet gotten used to her. Those who knew her repaid her with love in kind and with great respect. Both of these Eldresses were endowed with grace-filled gifts. They could see right through a person and foretold many things clairvoyantly but, having great humility, they lived under the guidance of Fr. Sebastian's eldership.

Then came the nun Vera, an intelligent and highly literate woman. She had previously served in Moscow in the Transfiguration Cathedral for Archbishop John and Metropolitan Nicholas of Krutitsa. Mother Cornelia arrived, an educated woman from the intelligentsia, and a highly spiritual nun. There came as well the nuns Marina, Maria "the lesser" (a quiet and humble nun), Olympiada, Tatiana, Eupraxia, Irene, Eugenia, and many other deeply religious people. Entire families came, having sold their houses in European Russia, in the Ukraine, in Siberia and in Orenburg. They all purchased houses in Mikhailovka near Fr. Sebastian.

Karaganda grew. It was built up on all sides, on the sites of the former villages of the old Molokan inhabitants (sectarians who had been exiled from what was once Imperial Russia). These settlements, then scattered among the districts of the steppe, with pit mines and mine shafts, were situated far from each other but had by now become districts of the city of Karaganda. The expanse between Feodorovka, Tikhonovka, Mikhailovka, and the Kirov and the Shakhtin regions was gradually built up. The first to be erected was "Dugout Town," which had once consisted only of half-earthen dugouts built by the first settlers, dispossessed kulaks,* in the years 1930-32. Then there arose the settlements of the first and second pits. The "old city" sprang up next to the large mine shafts, consisting at first of barrack-like houses, and then of the standard two-storey houses. During the time of the Second World War there arose the German settlement with its tile roofs, populated by those transferred from the German colony on the Volga—this was the settlement of "Maikuduk." It was already after the end of the war in 1946-47 that the "new city" began to be built with multi-storeyed houses. In this "new city" were built the Palace of Mines, a drama theater, a new railroad station, the Sports Palace, movie theaters, and later the Higher Institute, the Medical Institute, clinics, the Pedagogical Institute, and all the other schools which are located in a regional industrial center—technical schools, trade schools and a musical school.

Mikhailovka turned out to be the closest suburb, the one which most closely bordered the "new city." But a church was located only at the second pit. The church was large, and behind it was a large cemetery that led out into the steppe. But the church was far away from all parts of the city, as was the cemetery. Furthermore, there was practically no transportation to it. Very seldom did a bus pass by the church, from the old city to Tikhonovka, and when it did it was always overcrowded. It was with great difficulty that the inhabitants of all the regions fulfilled their religious obligations. One would have to go on foot more than half the way there, that is, one to two miles and even farther. In Mikhailovka a second cemetery was later opened, but that stood too far away from the church. How could one have a funeral? Funerals were either served in absentia or weren't served at all.

Once the Elder was walking with the nuns Maria and Martha to the cemetery which lay beyond Tikhonovka. There, in

---

*Kulaks were relatively well-off peasant farmers. They were exterminated as a societal class by the communists, mostly during the 1930s.—ED.

the middle of the cemetery, were common graves in which two hundred reposed peasants a day had been buried, who had died from hunger and sickness. They had been buried without funerals, without mounds, without crosses. The Elder, after seeing and hearing about it, said, "Here, day and night, over these common graves of the martyrs, there burn candles from earth to heaven." And Fr. Sebastian was an intercessor for them all.

But the Elder lived with the four nuns in Mikhailovka on Lower Street. He served Liturgy and Vespers each day in his cell. Mother Agrippina and Mother Barbara worked as nurses in the Mikhailovka Hospital; Mother Catherine cooked and prepared the meals; Mother Febronia washed the dishes, cleaned up, did the laundry and ironed. Everywhere there was sparkling cleanliness, order, silence and unusual calm such as I had never seen elsewhere. There were many icons in every room, and before them, with a soft light, glowed the flames of lampadas.

Ah, Batiushka! Batiushka! How gentle, radiant and loving! Whoever was once with him at Lower Street will never forget it. Soon the residents of Mikhailovka learned about him and began to invite him over to their houses with liturgical requests, since he could not receive them at home. After the daily refectory meal Fr. Sebastian would take the addresses which had been left for him and would go to conduct the requested services until evening. Permission to conduct the various services had not been given, but he went without refusing. The people in Karaganda were faithful then. "Don't betray him," they would say. Even the children, although they all knew, observed the rule "not to tell."

People in other suburbs also heard about him and strove to come to see him. Yea, and not only people, but even the beasts as well. When he, small and insignificant, walked with his quick, light stride along the street of Mikhailovka in his long, black overcoat and black skufia, dogs would crawl out from behind all the fences to see him. They rushed, fearing to be late, to miss him. When the gap in the fence was narrow and they could not crawl through it, then, having sniffed the Elder, they would dig a hole with their paws under the fence in order to force their heads through and would lie there, flat as a pancake. Laughing, their owners would tell of this, and I myself saw it. "When Fr. Sebastian walks by," the people said, "they crawl out like snakes." Where houses had low garden fences, the dogs would fly over them like birds. They would all decorously sit in front of their homes. They did not run out onto the street, nor did they bark at anyone. They would sit quietly, following the Elder with their heads as he passed by. What were they trying to express? Ah, the dogs of Mikhailovka! The dogs of Mikhailovka! How they impressed me with the keenness and depth of their dog souls and hearts.

The residents of Mikhailovka forcefully petitioned for the opening of a church—that is, the construction or remodeling of a house for one, even if it were not large. They petitioned obstinately. They sent representatives to Moscow, and in the meantime Fr. Sebastian went to private houses to conduct individual services as needed. Once, returning home from such services, he passed by a store where certain food products and beer were being sold. The store had a wide porch with tall steps on which there were, as always, many people—for the most part men. The Elder was walking hastily, without glancing anywhere, along the sidewalk. Suddenly he raised his head and looked attentively at the entryway of the store. On the stairs stood a twelve-year-old girl with a satchel in her hands, looking at him very intently. Noticing that he looked at her, she quickly descended the stairway and followed him. He glanced back and again looked at her. She walked up alongside him.

"Where are you going?" he asked her.

"I want to see where you live."

"What for?"

"To know."

"Well, let's go."

They walked to his house. Fr. Sebastian stopped.

"This is where I live."

"May I come in?" the girl asked.

"A guest has come to us," said the Elder as he entered the house with her.

"Come in," said Mother Agrippina gently.

The girl stood there and with great interest looked all around, at the long table, the icons and the burning lampadas. Mother Barbara was reading prayers. The Elder came out of his cell in a bright podrasnik with combed white and gray hair. They all sat down at the table. And Batiushka! His face looked so much better, so much more wonderful, so much more radiant than it had on the street.

"I have to go, to bring home what I bought. It would be better for me to come visit you tomorrow."

"Come at this time again," said Fr. Sebastian. "And what is your name?"

"Vera."

The next day Vera came. She came much earlier. She began to come almost every day. The nuns were kind to her, and she began to help them. This continued for a long time. Once Vera said to the Elder, "I want to live here with you."

"Tell your mother that she should come to see me," he replied.

Vera was overjoyed: "Mother will agree; she has a large family."

Her mother came and readily agreed to let Vera go.

Vera quickly came to feel at home. The nuns taught her much and cared for her, but in soul Vera was drawn only to Fr. Sebastian. He trained her quietly and gradually. She accustomed herself to submit to him without murmuring. He would assign her something to read daily—spiritual booklets, Lives of Saints, a certain daily portion from the Gospels, kathismata from the Psalter, and prayers. She had a good, resonant voice and sang at all his services. She gradually began to try to do more and more on her own for the Elder— to clean up his cell, and to iron his clothing and podrasnik. Sometimes she would cook something for him apart from the common meal, serve him, and so on.... She was wonder-struck by him once and forever—by his love, his meekness, his gentleness and kindness; by everything which she had never been able to see before, and which she never before could have imagined. In him lay all of her interests.... When they opened the church, Vera was one of the first in the church choir. Her resonant young voice sounded beautiful. She would be absorbed the entire day in the church services and in caring for the Elder.... Young, quick and adroit, she cared for him as for a little child.... She understood him without the need for words. She was endlessly devoted to him, and became indispensable and close. She was, as it were, Fr. Sebastian's very own daughter.

They petitioned for the opening of a church for more than a year. Finally, in 1952, the authorities allowed us to open, not a church, but a prayer house. It was permitted to celebrate all the services for special needs there—baptisms, marriages, funerals, common prayer, and confession. But it was not permitted to celebrate the church services. There was no Holy Communion. Still, half the work had been accomplished. Fr. Sebastian persistently pressed forward in his greatly needed activity. Accommodations were needed.

One deeply believing Mordvinian woman vacated her house and gave it, with its large yard, to the Elder. Yet another family of believers vacated their large house, not far from the Mordvinian woman's house, for his needs, while they themselves moved into a smaller house that they had purchased next door.

The Elder began to equip the "prayer house." They knocked down the partitions between as many rooms as they were able without weakening the structure of the house. Mother Agnia began to paint large icons for the iconostasis—at first icons of Christ and the Theotokos, very beautiful ones; then of the Most Holy Trinity, the Ascension, the Flight into Egypt, and the Resurrection of Christ—these icons were especially loved by the Elder. They were done with talent and skill; spirituality and warmth exuded from them. She then painted many more icons. The entire church was adorned with her icons. The old women had preserved a few more icons at the closing of the old Mikhailovka parish church. The first icon, "Quick to Hear," had once been ordered from Mt. Athos, by the first migrants from Belorussia to Mikhailovka. It was an icon of wondrous beauty, and very large. The Elder decided to place it in the iconostasis. Mother Agnia painted one of identical size, a very good one, of the Savior with the Gospel. She also painted an icon of the Old Testament Trinity, and (considerably later) icons of the New Testament Trinity, the Resurrection, Christ's prayer concerning the cup (for the altar, which Fr. Sebastian placed over the table of preparation), the Savior in purple and a crown of thorns, and other icons. An icon of the Trinity, the first on the right of the Savior, was painted by a nun Nektaria, a spiritual daughter of Elder Nektary, who came twice to see Fr. Sebastian, but for some reason did not get along here.... In addition to the icon of the Trinity, she painted a few more large icons, but they were all later replaced; the Elder did not like her work. There remained only the one on the iconostasis.

Now a far greater number of people were able to turn to Fr. Sebastian with their liturgical needs. An especially large number came for baptism each day. Many children had already grown up unbaptized, and they were all brought to be baptized. There were many other liturgical needs as well, but he was alone; only

Icon of the holy
Martyr Sebastian of
Rome, the heavenly protector
of Elder Sebastian. Painted
by Eldress Agnia for the
church in Mikhailovka.

the nuns assisted him. The main problem, however, was that church services were not permitted. After an exhausting day of work, after prayer in his cell, each night at three o'clock the Elder would walk along the dark streets (street lamps were few)—not to the prayer house, but to the other—to serve Liturgy.

On feast days he began serving the All-night Vigil together with the anointing with oil at 1:00 a.m. and, after a short break, the Liturgy. The windows were all tightly covered with blankets so that no light would filter through to the street. Inside the house it was bright, warm, and filled with people. The radiant, loving Elder, kind towards everyone, was accessible to all. Often he would give someone a small roll or an apple, or a packet of cookies. He wanted in some way to console, to show kindness or be of help. But when I began to go to his nighttime services I did not understand this. I saw that the people took the gifts with joy. But when he would give me something, I would refuse, saying, "I don't need it, Batiushka, I have some." Smiling, he would say, "It's good that you have some, and this will also do you some good." Later the women explained to me that one must not refuse, that it's considered a great joy when the Elder gives you something; it's a blessing from him.

The service would finish before dawn, and the people would walk home along the dark streets—only not in groups, but alone or in pairs. In the summer, when the nights are short, it would already be broad daylight and there would be many people on the streets; someone would be hurrying to the market, another to work. That's the way it was for three years, and everything went well.

But efforts to open a church continued. Alexander Pavlovich Krivonosov, a learned agronomist who was very dedicated to the Elder, travelled to Moscow again and again and finally, in 1955, brought back a document of permission to open a religious community in Mikhailovka.

Work started rolling at the prayer house on West Street in Mikhailovka to turn it into a church building. Partitions between the walls were removed. They mounted a blue cupola on the roof, and later a second, like on the churches of the old wooden sketes. They installed a fan in the ceiling so it wouldn't be stuffy. They began to build an iconostasis. Then they added a room and two vestibules. Fr. Sebastian gave everyone instructions, directing everything personally.

The representatives of the local authorities vigilantly observed the progress of the work. They categorically forbade them to raise the roof even one inch. Then the Elder blessed the people to gather secretly one night. And during that night they lowered the floor of the church by one yard. People took up shovels, and in one night fifty cubic yards of dirt were carried off by trucks. In this way the ceiling was one yard higher than it had been before. The floor was quickly covered with boards, and by morning they were already serving a Moleben.

By this time Mother Agnia had already painted many beautiful icons. Then in 1955 the day arrived for the consecration of the church in honor of the Nativity of the Most Holy Theotokos, the same as the old church of Mikhailovka, which had been closed in 1928. Church utensils, service books and patristic books were sent from Moscow by a former Karlag prisoner, Archdeacon James.

They built a house in the yard and called it the "lodge." They gradually added four rooms onto it. The first one from the vestibule was a large room which served as the refectory. A large corner near a window served as the kitchen; and opposite, in a dark corner, was the bed of one of the cooks, Matrona. The other cook, Maria, lived in her own home. They served as cooks alternately. They were both quiet, meek and amiable—very memorable. There was also a cell for the cell-attendants, and a large, bright room with a warm vestibule, which became the

Church of the Nativity of the Theotokos in Mikhailovka,
the remodeled "prayer-house" on West Street.

Elder Sebastian and Mother Anastasia in the church courtyard.
Photograph from the 1950s.

Elder's cell. Further on in the yard they built an open chapel for Paschal services and for the blessing of water on Theophany, since on those days all the worshippers would in no way fit into the church. Bunk beds were placed in the kitchen for visitors, of which there were many on great feasts. (A few years later the beds were removed by order of the municipal soviet.)

Across the entire length of the room, opposite the windows, stood a great, long table, alongside which were benches and stools. Beyond the table, in a dark corner behind some curtains, stood the bed of Mother Anastasia, opposite a shrine with icons and a lampada. Mother Anastasia was in charge. She knew about everything, ordered the affairs of the refectory and kitchen, and looked after the preparation of the food to make sure that everyone was fed—both those who came regularly as well as visitors. Sometimes she would personally help the cook serve the food onto serving dishes and place them on the table. She always walked about in very long, broad, black skirts or dresses which reached the floor. On her head she would most often wear a not-very-clean white cotton kerchief, and on her feet felt boots of an unbelievable size. Very often on one foot would be a felt boot while on the other something different. She hid her care for everyone, her angelic kindness of soul.

Mother Anastasia foresaw much, yet she never spoke directly. Instead, she would do something, and later one might come to understand or figure it out as one was able. She had a fine voice and sang often, but not always, in church. She would stand on the left kliros, with a long, white prayer rope in her hand, which stood out against the black background of the workdress she usually wore, and with an incredible felt boot on one foot.

Once the nuns Tatiana and Irene saw through the window that Mother Anastasia was hurrying towards them. They had just finished planting some tomato seedlings in a garden bed and had sat down to eat. It was a warm, clear, sunny spring day. They invited Mother Anastasia to eat with them.

She answered them, "I have no time."

She went out to the garden and pulled all of the transplanted seedlings out of the ground, then dumped some earth on the roots, placed the box of them on the porch and said, "Let them grow here." They were of course dumbfounded, but kept silent.

She quickly turned and left. Towards evening there arose a strong wind, the kind that blows only in Kazakhstan. Dark clouds gathered, and a rainstorm poured down with large hail-stones. The hail destroyed the young sprouts in the garden, turning them into mush together with the earth. In the morning, however, Mothers Tatiana and Irene transplanted their to-mato seedlings from the box into a bed, awestruck and amazed. But it was impossible to say anything to Mother Anastasia about it—she would frown and turn away.

From the refectory a door led into another room, well lit with a high ceiling and with an enormous icon of the Kazan Mother of God. In it lived the two young women who served the Elder—"Batiushka's Vera" and Maria Obraztsova—who were almost the same age. Next to the window stood a four-legged table, always covered by a new oilcloth, upon which prepared food would be placed before they gave it to Fr. Sebastian. On this table stood an icon and an ever-burning lampada. Finally, a door led into a large, airy room with a heated vestibule, which in turn led into the Elder's cell. When the cell was built on, he im-mediately moved there, while his nuns remained on Lower Street for a long time, five or six years.

Fr. Sebastian selected his priests himself. Initially he would scrutinize one of his parishioners, then summon him and say, "You must be a priest." This was what happened with regard to Alexander Pavlovich Krivonosov, the learned agronomist, who had a good position monitoring rural agriculture on the Regional

Executive Committee. The Elder himself had blessed him a short time earlier to take this job. Alexander Pavlovich had been the one who had gone to Moscow to obtain the approval for the opening of the church. He was frightened by these words, not wishing to change his profession of agronomist, which he dearly loved. (He had graduated from the Moscow Timiryazev Academy.) He went home and thought for a long time; he couldn't sleep, and wept. But he dared not disobey. He came to see Fr. Sebastian and said, "Bless—I agree to it."

"Well, that's good; now, for the time being learn what you need to, and then you'll go to Alma-Ata for ordination."*

---

* A letter of Elder Sebastian's to Metropolitan Nicholas (Mogilevsky) of Alma-Ata and Kazakhstan has been preserved: "Your Eminence, holy Vladyka Nicholas, I beg your holy blessing. This is your obedient servant, the unworthy Sebastian. Holy Vladyka, I entreat you earnestly, if it is possible, to ordain to the priesthood Alexander Pavlovich Krivonosov, in view of the fact that my health is weakening and it is with great difficulty that I serve the parish. Now the holy time of Great Lent is approaching, and there will be many people to confess and commune, and therefore it would be very difficult for me to fulfill this holy matter alone. Thus I, the sinner, implore you not to refuse my request and that of my parishioners, to ordain Alexander Pavlovich a priest. Alexander Pavlovich is a moral man, sober, and in all regards worthy of the priestly calling. "

Alexander Pavlovich must be spoken of in more detail. In his youth he used to visit the Shamordino Convent, and Blessed Pelagia, who was living there, told him much about his life's path and about the future. Thus, she said that he would depart from Orthodoxy, would be attracted by various religious and political trends, but at the end of his life he would become the "Archimandrite of Diveyevo." Her words later proved true. He left Orthodoxy, joined the Old Believers, and was attracted by other religious currents. But when he encountered Elder Sebastian in Karaganda, the Elder affected him to such a degree that he was finally and irrevocably confirmed in Orthodoxy and became a priest. Fr. Alexander became a kind, loving pastor and doer of the Jesus Prayer. Up to his death he awaited the fulfillment of Blessed Pelagia's predictions and would say, "Everything she foretold to me has been fulfilled. Only one thing has not." But if one were to

Fr. Sebastian with co-celebrants. From left to right: Hieromonk Joseph, one of the Elder's acquaintances from Optina, Fr. Alexander Krivonosov, Elder Sebastian and Fr. Seraphim Trufanov.

It was the same with Seraphim Nikolaevich Trufanov, an economist by profession, also distinguished like Alexander Pavlovich. He had received the priesthood long before at the behest of his father, also a priest, yet he did not serve as a priest but worked as an economist. He, like Fr. Alexander, was single. The Elder drew him to the priestly service. These two priests served with him for a long time.

Then he sent the former church warden to Alma-Ata to be ordained. Fr. Paul Alexandrovich Kovalenko became the third

---

look in a broader sense, everything has been fulfilled. From this prophesy one may conclude that Elder Sebastian had created a "Diveyevo Convent" in Karaganda—that is, a women's community similar to that of Diveyevo. After the Elder's death Fr. Alexander became the Superior. So, in the eyes of God, he was the "Archimandrite of Diveyevo," which Blessed Pelagia had forseen. Fr. Alexander reposed in the Lord on June 5, 1971.

priest. He was a very pious and mature man. Even while still warden, he had competed several times, with the Elder's blessing, in debates with a Baptist leader who had come to the church courtyard to put the "popes" to shame in debate. But the Baptist himself had been put to shame by Paul Alexandrovich. Fr. Sebastian was appointed rector of the church and was the fourth priest. Bishop Joseph soon transferred Fr. Seraphim to Semipalatansk to be rector there. The deacon, Fr. Nicholas Samartsev, another of the Elder's candidates, was ordained as a celibate deacon. Basil Pavlovich became the church warden.

Elder Sebastian served as rector of the church for eleven years, from 1955 to 1966, until his death. In 1957, on December 9/22, the Feast of the Icon of the Theotokos "Unexpected Joy," he was elevated to the rank of archimandrite by Archbishop Joseph (Chernov) of Petropavlovsk and Kustanaisk, and was honored with an award "for zealous service to the Holy Church" by Patriarch Alexei. On December 18/31, 1964, on his nameday, he was awarded the mitre and an archpastoral staff. The latter award had no precedent. Three days before his death Fr. Sebastian was tonsured into the schema.

The Elder continued his untiring ascetic service to the Church from the time of his novitiate in the Skete of the Optina Monastery of the Entrance [of the Theotokos into the Temple] until the time of his rectorship of the church in Karaganda and his elevation to the rank of archimandrite—that is, for fifty-seven years, from 1909 until 1966.

Fr. Sebastian had an irreproachable fidelity to church rubrics, and allowed no omissions or abridgments in church services. For him church services were an inalienable condition of his spiritual life. He had a special reverence for the Feasts of the Lord's Ascension and Pentecost, as the culmination of the work of Christ the Savior, as the crown of all Christ's mysteries. In talks his favorite image was St. John the Theologian, whose commemoration he celebrated especially solemnly and reverently, requiring this of his flock as well. Appealing to his flock from the ambo, he would say, "Yesterday, on the day of the commemoration of St. Sergius of Radonezh (September 25/October 8), the church was bursting with people, but today (September 26/October 9), the day of the repose of St. John the Theologian, the church is half empty. How is it that you don't understand who is higher, whom should be more revered, and which feast is greater?" He likewise had a particular reverence for all seven feast days of the Forerunner and Baptist of the Lord, John, and for the feast day of the Holy Unmercenaries Cosmas and Damian (July 1/14), the protectors of his home village.

Fr. Sebastian's love was not condescending. He had the gift of great and profound discernment and exercised moderation in everything. He often said, "The more softly you go, the further you'll get," or, "The greatest virtue is discernment," or, "One must keep to the royal path"—that is, the middle way in everything. The main thing in him was his complete trust in God's Providence. Such was his pastoral image.

Each day after Liturgy the Elder would send Vera to distribute money to the poor near the church. Having overcome serious illnesses, he would often personally serve Liturgy and fulfill requested liturgical services. He especially loved memorial services celebrated according to the monastery custom he had inherited—he zealously served Pannikhidas daily, and continued celebrating funeral services until the end of his life. He said that he liked to commemorate and serve funerals for women more because among women there were far fewer sins. To him all the sins of people were visible. "A golden mean is needed in everything, along with moderation," he would say. "And regarding service to God and one's salvation, constancy is needed. This is the main thing, and there should be neither haste nor excess." Again he would repeat, "The more softly you go, the further you'll get." Once the Elder spoke about one woman, saying that she had begun to pray a great deal. He said, "Why are you doing that? There's no need, you might over-pray." "The Lord will not allow suffering beyond our strength, and so we must endure everything," he said. "But pride is more terrible than anything. It's a demonic characteristic."

Fr. Sebastian's spiritual loftiness was closely and powerfully felt and, as it were, awed people, instilling in them a pious fear. Great was his popularity, and even deeper was the respect toward him. He had a natural breadth of soul, a love for beauty in general and for the beauty of nature in particular. He felt compassion for animals. Once the following incident took place: The "kitchen cat" bore five or six kittens. The cook and someone else wanted to drown them. Somehow, suddenly the Elder appeared in the kitchen and heard this conversation. He was all atremble and almost screamed: "Don't you dare drown them! We'll raise them all!" All the kittens were kept, and when they had grown a little they were all snatched up, as "a blessing from Batiushka," by the Mikhailovka parishioners.

He felt great warmth and love for art. There was a certain special softness of soul in him. All of these qualities and all of his spiritual experience—acquired during fourteen years of life in the Skete and nineteen years of close daily interaction with the great Optina Elders, his life having passed under their guidance—predetermined his path toward active ascetic service to men, taking the most varied forms of help.

The Elder's health was weak. He especially suffered from a condition of his esophagus. Everyone knew that he could not be disturbed or distracted with conversations under any circumstances while he was eating. He would immediately begin coughing, which would sometimes end with vomiting. This illness was a result of nervous shocks, a multitude of which the Elder had endured during his long life. He was always in a tense state. When the church was not yet registered, and the Elder would serve Divine Liturgy with his closest people, he constantly experienced a feeling of fear. He would say, "'Well, then, Batiushka,' they say, 'serve!' But do you realize what I go through?" After all, he was breaking the law. At any time they could come and arrest everyone. Later, when they were serving openly in the church, the Elder's fear let up somewhat. It would happen that someone with military shoulder straps would drop by the church and Fr. Sebastian would already be thinking, "He could come up right now, interrupt the service and arrest us." Once one of his spiritual children said to him, "I'm afraid of such-and-such a person." And he would smile and say, "Really? But I'm not afraid of him. I'm not afraid of anyone. I'm afraid that they'll close the church. That's what I'm afraid of. I don't fear for myself, but for you. I know what I have to do; but what you're going to do, I don't know." These were the Elder's words.

When Elder Sebastian had strength, he would, after each Liturgy, serve a Moleben. The choir would sing, and they would read two Akathists. When he was in a weakened state, they would read only one Akathist. At the end of the Moleben he would offer the cross to be kissed and would unfailingly give a short homily. Though in a soft voice, he always gave some kind of edifying instruction. Of course, the whole church would remain for the Moleben. Many young people would be there. On the cliros alone a choir of up to seventeen young women would stand and sing. And they would all hide when the government representative came to check up on things. As soon as they heard, "The authorities!"—they would all hide. Up to eight people would come with the representative. They would come into the church and only old women would be standing at the cliros. The authorities kept dreaming of closing the church, and they often summoned the Elder "over there." He would go, and they would be unable to say anything. "What's with this old man?" they would say. "Why can't we do anything? Well, let him be an elder; but when his time as elder passes, then we'll close the church." The representatives of the local government preferred to speak with Fr. Alexander. They could obviously sense the Elder's spiritual loftiness, and it frightened them, instilling in them a reverent fear.

Once the plenipotentiary of religious affairs of the regional executive committee began to demand of the church warden of Fr. Sebastian's church that his clergy cease going to the city of Saran and the settlement of Dubovka, since they belonged to a different region. The warden passed this demand along to the Elder, and the next day he went, along with the warden, to the executive committee. When the Elder spoke with the plenipotentiary, the latter immediately changed his tone. He began to explain himself, and even apologized before the Elder. Fr. Sebastian then turned to him and said, "Comrade plenipotentiary, surely you'll give us permission, in accordance with the requests of the miners, to perform special services in Saran, Dubovka, and the other settlements. Sometimes a mother asks that a sick one be communed, or that a funeral be served for the reposed. " The plenipotentiary graciously said, "Please, Fr. Sebastian, fulfill their requests; don't refuse them." No matter what questions the Elder put to him, he refused almost nothing. And he never again mentioned anything to the church warden.

For the Elder's spiritual children his nameday and his birthday were festive events. Everyone wanted to go up to him and congratulate him, and give him even a small gift. But Fr. Sebastian did not like honors or special attention, nor did he like to receive gifts. Everyone would gather to congratulate him, but he would come home late in the evening or the next day. Once the Elder came home in the evening on his nameday, opened the door to his cell, and, without entering it, unexpectedly exclaimed, "Who?! Who has allowed my soul and my cell to be cluttered up?!" The cell-attendants, alarmed by such a reaction, glanced into the cell and saw that near his bed there stood some new felt boots. Someone had placed them there without the Elder's blessing.

The Elder likewise did not like it when someone was extolled. He would immediately say something about the shortcomings of that person. But if he saw that someone was being disparaged, he would quickly find in that person the very best qualities. No matter what kind of sins he had, the Elder would find something good.

The Elder expended much labor for the nurturing of his flock. The life of the parishioners close to him transpired beneath his watchful eye. He was gifted with a subtle sense of humor and liked to joke, but always very benevolently. He didn't begrudge his time in giving counsels and directions, in forbidding or absolving something; he diagnosed the proper matter for everyone. The lives of these people were models of virtue. They were called the "Batiushka-ites." The very least of his counsels, the smallest, were always profitable. Once he was walking with someone down the street and walked next to the pavement, on the ground, where the grass was growing. "It's better to walk here," he said; "it's softer on the feet and wears out the shoes less."

It was said that a good half of Mikhailovka was like a secret monastery in the world. In association with the Elder it would somehow become indisputably and even graphically clear, without any need for words, that the soul lives eternally—that our life does not die, it's only our body that becomes worn out; that the soul is not something vague but the whole man, the true person, the inner man. This was so simple and he spoke about this so simply, as about something ordinary, long known to everyone.

Fr. Sebastian often travelled to the settlements of Dubovka, Saran, Fyodorovka and Topar. He would baptize and serve funerals in homes. In those places which he would visit, parishes have been formed at the present time by his prayers. He would also go to the settlement of Dolinka, where he had served out his term of imprisonment. There was preserved in Dolinka a cross carved in a tree, which the Elder had carved with his own hand. The tree had grown since then, and the cross had grown along with it. In Dolinka, under almost every tree there was a person buried, a prisoner. There was a grave under almost every tree.

But the Elder especially liked to be in the settlement of Melkombinat. He would say that in Mikhailovka he had his "Optina," and in Melkombinat he had his "Skete." He gathered his orphans and widows there, bought them a house and became their guardian. When he would come to Melkombinat to pray, people would cast aside their work and cares and, one after another, would hasten to where Fr. Sebastian was, if only to receive his blessing and be consoled. He would meet each with love, and to each would say something edifying. A spirit of peace reigned here.

Overcoming illnesses, weakness, and old age, the Elder fulfilled his pastoral responsibilities until the last days of his life, relinquishing the secret desire of his soul, to lay aside the rectorship for retirement and receive the schema. At the Melkombinat settlement lived Fr. Sebastian's old widowed brother Hilarion, who would come to see him together with his youngest daughter and his granddaughter Thaisia, a wonderful young woman in all respects. Thaisia worked as a nurse. The Elder had bought them a large, comfortable home; he wished to go live with them in retirement. He liked the Melkombinat settlement, and it was there, on a quiet street, that he bought a nice home for Vera. Vera furnished it and settled two women there, but very seldom did she personally go there. Hilarion Vasilievich Fomin came to church on Sundays and feast days with his daughter and granddaughter. He would bow to the ground,

Fr. Sebastian in the midst of his beloved Melkombinat community. Sitting beside the Elder is Abbot Parmenas, also a former prisoner of the Karlag.

approach Fr. Sebastian for a blessing and reverently kiss his hand. He confessed to him kneeling, and with tears he would beg his forgiveness for past offenses. He was a real old-timer, ninety years old, tall and erect, whereas Fr. Sebastian was of short stature. Before the end of his life Hilarion was tonsured as a riassophore monk and is commemorated as such. His daughter was also getting on in years, and was very modest and quiet. He and Thaisia dearly loved the Elder.

None of his spiritual children took a step without his blessing. The Elder was very distressed when someone did not listen and carry out his counsel, because it was always to the harm and frequently to the misfortune of that person. In such cases, he often wept. He frequently wept during confession. Why? Either he was horrified by some sin, or he didn't see the requisite repentance, or else he foresaw something. His love was tender and considerate, and imparted joy and happiness. Sometimes he would grow angry, but this was seldom; he was always, as it were, hoping to make one obedient. This came out of him in a child-like manner. He would say, "Look, I'll take a stick and let you have it; boy, will I let you have it with a stick!" In such cases, people often fell to their knees and asked forgiveness; it was not the stick that they found threatening, but the thought that they might have upset him.

For thirteen and a half years I was Elder Sebastian's spiritual daughter. This happiness cannot be compared with anything. There was such total protection in everything, such love. No matter what would happen, if you would only manage to run to him and succeed in informing him, he would take everything away and right every wrong. He would even prolong one's life. As he once told me, or, to be more precise, as he once spilled out during a frank conversation, "How many lives I've prolonged."

He once told me about the arrival of Leo Tolstoy at the [Optina] Skete after his clandestine departure from "Yasnaya Polyana." It happened like this:

"When Leo Tolstoy came to the Skete on one of the last days of October, 1910, I was serving as Elder Joseph's cell-attendant. Leo Tolstoy had arrived in Optina from Kozelsk the day before, late in the evening, and had spent the night in the monastery guesthouse. The guest master, Fr. Michael, later related that, after tea, Tolstoy had questioned him about the Elders and asked which of them was receiving people, and if Elder Joseph might receive him, saying that he had come to visit and have a chat with the Elders."

Fr. Michael recounted the following:

> They came—there were two of them. They knocked. I opened the door. Leo Nikolaevich asked, "May I enter?"
> I said, "Please do."
> But he said, "Perhaps it's not possible for me; I'm Tolstoy."

"Why not?" I said, "we're happy to receive everyone who has a desire to see us."

Then he said, "Well, greetings, brother."

I answered, "Greetings, your Excellency."

He said, "You weren't offended that I called you brother? All men are brothers."

I replied, "Not in the least; and it's true that all are brothers."

Well, that's how things stood between us. I conducted him into the best room. Early in the morning I sent an assistant to the skete Superior, Fr. Barsanuphius, to warn him that Tolstoy was coming to the Skete to see him.

About what happened afterwards, Fr. Sebastian himself recounted the following to me:

"Elder Joseph was ill, and I was sitting beside him. Elder Barsanuphius called on us and related that Fr. Michael had sent to warn him that Tolstoy was coming to see him. Elder Barsanuphius said, 'I asked him, "Who told you?" and he replied that Tolstoy himself had said so.'

"Hearing this, Elder Joseph said, 'If he comes, we'll receive him with affection, respect and joy, even though he's been excommunicated. This time he came on his own—no one indeed forced him to come, otherwise we couldn't receive him.' Then they sent me to look outside the skete enclosure. I saw Leo Nikolaevich and reported to the Elders that he was walking close alongside the house, at first approaching, then stepping back.

"Elder Joseph said, 'It's hard for him. He's surely come to us for living water. Go and invite him in, if he's come to see us. Go ask him.' I went out, but he was no longer there; he had left. He could only have just gone off but, after all, he would have been on a horse, so I couldn't have caught up with him. Later there was a message to the Elder from Tolstoy's sister, the Nun Maria, that he had left her from Shamordino. Then from the Astapovo railroad station a telegram arrived for us concerning the illness of Leo Nikolaevich in which, in his name, the Elder was asked to come to him. Fr. Barsanuphius immediately left, but those who surrounded Tolstoy would not let him see Leo Nikolaevich. Fr. Barsanuphius passed a letter in to his daughter Alexandra.

"He wrote to her that 'it was, in fact, the will of your father that I come.' All the same, they didn't let him in. Nor would they allow in Tolstoy's wife Sophia Andreyevna. She had come in her own train-carriage and lived at the station in it. This was a very difficult experience for Fr. Barsanuphius; he returned nearly ill and always became upset when he recalled it. And he said, 'Though he was a lion,* yet he could not break the chains. It's a pity, a great pity.' Elder Joseph also felt deeply for him.

"Fr. Barsanuphius said that it was not true that someone had sent him. 'It was solely because of the desire of Leo Nikolaevich himself that I went to Astapovo,' he affirmed."

The Elder's constant care was to establish deep peace in people's souls through the cutting off of one's will. He tried to bring his own life and the life of his flock in line with monastic life. He was always greatly distressed if someone did not obey him and did not fulfill his counsel. This was always dangerous and often to a person's misfortune. Sometimes he even became angry. He would turn away, move aside and would not bless. If he would see that there were tears or that the person was changing his mind, he would feel sorry for him and at a certain point would unfailingly cheer him up somehow. If he would see that a person heeded his counsel in the end, he would greatly rejoice, even becoming totally radiant, as sometimes happened. Once I heard how he spoke to one young woman: "You haven't been obeying me. Why are you coming now, weeping and pleading? Now you'll have to endure." And turning to the other young women, he said, "Why don't you listen? You see, I'm..." he stumbled, "not always wrong...." Such was his humility.

---

*Tolstoy's first name in Russian, "Lev," means "lion."—Trans.

Elder Sebastian in his cell. Above him is a portrait of his beloved Elder Joseph.

My first meeting with Elder Sebastian took place in 1952 and was a shock to my soul. I had arrived in Karaganda eight years after him, on August 31, 1952, having been forbidden to go home to Moscow. At first I wanted to find a place to live in the city of Kokchetav. There was a good, healthy climate there, and forests. It was in the proximity of the Kazakhstan oasis—the Borovov resort with its lakes and pine forests—but none of my friends were there. However, my very closest friend had settled in Kazakhstan one and a half years before my arrival. This was the Doctor R. G. L., with whom I had worked for eight years in the camp hospital and had lived for five years in the same room. We had been through a lot together. All paths led to Karaganda, and I finally dropped in on her. We settled there and continued to be friends. Karaganda was not strange to me; it was somehow like a second homeland. Thus I remained in the sooty, dusty coal-mining town of Karaganda, with its burning, purple gas fires above the mining wastes. I was no longer drawn to the pine-fresh air of Kokchetav, thanks to the friendly warmth and closeness of soul of tried, faithful friends. And I found work according to my desire, which was interesting as well.

During the third week in October, R. G. L. was terribly ill with malaria. Her temperature of over 104° fell for a short time, and again another such severe attack began. When the attacks overcame her, there suddenly began a heavy delirium of severe psychosis.

She lived in another district of the city, far from me. Her daughter could not cope with her. They called an ambulance, and that night she was taken to the psychiatric hospital twelve miles away in Kompanaisk. When I arrived there with her daughter, we were absolutely dumbfounded and over-whelmed. It was not her; her appearance was frightening. She was like an animal—she took the food which we had brought her from our hands; she crammed it with rapidity into her mouth and again took more. Then she began to walk around us on all fours. The orderlies carried her into the ward. Her daughter sobbed inconsolably.

I took her to my home. We arrived worn out, tired, not feeling like ourselves. My housekeeper, learning what had happened, began to say to me, "Don't despair. I advise you to do this—tomorrow take the following trip…. We have a suburb, Mikhailovka; a Batiushka lives there, a monk—he's absolutely special. Many now fervently trust in him, that he can help in misfortune. Ask him, and he'll pray and help your sick friend. Go—don't doubt, and don't be afraid. If he agrees to pray, everything will go well with your sick friend. Ask him—explain everything to him." She didn't know the address, but said that in Mikhailovka everyone knew him and would show me where he lived. When I had come to Karaganda, I went to church at the Second Mine every Saturday and Sunday. I had become acquainted with many people there, but no one had spoken to me about a priest in Mikhailovka.

The very next day I went to Mikhailovka. Some woman did in fact show me immediately where the Elder lived. He lived at the very beginning of Mikhailovka, on Lower Street. Mother Agrippina opened the door for me, but Fr. Sebastian was not at home. I told her why I had come. She was friendly with me and said, "Yes, you must definitely speak with Batiushka; tell him and ask his help." She gave me the address where he had gone to serve a short service, saying, "There's a bench outside this house. Sit there, and watch. When you hear them singing, this means that the memorial meal has ended and Fr. Sebastian will come right out. He might not want to stand with you; he doesn't like to stop in the street. But walk alongside him and tell him your need. Tell him—tell him everything you need. Although he'll be walking, he'll listen to you."

This is exactly what happened. I sat, agitated, on the bench. Then they sang inside the house. Just as they finished singing, right out through the gate walked an old man of medium height with a gray beard, in a long black overcoat with a little black cap. Without lifting his eyes and without glancing at me he walked on along the street, with a light, hasty pace. I walked alongside and told him why I had come. He walked silently, without slowing his pace, but listened attentively to me. When I began to ask his help, he stopped, looked at me with his kind, extraordinary eyes, with a gaze which penetrated into my soul, and quietly, simply said, "But she's neither Orthodox nor a believer."

I was terribly startled. "Yes," I said, "she's a Lutheran. Her father was Estonian and her mother was Russian. She's not opposed to the faith, but she's far from it. She's a good, kind person."

The Elder was again walking at the same quick pace. "It's not a problem that she's a Lutheran. Lutherans are also Christians," he said. He looked at me again and said, "All right, I'll pray. Visit her in two or three days. And you yourself should pray fervently, too. Well, here I am—this is my house. Good-bye."

In three days it was Sunday, and in the morning we went by train to Kompanaisk, to the hospital. Everything there was somehow like in a family, not like in a big city. There were low, single-storeyed little houses in a green courtyard, and in the courtyard many benches. Through the courtyard various medical personnel in white smocks passed hurriedly from house to house. On the many benches sat visibly recovering patients who were out for a walk. The senior nurse met us outside and began to smile at us. "I can cheer you up," she said. "It's been two days since your sick friend 'woke up.' They've already moved her to the separate convalescent ward—the sanitarium, as it is called. There it is, the second house on the left. Go over there. She'll make you happy."

They let us right into her quarters. R. G. was sitting on her bed, her hair combed, neat, in a new gown, with her former countenance, and drinking tea. She really cheered us up. "How did I wind up here? What happened to me?" she asked us. Of course we

84

were both joyous and astonished—such a change in two days! On the return trip in the train I sat in the corner, turned to the window, and wept. Dear Batiushka! What a miracle!

The next day I just couldn't work. Immediately after making my rounds of the sick I left the hospital to thank the Elder. At home he was totally different than out on the street—kind and amiable. He requested that I stay with them for lunch. He told a story, was joyful and asked about many things.

I no longer went to the church at the Second Mine. Mother Agrippina gave me an address where I could spend the night, with Nun Maria, whenever I could come to the Elder's services at night. Soon I became his personal physician and spiritual daughter. My life flowed along in a totally different direction than before. I became a "Batiushka-ite."

I'll always remember the first case of the Elder's clairvoyance that I witnessed. He was serving a Pannikhida and was reading the lists with the names of those who were being commemorated. During the reading of the lists he stopped, and, holding one in his hand, looked around. "Who submitted this commemoration: 'John, Simeon, Olga, Maria'?" "I did, Batiushka!" responded one woman. "And when did this Simeon die?"

"A long time ago, Batiushka."

"Take this slip," said Fr. Sebastian, "I can't commemorate him. Bring me a certificate of his death."

The woman flared up. "What do you mean, Batiushka? I'm not some little girl that would do a thing like that."*

"That's very nice; now bring me a certificate." Fr. Sebastian didn't know this woman; she was a newcomer, otherwise she might not have dared to deceive him.

---

*There exists a crude superstition that if you write down the name of a living person in the commemoration "for the reposed," that person becomes strongly troubled and is drawn towards the person who commemorates him in this way.

I was struck not only by the Elder's clairvoyance, but also by how he focused on each name he commemorated. How great was the power of his commemoration in prayer!

Here is another instance: There sang in the Elder's choir a young woman—Marusya Stakanova. She was from the children's home, where she ended up after leaving the foundlings' home. She was an orphan and knew nothing about her parents, even their nationality, but she was a brunette, with very dark skin, hair and eyes. When she was still in the children's home - they called her "Marusya Stakanchik" (the little drinking-glass).

Once she approached Fr. Sebastian and told him that she was grieved that she did not know the names and nationalities of her parents and was unable to commemorate them or pray for their repose. "I have no time now," said the Elder, "I'm going to be busy. Come tomorrow, we'll have a talk." The next day he himself called her and said, "Marusya, your parents were Orthodox, Russians and exiles." Then he gave her father's name, as well as her mother's. Marusya greatly rejoiced and began to submit their names for commemoration.

Mother Maria, with whom I spent the night when I came for the Elder's services at night, was old, quite hunched-over and thin, but tireless and a quick worker. She was Fr. Sebastian's altar-attendant. She had known him from his youth and, finding him after his imprisonment in Karaganda, she had come to him for good. She bought a small house in Mikhailovka. In a large room she placed two iron beds, two narrow couches and, behind them, several closed-up folding beds—these were all for overnight guests. She herself, when there were many such guests, lay on a trunk, on some sort of rolled-up bedding with a ball of yarn for a pillow. When we, the night-guests, came to her in the evening, tea was always boiling on the stove. She poured tea for all, and most comfortably and solicitously made everyone's bed for the night.

In Karaganda, far from the Mikhailovka suburb, in a hospital amidst massive coal mines, I headed the large therapy division. Once a commission from the Regional Health Department came to me to verify the division's work. It was headed by a Dr. Olga Fyodorovna Orlova, a therapist from the Regional Hospital and the Clinic of the Institute for Nurses. The commission inspected the food service area, the chambers, and the case histories of the sick for a long time and finally left.

The next day I arrived to spend the night at Mikhailovka. Everyone was already drinking tea at Mother Maria's; some were even asleep. Some other people had arrived as well. There were quite a few people; all the spaces were occupied. I slept on an iron bed, as if on a comfortable and privileged spot. Mother Maria came up to me and began to whisper, "Tatiana Vladimirovna, excuse me. A woman has come, and there isn't any other place for her to lie down. Move over toward the wall. She's very clean, neat, and cultured...." I didn't catch any more of her words and, without opening my eyes, so as not to interrupt my sleep, I moved over against the wall.

Someone slid against my back underneath the blanket, and I went to sleep. And what was our mutual surprise, when Mother Maria awakened us, and my eyes met those of the one who slept behind my back. It was Olga Fyodorovna! We were both bewildered, even frightened, and then burst out laughing.

We headed out together into the night along the dark street which was illumined solely by the stars of the frozen, wintry sky. We soon reached the warm, heated house, with the tightly covered windows, and within it the Elder and the services in the dead of night.

In 1955, Mother Maria's upper lip began to hurt her. The lip was deformed by a growing tumor, dark blue and unpleasant. She was taken to a surgeon, who said that it was necessary to operate immediately and set forth the procedures to the oncological staff. My suspicion, that it was cancer, had been confirmed.

She went to obtain a blessing for the operation but the Elder said, "The tumor is now large; they may cut open the lip, but such a spot can appear in another place. No, an operation isn't necessary. Go venerate the icon of the Holy Trinity that's on the pannikhida table.* May God grant that it will pass."

Mother Maria became cheerful. I thought there wasn't any hope for improvement and that her days were numbered. I soon left for two months on vacation. When I returned I saw Mother Maria just as busy and fussy as before. She had just lit the censer that the Elder used for memorial services, and on her lip there wasn't any trace of the tumor. "How did you treat your lip?" I asked. "I didn't treat it; I just venerated the icon of the Holy Trinity as Fr. Sebastian blessed me to do, and the tumor gradually got smaller and totally disappeared. Glory be to God!"

There was another, similar instance. Riassaphore-nun Paraskeva, who always read the Psalter for the dead, had on her chest, below her neck, on the left side, a blue-colored blemish. It began to grow and turn dark red. Paraskeva went to the hospital, to the outpatient clinic. They immediately told her that she must be quickly operated on, with the understanding that this was cancer. Bursting into tears, Pashenka walked to the gates of the church. There she was met by a woman, a believer, who had great faith in the power of the Elder's prayers, and she advised her not to cry, but to go to Fr. Sebastian. Paraskeva heeded her. She came away from the Elder radiant: "Batiushka said, 'Cancer, cancer—you fool!** Don't go anywhere, it'll pass.'" And, what do you know? The blemish began to grow pale, became

---

*In Orthodox churches there is a table, usually before a depiction of the crucifixion, where Pannikhidas are celebrated and candles are placed to commemorate the dead.—ED.

** In Russian, this statement rhymes: *"Rak, rak—durak!"* —TRANS.

smaller, and soon disappeared without a trace. And that riassaphore-nun lived for another thirty years, to a ripe old age, and was tonsured.

The Elder never healed or cast demons out of anyone openly. Due to his modesty and simplicity he would always say, "I don't heal anyone, I don't exorcise anyone—go to the hospital." "I," he would say, "am like a dumb fish." That is how he would abase himself. He would help people by his secret prayers. Concerning the possessed he would say, "Here they suffer, but there, they'll pass through the toll houses painlessly.... I don't want to take your cross from you. You'll suffer here, but in Heaven you'll obtain a greater reward." And he would console them, the sufferers.

The Elder possessed spiritual wisdom and great patience. When someone would murmur against his neighbor he would say, "I endure all of you, but you don't even want to endure one person." If people were unable to get along, he would become anxious: "I'm the Superior, yet I obey all of you." He took care for the salvation of each person—that was his goal. He implored them, "Live more peaceably." Once he went to serve a special service and forgot the censer. Everyone began reproaching one another. Fr. Sebastian said, "I myself am to blame," and they all fell silent. The Elder would say, "Well, I've assembled all of you here—the blind, the lame and the half-baked. I myself am sick, and I've gathered the sick." Fr. Alexander, who served with him, did not have much of a voice, and Fr. Paul also had a weak voice. "Well, we've gathered together here, and we'll serve in our own small way, no matter how half-baked we are!"

Fr. Sebastian did not bless people to travel to different monasteries. "Here," he would say, is the Lavra, and Pochaev, and Optina. Services are going on in the church—everything is here." If someone was preparing to move somewhere, he would say, "Don't go anywhere; there will be danger everywhere, disorder everywhere. But it will only graze the edge of Karaganda."

His Holiness Patriarch Alexis I greatly desired to see the Elder and speak with him. He blessed Bishop Pitirim (Nechaev) to bring him, even if by plane. But Fr. Sebastian was already weak and did not consent to it. "I'm not fit to take a plane," replied the Elder, and he stayed in Karaganda.

Elder Sebastian attributed great significance to the veneration of icons and the placing of candles before them. Sometimes he would summon a certain spiritual child or parishioner and give a bunch of candles, at one time more and at another time fewer. And he would say, "Pray—light candles more often." Either he felt that something ominous would happen to this person or he saw something else, since the person would seldom light candles before the icons. Often the explanation would later be revealed. But, to one of his spiritual daughters who had monastic inclinations, he said on one occasion: "You don't need to light candles—you yourself will be a candle."

If he noticed that someone did not venerate icons he would tell him, "When, my dear one, you are pondering or deliberating something, keep a correct discernment in your heart and mind. Discernment is the highest virtue." He would tell this to many. I heard how he said to one person, "My dear, understand first of all that it's difficult for you to comprehend much, and therefore it's easy for you to be mistaken. For it's in this way that people often take their ignorance for wisdom." He once told me that Elder Nektary always said that wisdom, intellect and discernment are gifts of the Holy Spirit that lead one to piety, and that a person deprived of the gift of discernment often imagines himself to be superior to others. He further added, "With what is one's defense from evil sought? Not in pride, but in humility is it bought."

The Elder always spoke about icons with reverence and love. He would say, "On the feast of the Triumph of Orthodoxy what do we celebrate? That the iconoclast heresy was overthrown! The grace of God lies upon icons. They protect us from the dark powers. They are given to us as a help from God. There are certain holy things in which the grace of the Holy Spirit accumulates. And the icons especially imbued with grace are those before which the faithful have prayed throughout the centuries, the wonderworking icons. Icons, like little hands from the Lord, bring us grace. One must regard an icon with reverence, with love and with thanksgiving to God."

Fr. Sebastian would often repeat how one must carry out one's duties unwaveringly. I once said to him after a Pannikhida, "You're very tired again today. You took such a long time serving the Pannikhida." He grabbed a small bundle of lists for commemoration from the pannikhida table and showed it to me. "Here, look; I have to pray through every such stack."

In accordance with the monastic custom he had inherited, the Elder especially liked to celebrate services for the reposed, and he served Pannikhidas daily. He would say that he liked to serve funerals and Pannikhidas for women more, because they had far fewer sins. The sins of the reposed were visible to him. It would happen that he would get his novices up at three or four in the morning and have them bring him lists of the reposed for him to commemorate. After Fr. Sebastian's repose, people had dreams like this: Many churches would be standing, all in gold and tall, and amidst them one small church covered with crosses. The people would ask, "Whose church is that, with the crosses?" "This," would be the reply, "is Schema-archimandrite Sebastian's church. He loved to pray for the reposed, and therefore this church is completely guarded by crosses, so that no one will be able to do anything to it." And it has stood there for forty years already.

Elder Sebastian was simple and accessible. And all the same I always experienced trepidation before his incomprehensibility. My heart always shrank when during services he would walk out of the altar through the pannikhida chapel and, standing in the doorway which opened into the church, would look out. He would gaze attentively for a long time at the people who were standing in church. The Elder's gaze would vary—at times it would be severe and penetrating, at times vague as if he noticed no one, at times reaching somewhere afar off and seeing something in the distance. Sometimes his gaze reminded one of that of a bird, when it was impossible to figure out whom or what he was looking at. When Fr. Sebastian looked directly at one, then his gaze was "present," always friendly and kind. And it was then easy to be with him and to be joyful. And such was the love expressed toward him—radiant and joyful and light. Only such love as this could fill one's soul. What happiness!

Once his gaze fell upon me under unusual circumstances. A great unpleasantness had come to me—not merely an unpleasantness, but a great trial had befallen me; it was like an unexpected misfortune, and it was no one's fault but my own. I came to church and the Elder was serving. I went to the furthest corner, to the only hidden recess. At the back of the right cliros stood a large crucifix, which enclosed the cliros, and to the right of it near the window was a secluded corner. I knelt and prayed ardently; my face was covered with tears. Suddenly, raising my head as if I had been shoved, I caught sight of Fr. Sebastian, or, more accurately, of his eyes, fixed on me. He stood at the corner of the cliros against the outside wall, in a small nook between the crucifix and the wall; and he looked at me directly, seriously, and with alarm. I was conscious that he was coming towards me, troubled at the condition of my soul. He came—he hastened to catch from me the sound of my silent account of everything that had happened. He was coming to me! He never went to the cliros during the services, even less so to that far corner. I looked into his eyes. Not I, but my soul which was opened to him, looked at him. And the tears which poured forth from my eyes were now totally different, but perhaps I was no longer crying. No, I wept. I wept from love, out of holy love for the Lord. And thereby it was easy to entrust my sorrow into his hands, since he was here for my sake and not for anyone else's, and also because it was so radiant in the church. But the important thing was that he existed at all, and I understood how the Lord "resteth in His saints."

But from whence was all this given to me, and for what reason; "And whence is this to me…?" (Luke 1:43). The Elder had already left and had made the priest's exclamation from the altar. He had been there only for a very short moment, yet I was still weeping softly, more and more quietly, not getting up from my knees.

There lived in the settlement of Tikhonovka the Hieromonk Tryphon, who had lived in the Monastery of St. Peter in Moscow until its closure. He was often at the Elder's place, especially on feast days. He had a pleasant voice, so he sang in our choir and would sing solo as well. An incident occurred involving him which Fr. Sebastian strictly forbade him to make known. "Only when I die," said the Elder, "then you can tell." After his death, Fr. Tryphon related this incident in detail to both Fr. Alexander Krivonosov and me.

After the opening of the church in Mikhailovka, Fr. Sebastian, with the help of the rector of the church at the Second Mine, managed to organize prayer houses in Tikhonovka and Fyodorovka where Fr. Tryphon served with the Elder's blessing, since he was the only free priest, that is, the only one in Karaganda not assigned to a parish. He himself lived in Tikhonovka and would go to Fyodorovka, which was far away, on certain days to serve specific liturgical needs. Monks lived and conducted the services in these houses.

Although Fr. Tryphon was old, he was in good health, and, more importantly, he was deeply devoted to the work of the Orthodox Church and to the Elder.

One Sunday after the service he approached Fr. Sebastian to get a blessing to travel that day to Fyodorovka. The Elder looked at him attentively and, blessing him, said, "I wanted to personally send you there today, but don't ride there. Go on foot straight through the Park Preserve." He said this sternly. Fr. Tryphon was amazed because, although the Park Preserve lay directly ahead, the path was very long and tiring. But, of course, he went as the Elder had blessed him.

The Park Preserve occupied a very large sector of the city—it was a massive nursery for trees which were grown to supply greenery for the parks, streets and courtyards of the city. Beyond it stretched the territory of two Pioneer camps, and beyond these stretched the Botanical Gardens, which were affiliated with the Botanical Gardens of the Academy of Sciences in Moscow. Then began the last part of the road which ran along the highway to Fyodorovka, past the prison. The route was very long. But by the highway one could travel directly from Mikhailovka to Fyodorovka.

The Park Preserve had first begun to be planted in the 1930s. There were many old trees, under which open paths stretched from one end to the other, and there was much thick undergrowth.

As Fr. Tryphon traversed the Park Preserve he didn't encounter a single person on the path. But suddenly from behind a dense bush a sturdily built young man jumped out in a very excited state. The man grabbed him by the hand and pulled him into the woods, off the path. Fr. Tryphon was very frightened, but was forced to submit, hurrying after him into the heart of the woods. The man pulled him along, "Let's go, Father, let's go; I've been waiting for you for a long time. I've totally worn myself out." "I thought my end had come," Fr. Tryphon told us. When they entered into the thick of the forest, the man let go of Fr. Tryphon's arm and said, "Well, Father, sit on the stump.

Hear me out and decide my fate. On the path our conversation might have been disturbed." He began to tell his story:

"I dearly love my wife. She's beautiful, young, intelligent and a good housekeeper. We live amiably, amidst plenty. I very much want to have a child—and not only one—but we have none. Suddenly, yesterday, I found out from a nurse that last week my wife had an abortion. Fortunately, my wife had gone to work at her shift. I suffered alone all night with my thoughts. 'What does it mean?' I thought. Perhaps the baby is not mine. That means she's been deceiving me. And if it is from me, then she doesn't love me and decided to do away with it. All these years she's been lying to me. And because of her lie, because she's committed such a crime, to kill such a long-awaited baby, I've decided that I can't forgive her, no matter what. And to live without taking revenge on her—this I can't do. I decided that I have to kill her. As I came to this firm decision I began to feel a little more peaceful. I don't know whether I dreamed or dozed off, but I dreamed that a little old man of medium height with a large beard said to me, 'What's this? You've made this decision on your own, without taking counsel with anyone; this can't possibly be done. You have to get some advice first,' he said. 'Ask counsel; tell everything to the first old man you meet on the road. And do as he tells you.' And he spoke so sternly. 'If you've decided correctly, the man will tell you so; but since you're in a frenzy now, you could easily make a mistake.'

"I was sitting on the bed, and there wasn't anyone there. But I had clearly heard the voice. I jumped up from the bed and ran from the house before my wife came home from work. I walked along the street and thought, 'How could I possibly tell anyone on the street and pour out my soul? Who could stand to hear me out and get involved in my predicament? People are busy with their own affairs; most likely the man would call the police and turn me in.' And so I decided to walk to the Park Preserve and wait until an elderly man passed by, since I could talk here un-hurriedly and force him to hear me out, and there are no police. And I could force him to give me a proper answer. All this would be possible here. Only tell me the truth, the very truth as you un-derstand it concerning my wife. Why did she do such a thing? Tell me what you really think, or it'll go badly for you. I can fig-ure out if you're beating around the bush."

"What's your name?" Fr. Tryphon asked him. "Nicholas." "Well then, wait a minute," said Fr. Tryphon, "and I'll pray to your Saint, Nicholas the God-pleaser. You see, I'm a monk. I'll pray to St. Nicholas to reveal the truth to us."

After prayer Fr. Tryphon told the man reassuringly, gently, "Well, here's how it is, Kolya! Your wife is already repenting. She loves you. She's faithful to you; she's weeping right now. She regrets that she wanted to continue living freely, without cares. She treasures you. Go home peacefully; forgive your wife. Make peace and live together in harmony." The man's face brightened up; his temporary madness left him. "Soon a child will be born to you. This is what St. Nicholas told me. I'm not saying this of myself."

The man began to tremble all over, sobbing, and falling down at Fr. Tryphon's feet. He began to ask forgiveness and to thank him. "After all, I might have killed you if I had decided to kill my wife. I would have feared you as a witness; I was crazy."

"Well, go calmly, Kolya; go in peace. I forgive you."

Fr. Tryphon walked to Fyodorovka not feeling like himself, and thought, "How could the Elder have blessed me to walk through the woods? Such danger lay in wait for me there." When Fr. Tryphon next saw Fr. Sebastian, the latter met him with a smile, "Well, did you survive?"

"I was so stunned that he knew everything," related Fr. Try-phon, "that I froze on the spot. 'Yes, Batiushka, I survived,' I said, 'but I could have died.'"

"What are you saying, Fr. Tryphon? I was praying the whole time—what was there to fear? After all, two souls had to be saved, to be delivered from such intense demonic delusion."

The Elder forbade him to speak about this to anyone. "As long as I'm alive, don't say a word about this to anyone. But when I die, do as you wish."

At one of the health centers of our hospital a nurse named Sophia Vasilievna worked. Her husband was the accountant general of the Regional Trust. It is hard to imagine how much grief this family had borne. Seventeen years ago they had tragically lost their only son, twelve years of age, in whom was all their life. The wound did not heal. The boy had walked out onto the balcony to water the flowers in the pots. Wanting to fix something, he had leaned over through the railing and fallen from the fifth floor. His parents had been sitting at the dining room table, and he had been talking with them from the balcony. Suddenly the doorbell rang, and the youth was brought in dead.

Later new sorrows began to befall them. Soon, in 1937, the father was arrested and sentenced to ten years. For Sophia Vasilievna, years of isolation, persecution, unemployment, hunger and cold began. Now all this was long behind them. Bearing everything stoically, they had managed to survive. They lived in great abundance, built themselves a nice stone house, and planted a garden. But the long years of childlessness crept up on them, and they wanted to adopt a baby—a little boy. In Kuibyshev there was a large children's home where orphans under the age of seven were gathered. These children were given to those who wished to adopt a child and who presented the necessary certificate and documents. Those children whom no one had chosen were taken, at age seven, to an orphanage for older children. They arranged to go there and select a little boy for themselves. I told Sophia that if she wanted this child to be to their good fortune, they should go to Fr. Sebastian and ask his blessing. They had already purchased their tickets, but the trip was still a day off so I went with her to see the Elder.

We were told that he was ill, lying down, and wasn't receiving anyone. We stood, crushed, at the door of his cell. Suddenly the Elder rang the bell from inside his cell. He asked who had come and told us to come in. We entered and knelt next to his bed. He attentively listened to my account and our requests and, not lifting his head from the pillow, he said, "It's a good idea; you should go. You can adopt a child, but only a little girl. You mustn't take a little boy." And blessing us he said, "I bless you to adopt a little three-year-old girl." We thanked him and immediately left. The next day they departed. I was uneasy as to how the father would give up his dreams of a boy.

Within several days they returned, bringing home a three-year-old girl. She was friendly and loving; best of all, she clung to the father. But she was very homely. It was not that her facial feature, taken separately, were poor; this was not the case. She was just generally a homely child. Yet the parents were pleased and didn't notice this. Her co-workers marveled: "Well, why did Sophia Vasilievna choose such a homely little girl?"

They related to me how everything had transpired during the selection of the child in the children's home. When they filled out the adoption papers in the main office, they were told, "Now go on; select whichever child you want, whichever one pleases you. None of the children have sicknesses. We admit them only after verification of the medical examination. Now they have just awakened the children after their daily nap, and the children are going to the potty; but please walk among them and choose one."

"We hadn't managed," said Sophia Vasilievna, "to pass by one wall of the 'potty-room' when a little girl from the other end of the room rushed toward us, grabbed my husband by the legs with her little arms, snuggled her face against his knees, and, quivering throughout her whole body, shouted out, 'My daddy has come, my dear daddy has come....' The matron was barely able to pull her aside, grabbing her arm and saying to us, 'Don't be confused; choose, have a look.' 'No,' the father said, 'We won't have to look any further. She herself has chosen us. Expedite the paperwork on this little girl for us.'" Thus they brought home the homely little girl and didn't notice her appearance. They loved her because she "recognized" them.

The little girl grew up to be joyful, very obedient, loving, friendly to all and helpful. She adored her father. I saw how she would rush to take off his boots and bring his slippers from the bedroom when he came home from work. She tried to help her mother, grabbing the broom and trying to sweep the floor, even though she didn't yet know how. Sophia Vasilievna said, "We didn't teach her to do this. She thought it up all on her own." But, of course, they showered so much love, warmth and kindness on the child that she, not having seen this in the children's home, drank it all in as a flower does water. Their home became happy; everything became somehow radiant. When after four years she went to school, she proved to be very capable and diligent, and so she learned well. She also did everything in the house, helping her mother joyfully. She loved to sing. She began to shape up and look nicer. It's simply astonishing how her homeliness vanished and how she became in every sense attractive. I told Sophia Vasilievna, "Your daughter is becoming very pretty." She replied, "She's always been a fine girl." Here it was—the Elder's blessing and obedience to him.

But what disappointments, what difficulties, grief and misfortunes did people suffer when they acted counter to the Elder's counsel! I came to observe a great many of them (especially in respect to marriages), about which it's painful even to reflect upon. Someone would come to ask his blessing, and he would tell them straight out, "Never enter into marriage with him."

But the self-willed young one would counter, "I love him," or "I'll shape him up." And then, alas! The most difficult life would ensue. If the family situation became unbearable, the Elder would never counsel them to endure it any longer, even for the children's sake. He would listen to the whole account and say, "Well, all right, you can leave him; you can separate." He would say this in rare instances.

I'll relate only one tragic story. At the very beginning of Fr. Sebastian's pastoral service in Karaganda he had a spiritual daughter named Tanya. She was an amazingly intelligent, beautiful and pleasant young woman with a sympathetic, kind heart. She was very attached to the Elder. And he loved her especially strongly, so they said. She planned to enter into marriage with a handsome young engineer from Alma-Alta. The Elder wouldn't bless her. She at first obeyed, but later she again began to ask for his blessing. He categorically forbade her, insistently and sternly. She tried to be obedient, to give up the idea. Fr. Sebastian spoke a great deal with her and tried to persuade her. In the end she said, "I love him, and I'll endure everything." When she was leaving to go to her fiance, Fr. Sebastian wept; he begged her to think it over. He went to the railroad station to see her off and at the station begged her to get off the train in Alma-Alta and then return. No one had ever seen him so persistent. She did not return. Her life unfolded very unhappily. She endured much suffering, fell ill and after two and a half years died from tuberculosis.

Fr. Sebastian saved us, his spiritual children, from many misfortunes, but we were unaware of it at the time. Later when we became aware of his intercession we were astonished. Sometimes he would require of us some kind of decisive act, but more often everything went along somehow quietly, peacefully, as water flows in a stream. His guidance and intercession went unnoticed. Three times death approached my threshold in Karaganda, but he did not give me up, and prolonged my life.

I was once greatly awestruck at how the Elder heard those who mentally besought his aid. One time R. G. and I were traveling together to the city of Saran to visit some old friends. The bus ran every hour. We were to return before evening. The driver was a young Chechen (a people of the Caucasus). On the way another bus passed us whose driver was Russian, also a young fellow. He stuck his head out of the driver's window and shouted with a laugh, "You're dragging like an old nag!" This really got the goat of our Chechen. He stepped on the gas and raced ahead in order to overtake his offender, while the latter sped even faster. The vehicle hurtled along; it lurched from the unevenness of the pavement so that the people who were standing in the aisle bumped their heads against the roof. A horrible fear gripped my heart. And then where the highway makes a large bend, skirting a field in which wheat had recently been harvested, to my horror I saw that our driver had driven down off the highway onto the field. He was racing the vehicle along the rise in the field so as to bypass the curved section of highway and come out ahead of the first bus. The bus bounced along the rise, tossing from side to side. All the children were crying. The wheels were just about to come off the bus, and the bus was about to collapse and crush our bones. Everyone begged the conductor to stop the driver, but she, as white as a sheet and terrified, could only reply, "When he's this frenzied, who can stop him?" I understood that we were on the verge of death. Fear gripped my heart, and I began to pray, mentally calling out to the Elder, "Batiushka, save us; Batiushka, help! Batiushka Fr. Sebastian, save us!" I looked through the window and saw the first bus standing still on the highway. All the passengers had disembarked and were now crowding around it—it had lost a tire. Our driver began to slow down, got on the highway and drove past the first bus silently, without even sticking his head out of the driver's cab. Everyone began to come to themselves, to calm down.

The next day there was an All-night Vigil for a feast. I rode to Mikhailovka early and waited outside for the Elder to go to church. He left his room and approached me. I wanted to tell him how yesterday I had had a terrible scare, but he asked me first: "Was that you who was shouting at me yesterday, 'Batiushka, save us, help!'" I said, "Yes, it was I, Batiushka."

"When you call for me, you should tell me everything—who is calling, and what to save you from—or else it's very difficult for me. I hear 'Save me,' but one should say who, and from what. Well, did you arrive safely?" I was absolutely stunned.... "Yes, safely!"

The Elder prayed for and healed not only those who were near him and personally asked his help, but even those who called out to him from somewhere far off. The following occurred to Barbara Petrovna Dronova (†1981): In 1961 she gave birth to a daughter, Lena, the third child in the family. The little girl grew and developed well, and had already begun to walk. But she suddenly came down with a terrible illness. Each day in the evening she would begin to have attacks of convulsions, which cramped her legs and arms, and she would become as if dead; her arms and legs would cease to move. They showed her to a doctor. The doctor said that this disease almost never yielded to treatment, and that the girl would probably die. Thus it continued for two weeks—each day there was an attack in the evening. The girl weakened, stopped walking and ate nothing, but only lay in her little bed almost motionless.

The young mother was in a state of great sorrow. She wrote a letter to Fr. Sebastian in which she described her grief and asked him to pray. The letter was not addressed to the Elder personally, but to Deacon Nicholas Samartsev. At the very moment that she let the letter drop into the mailbox she felt somehow very light in soul. That evening there was no attack. And there never was another one after that. The little girl again began to grow and develop normally. Two months later Fr. Deacon Nicholas sent a letter to Barbara Petrovna in which he wrote, "After receiving your letter I wasn't able to read it in a timely fashion to the Elder. I carried it around with me all the time, and it got torn up in my pocket. Later I told the Elder anyway, 'Matushka Barbara sent you a letter. Should I read it?' But he replied, 'It's no longer necessary.' He's probably angry at you for some reason."

In actual fact, the request that had been directed to the Elder had been heard and fulfilled. While the letter was still lying in the mailbox in Lipetsk, the little girl had already been delivered from the terrible illness.

A year later Matushka Barbara herself took sick. She had a serious attack of liver disease. She could eat almost nothing. She greatly weakened. In 1961 she travelled to Karaganda to see Fr. Sebastian. She told him that she was extremely ill and that she would probably not last long, that she was preparing to die. The Elder objected, "What do you mean, Mother, you still have children to raise." Having spent a few days in Karaganda she returned home to Lipetsk. It was then Great Lent. There were no attacks of the illness during the whole of the Fast.

On Pascha, when everyone was breaking the Fast, Barbara Petrovna tried to eat half of an egg. (It is contra-indicated to eat eggs when one has liver disease.) No attack followed, and there were no further attacks of the illness.

In 1966, not long before the Elder's repose, Matushka Barbara went to see him in Karaganda. She saw that he was quite weak, and she had a premonition that he would soon die. Saying farewell to him, she said, "We probably won't see each other again." Fr. Sebastian replied, "We'll see each other in the next world." At parting the Elder gave her his shirt, which he had worn for a very long time. When Barbara Petrovna was returning to Lipetsk from Karaganda, while she was in the plane her tooth began to hurt very much. She placed the Elder's shirt against her cheek and called to him mentally for prayerful help. The toothache began to diminish, and gradually subsided altogether.

There were later other incidents of healings from the Elder's shirt for Matushka Barbara and other members of her family.

Miracles took place around Fr. Sebastian all the time, but we did not always see or comprehend them. On another occasion when he was asked something point-blank, how did he answer? He said, "But how should I know? I'm not some kind of prophet! I don't know anything about it." That's all he would say. Another time he would even frown and would only explain later.

In 1956 I had a severe heart ailment. I was greatly distressed, since I was awaiting a reply about my political rehabilitation and had become very exhausted at work. I lay at home, and with difficulty I was able to pull through this illness. I had a severe weakness of the heart. All of a sudden my temperature unexpectedly began to rise. I was taken to my hospital with great difficulty, though it was very close by. My condition was grave; my temperature was 104°. It appeared that I had typhus. My situation was catastrophic, hopeless. There was little hope that my ailing heart might cope with such a severe illness.

My general awareness had become obscured. I couldn't explain anything about my state, but Fr. Sebastian himself had inquired how I was, and Fr. Alexander and Mother Anastasia came to the hospital to visit me. I lay alone in an isolation ward. As soon as I saw both of them beside me, my consciousness cleared up. I told the nurse that no one else was to enter my room. Fr. Alexander confessed me and gave me Communion. On my own I read the Elder's letter to me that he had sent with them. It was short, but it gave me hope and strength. He had written just a few lines:

"Christ is in our midst, deeply respected and dear Tatiana Vladimirovna! Your grave illness is not unto death but to the glory of God. There yet lies ahead of you much to endure. And now we are caring for you.

Hieromonk S. Fomin"

After Communion Fr. Alexander and Mother Anastasia sat a while longer and prayed with me in the room; they read the Gospel and some prayers. I understood everything clearly. Before nightfall my temperature began to subside, and the next day it became almost normal. I began to recuperate slowly, but surely. After two months I received my documents of rehabilitation and traveled to Moscow to secure all my new privileges. I returned to Karaganda before finding living space in Moscow.

During the month of September, 1958, I made haste to travel on vacation to Moscow so as not to postpone the processing of an order for a room and a residence permit. Then I had to return to Karaganda since I had promised to allow the head physician to go on leave, that is, to remain in his place at work (there wasn't anyone else who could do so), and then afterwards depart for Moscow for good. It was difficult to purchase tickets during these months, and the individual through whom I could ordinarily order a ticket on any date I wished had also gone on vacation. I had to go to the downtown station and, registering my name on the list, sit there the entire night, since every two hours they make a roll call of those who are registered.

It was a tormenting, sleepless night outdoors. I was very cold, and there wasn't anywhere even to warm myself. Totally worn out, in the morning I finally received a good ticket in a second class car and went straight to work, hungry and chilled to the bone. The next day I went to the Elder's services at the church and shared my joy that I had obtained a ticket.

Fr. Sebastian was already in church, but the services had not yet begun. He greeted me, smiling: "You got a ticket—good, good, we'll serve a Moleben for travelers. But what day is the ticket for?"

"For Wednesday, Batiushka." He raised his eyes and began to look upwards. Suddenly he frowned, turned his gaze towards me and said sternly: "Don't rush—Wednesday is too early to travel."

"How is it too early, Batiushka? How is it early? My vacation begins then. I can't be late in returning home, and I need to accomplish everything that I'm going to Moscow to do. I bought the ticket with great trouble; why should I wait?"

He openly scowled: "You have to sell the ticket. Wednesday is too early to travel. Right after the service go to the station and give the ticket back."

"But I can't do it, Batiushka. I can't possibly postpone the trip!"

"I order you to turn in the ticket; turn it in today, do you hear?" And in a fit of anger he stamped his feet at me. I came to my senses.

"Forgive me, Batiushka, forgive me. Bless, I'll go right now and turn it back in."

"Yes, go now, and then from there return to me. You'll still be able to catch the service," said the Elder, blessing me.

He had never behaved like that towards me before. After turning in the ticket, I returned to church. I was in a peaceful state; I was glad that I had obeyed the Elder. What would he say now?

He greeted me joyfully, in a pleasant way. "You took it back—that's good. Now when are you thinking of departing?" I was very surprised.

"How am I supposed to go? I just returned my ticket."

"Well, what of it? Go tomorrow and get a new one." My astonishment knew no bounds. "You can do it now on your way home. Stop in at the downtown station and register in the line. You don't need to stay there all night; go sleep at home. In the morning go and get your ticket."

All I could say was, "Fine." And I didn't ask anything. I left and thought: Batiushka always feels so sorry for me, why is he now pushing me so, unless he doesn't want me to leave Karaganda; but all the same I'll be returning again.

I arrived at the downtown station, and a man was already standing there with a list. He had only just begun to register names; I was the seventh. He appeared to be a teacher. I told him that I had already endured one night there. He said, "I'm not going anywhere—I want to make sure they don't start a new list. Go home, and I'll note you down at the roll call." He took down my last name. "Come tomorrow by eight o'clock." I thanked him and left. In the morning I came, stood in line and obtained a good second class ticket. Before my departure a Moleben was served. Fr. Sebastian gave me a large prosphoron, blessed me, and I left.

When our train approached the Volga and stopped at the Chapayevsk station, I was sitting in the compartment. The door into the corridor was open, and I saw that all the passengers were leaping out of their seats and pressing against the window in the corridor. I also went out. "What's the matter?" I asked. One passenger made room for me at the window. On the next track the passenger cars were piled on top of each other. They had hit the next line of track, as well. Several cars stood vertically in a pile. Fear seized everyone. They ran to the conductor with questions. She explained, "This was an express train, one like ours—it was the one that left Karaganda on Wednesday. It had a huge collision—it ran full speed into the rear end of a freight train. That's why the cars are lying on top of each other. It was so horrible that they brought in hospital trains from Kuibyshev. But as you can see, they won't be able to pull the cars apart very soon. There's a lot of work to be done on them. The freight trains aren't running through Chapayevsk; they're rerouting them." I withdrew to my compartment, lay down on my berth with my face to the wall and wept. "Bati-ushka, Batiushka, dear Batiushka."

Three months later I left for Moscow for good. Fr. Sebastian saw me off, saying only, "Come back often." It was now 1959. I came to see him on vacation a year later. He said that this was too seldom. I was with him again in 1961 and in 1963, but in 1965 they began to write me from Karaganda that the Elder had begun to feel significantly weaker. I wrote him a letter stating that I wanted to live near him for a longer time, and asked his blessing. In reply I received a telegram: "The Elder blesses. Come, we're expecting you." I left work with joy in the autumn of 1965 and departed for Karaganda.

At first, the Elder seemed the same as he had been on my last visit to him in 1963. He likewise continued to serve daily—both in the morning and in the evening. He would say, "What kind of priest would I be if I stayed home for the Divine Liturgy or Vigil?" He conversed at length with people, especially with those who had come from a distance. In church, in the church yard, in the "lodge," everything was the same as it had been before. Therefore it seemed that it would always be this way, un-wavering and unchanging; that Fr. Sebastian would be with us, and that it couldn't be otherwise. So, I didn't begin to under-stand right away that he now had but little strength left, nor did I understand what exertion of will it cost him to keep himself go-ing and to direct everything.

In church, behind the pannikhida table, a partition was set up and a small room was equipped for him, which they called the "stateroom." Next to the back wall, behind a curtain, there stood a bed on which he could rest during the services, when pain or severe weakness would plague him. Before the win-dow a small table and an armchair also stood, where the Elder could receive penitents for confession, converse with new arrivals or with his spiritual children and the clergy from the

The "lodge"—Elder Sebastian's cell in the courtyard of
the Mikhailovka church.

church. At the table a second chair stood ready, but those who
came to confess stood kneeling before his armchair, with their
forehead against his knees. It was easier for him to bless them
like that.

His vestments were hung on the walls. In the front corner,
on the second table, were a number of icons, among which there
stood out a large, ancient, dark brown Tikhvin Icon of the
Mother of God, obviously from the old church. Above all the
icons was one of the Ascension. In front of them colored lampadas always burned, atop engraved, polished, silver stands. Also
on the table were a Gospel, a cross, and many blessed prosphora
which he would give out. Sometimes there lay several small rolls,
candies, apples and cookies from the pannikhida table which he
would distribute also.

It struck me how Fr. Sebastian penetrated into everything,
into every detail of church life. Each day he would personally

Contemporary photograph of the interior of the church in Mikhailovka. At right is the area in which Elder Sebastian would serve Pannikhidas.

serve a Pannikhida, sitting in an armchair in front of a huge icon of the Most Holy Trinity (a truly remarkable icon, which Mother Agnia had painted not long before 1965). He read each commemoration sheet himself. When the Pannikhida ended he would move up to the pannikhida table from which the worshippers would take only the *kutya* (sweetened boiled wheat). What remained he moved to different parts of the table saying, "Take this to the poor in the courtyard," "Take this to the refectory," "This is to be divided among the sick," etc. He often walked into the baptistry, then into the refectory, and looked to see who was sitting at the table. Then he would remind us, "Call such and such and so and so; see that they don't leave without supper, since they have a long way to travel." Nothing escaped his eyes. In the morning, before services, many parishioners would bring groceries to the refectory, one offering vegetables, someone else fish, another flour. At every feast, he would send someone to distribute money to the poor. He only served the Divine Liturgy on feast days.*

Sometimes the Elder would give the priestly exclamations lying on his cot. Under his feet they would place a bolster to make his feet a little higher. He would be in a half-mantia, epitrachelion and cuffs. He sometimes read the litanies lying

---

*A letter from that time has been preserved, from Elder Sebastian to Archbishop Joseph (Chernov) of Alma-Ata and Kazakhstan:

Your Eminence, Vladyka Joseph. I beg your holy blessing for all of us and I beg your forgiveness for the fact that up to now I have not been able to write a reply to you. For a long time I kept intending to write to you and congratulate you with the feast, but it has not worked out. You congratulated us by telegram, while I keep delaying my reply. Sickness and physical weakness, as well as services, management cares and special services all exhaust me, the sick and weak one. Illnesses give me no rest at all, even at night. Coughing and my hernia bother me a great deal. But time moves on—it does not wait. Not long ago it was Christ's Nativity, and now three weeks have already gone by since then. We spent the feasts well and happily. We still live and serve in peace and harmony. I would have liked to have Fr. Nicholas ordained to the priesthood and the church warden Paul Alexeyevich to the diaconate—he is very zealous in reading and singing, and such believers and zealots are few now. But later—however it pleases God, and however Your Eminence blesses. As regards the construction, nothing is moving for the time being. Glebov, who, thanks to you, received Fr. Alexander and Fr. Andrew, is sick all the time; yet we would like to find out the exact result—where they will permit the construction, whether in the old location, or in another place, or whether they refuse altogether. We are collecting building material gradually, but inasmuch as the place has not been designated, we do not know where to store and keep it. Your Eminence, Vladyka Joseph, I beg your holy blessing to retire and devote myself to my own soul, and for Fr. Alexander, Fr. Seraphim or Fr. Nicholas to be the Superior. My mind is now weak, and my ill state does not allow me to cope with matters. Bless me to retire and to make Fr. Alexander the Superior, with your blessing and the consent of the parishioners. All of us—myself, your unworthy novice, as well as Fr. Alexander, Fr. Seraphim, Fr. Nicholas, the rest of the parish clergy, and all the parishioners bow before you and ask your holy blessings and prayers.

down. He always got up for the Gospel, and read the Gospel in his phelonion.

At the beginning of December of 1965, a severe frost began, with temperatures reaching -40°. Fr. Sebastian's lungs became weak. When he walked across the courtyard to church and breathed the icy air, he began to cough so hard that for a long time he couldn't utter a single word. I told Olga Fyodorovna that he should be carried through the courtyard on a light chair with his mouth covered.

"I've already spoken to him about this," she said, "but he won't hear of it, he gets cross." I said, "Batiushka, it's not right for you to walk across the courtyard in such a freeze." He looked displeased. "I'll fly across." I began to consider how I might persuade him; his temperature had begun to rise due to the worsening of the illness, no longer simply a cough.*

Once I came to the Elder when he had just finished lunch and was still sitting at the table. I knelt before him. He blessed me and asked, "Have you eaten?"

"Batiushka, dear, I've seen how for fourteen years you've grieved, how you've suffered when people haven't listened to you, and you've seen how a person's disobedience destroys him. You've seen how it will be bad for him because of it. You've seen it all. Why can't you see how Olga Fyodorovna and I suffer because you walk through the courtyard in -40° frost, and don't try to cover your throat. You breathe the icy air, and because you overwork your body from walking, she

---

*Olga Fyodorovna Orlova, the Elder's main physician, diagnosed the following illnesses: chronic bronchitis with chronic dilation of the bronchial tubes and tiny abcesses, emphysema, constriction of the epiglottis, a benign tumor of the prostate, inflammation of the pelvic lining, symptomatic hypertension, and inguinal hernias on both sides with frequent partial strangulation. He suffered from these infirmities for several years.

and I, both doctors, understand how dangerous this is for your sick lungs. You need to be carried through the courtyard with a warm scarf wrapped around your mouth." He was silent. I began to cry. He placed his hand on my head and said, "Don't cry. Let them carry me."

Our youngsters, the subdeacon Peter Goroshko,* Alexander Medvedev, Alexis Veretennikov,** and Basil Pisarev,*** all novices of Fr. Alexander Kiselev,**** soon fashioned a lightweight armchair out of aluminum tubing with four handles (two in front, two in back) and in the evening carried the Elder to church. He smiled and joked each time Vera dressed him, saying, "Well, I'm ready—where are my ponies?"

Once I was with the Elder when his health was not good, and they were preparing to carry him to church. I passed through the courtyard and came up alongside of him. Fr. Sebastian said, "Well! Now here's the pace horse!"

Fr. Sebastian respected medical personnel and appreciated their labor, from orderlies to physicians. When he was to bless someone for studies, he would most often bless them to go to medical school; from time to time he would bless them to go to the institute, and he would bless them to work as orderlies in hospitals. "It's not a sin to receive medical care," he would say. "Whoever works in a hospital is doing something salvific. It's a good deed to take care of people." He would recommend surgical treatment in cases of particular necessity, when he knew that conservative treatment would not help. Those who were operated on with his blessing recovered completely. The Elder was himself a good diagnostician. Sending a patient to be examined by

---

*Now Abbot Peter. He still serves in the same church.

**The now-reposed Hieromonk Herman.

***The now-reposed monk Basil.

****At the present time Archpriest Alexander, the Superior of the Church of the Nativity of the Most Holy Theotokos.

his chief physician, Olga Fyodorovna, he would say, "Olga Fyodorovna, please examine this patient. I think he has such-and-such an illness." And the diagnosis stated by him would be confirmed.

Fr. Sebastian was so gentle, and had such a soft heart. I often saw how he strove to caress and comfort. One time he said to me, "It's forbidden to caress monks and cats. You can shelter them or feed them, but it's forbidden to caress them."

My winter coat was light yellow, like a downy chick, with a furry collar. When I came to church and to his room for a blessing and stood before him on my knees, he would look at me so kindly, stroking the fur collar, and say, "What a beautiful little collar, a very beautiful little collar." When the apple trees blossomed in the church garden and next to the home of Matushka Vera, the Elder, passing by, would always stop before the blossoming trees, gaze at them for a long time and admire them.

Elder Sebastian grew noticeably weaker. He began to talk less with visitors, spoke more briefly and didn't receive everyone. Only those from other cities would not be refused: with them he sometimes spoke at length. And there were many who came. Then he began to shorten his conversations, especially if several had come. His subdeacon-novices—Alexander, Alexis, Peter and Basil, would make sure that no one would linger with him. Sometimes they would crack open the door and remind one that the Elder was tired, and sometimes they would simply not admit anyone, saying, "Batiushka is resting." One of them would always be on watch at the door to his room in the church when he was there.

In February Archbishop Joseph came to Karaganda. Fr. Sebastian, although he was weak, served together with him. When he said farewell, the Archbishop said, "Now I'll come after Pascha and I'll bring you a reward—a basket of grapes." Everyone understood that tears awaited us.

Elder Sebastian with clergy and parishioners of the Mikhailovka church. At far left is Fr. Alexander Krivonosov. Wearing a klobuk and holding a staff is Bishop Joseph (Chernov, later Metropolitan of Alma-Ata). Photo from 1950s.

The Elder often recalled death and the passage to eternity. When people addressed the question to him, "How will we live without you?" he would answer sternly, "Who am I? And what? God has been, is and shall be! Whoever has faith in God, though he be thousands of miles from me, will live—and be saved. But he who even pulls at the hem of my ryassa, but does not have the fear of God, will not receive salvation. Those who have known me and seen me will, after my death, value me less than those who neither knew nor saw me. Familiarity breeds contempt."

It was no longer as simple as before to get to see him; for some it was quite difficult to get through to him. All this was new and unusual for Fr. Sebastian, but it still did not seem constricting. It was thought that all this was temporary, for as long as the Elder would be sick; then, when he would improve, everything could again be as before. Sometimes it appeared that he was getting better, and that soon he would again be easily accessible to everyone. That is how it seemed, but it did not turn out that way....

Elder Sebastian in the late 1950s.

4

Last Days

I WANTED TO RETAIN everything in my memory about the Elder, to collect his every word. And I began to keep a daily journal, writing down therein everything that I saw or heard from him.

*The beginning of Great Lent. February 7—Forgiveness Sunday:** Fr. Sebastian served Liturgy and in the evening conducted the Rite of Forgiveness. He was strong and his countenance shone.

February 9. Tuesday: The Elder read the Canon of Andrew of Crete.

February 10. Wednesday: He finished the Canon. His voice was clear, distinct.

February 11. Thursday: During the first four days of the first week of Great Lent, on the days when the Canon of St. Andrew of Crete was read, there were no meals. The Elder didn't allow anything cooked, except for soup after the Presanctified Liturgy on Wednesday, and even tea was not made. On Wednesday he blessed the weak to receive Holy Communion. On the table in

---

*All dates given in this journal are according to the Church (Old) Calendar.—ED.

the refectory stood pitchers of kvass, dishes with sliced black bread, sauerkraut in bowls, and plates of pickled cucumbers and raw onion. In the ash pit of the stove were warm baked potatoes and onions, and the Elder blessed people with weak stomachs to eat these. There wasn't any other type of food set out.

On Friday at the Presanctified Liturgy there was an enormous number of communicants. (After four days of standing for the Canon of St. Andrew and such a strict fast.)

February 12. Friday: After Liturgy there was the first refectory meal: mushroom soup and buckwheat kasha with sugar. In the evening—kasha from lunch, tea with sugar, and dried and fresh white bread. Fr. Sebastian served daily, and he read the Canon of St. Andrew of Crete all four days. He permitted those who were going to receive Communion on Saturday or Sunday to eat their first meal on Thursday, February 11.

February 15. Monday: The Elder was not brought to church. All day he neither conversed with nor received anyone.

The entire second week, until March 3, passed as usual. At ten o'clock in the evening, before sleep, all those closest to the Elder gathered in the room in front of his cell. He opened the door and we saw him standing before the icons and the lit lampadas. Maria Obraztsova read the Prayers Before Sleep. What calm and grace were poured forth....

Those evening prayers with him will be forever unforgettable.

February 21. The Second Sunday of Great Lent: Fr. Sebastian served Liturgy. After Liturgy, he received those who had come to see him. He blessed several people, who had come earlier, to leave. In the evening he served the Rite of Passia.*

---

*The Rite of Passia (Passion) is a little-known Lenten service consisting of several of the hymns from the end of Passion Week and the reading of the account of Christ's Passion as set forth by each of the evangelists on the second through the fifth Sundays of Great Lent.—ED.

February 22. Monday: Those who were visiting Mother Agnia told the Elder that Maria, who lived with her and who sang in the choir, was being very difficult with the Eldress and even rude; that Maria often didn't listen to her, and wasn't doing what Mother Agnia asked her to do, but did things her own way. Mother Agnia had been treating her as one of her own relatives and caring for her. She would try to prepare something for her arrival, but Maria would push aside her attention saying, 'I don't want it, I don't need anything.' This grieved the Eldress. But Fr. Sebastian had blessed Maria to live with her and, of course, to undertake all the household chores and responsibilities, considering that someone like Maria, an orphan, needed Mother Agnia's good-naturedness, warmth and care after having been in the children's home.

After the services, the Elder summoned Maria to the pannikhida table and asked her, "How are you and Mother Agnia getting along?" She muttered something in reply. "Is that how you're going to talk with me? You dare to speak to me that way? If you answer *me* so disrespectfully and brazenly, then I can understand how you speak with Agnia. You should regard it as a great happiness that you are living with Mother Agnia. It's a rare good fortune." And he began to scold her. It was the first time that I had heard him speak so sternly. "You know what kind of person Mother Agnia is? Mother Agnia is a saint." Maria stood there, kept silent, and only dropped her head lower and lower.

February 28. Third Sunday of Great Lent: A young hierodeacon from Kiev, Fr. Paul (in baptism Anatole) came to Fr. Sebastian. He had been born in Paris, and his family had returned to Russia ten years ago. His father was an eminent, learned professor of the Kiev University. The Elder gave him living quarters in the church courtyard, in Mother Vera's house. Throughout the fourth week, Fr. Paul read in church very beautifully, expressively, enunciating every word, as no one before him had done.

He served the Elder as a subdeacon in the altar and tried as much as possible to be at his side. The Elder would converse with him at length. Not only Fr. Sebastian, but absolutely everyone who lived around him loved Fr. Paul. There was something especially attractive about him, a touching charm. He would also go to see Mother Agnia. He was very modest, but one could sense his highly cultured European education and broad outlook. The Elder watched him closely. In the evening he served the Passia.

March 3. Wednesday: Fr. Paul was very active in the church services. He read much from the ambo, assisted in the altar and sang in the choir. In the evening he conversed at length with the Elder in his cell.

March 7. Fourth Sunday of Great Lent: Fr. Sebastian celebrated Liturgy and served the Passia in the evening. He felt well all day and did not go to his cell in church.

March 8. Monday: Fr. Andrew came from the village of Osakarovka, in the central region of Kazakhstan. He asked Fr. Sebastian to give him somebody to help with church reading and to direct the choir. He had no one; he was alone in the church. The Elder blessed one of the women from the choir to go—an experienced singer, thirty to thirty-five years old, by the name of Anfisa. She could also lead the services. And suddenly he blessed Fr. Paul to go with her to Osakarovka. A conversation took place between him and the Elder that distressed them both. Of course, Fr. Paul had left Paris for Russia, had become a monk and had come to Fr. Sebastian not just to wind up on some obscure part of the steppe. He had come here to be at the Elder's side, but now that he was sending him away, he said, "Bless me to return home, to Kiev. I'll go back to my hermitage near Kiev."

Fr. Sebastian said, "I'll give you a hermitage! You came to me and I accepted you. You came of your own free will. I didn't summon you. You'll have a hermitage here in Osokarovka." Fr. Paul said, "Let me go—bless me to leave you for good!" Fr. Sebastian, upset, said, "I'll give you Kiev; I'll give it to you with a stick! I'll give you a stick and I'll grab a birch rod on top of that—yes, even a birch rod! Are you a monk?!" Fr. Paul fell at the Elder's feet: "Forgive me, bless me; I'll go to Osakarovka." He ran to his room for his icon, with which his father had blessed him to enter a monastery when he was still a boy. He took nothing more. Everyone felt sorry for him. All were upset to the point of tears and lamented to Fr. Sebastian. Vera said to him: "You're dispersing all of your own people—you're scattering them! We need Fr. Paul ourselves—how he reads, how well he sings in the choir! We have virtually no male voices! And everywhere, everywhere he does everything so well, so quickly; in the altar, in the vestry. The nuns are already so old. We need him so! Why do you give everyone away?"

Sasha and Pasha came to Fr. Sebastian and said that Fr. Paul was needed very much for the choir. "Let Fr. Andrew look for and choose someone for himself. Others will come to beg from you in the same way." The Elder was silent. Fr. Andrew was in a hurry to leave today. Everyone came to see Fr. Paul off. Everyone reproached Fr. Andrew. Fr. Paul had a stunned, dishevelled look. Fr. Sebastian did not come out of his cell. Vera gave Fr. Paul twenty rubles: "This is for you, for the road, for when you want to come to us. And if it's bad for you there, come immediately and tell the Elder." Fr. Andrew, Anfisa and Fr. Paul left for the train station. Before the All-night Vigil Fr. Sebastian drank tea and did not speak with anyone. The next day was the Feast of the Forty Martyrs of Sebaste. During the Vigil the Elder was agitated and "ferocious," as the nuns put it. Fr. Alexander caught it for the fact that he asked whether to sing or read the Great Doxology, and Fr. Alexander and Alyosha Vedernikov caught it when they were supporting the Elder so he could cense the church. He said angrily, "Bless—I'll go cense by myself." He himself went around, censing the whole church.

March 9. Tuesday: The Elder performed the funeral of one of his spiritual daughters, a middle-aged woman. During the service he wept.

March 10. Wednesday: The Vigil of St. Mary of Egypt. Fr. Sebastian read half of the entire Canon of St. Andrew of Crete. He read very well, very distinctly—better than Fr. Alexander. A possessed woman was brought from Siberia.

March 11. Thursday: In the morning, during the Presanctified Liturgy for the Feast of St. Mary of Egypt, Fr. Sebastian served. The entire time the possessed woman meowed, bleated like a sheep or a goat, crowed like a rooster, barked like a dog or neighed—for the whole service. They dragged her to the narthex. This was not difficult; she was extremely weak and exhausted—her face looked worn out, full of suffering. Towards the end of the service she lay in a corner, prostrate, unable to remain on her feet. Beside her sat the two women who had brought her.

In the evening there were not many people in church. When all had already dispersed, the Elder was still in his cell, though he had not served. I was detained, speaking with the mother of the deacon, Fr. Nicholas Samartsev. I was copying out a recipe for her. There was no one else in the church except for the possessed woman lying quietly in the corner, and one woman who sat with her. Suddenly the Royal Doors opened and the Elder came out in full vestments, with mantle and staff. The possessed woman got up from the floor and went, barking, meowing, and crowing like a rooster, towards him. Before reaching him, she crowed loudly. *"Nu!"* ["Well!"]—said the Elder threateningly, and I didn't even recognize his voice. She crowed once again, but much more softly. *"Nu!"*—he repeated. She crowed very quietly, as if from afar. *"Nu!"*—said the Elder. She was silent. Then she said: "You are Joshua the son of Nun."

Fr. Sebastian in archimandrite's mantia, as he appeared
to the possessed woman (see previous page).

"I am not Joshua the son of Nun, I'm Sebastian," he said authoritatively. "Tomorrow morning come here to the priest, confess and then receive Communion."

March 12. Friday: Fr. Sebastian didn't serve, but sat in the altar during the Liturgy. He served only a Pannikhida. The formerly possessed woman stood calmly during the service and quietly received Communion. In the evening they took her back home, to Siberia. The Elder served the Vigil—the Laudation of the Most Holy Theotokos. He read half the Akathist, then left for his room and lay down.

March 13. Saturday: He served Liturgy. He was in the altar for the whole Vigil but did not vest, and after "Glory to God in the highest..." he went to his room and asked that a woman and her daughter, who had come from somewhere far away, be summoned to him. He spoke with both of them. I dropped in to see him when they had left. I said, "Batiushka, bless! I haven't visited with you for a long time."

"Ye-es," he said slowly, "we haven't seen each other but I've visited with you every day." He blessed me. I asked, "Batiushka, are you feeling any better?"

"Yes, I'm just tired." He began to bless many of his visitors to go home. I said, "Batiushka, decide my fate, too. I've been living here a long time already."

"You've been living; go on living," he replied and, displeased, he turned away. I was satisfied. "I haven't been pestering you, have I?"

"What did you say that for?" He turned to me, somewhat pensively. "You'll live here until Pascha and after Pascha, too."

March 14. The fifth Sunday: At the Liturgy, after "Holy things are for the holy..."* the choir sang, for the last time, "Open to me the doors of repentance." This was done at the

---

*That is, while the clergy commune, before the faithful receive Communion. —ED.

Elder's request. He did not vest, but sat in the altar in an armchair. From this day I could clearly see and understand how he was weakening. In the evening he was not brought over at the beginning of services, but much later. He lay on the bed in his cell.

March 15. Monday: Fr. Paul arrived, with something Fr. Andrew had sent with him. The Elder was very weak and lay all day in his cell. Fr. Paul sat beside him for a long while.

March 16. Tuesday: Fr. Sebastian was at home the whole day. I went to see him.... He blessed me twice and said, "There will still be time for us to talk; don't worry, we'll talk—let Fr. Paul come in." He told him that he would soon call him back from Osakarovka for good. During the Vigil he sat in the altar in the armchair. Before the anointing with oil he vested, and then went out and did the anointing, sitting in the armchair. Therefore everyone had to kneel to be anointed, so a small, soft rug was laid there.

March 17. Wednesday: The commemoration of St. Alexis the Man of God. There was a solemn, festive Liturgy and there were many communicants. The Elder neither served nor vested. He sat in the altar and did not go into his room. During the middle of the service, Fr. Paul left for the train. Fr. Sebastian went out to serve a Pannikhida and served, as always, sitting in the armchair. He repeated the hymn "Memory Eternal" several times. The choir would finish singing, and he would again say "Memory Eternal." They would finish, and then repeat it again.

March 18. Thursday: At three o'clock in the morning Fr. Sebastian woke Vera and said, "I feel worse than I ever have before. My soul will probably leave my body." They called me and we sent Petya in the car for Olga Fyodorovna. I gave him an injection and some medicine to drink. He was breathing with great difficulty and waited impatiently for Olga Fyodorovna; he kept asking for her. She, as soon as she arrived, immediately sent the car to the hospital for an oxygen tank. The Elder began gasping for breath. Petya quickly brought the oxygen and we set up a supply of humidified oxygen and an apparatus for intravenous medication. His temperature was 101.5°. After half an hour the oxygen tank was empty, since it was a previously used tank. We sent Petya for a second tank, but it was only enough for three hours. Then Olga Fyodorovna sent the car not to the hospital, but to the place where they fill the tanks, since it was already approaching the end of the working day. The third tank was finally a freshly filled one. We gave him a few injections that day. He was semi-conscious, but breathing evenly and peacefully. Olga Fyodorovna went to work and I sat beside him, gave more injections, and checked his pulse. At ten o'clock he opened his eyes and began to speak. His temperature dropped and I again gave him medication. At twelve o'clock he asked to eat and towards evening his temperature dropped even lower. Olga Fyodorovna returned from work; I went to rest, while she remained to spend the night.

March 19. Friday: His temperature in the morning was normal. He ate, lying there in a light-blue podrasnik, and read. The day went well.

March 20. Lazarus Saturday: At night something very significant for the Elder happened, something exceptionally important and joyous in the extreme. In the evening he peacefully fell asleep and slept well. At three o'clock in the morning he awoke Vera with the bell and told her to awaken and bring Fr. Alexander. He was radiant and trembling with joy. What he told Fr. Alexander—his confessor—and what they talked about, nobody knew, and we still don't know. We only know that he requested confession and Holy Communion, since Fr. Alexander went into the altar for the Holy Gifts. After Communion, Fr. Sebastian began to sing "Christ is Risen" and sent Vera to awaken and bring the girls from the choir, so they could sing the sticheron before Matins from the Paschal service for him. The girls came, all in white kerchiefs, and began to sing the Paschal troparion, the sticheron before Matins, and the irmoi of the canon. He said to Fr. Alexander in front of everyone, "Well, you've never before greeted Pascha the way you will this year!" Fr. Alexander said, "Batiushka, stay alive—you're so needed, not only by us in Karaganda, but by the whole Orthodox Church. Who besides you can establish the monastic way of life in the world?" When the girls had sung everything, the Elder said to Vera, "And now, give me some red eggs."

In the morning he asked Vera to bring him some milk. "Now look, " he said, "all I get is kvass and cold soup. Why do you keep pushing kvass at me? You should give me some milk." Vera went to the store and brought back some milk. No one contradicted the Elder. She poured some milk into a cup and said, very timidly, "Today, Batiushka, is really only Lazarus Saturday. Then it will be Great Saturday, and only then Pascha. If today had been Pascha, then there would have been kulichi and a lot of red eggs on your table—and you see, we still have nothing. The Elder smiled: "I know, I'm not off by a whole week. For me today is Pascha. If only you would dye three red eggs for me." "Right away, Batiushka, I'll dye them," said Vera. During the day he felt better; he even read the Liturgy in bed. He got up to eat at the table in his light blue podrasnik. He ordered dinner to be prepared for everyone with caviar, and soup with caviar. "And fish for tomorrow, cook it for tomorrow, for Palm Sunday." He lay quietly, and spoke little. His face was very bright. At the time of the common meal he asked Vera, "Who's sitting at the table?" Vera said, "Besides all of us who live here, there are all four of our subdeacons, Olga Fyodorovna, Tatiana Vladimirovna and Fr. Tryphon." He was pleased.

In the evening the Elder sat at the table by the window and watched the people going to church with palms. "The people are

Elder Sebastian's choir, seated before the royal doors
of the Mikhailovka church.

getting ready for the Vigil," he said. "But I need to prepare to see my
fathers and forefathers, my grandfathers and great-grandfathers."

Before six o'clock in the evening, he drank tea and asked to
be dressed and brought to church. He served the Vigil with great
difficulty and rested often. He went out for the anointing, but
only anointed a few—the men, and me and Elizabeth Fyodorovna.... After us he let Fr. Alexander continue the anointing, and he went to his room and lay down; he had an emaciated
appearance.

March 21. Palm Sunday: At night we again repeated the
singing of the Paschal canon and irmoi. He told Vera to boil
three kinds of eggs: soft-boiled, medium-boiled, and hard-
boiled; and that they should be distinguished by color so that
each person could eat the kind he liked. In the morning he
awoke early and spoke with Vera, and was concerned that she
feed everyone fish at dinner. His general state became better. He

served the Liturgy and himself gave Communion to a portion of the people. Then he rested in the altar in the armchair. He served until the end, and then immediately told them to bring him home. I walked alongside through the courtyard and asked him how he felt. He said, "Not badly, it's just that I'm very weak." When they carried him up to the doors of his cell and were going out to the courtyard, he gave a blessing and said, "Go have lunch—they've prepared some nice fish today." After lunch he lay down, and did not get up from bed until evening prayers. He was not brought to church in the evening.

March 22. Monday of Passion Week: The Elder was brought to church for the Presanctified Liturgy. He was weak, and did not attempt to vest, or even to sit in the altar. He lay in his cell in bed and occasionally dozed. After the service I went to him to ask him how he felt. He said, "Olga Fyodorovna came in the morning and gave me an injection—nothing hurts. Don't be sad, it's only weakness." I said, "Batiushka, I received a letter from my brother in Moscow. He writes that he's glad I'm staying with you for Pascha, that through me grace comes to him from you; he wants me to be at peace that all at home are well." I said this, and all the time thought to myself to ask him to pray for my brother, but decided not to ask, so as not to trouble him. But he said, "Well, glory be to God! How good—now you'll live in peace here." And then he looked at me and immediately sat down on the bed and began to cross himself and say quietly, "Save him, O Lord, grant him understanding, O Lord, protect O Lord, Thy slave Vladimir, not only in this life, but also in the future age; in eternal life grant him eternal joy!" Then he whispered something else, but I didn't catch it; I was weeping. He blessed me twice, and I left him. Different feelings crowded each other in my breast—joy, and sorrow, and grief.

March 23. Passion Tuesday: The Elder was brought to church in the morning and lay on his bed. Having heard that they had brought in someone who had died, he said that he would personally serve the funeral. He went out to the pannikhida table and sat in his armchair. He gave the first exclamation to the choir. He was unable to do more. He read the Gospel and helped Fr. Alexander to read the service for the dead. After the end he said to Fr. Alexander: "Go right now, quickly, to the telegraph office, and send a telegram to Osakarovka for Fr. Paul to return permanently."

March 24. Passion Wednesday: Fr. Sebastian was brought to church and lay in his room, and asked that lunch be brought to him. Vera came running with lunch. He stayed here to rest until evening, until services. He served the Vigil for Annunciation and did the anointing himself, sitting in the armchair, and those who came up knelt before him. He anointed not only the men, but also many women. When I came up he said, "You mustn't be sad." He went back into the altar entirely devoid of strength.

March 25. Annunciation. Passion Thursday: There were two Liturgies. At the late Liturgy he sat in the altar in the armchair, and during the Hours he himself took out particles from the prosphora. There were a great many prosphora; besides those from the people in church, there were large trays of church prosphora from the Elder. Then they cut them in half in the narthex and brought them on the big tray to give out to everyone in church, saying, "From Batiushka." He stood in the doorway and watched attentively how they gave out the prosphora from which he had taken out the particles. Afterwards, he was not brought home. He had lunch in his "state-room" and rested after lunch until the Vigil, with the reading of the Twelve [Passion] Gospels. He put on his mantia and read the first Gospel, then rested in his room, and then read the eleventh and twelfth Gospels. When he was led by the hand into the altar, he gave all a general blessing. He looked better, stronger, and read the Gospels well, very clearly and distinctly.

Elder Sebastian in his cell. Passion Wednesday, 1966.

March 26. Passion Friday: The Elder was brought to church in the morning. After the Hours, until the bringing out of the Winding Sheet, he rested in his church room. At the time of the bringing out of the Winding Sheet he stood in his vestments in the altar with a large candle which, it seemed, he was barely able to hold in his hands. He watched through the north [deacon] door as Fr. Alexander and Fr. Paul brought out the Winding Sheet. On his face were sorrow and anxiety. When the people began to venerate the Winding Sheet he stood at the royal doors and looked out at the church. Lunch was brought to him in his church room, and he rested there until the Burial Service. After the Burial Service he did not go home, but remained to spend the night alone in the church room. The door from the narthex to the courtyard was left unlocked. The night-guard, Anfisa, came by and looked in. Vera arrived and also had a look. The Elder slept peacefully.

March 27. Passion Saturday: Fr. Sebastian lay in his room during the Liturgy. After the end of the Liturgy he put on his mantia and klobuk and went out to say farewell to the people. He spoke of his grievous illness. He congratulated all with the approaching Feast of Pascha and said, "I'm leaving you, leaving earthly life. My time has come to part with you. I promised to say farewell, and now I'm fulfilling my promise. I beg one thing of all of you—that you live in peace. Peace and love—this is the most important thing. If you will have this amongst yourselves, then nothing more is needed and you will always have peace in your souls. Now we await the Bright Matins—the coming of the Feast of Pascha. But this Pascha is of temporal life; we must attain to the eternal Pascha of the salvation of the soul for eternal joy. And how is it possible to attain it? Only through peace, compassionate love, and sincere, heartfelt prayer. Nothing outside of you will save you, only that which you achieve within yourself, in your soul and your heart—the peaceful stillness of love, so that you will never cast a suspicious glance at anyone. Look straight ahead, and be ready for every good response, for every good undertaking, with heartfelt sincerity. As my last request I beg you for this. And I further implore you—forgive me." He bowed from the waist and staggered. Quietly, he was barely able to return to the altar, and he asked to be brought back to his cell. The people did not disperse—everyone was weeping.

The night of Pascha, 11 pm: The Elder wanted to be taken to church; the boys came for him, but he was unable to get up, so he sent them to church. They stood in church for half an hour and again went to get him, but they returned to the narthex alone. Everyone who was in the narthex was waiting for him—all of his close ones became troubled in soul. Matins proceeded, and sorrow lay upon our hearts. I barely managed to make my way through the narthex to the door, since a large number of people were standing there, and ran to the Elder. Beside him sat Vera, and in the big room Maria Obraztsova kept watch. He looked at me and said, "What have you left the church for? I'm not dying yet.… I'll still manage to greet you with Pascha here, and the dead as well—go back to services. Be calm! When you left, what were they singing in church?"

I replied, "Having beheld the Resurrection of Christ."

"Well, that means that Matins is not over yet—go." I returned to church and reassured everyone. When the Liturgy had just begun, Maria ran into the narthex from the Elder and summoned Olga Fyodorovna. She did not come back for a long time. Everyone began to beg me to go find out what was going on with Batiushka. I went into the first room—the door of his cell was open. Beside him stood Vera, behind her Olga Fyodorovna, and by the door stood the boys. I entered and stood next to Vera. He opened his eyes, looked at me, and said, "Is Matins over yet?"

His state was calm, even joyful. I understood that this was after a pain-killing injection. He turned to me, "I want to go to church. You know, I used to sing well myself. The whole week of Pascha, every day I would sing the whole Paschal service by myself in my cell. Now you have to beg me to sing. But I don't want to sing here, I want to sing in church. Right now, after the injection, I'll sleep a little, ten minutes; I'll rest and then you can dress me and bring me to church." Vera said, "If you take a nap right now, Batiushka, then it will be until morning." He said, "Well then, take me right now. Dress me. I want very much to wear my mantia and klobuk and sit in church, even if only for Liturgy, but I'm simply unable to serve; I'm just too weak." I said, "But how well you read the Gospel on Thursday, Batiushka, how well. So clearly, expressively and loudly; everyone was overjoyed. You read much better, more clearly, than either Fr. Alexander or Fr. Paul. Only Fr. Vladimir read more loudly than you." He rejoiced at my words: "Really? I was worried that I read poorly and couldn't be heard. Well, the Lord save you." Vera began to dress him and he continued to speak: "Now I beg you all to console one another, to live in love, in peace, and never raise your voice against one another. I demand nothing more of you. This is the most important thing for salvation. After all, everything here is temporary, all is fleeting. What is there to worry about—what is there to gain for yourself? Everything, everything quickly passes away. You must think about that which is eternal."

We dressed him and the boys carried him to church. At his order they brought a large tray of prosphora to his room and he took out particles; there were very many prosphora. Most of them he ordered to be cut into four pieces and sent to the church to be distributed. He ordered that whole prosphora be given to those who had come from afar and to certain others who were standing by the pannikhida table. Then he took a piece of antidoron from the Feast of Annunciation from a box on the table, divided it into small pieces and sent it to the choir and to those who stood selling candles. He was very tired and lay down on his cot. Then he quickly arose and put on his mantia, but was unable to put on his klobuk. He lay down again and said, "Never mind, I'll sit like this." He sat up with difficulty for a little while and closed his eyes. Olga Fyodorovna said that his pulse changed. She wanted to give him an injection right then, but decided to bring him back to his cell and do it there. I also left with them. Soon the Liturgy ended, at which Vera sang in the choir.

The door of the Elder's cell was open, and we drew near and looked at him. He was sleeping, and breathing evenly and peacefully. Later, at one in the afternoon, I came to see him. There was no one in his cell or in the first room. He was lying in a new, cream-colored, silk podrasnik. I said to him, "Christ is risen!" He responded, "In truth He is risen!" and then said, "Take an egg from the table and move the chair a little closer to me; sit beside me. I was just lying here remembering how the Elders died in Optina. Fr. Joseph was sick for a very long time, but Fr. Anatole 'the Younger' was never sick for even one minute. He died in a miraculous way; this was a mystery ... quite wondrous. By his great humility he was closer in spirit than anyone to my Elder Nektary. After the revolution two of the Elders died and were buried in the Optina cemetery. Fr. Theodosius, the skete Superior, died in 1920 when everything in Optina was still like it was in the old days—no one had touched anything or persecuted anyone. But as the civil war ended in 1921 everything changed, and there was a great deal of persecution, particularly in 1922. There were searches and many arrests, and then it was Elder Anatole's turn. They came to him on July 29, conducted a lengthy search, cut his hair and shaved him. He bore it all patiently. Then they said, 'Well, get ready to go.' He begged them to let him postpone his departure until morning. They agreed, and told his cell-attendant to get him ready to leave early in the morning. They gave him a strict warning about this and left. Elder Anatole began to pray. His cell-attendant waited for two hours—the Elder was praying the whole time—and then he went in to him and said, 'Well, Batiushka, let's get ready.' But Fr. Anatole answered, 'Go away, don't bother me.' He left. He came in after another two hours and begged, 'Batiushka, let's get ready.' And he responded, 'What are you getting so upset about? I'm not going anywhere with them. Go away.' He left again and the third time he came in, Fr. Anatole was lying on his cot with his hands folded on his chest—dead. Well, the cell-attendant called the necessary people and they vested the Elder, placed him on the table, lit the candles and began to read the Psalter and the Gospel. Soon they came for him. They said, 'Are you ready, Elder?' The cell-attendant answered, 'He's ready, come in.' They entered, and there he was, lying dead on the table. Well, they went away, of course, probably quite amazed, and Fr. Anatole was the last one buried in the Optina cemetery, next to Elder Macarius. When they were digging the grave they damaged Elder Macarius' coffin and uncovered his incorrupt relics."

He was tired after the long talk, and closed his eyes and began to doze off. Vera arrived and I left silently, going to Mother Agnia's. The Elder was brought to church, but not at the very beginning of the service. He was sleeping and they didn't want to disturb him. He listened joyfully to the singing of the choir in church, but didn't sit up, since his feet and hands were very swollen.

March 29. Bright Monday: He lay at home until evening and received visitors. They brought him red eggs and pisanki [Ukrainian decorated eggs]. He also gave out red eggs. Kulichi stood on the table, on a snow-white tablecloth, and there were numerous red eggs in a bowl. In a small, light blue vase were the first Siberian snowdrops.

I entered his cell, congratulated him with the Feast, went up for a blessing and said, "Mother Agnia with joy sends you her

best wishes with the Resurrection of Christ! And here is an egg."
He beamed with joy, "Save her, O Lord, and bless her. How
much she's done for our church! No one has done as much as she
has. She's done so much that's beautiful and good during her
whole life—she's a saint. I'm dying; turn to her for everything
now. "

He was brought to the beginning of Matins at six in the
morning. He was filled with joy, but soon became tired and was
brought home before the end of the service. He was very weak.
Olga Fyodorovna remained to spend the night in the first room.
At three in the morning he rang and when they ran to him he
was covered with blood. A hemorrhage had opened up in his
throat after coughing. He was silent and his eyes looked anxiously at us. Olga Fyodorovna's hands and knees trembled as she
gave him an injection to stop the bleeding. Vera carefully and
slowly changed his clothes. He was very weak and began to fall
asleep. He was not brought to church that morning or evening.
No one went into his room except Vera.

We called Archbishop Joseph in Alma Ata and he said, "He
won't die yet this week, but death is already at the threshold. I'll
fly in to see you."

March 30. Bright Tuesday: He awoke in the morning breathing calmly and freely; he wasn't coughing. He said, "Vera, put
my boots on. I have to go to church to greet the people with Pascha and bid farewell to everyone. I promised them. I'll tell them
everything right away. I'll tell them that which is most important."

"Batiushka, what do you mean, boots? I can't even put your
slippers on, your feet are so swollen. You already said farewell."

"No, no, I haven't fully taken leave; the most important
thing, I have to tell them the most important thing. Dress me."

Vera began to dress him and obtained some kind of closed
slippers and cut them at the sides. The boys carried him to

church. He sat for a little while in his armchair dressed in his mantia and then asked to be carried over to his bed. At the end of the service they carried him in their arms into the altar. He sat for a short time by the Holy Table, then arose and went out through the royal doors to the ambo. He stood there, leaning on his staff, and again began to say goodbye to the people. "Farewell, my dear ones, I'm departing now. Forgive me if I've angered you in any way. For Christ's sake, forgive me. I forgive all of you for everything. I feel so sorry for you. I want one thing from you. I beseech you about one thing. I demand one thing—love one another, so that there will always be peace among you. Peace and love! If you will obey me in this—and I implore you to do this—then you will be my children. I am unworthy and sinful, but the Lord has much love and mercy. I place my hope in Him. And if the Lord will vouchsafe me His radiant abode, I'll pray for you unceasingly. I'll say, 'Lord, Lord! I'm not alone; all my children are with me. I can't enter in without them; I can't be alone in Thy radiant habitations. They were entrusted to me by Thee.'" And then he added quietly, barely audibly, "I can't, without them."

He said this and wanted to bow down, but was only able to incline his head. The boys grasped him by the arms and led him back into the altar. Throughout the entire church one could hear tearful sniffling, convulsive sighs and restrained sobbing. When he was being carried through the courtyard I walked alongside. He looked at me and made the sign of the Cross over me twice.

He lay alone in his cell until evening, was quite weak, and breathed with his mouth open. We looked at him only through the crack in the door. He was not brought to church in the evening. During the service three young women from the choir came to sing Matins for him in his cell. I came in with them along with all those who lived in the lodge, and subdeacons Alexander and

Alexei, and Fr. Paul. Everyone sang Matins. The Elder blessed all who were there. He had a peaceful night and breathed easily.

March 31. Bright Wednesday: Fr. Sebastian was brought to church at the beginning of the Liturgy and lay in his "state-room." Bishop Pitirim's sister, Nadezhda Vladimirovna, arrived with his favorite pupil from the Theological Academy, Anatole Ivanovich Prosvirnin.* After services Nadezhda Vladimirovna went to see the Elder in his state room and they spoke at length.

In the morning Vera was very disturbed and nervous, and became angry at everyone. She jumped at Petya and yelled at him. She didn't leave, as usual, to go and prepare for when they would bring Fr. Sebastian home, but stayed in the narthex and in his room. He called her in and said, "Help me to sit up." She put her arms around him, sat him up, lowered his feet from the bed and put his slippers on. The boys brought in his armchair. He wanted to get up on his feet to shift over to the armchair, as always, but was unable to stand up. This was the first time—before this he was always able to get into the armchair himself. Vera again put her arms around him, lifted him up, and sat him down in the chair. When he was carried out I also went through the courtyard, but not alongside him; he turned his head and searched for me with his eyes. I ran up to him and he blessed me, gazing at me long and attentively, but it was difficult for him to raise his hand. This was also the first time this had happened. His glance was somehow penetrating and consoling. When they brought him into the cell he requested to be reseated immediately at the table. "I fall asleep on the cot," he said.

Vera allowed the Elder's spiritual daughter, Elizabeth Fyodorovna, a nun from Moscow, to see him, while she prepared his food in the first room, straining it and putting a portion in a small dish. She gave him everything in a tea saucer; only the soup was in a small children's bowl. She made it all very tasty but even

---

*Later Archimandrite Innocent (†1994).

so, he sometimes didn't finish half his portion. Vera let Elizabeth Fyodorovna in and she fell at the threshold on her knees and began to weep. He said, "Why are you acting like this? None of this is necessary."

She said, "Batiushka, how poorly you look."

"Well, make it so I'll be better." She rose from her knees, came closer to him, and again knelt. He blessed her. She begged him to accept what she had brought for him from Moscow—black caviar and orange juice. He responded, "Treat those with whom you're living here—I no longer need anything. I have everything." She put the packet on the table anyway. He blessed her two more times and said, "Go out and tell everyone that I bless them to sit down and have lunch." I stood beside Vera; the door to the cell was open and therefore I heard and saw everything. Vera went to feed the Elder with the little bowl and saucer, and we all left for the refectory to have lunch. After his meal Vera and Maria carried him over to his bed and he instantly fell asleep. During the day they looked at him through the crack, but he slept the whole time. Nadezhda Vladimirovna opened the door a little to see him, but I had already grown accustomed to looking through the crack.

There was a call from Alma Ata saying that Archbishop Joseph had become very ill. His temperature was 104°, so he would not be able to fly in. Vera called me over to the table at which she prepared Fr. Sebastian's food and showed me the two little dishes of his food and a piece of bread that sat under the napkin. Today he had eaten extremely little. Olga Fyodorovna and I took the opportunity to finish his food. We left the small piece of unfinished bread for others. Had I not been there, Vera would have finished all of his food herself. After his meal none of his food was thrown out, as if it were sanctified.

When the Elder awoke, Vera dressed him, combed his hair, sat him up on the bed, placed a pillow behind his back, let his feet down from the bed onto another pillow and invited the photographer in. Anatole Ivanovich took a few different shots of him, both with and without his klobuk. In the evening he was not brought to church. He again spoke with Nadezhda Vladimirovna, but not for long.

The door was open just a little, and when I saw that he had blessed Nadezhda Vladimirovna, I went in and also approached him for a blessing. He looked at me kindly and blessed me twice. He said, "Take an egg from the table," so I took it and gave it to him, and then received it from his blessing hands. Then he said to me, "Open my door; I'll bless everyone in there from here. I'm already tired." I opened the door; in the first room, besides our own people, there were also three newly arrived nuns. Everyone approached the open door. He blessed them all three times with a sweeping sign of the Cross and said loudly, "I forgive everyone; for the Lord's sake I forgive everyone; I forgive everyone everything, whoever is sinful in whatever they have sinned." He blessed them once again and laid his head on the pillow. Vera closed the door.

April 1. Bright Thursday: The commemoration of St. Mary of Egypt. At two in the morning he felt very poorly. He coughed, and breathed with difficulty. At four in the morning blood and phlegm came up. I gave him styptic medication and an injection. Towards six the bleeding stopped, and he ceased coughing and fell asleep, breathing calmly. At noon he ate a little and again dozed off.

An hour later Fr. Andrew arrived from Osakarovka and Fr. Sebastian spoke with him. Before evening Maria Alexeyevna Ovchinnikova arrived. She was the wife of Fr. Nicholas Ovchinnikov, the head priest of the cathedral in the city of Elets. Both of them, Fr. Nicholas and Maria Alexeyevna, were physicians. They were my fellow students at the University of Moscow Medical School, and graduated in 1930. He worked as a surgeon

Fr. Sebastian, photographed in his cell by Anatole Ivanovich
Prosvirnin on Bright Wednesday, 1966, less than a week
before the Elder's death. One of the last photographs
taken of him during his life.

and she as a therapist. Maria Alexeyevna had a strong, beautiful voice. She had graduated from music school as a vocalist. When her husband became a priest in the cathedral she began to sing in his choir. They also continued to treat the sick, especially believers. They were renowned as specialists.

Fr. Sebastian was not brought to church, but lay at home in his cell. At eight in the evening he received Maria Alexeyevna and spoke with her. She had brought him a very beautiful egg—a pisanka. After she left Vera went in to feed him. After fifteen minutes she came out with her eyes full of tears. She said in the refectory, "Go, call all of our girls and boys." They ran for them at once. Nadezhda Vladimirovna went in to the Elder's cell and didn't close the door. He smiled affectionately and said, "Today I want to bless everyone separately." He then spoke with her about something for a little while, and said, "Let them come in now one at a time."

I went in next to last. Only Fr. Paul stood by the door behind me. When I went in the Elder's head was bowed; he lifted his head and smiled warmly. I said, "Christ is risen!" He looked at me brightly and exclaimed, "In truth He is risen!" He blessed me with a large sign of the Cross and gave his hand to be kissed. Then he took an egg that was lying on his lap—the egg that Maria Alexeyevna had brought—and gave it to me. I thought that everyone had already received a blessing, but he had saved the egg for me, and I began to cry. He shook his head and said three times, "Matushka Agnia, Matushka Agnia, Matushka Agnia." I asked, "What? What about Matushka Agnia?" "Our Matushka Agnia also paints very beautiful eggs. Everything, everything she does so beautifully, so beautifully. Save her and bless her, O Lord! I wanted to buy a house for her in Melkombinat, but she didn't want it. She knew that it's not our lot to live in retirement. Now I'm already going away and she needs to be closer to the church." I started to get up from my knees, and could not see anything because of my tears. Someone fell on his knees beside me. Later, when I was leaving, I saw that it had been Fr. Paul. After him, Mother Anastasia came out of the refectory with her wide gait and went in to see him. They allowed none of the later arrivals to see him. Vera closed the door. We sat down in the refectory and calmed ourselves from our tears. We dispersed at eleven.

April 2. Bright Friday: The feast of the icon of the Mother of God, "Life-giving Spring." The Elder hardly slept at all at night. This was his second almost sleepless night. Olga Fyodorovna spent the second night here. He was suffering and said, "In my whole body there isn't one living part that doesn't hurt. My spine is burning like red-hot iron. It's impossible to breathe." He gasped for breath and said, exhausted, "But worse than everything is agony of spirit." He kept asking what time it was. Olga Fyodorovna was giving him an injection every three hours; they relieved him, so he awaited them. Towards morning he felt better and fell asleep.

At the end of Liturgy the nuns got together and visited him: Mothers Febronia, Kira, Maria, Eupraxia, Maria Ilarionovna and Catherine Alexeyevna. Vera was singing in the choir. When Mother Febronia went in to see him, he looked at her with a long, steadfast gaze, blessed her twice and said, "May the Lord save you for all your good deeds and devotion. I have great faith in you; the Lord save you." As she went out he made the sign of the Cross several times behind her. He blessed her two more times and closed his eyes. The remaining ones came up and kissed his hand. He neither opened his eyes nor raised his hands.

Another oxygen tank was brought. After he received the oxygen he opened his eyes and said that everyone should immediately put together a festive dinner and set the tables in the first room and in the refectory, since today was the last Paschal Matins service before the end of Bright Week. They placed tables in the first room. Two kulichi were brought from his cell and a tablecloth was put on the table. Vera seated everyone—there were twelve people. The rest had dinner in the refectory. After dinner, the three of us who were physicians went out to the courtyard and sat for a long time, talking. Tamara came from Matushka Agnia and said that she had locked herself in her room and would receive no one.

In the evening we looked at the Elder through the crack in the door. He lay with his eyes closed. Then everyone went to the last Matins.

At ten in the evening Abbot Dimitry, who had flown in from Kokchetavo, arrived and spoke with Fr. Sebastian and Fr. Alexander. He spent the night at Fr. Vladimir's. They called Archbishop Joseph and asked about his health. They said there that he was still sick; his temperature had gone down but he was unable to fly in. Then they asked his permission for Abbot Dimitry to tonsure the Elder into the schema. Archbishop Joseph replied that it was not necessary—that Bishop Pitirim would be flying in tomorrow from Moscow and would do everything himself.

We asked the Elder, if possible, not to change his name at his tonsure, since everyone knew him by this name, and a change of name would be an additional suffering for everyone. The Elder consented and said that he would ask Bishop Pitirim about this.

"The day of my repose is approaching," he began to say to those around him. "I'm very happy that the Lord is making me worthy to receive the schema. I've awaited this day for a long time. I feel sorry to be leaving you all, but this is the will of God." "Batiushka, to whom are you leaving us?" The Elder was silent and concentrated and then said, "Don't be grieved. I leave you in the care of the Queen of Heaven. She herself will direct you. But you should try to live in peace one with another, to help one another in everything that is within your power. I won't forget you—I'll pray for you, if I obtain boldness before the Lord. And you should pray. Don't abandon the church—try especially to be there on Sundays and feast days. Observing this, you'll be saved by the mercy of God and by the intercession of the Queen of Heaven."

Late in the evening Olga Fyodorovna and I went in to see him. She gave him an injection and I held the tourniquet. He began to speak to me: "Here you are, doctor; my dear old doctor. It's hard for me to utter a word but I want to tell you something. My tongue doesn't move and my mouth is all dry. Everything hurts. You couldn't find a pin-point that doesn't hurt. My legs no longer hold me up. There's such weakness in my whole body, even in my eyelids, and it's hard to lift them up. But my head is lucid and clear; my thoughts flow distinctly, deeply and calmly; my consciousness has not darkened or changed—no, there's none of that. I see everything that all of you are doing. I lie here and think—and this means that thought does not depend on the body. And the brain is part of the body. In my body there would no longer be any strength for thoughts by now. Thoughts come from the soul. Now this has become understandable. Well, glory be to the Lord, I barely managed to tell you everything. I hope you're getting all this."

No one was allowed to see him the whole day. We sat in the refectory. Fr. Paul went past everyone with an armload of firewood for the Elder and, smiling, indicated the firewood with his eyes and said to me and to Nadezhda Vladimirovna, "Trojan Horse." This was in the evening.

April 3. Bright Saturday: At three in the morning Fr. Sebastian had us call Fr. Alexander. He received Holy Communion and said, "Anything might happen; it's not necessary to wait until morning." After Communion the rest of the night passed easily, and he asked us, "How is it, is it easy for you to breathe? Do you have enough air?" Olga Fyodorovna and I said, "There's enough for us, but how about you, Batiushka?"

"There's enough for me, too." He fell asleep peacefully and slept until 8:50 in the morning, when Olga Fyodorovna gave him an injection. He asked, "Where is Tatiana Vladimirovna?"

Olga Fyodorovna said, "She was here not long ago; right now she probably went to church for services. Shall I call her?"

"No, it's not necessary, it's not urgent."

At nine Bishop Pitirim arrived from the airport and went straight to see Fr. Sebastian. Astonished at his appearance, he said to us, "I've never seen him like this, not during any other of his illnesses." He then spoke with him for a long time. He was alone with him; no one came in.

At eleven Vera brought the Elder's food in. The Bishop himself fed him with a little spoon. Nadezhda Vladimirovna, Maria Alexeyevna and I came to the lodge from church. Nadezhda Vladimirovna said, "Well, now everything will be in order." Vera brought out the Elder's dish and closed the door. Maria Alexeyevna and I wanted to leave, but Mother Anastasia did not let us. I sat down at the table in the refectory. In the kitchen they washed and dried a beautiful serving dish to be used to serve lunch to Bishop Pitirim. Olga Fyodorovna and Nadezhda Vladimirovna went to the room in which the Bishop was staying, in Mother Vera's home. Fr. Alexander came and sat with us at the table in the refectory. Then Fr. Paul arrived. Fr. Alexander seated him at the table as well. We were waiting for Vera, with Fr. Sebastian's blessing, to begin lunch, as she had always done. Vera came in and told us that she had barely opened the door to his room when he immediately looked at her. The Bishop was reading the Gospel to him and she, in pantomime, had asked a blessing to begin lunch. He instantly understood her and gave a blessing. The boys Alyosha and Alexander arrived. Mother Anastasia served the food and then sat down. When we had finished

Fr. Sebastian and Bishop Pitirim (here still an
archimandrite) with Mother Agnia. Photo
taken April 29, 1963.

lunch Bishop Pitirim came out and blessed each of us as we came
up to him, then went to his room. Everyone dispersed. I went
out to the first room and only Maria Obraztsova was there.
Thirty or forty minutes later the Elder suddenly rang. I leapt towards him. He was deathly pale and said, "It's bad," and was unable to say more. His pulse could barely be felt. I quickly
checked his blood pressure, and it was very low. Marusya and I
were completely incapable of turning on the oxygen tank. As
luck would have it, Petya was in the refectory and turned the
tank on right away. I asked him to call Olga Fyodorovna, who
was having lunch with Nadezhda Vladimirovna in the Bishop's
room. I gave the Elder heart medication. As he breathed the oxygen he quickly began to feel better. Marusya stood beside him
and suddenly began to stroke him. He frowned and, taking the
oxygen tube out of his mouth, said, "What are you stroking me for?
Go away." Olga Fyodorovna arrived and gave him intravenous

medication. He completely recovered and began to speak: "The Lord save you!" Then he dozed off.

We all quietly left and sat in the first room. Then Olga Fyodorovna sent me to see him: "Go ahead, go ahead. In the morning, before the Bishop arrived, he asked me to call you." I went in. Fr. Sebastian blessed me twice but said nothing; he only looked at me intently. When I went out, Petya stood in the doorway, unable to decide whether or not to go in. I pushed him in. Vera returned and went in too, as Petya left. Mother Anastasia wanted to go in, but Vera didn't let her, and she herself came out and shut the door tightly. Twenty-five minutes later the Elder rang, and Vera went in. He urgently told her to ask the Bishop to come to him. He came, and Fr. Sebastian requested him to begin the service of tonsure to the schema without delay. The preparations began. Olga Fyodorovna had put syringes on to boil, but did not return to get them, since she was with the Elder. I brought the boiled syringes to her and saw the beginning of the preparations. They seated him in the armchair. Just in case, Olga Fyodorovna prepared everything needed for injections and infusions. Bishop Pitirim went into the first room and asked all who were there to leave. The boys and the subdeacons were also there. Everyone left; the Bishop said nothing to me but I went out of the cell. Mother Anastasia anxiously drew me behind the curtain where Maria's bed stood, and said, "Don't leave—we'll hide here. They'll probably open the door, and that way we'll see him being tonsured." I said, "No, I'm leaving right now. Forgive me, but I won't stay with you." She sat on the bed in an agitated state. The Bishop came out and summoned Mother Anastasia, and we both went in. I don't know how it escaped from me: "Aren't you going to call me?" The Bishop responded, "What do you mean? This is not from me, it's the Elder's will that only those allowed by the rubrics be present." I went out to the refectory. The whole lodge was empty; not a soul was there, except the downcast, sorrowful boys sitting in the refectory.

After the tonsure the Elder spoke very little. His face and his whole appearance were amazingly transfigured. He was filled with such grace that one's soul would tremble at one glance at him, and one would keenly sense one's own sinfulness. This was a majestic Elder, no longer an inhabitant of the present world.

April 4. Thomas Sunday (Antipascha): During the Liturgy Nadezhda Vladimirovna, Olga Fyodorovna and I stood in one corner of the narthex. Maria Alexeyevna sang in the choir. Olga Fyodorovna said that early in the morning she had given the Elder intravenous medication, and his face had become unrecognizable. Nadezhda Vladimirovna said that his hands in particular had changed. I stated that a man's hands are most expressive—they're alive, they move. You can follow a man's face, but not his hands. Whole prosphora and antidoron were brought out from the altar and distributed to those in the narthex "from Batiushka." Nadezhda Vladimirovna did not take the antidoron, but took a prosphoron and went to hand in commemorations for the Moleben and Pannikhida. She distributed prosphora there and left. Tasya came from the Elder, and Olga Fyodorovna and I asked how he was. Tasya said that he was like yesterday, only a little weaker. Olga Fyodorovna related that at three in the morning he had felt very poorly. He requested that Fr. Alexander be awakened, and he confessed and received Holy Communion. He told him that he was experiencing anguish of soul and body. Services had already ended, and I went home and sat down to write in this journal. After recording everything I went to Mother Febronia's house, to see Maria Alexeyevna. She didn't appear to be at home. I dropped by the lodge; Olga Fyodorovna was in the refectory and she invited me to sit with her and have lunch. I declined and she began to detain me; she took the kerchief from my head and started to unbutton my overcoat.

Mother Anastasia approached and said to me insistently, "Sit down, do sit down." By her glance I perceived that she empathized with me in soul, felt sorry for me, and understood. At this point the unfathomable depth of the goodness of her soul became clear to me. And how she always strove to hide her goodness. She sought for a hidden life. "Thank you, Matushka, thank you. Very well, I won't go," I said to her.

Fr. Alexander came in and said that without Fr. Sebastian he did not wish to continue serving here—that he would leave us. We said that while the Elder was still living it was not up to us to think about anything; we had only to wait for what he would say and what he would bless. Olga Fyodorovna asked me, "Do you want to see him? Now's your chance, since you haven't seen him today. Let's go." She opened his door and we entered, without asking anyone. He was breathing with difficulty and lay with his eyes closed and his hands resting on the blanket. He ran his fingers over the blanket as if over a keyboard. Then he opened his eyes and looked past us with distant, sorrowful eyes. We went out. Bishop Pitirim was walking towards us. I bowed low before him and said, "Forgive me." He looked at me tenderly with his kind, sparkling eyes and said, "No, you forgive me."

We returned to Fr. Alexander in the refectory and sat at the table. He reproached me for my frame of mind. I answered, "I've already figured everything out—the Elder is dying and that's all there is to it." And I began to weep. Fr. Alexander gave me the key to his room and told me to go down and take all the eggs from the bowl on the table for Mother Agnia, as well as a packet marked "Mother Agnia." When I passed by the Elder's cell his door was slightly open and I saw that the Bishop was sitting beside him and saying something to him, and was holding a Gospel in his hands.

I returned to the refectory, wrapped the eggs in paper for Mother Agnia, and we three sat down for lunch. The rest had eaten long before. The package for Mother Agnia was fairly large and full, and I placed it on the window sill. Fr. Alexander said, "Don't throw that package like that—it's wrapped up money." I thought that it was probably from Fr. Sebastian. We had just finished lunch when we heard a ring from the Elder. The Bishop came through the door and said, "Where is Tatiana Vladimirovna? Tatiana Vladimirovna—go, he's calling you."

I went in and knelt before the bed. He said so affectionately to me, "My old doctor, help me. It's very hard for me, very hard; I'm very sick." My heart stood still and my eyes grew cloudy. I said, "Alright, Batiushka, alright. We'll help you right away. Where does it hurt?" He indicated his hand, bandaged after an intravenous infusion. It was already difficult to locate the veins. I said, "Right now I'll give you a pain-killing injection and the pain will pass; this medication goes under the skin—all the veins have already been pricked all over. The pain will go away after the injection."

He said, "This is not the chief pain; the main thing is anguish of soul."

I said, "What for, Batiushka?"

He replied, "Do you think death is a joke? I have many sins and few good works," and he placed his hand on my head.

I said, "Batiushka, your sins couldn't be found with a microscope, and you have a whole sea of good works. So many towards me alone. You saved me from certain death three times—from a fatal illness, a train wreck, and a bus crash. And how much, how much more! You not only saved my life—you prolonged it and set it in order. All of this can't be counted, as the water in the sea can't be measured."

"But what have I been doing? I wanted to live a strict and modest life, but nevertheless I've taken delight in joys and pleasures. I have admired much of what is beautiful, especially nature."

"Batiushka, isn't beauty grace from God?"

"The grace of God is joy from God. But accomplishments—I have no accomplishments. And it often happens that this is unforgivable. And no podvig. A man lives, and for what? Everything comes from God, but what is there to give to God?"

"Batiushka, perhaps you are saying this about me?"

"No, not about you, about me—but of course, it applies to everyone. All the same, the passage yonder is unavoidable. All here is temporary, fleeting. And for what must a man travel his life's path? For love, for good; and he must suffer for them, and must patiently endure sufferings. Then he can pass over into eternal life for joy, and not for torment. One must expect joy there, and strive for that eternal joy. You say that I've lived and done good, but then I've also sinned. A man cruelly makes mistakes and is not forgiven, and loses all he has acquired. I've suffered much; I've carried my cross—not a light one. Monastic life is difficult, but it's also the easiest, and I have sometimes murmured; and from this—from murmuring—everything is lost and no merit is granted. Thus there's torment of spirit in place of joy."

"Batiushka, I understand what power there is in repentance. But I clearly understand that you're saying all this about me. Dear Batiushka, thank you for everything, for everything you've done for me. Forgive me for my unworthiness and my ingratitude and my disobedience; for everything that was not right, that was not as it should have been. Tell me, how should I live?" He was silent. I continued, "I also want to tell you how many people are praying for you, how many people..."

"You ask how to live? Live as you're now living. All are sinners. Only don't commit any great sin." He placed his hand on my head, then blessed me three times. "Well, we've had a talk together; you were always asking to have a talk. Today it's easier for me to breathe and talk. Christ be with you." I arose from my knees; my breast was bursting. Bishop Pitirim had listened attentively to our conversation. I went up to him and he also blessed me. I went towards the door. How is it possible to live without the Elder? How can we retain him and not lose him after his death? How can we be with him always, in a way that we were unable during his life? I went out into the first room. Vera brought tea in to him. He agreed to eat one soft-boiled egg and half a dish of cottage cheese with milk. He said, "I feel a little better today."

The Bishop left to serve Vespers. Fr. Sebastian said, "The choir is busy—let our own people come in and sing a bit for me." We all went in and sang. Maria Alexeyevna sang better than anyone and led us. He fell asleep during the singing. I went to Mother Agnia with Fr. Alexander's package.

April 5. Monday: He spent the night quietly. He slept and breathed peacefully. In the morning he asked to be brought to church. At first they brought him to his "stateroom," to bed; but soon he asked to be brought into the altar, to the Holy Table. He sat in the armchair in his podrasnik. He crossed himself, kept falling asleep, and simply drooped. When the Gospel was being read, he opened his eyes and lifted his head. Fr. Alexei approached and said something to him. He waved him away with his hand. He no longer dozed, but listened to the Bishop serving. Fr. Vladimir drew near and spoke very briefly with him. After Liturgy the boys came up and suggested that they take him home. He said, "All right," and had them move him right up to the Holy Table. He wanted to venerate the Holy Table but could not, so he took the cross from it and kissed it. He said, "Let's get ready." The boys asked, "Are you going to give a general blessing?" "Yes, yes," he replied. "Should we bring you out to the ambo?" "No, only bring me out to the Royal doors." He blessed everyone standing in church, on all sides, three times. While he was being carried through the courtyard he blessed everyone, turning to either side and looking at everyone. They brought him into his cell half dead. Vera put him to bed. He fell asleep instantly. Bishop Pitirim went in to see him and returned. He sat in the courtyard on a bench in the sun, under Fr. Sebastian's window. The day was warm and sunny. The Elder called Vera only at four in the afternoon. He ate a soft-boiled egg and drank half a cup of tea. The Bishop went to him at 4:30 and was with him until six.

At six a great, festive service began—the Parastasis of Radonitsa.* A little after seven Fr. Sebastian requested that he be brought to church. He lay in his room and neither said anything nor looked at anyone. He frequently crossed himself, listening to the hymns, to the service. After they had finished singing "Memory Eternal," he asked to be carried home. He was very weak and said nothing. After the service had ended the Bishop came to him, sat beside him, and read to him. After ten in the evening Fr. John, who had flown in from Michurinsk, arrived from the airport. The Elder received him joyfully and spoke with him. After him he received Maria Alexeyevna who was preparing to leave the next day, and blessed her for the road. The Bishop sat beside him for a long while. The Elder was uneasy and did not sleep.

Fr. John sat with us in the first room. He was well acquainted with Maria Alexeyevna and Mother Agnia. He related to us what the Elder had said to him, and how happy he was to find him alive. The Elder had said, "I'm very happy to see you. How good it is that the Lord helped you to find me still alive. You succeeded in coming to me. And I managed today to greet all of my reposed ones with Pascha and to pray for them. What a truly good day this is. Today the Bishop also prayed and tomorrow will pray for all my reposed children. I have lived until Radonitsa. The

---

*Radonitsa is the Tuesday following Bright Week, the first occasion after Pascha on which the dead are commemorated. A Parastasis is a special service for the dead.—TRANS.

Lord is merciful. It's so necessary for the dead—the prayers of the living are so valuable to them. I always prayed for the dead more than for anyone. And I exhort you, Fr. John—pray for the dead more than for anyone. For everything, glory be to God. Glory be to God for everything!"

These last days of the Elder's life many of his spiritual children, not wishing to abandon him, spent the night at the church. Today after the usual evening prayers (the beginning of Thomas Week) the Elder asked that the Paschal Hours be read, after which everyone dispersed to their homes, and I went to mine. Olga Fyodorovna remained to spend the night in the first room along with Fr. Sebastian's granddaughter Thaisia.

April 6. Tuesday: Radonitsa. All that I am now writing was related to me by Olga Fyodorovna. The Elder was not as weak as he had been two or three days ago but he slept uneasily, tossing and turning.

In the evening Fr. Sebastian blessed Vera and Maria to read Akathists: one to the Dormition of the Mother of God and one to the Most Holy Trinity, which he especially loved. When, during the reading of an Akathist, he was lying in bed with closed eyes, Vera thought that he had dozed off and began to read more quietly, but he said, "Vera, read more loudly—I really am listening and praying." He retained his hearing and consciousness to his death.

Olga Fyodorovna twice looked in on him and watched how he slept. At four in the morning he rang. Vera went in, gave him something to drink, and went out. Olga Fyodorovna went up to him, and his appearance was full of suffering. She asked him, "Batiushka dear, do you feel poorly?" He nodded his head in the affirmative, "I feel miserable; my suffering has become grievous."

"Shall we do an injection?"

He consented: "Yes, please, do it." Olga Fyodorovna gave him the injection, moistened some gauze and placed it on his head, and gave him something to drink. She asked, "Is it good like that?" He replied, "The very best, the very best. The Lord save you." Then he suddenly asked, "Olga Fyodorovna, with whom do you live?"

"With my father, mother and brother."

"I know, and I even remember your distant relative, A. N.; I'm asking something different—with whom do you live?" Olga Fyodorovna was silent; she did not understand what he was asking. Vera entered, brought something in a glass, and gave it to him to drink. Five or ten minutes passed; The Elder was silent, then asked, "What time is it?"

"Four-thirty."

"What, what, already?" His breathing immediately became labored and bubbling. He sat up in bed with a jerk and leaned on his elbow. He began coughing hard and bleeding from the throat. At first it was a great deal. He spat it out twice, and then the bleeding lessened. His chest was all spattered with blood. Suddenly he inhaled deeply, tried hard to breathe, but was unable. His eyes were wide open. His gaze strained into the distance, as if he saw something and was amazed. This was only for an instant. Olga Fyodorovna began to administer a strong stream of oxygen through his mouth and nose. Nothing helped; his lips turned white and his eyes began to change. Olga Fyodorovna tried to give him artificial respiration. He exhaled convulsively, dropped his head on his chest, and did not breathe again. It was all over. The time was 4:45.

Olga Fyodorovna cried out, and in an instant Thaisia and the cell-attendants ran in. A lamentation went up and things became chaotic. They called Bishop Pitirim and all who were at hand that night. The rest took its course.

The guard who was on duty, Anfisa, came running for me, knocked on the window and said, "Batiushka has died." When I went in the Elder was lying on top of a white bedspread in his new cream-colored silk podrasnik. The same kind of cream-colored material covered his legs, and a kerchief of the same sort covered his face. I looked around and no one was looking at me, so I lifted the kerchief. His face was peaceful and as if alive. I knelt and kissed his hands. They were placed crosswise on his chest and were warm, also as if alive. I absolutely do not remember who was in the room. No one stood beside him, no one wept. There was a kind of terrible and solemn silence. A kind of peace enveloped the soul, and not sorrow. Our Batiushka was with us, so close—only dead—but we were with him all the same. And the awful suffering was over at last. Bishop Pitirim began to serve a Pannikhida. It was 5:30.

After the Pannikhida everyone left the Elder. They closed the door and began vesting him. I, of course, did not see this but Fr. John described it all for Mother Agnia on a sheet of paper—she probably requested it as a remembrance. She gave it to me to copy. Here is the description: "At 4:40 Petya came to us and said that the Elder was very bad, extremely bad. By the time we dressed ourselves and got there, he had already reposed and they had already changed his clothes. When we went in he lay on the bed on a bedspread in a silken cream-colored podrasnik, with his face covered. Bishop Pitirim began to serve a Pannikhida. After the Pannikhida we began to vest the Elder. He was still quite warm. At the beginning we rubbed his body with olive oil. He hardly had a body, only bones. We clothed him in a hair shirt, paramon, riassa, woolen socks, and slippers. Then the great schema. The Bishop covered him on top with the mantia and covered his face with the klobuk. Afterwards, when they place him in the coffin, the Bishop will give him a mitre, as the Elder had willed it, and will carry him to the cemetery with the mitre on. And there they will take it off and put on the klobuk. The Bishop did not dress him in the mantia—he said that the Elder did not will it. Here is everything that I saw, in which I myself took part, of which I am unworthy on account of my sins. Forgive me. Unworthy priest John. The Lord save you."

The door of the Elder's cell was opened; he lay on the table in his klobuk. Everything, including his head and klobuk, was covered by his mantia. Candles were burning and they were reading the Gospel. Under the black mantia on the table lay our Elder. Our precious Batiushka—love for whom, and whose own love, surpassed every possibility of love on earth. He was the most beloved of us all; and each of us, his spiritual children, was for him the most beloved. Yes, not one of his favorites, but precisely *the* favorite. Such was his love, that this impossibility became possible. Not only possible, but even comprehensible and natural. And here a black mantia covered something on the table. Everyone knew that it was the Elder on the table—it was surely he. Strictness and greatness had attained its limit. But all this was no longer Fr. Sebastian. An unfamiliar priest was reading the Gospel. Between that which was lying under the black mantia on the table and me was an uncrossable boundary, deeper than the deepest abyss.

The Bishop served a Pannikhida. Then they again read the Gospel. Again, a newly arrived priest served another Pannikhida. Again they read, then sang. New candles were lit and placed. All was quiet, quiet....

In church, Bishop Pitirim served the Radonitsa Liturgy for the dead. In the cell they read, *The earth is the Lord's and the fullness thereof. The world and all they that dwell therein* (Ps. 23:1). Black kerchiefs, black scarves, black dresses.... *Precious in the sight of the Lord is the death of his saints* (Ps. 115:6). *For though I should walk in the midst of the shadow of death, I will fear no evil, for Thou art with me* (Ps. 22:4).

At five in the evening they brought the coffin, covered in black. They laid the Elder's body in it and carried it to the church with the hymn, "Helper and Protection." Again the words of the hymns and psalms, marvelous to the soul; whole depths of sorrows and consolations, and hope for the radiant, the effulgent, the incomprehensible.

The cruel sufferings of our Elder have ended; the cross-sufferings of his sacrificial love. Is it possible to grieve? Over what? His physical sufferings have been cut short, and his "anguish of soul." His spirit is in freedom. But is it possible to sever the spiritual link with him? How much he promised us—how much consolation.... How many of those he comforted did he leave in hope. It's sinful to grieve, to weep, to suffer. What is gone is that happiness that it was always possible to ask him about everything. No matter what would happen in life—if only one would manage to reach him and tell him, then all would fall into place, all would be made right. This happiness is now gone, as all happiness on earth goes. His voice, with the prolonged final verse during the reading of the Gospel, his tender glance—this has also gone, as all here passes. Contact is now possible in an entirely different way ... through prayer.

Many priests came from different cities. People, having received notice, kept on coming. Our priests and those that came served Pannikhidas each hour, all night. The choir often sang "Having slept in the flesh as a mortal...."* The whole church was aflame with candles and lampadas. Fr. Sebastian's head was already entirely covered by his black velvet mitre, encrusted with sparkling stones. At first he was covered with a dark embroidered covering, then with a white one that was painted all over with pictures—the ends were easily visible. On top there was a black church covering with a white cross.

April 7. Wednesday: The Bishop served the Liturgy. How good this was, how consoling! I know how the Elder had loved him, and how his soul, loving beauty and harmony, rejoiced, finding such accord in the handsome, majestic, and austere figure

---

*Exapostilarion of Pascha.

Bishop Pitirim serving the Elder's funeral in the
Mikhailovka church. April 8/21, 1966.

of Bishop Pitirim. His soft, deep voice, penetrating into the soul, revealed his goodness, pacified pain of heart, and healed pain of soul, as did the words of his sermon, in which he related what sort of person the reposed Elder was, especially for us. He spoke of what he wished from us, how we must build our lives, what guidelines to hold fast to, how to act; for we had been deemed worthy of the good fortune to have been under the Elder's spiritual guidance.

Again, all day and night they served Pannikhidas, read the Gospel and lit candles. Fr. Sebastian had reposed, surrounded by his close spiritual children, among parishioners who honored and loved him, and among those people who flocked together to him under the grace-filled protection of his church from many and diverse cities of Kazakhstan, Siberia and European Russia.

A telegram was received from his Holiness the Patriarch: "I express my condolences to the parishioners of the church on the occasion of the repose of the blessed Elder, Archimandrite Sebastian. His Eminence Pitirim, Bishop of Volokolamsk, is blessed to serve the funeral of the reposed-in-God. Patriarch Alexei."

April 8. Thursday: On the third day they buried Fr. Sebastian in the Mikhailovka cemetery. The hierarchical service for the dead and the burial were served by Bishop Pitirim with the participation of all of the Elder's former co-celebrants at the church—Fr. Alexei Ulovich and very many priests who had traveled from various cities, and from near and distant regions of Russia. After his sermon the Bishop asked all present to calmly and quietly come up to take leave of Fr. Sebastian, since the reposed Elder could not tolerate disorder and noise in the church. This went on, decorously and calmly, for about two hours.

The earthly path of his half century of pastoral care and twenty-two years of guidance of eldership was completed in the church in Mikhailovka in the city of Karaganda, whose cemetery will always be famous, and where a white marble cross shines

The Elder's coffin being carried from the church to the cemetery.
Photograph by Anatole Prosvirnin.

over the grave of Elder Sebastian. The sacred podvig of the blessed Elder, who had acquired great gifts of grace from the Lord, was now completed. His service to God, through upholding the good in mankind for the salvation of souls, had come to its end, and his superb example of holy spiritual love was concluded—*his fruit is unto holiness and the end everlasting life* (Rom. 6:22).

Fr. Sebastian often spoke of eternal life and the kingdom of God, and this found its expression through a certain concept of his—the "Great Family." Once, not long before his death (I did not note the date), to my words, "Batiushka, stay alive with us," he replied, "They're already waiting for me there."

After the funeral Liturgy there was a break of an hour and a half, and the clergy and singers had lunch. Fr. Sebastian was photographed in his coffin in the church courtyard from above.

Anatole Prosvirnin climbed onto the roof of the lodge with a camera. At three o'clock they carried the Elder to the cemetery. The faithful brought the coffin out of the enclosure and placed it in a hearse. The clergy sat around it. The Bishop was taken to the cemetery in the church vehicle by a circuitous route; he met the coffin at the cemetery gates. Before this the city council called the church, asking if any kind of help was needed from them for the burial. We asked them to send buses to convey the old and sick to the cemetery. Three of the better buses were sent at once, in which people were dispatched earlier, before the body was carried out of the church. It would have been impossible to drive down the street afterwards. This was surprising, and indicative of the kind of trembling respect Fr. Sebastian had enjoyed, not only from believers, but even from those far from the faith. One of the parishioners, whose husband managed a garage, succeeded in persuading him to send a few more vehicles to the church, to take passengers for whom there was no room in the buses. The Elder was carried in the hearse for only a small part of the distance—along the highway and from the town of Saran to Shakhtinsk. Then, turning off the highway to the cemetery, they removed the coffin from the hearse and it was carried on outstretched hands in such a way that it seemed to float over the crowd. His black mitre with glittering stones was clearly visible from everywhere. All movement, usually very brisk on this thoroughfare, was stopped while the coffin was being carried, since the crowd moved like a solid wall on the road and sidewalk. The windows of the homes were open and people were looking out from them. People also stood at the gates of the houses and on benches. When they carried him past the cement factory, the entire fence was filled with people sitting on it; and when the procession, with its loud continuous hymns drew closer, all the shifts, in overalls spattered with wet cement, poured out

Funeral procession down the central street of Karaganda.

into the factory courtyard. Those carrying the coffin were frequently replaced. People made their way through the crowd to the coffin just to touch his hand, and then immediately moved away, yielding their place to others, and so that they would not bother the clergy and the Elder's close ones and the choir of young women in black kerchiefs, who were walking behind the coffin.

When they turned onto the quiet cemetery street the choir began to sing "Christ is risen"—and not only the choir, but the whole crowd, as well as the old folk, and even drivers sitting in their trucks. With hymns they brought him up to the cemetery, and through the cemetery up to the grave. Numerous people had gone ahead and waited there to see the burial. The grave was dug at the edge of the cemetery, and beyond it began the fragrant springtime Kazakhstan steppe, where Siberian pea shrubs [karaganniki] were already beginning to bloom on the hillocks, along with aromatic sage and thyme. Further on in the steppe small lakes shone. A cross lay on the ground beside the open grave.

Bishop Pitirim went up to the coffin, which was lying on the ground, and began serving a Pannikhida. After it was over, many took their leave of him. At five in the afternoon they lowered the coffin into the grave. It was let down gently with boards. The soil from the bottom, which had been thrown out last when the grave was being dug, was unexpectedly of a white color.

They buried the coffin with the Elder's body, filled in the grave mound, and set up the cross with the inscription and a very small icon of the Savior. But he has remained with us always, wherever we have lived. If only we would live as he had commanded us, as he had begged us to live, as the dying man had given us as his testament. If only we would not forget this, then he will not forget us. In dying, he carried away with him his care for us. "Only don't commit any kind of big sin," he had said, as though forgiving me. And he bore away our love for him to the Lord as well.

May eternal memory in the Lord be with him. May eternal memory be between us. Eternal, eternal memory....

By the time we arrived on the bus from the cemetery everything was already prepared for the commemorative meal.* Laden tables stood not only in all the rooms of the church house, but also throughout the entire courtyard. They began to seat the people right away. Parishioners of the church were seated in the courtyard. How were they able to cook that much food, collect that many dishes, bake such mountains of bliny!? Yet I watched the parishioners bringing heavy baskets to the lodge. The funeral feast continued for another three days—Friday, Saturday and Sunday. After the service in the church, tables were again

---

*It is customary after Orthodox funerals to serve a commemorative meal in the name of the reposed, at which the poor are fed. Such a good work performed in his name is of benefit to his soul.—Ed.

placed in the courtyard. But, of course, there were already fewer people; those who had come from afar had dispersed. All the poor were seated at the table. There was another big funeral meal given on the ninth day. Up to and including the ninth day, the priests and the Elder's close ones went daily to the cemetery to serve Pannikhidas.

I went home to Moscow on the tenth day; I had wanted to stay until the fortieth day, but I had nothing to wear—it had become warm, even hot, and I had come in all my winter clothes.

I stepped out into Moscow from the Kazan station on Komsomolskaya Square. It was the first of May, so there were no taxis, and I went by metro. Everything was familiar, ordinary from childhood, but somehow distant. How would I get used to it? How would I live so far from Mikhailovka, which was so close to my heart? My heart was constricted with pain and repentance. I remembered how the Elder was once displeased, and how he said, "Again you haven't been here for five years." "What do you mean, Batiushka, what five years?" He was displeased that I, coming from Moscow, did not come to him each year. Oh, if it were only possible to relive those years!

Batiushka dear, forgive me. Help me, that my worldly interests and obligations do not bind me again to the earth. That they do not distract my soul and my thoughts; do not separate me from you.

Marble cross over the grave of Elder Sebastian
in the Mikhailovka cemetery.

5

Canonization

Time went by. The memory of the holy Elder Sebastian, far from dimming with the passing of the years, still burned brightly in the memory of those who knew and loved him. Accounts of his grace-filled help were handed down from one generation to the next, while the reposed Elder, having obtained boldness before the Lord's throne, continued to work wonders in the lives of those who called upon his aid with faith.

Shortly before his repose, Fr. Sebastian had told some of his spiritual children that communism would one day come to an end and even that "in thirty years my body will be raised from the earth." This seemed unbelievable to them, since the soviets had been in power for almost fifty years by that time, and many of them had never known any other life than the repressive atheism of the communists. But, ultimately, *God is not mocked* (Gal. 6:7). Beyond the expectations of all, in 1991, the soviet edifice, built upon the shifting sands of falsehood, crumbled into dust.

Several years after the Elder's death, Sasha (Alexander) Kiselev, one of Fr. Sebastian's "ponies," who helped carry him in his chair to and from the church towards the end of his life, was ordained to the priesthood. By 1991 he had already become rector of the Church of the Nativity of the Most Holy Theotokos in Mikhailovka. It was in that same year that a blessing was given to begin the construction of a new cathedral in Karaganda. On July 1/14, 1991, the Feast of the Holy Wonderworkers and Unmercenaries Cosmas and Damian (the heavenly protectors of Elder Sebastian's home village), the cornerstone was laid for the new church.

By 1995 services were already being held in the unfinished, as yet unconsecrated, but nevertheless magnificent cathedral. That year Patriarch Alexei II came to Karaganda—the first time a Patriarch had ever been to that region. He served a Pannikhida for all those victims of the red terror who had suffered in the Karlag and were buried in the mass graves located throughout that area. He also made a pilgrimage to the grave of Elder Sebastian.

Finally, with the blessing of the Patriarch, on September 29/October 12, 1997 the canonization of Elder Sebastian took place, along with that of Hieromartyr Pimen (Belolikov) (see below) in the Ascension Cathedral in the city of Alma-Ata. The triumphant service was led by Archbishop Alexei of Alma-Ata and Semipalatinsk, whose Act of Canonization follows:

> The holy Orthodox Church of Christ, which from the beginning has placed its hopes in the prayerful intercession before the Throne of Grace of the holy people of God, bears witness, through the conciliar mind of the Russian Orthodox Church, to the appearance in its bosom of the great throng of new martyrs and confessors of Russia, who suffered in the twentieth century at the hands of the godless authority. The God-loving plenitude of the Russian Orthodox Church reverently preserves the holy memory of the pious life, the suffering-filled labors of confession of the Faith and the martyric end of many hierarchs, clerics, monks,

Laying of cornerstone for the new Karaganda cathedral in 1991.

nuns and Christian laymen, who, in the present century, within the boundless expanses of Holy Russia, affirmed their faith, hope and love toward God and His holy Church even to the point of death and left for the next generation of children of the Church the spiritual testament: *For whether we live, we live unto the Lord; and whether we die, we die unto the Lord* (Rom. 14:8).

By God's Providence the land of Kazakhstan was manifest in the twentieth century as one of the many Golgothas of Holy Russia. Many of the New Martyrs of Russia finished the course of their lives in the boundless expanse of her steppes, in exile and in concentration camps, selflessly standing for Holy Orthodoxy. This land, which has received in its bosom their confessing bodies and has drunk in the streams of their martyric blood, truly shows itself to be a vast Antimension stretched out beneath the vault of heaven; and its air is sanctified by the ascent of their holy souls into the shelter of heaven.

An outstanding testimony of this is the ascetical life, suffering and death of the ever-memorable Bishop of Vernensk and Semirechia Pimen (Belolikov, †September 3/16, 1918), and that of the Karaganda Elder, Schema-archimandrite Sebastian (Fomin, †April 6/19, 1966).

Bishop Pimen (Belolikov) was the first archpastor of Vernensk and Semirechia, the vicar of Turkestan, the spiritual son of St. John of Kronstadt and the co-ascetic of Archbishop Andronicus of Perm (well-known for his lofty spiritual qualities and his martyric end). In the rank of bishop he headed the Urmisk mission in Persia. When he entered upon the direction of the parishes of Semirechia he showed himself to be a firm confessor of Holy Orthodoxy, a solicitous and considerate father of his flock, a steadfast preserver of Church unity and obedience to His Holiness Patriarch Tikhon. He received a martyric death for Christ's sake by shooting on September 3/16, 1918.

Schema-archimandrite Sebastian (Fomin) was an inhabitant of the Optina Monastery of the Entrance of the Theotokos into the Temple and a spiritual son of the last Optina Elders, Nektary and Joseph. After the closure of the Monastery and his service in the Tambov diocese he was exiled to the Karaganda concentration camp—the Karlag. He spent his time in bonds courageously, preaching Christ to the prisoners. After the end of his exile he established the community of the Nativity of the Theotokos in the city of Karaganda, which up to now preserves the traditions and rule of Optina Monastery. He gathered around himself many exiles and guided them in the spiritual life.

Having attained deep old age the Elder, who was honored by a multitude of spiritual children, peacefully departed to the Lord, Whom he had zealously served, during the radiant days of the Paschal celebrations in 1966. After his repose the Lord has glorified His servant and saint with many signs

Procession with the relics of St. Sebastian after their uncovering.

Reliquary of St. Sebastian in the Mikhailovka church.

and miracles, poured forth through mediation upon all who with faith seek his intercession.

With the blessing of His Holiness, Patriarch of Moscow and All Russia Alexei, after having examined the material presented to me by the Diocesan Commission for the Canonization of Saints on their pious life, ascetical service and confession, and martyric and righteous death, I now decree:

1. That the local honorable veneration of Hieromartyr Pimen, Bishop of Vernensk and Semirechia, and of our holy Father Schema-archimandrite Sebastian the Confessor, Elder of Karaganda and successor of the grace of Optina eldership, is blessed.

2. That the honorable remains of Hieromartyr Pimen, located in an unknown grave, are henceforth known as holy relics. If it is possible to uncover them they are to be given due reverence.

That the honorable remains of the holy Father Sebastian the Confessor, buried in the Mikhailovka cemetery in the city of Karaganda, are henceforth known as holy relics, and after their uncovering are to be given due reverence.

3. That the services to Hieromartyr Pimen and St. Sebastian, composed by Archbishop Alexei of Alma-Ata and Semipalatinsk, are blessed for use in the divine services on the days of their commemoration.

4. That the memory of Hieromaryr Pimen, Bishop of Vernensk and Semirechia, be celebrated on the day of his martyric death, September 3/16.

That the memory of our holy Father Sebastian, Elder of Karaganda and Confessor, be celebrated on the day of his righteous repose, April 6/19.

5. That icons be painted of the newly-canonized Hieromartyr Pimen and St. Sebastian the Confessor for veneration in accordance with the decree of the Seventh Ecumenical Council.

Interior view of the newly built Cathedral of the Nativity
of the Theotokos in Karaganda, wherein the relics of
St. Sebastian now repose.

6. That the Lives of Hieromartyr Pimen and St. Sebastian the Confessor, with their detailed biographies, works and letters be published for the edification of the children of the Church in piety. That the services of the newly canonized saints be published separately.

7. That the Reverend Archpastors of the Kazakhstan Diocese of the Russian Orthodox Church and the Synodal Commission for the Canonization of Saints be informed of this grace-filled spiritual joy.

By the intercessions and prayers of Hieromartyr Bishop Pimen and holy Elder Sebastian the Confessor, may the Man-loving Lord strengthen the Orthodox Christians of Kazakhstan and send down upon them His blessing. Amen.

—Archbishop Alexei of Alma-Ata and Semipalatinsk
September 29/October 12, 1997

Finally, several days after the canonization, on the eve of the feast day of St. Ambrose of Optina, whose memory the Church celebrates on October 10/23, the uncovering of the relics of Elder Sebastian took place. Early on the morning of October 9/22, in the presence of a large crowd of believers, the assembled clergy, led by Archpriest Alexander Kiselev, served a Moleben and then began the uncovering of the holy relics of the Elder. That evening the relics were brought to the Church of the Nativity of the Most Holy Theotokos in Mikhailovka and placed in a reliquary. Just after the thirty-second anniversary of Elder Sebastian's repose, on April 19/May 2, 1998, the relics were solemnly transfered to the new Karaganda cathedral and placed permanently by the left side-altar, which was then consecrated in honor of St. Sebastian, Elder and Confessor of Karaganda.

Thus were the Elder's prophetic words fulfilled. *No man, when he hath lighted a candle, putteth it in a secret place, neither under a bushel, but on a candlestick, that they which come in may see the light* (Luke 11:33). Now this luminary of suffering Russia has been set before all as an intercessor for his people at a crucial moment in their history. And, indeed, he is a prayerful supplicant before God in these apocalyptic times for all Orthodox Christians who call upon his aid with faith.

A MIRACLE IN AMERICA

When the Akathist found at the back of this book was received, it was sent to the translator of this book, who lives in Maine. Having great love for Elder Sebastian, he dedicated his Orthodox mission house to him and had even made a pilgrimage some years earlier to Karaganda to venerate the relics of the newly canonized saint. He wrote the following, shortly after receiving the Akathist:

"I feel I should report to you an event which, in my opinion, is a miracle of Elder Sebastian here in Maine! A couple of weeks ago we had a terrible forest fire on the coast of Maine. This spring had been the driest on record. I heard about the fire from a Serbian woman who lives in that area. Her voice on the phone was trembling. The fire was only a mile from her house, and she and her neighbors were all evacuating their homes.

"There were ten fire divisions fighting the blaze as well as a few helicopters. When she called, the wind was still blowing out to sea, which was keeping the fire from spreading. They were expecting the wind to change, however, and blow inland, which would have caused the fire to spread into the vast forests in that area and would have caused a disaster.

"After the Serbian woman informed us by phone about the danger she was in, I and a couple of the members of our community read the Akathist to Elder Sebastian, asking him to pray for all the people in danger from the fire and for all those who were fighting the fire as well.

"At that time, apparently, the helicopter operators noticed on their wind gauges that the wind was indeed shifting and starting to blow inland. But then it shifted once more and began blowing steadily out to sea. It blew out to sea for the rest of the day. Also, apparently up to that point the firefighters had felt that the blaze was quite dangerous and uncontrollable, but at a certain point (also about the time when we asked for Elder Sebastian's prayers) everything became easier for them and they were able to control the fire without difficulty. The amazing thing is that nobody in that area, which is quite poor, lost anything. Not a home, or even a pet, was lost. Many of the people felt they had experienced a miracle, because the fire had seemed so dangerous at first, but then stopped spreading and lost all its force. It is interesting that the change happened at the same time we were reading the Akathist to Elder Sebastian.

The new cathedral in Karaganda.

"It is inspiring to think that Elder Sebastian, our patron Saint, has been looking out for us and protecting us as his flock, even in Maine!"

May others, likewise inspired by the life and example of Elder Sebastian, turn to him in prayer. As one who lived through the fiercest persecution of Christianity in history, he is especially close to us, who stand on the threshold of an uncertain future, and who are witnessing the evaporation of true Christianity from the face of the earth.

Holy Elder Sebastian, pray to God for us!

PART II

*Accounts of Elder Sebastian's
Spiritual Children*

Elder Sebastian.

Accounts of Spiritual Children

1. THEODOSIA FEDOTOVNA PROKOPENKO
(SHVAGER)

They brought us to Settlement 5 in Osakarovka on August 1, 1931. Our mother was with us, and there were seven of us children. My older brother Paul was sixteen years old, I was twelve, then there was my younger brother Zhenya, and my younger sisters Nadya and Barbara, then Vanya and the youngest child, Grisha. It was a large family. They had taken Papa before us, and we didn't know where he was.

We used to live in the Stalingrad Province and our father worked in the village soviet. When they began accusing the surviving peasants of being kulaks* in 1929, the committee enlisted my father as a committee activist. Papa declined the job, which was to take away property from the peasants, saying, "I won't go; I can't do it." Then they seized Papa and all of us as kulak supporters. We were powerless peasants, the "middle ones" as they

---

The soviet seven invented a word for this—"raskulachivat."* A family would be accused as kulaks, and this entitled the accusers to strip them of all their possessions, often leaving them with nothing but the clothes on their backs.—TRANS.

ВОДЫ, ВОДЫ!

WATER! WATER!

[*This drawing, as well as those which follow throughout the rest of this book, is the work of artist Leo Premirov, a former prisoner of the Karlag, who drew them based on his own experience. The prisoners depicted here are being transported to the concentration camp by cattle car.*]

used to say back then. We had a small earthen dugout for a dwelling, a cow, a couple of horses and a few sheep. Papa was put in solitary confinement for a year. At first they moved us twenty-four miles from Stalingrad, and in 1931 they brought us to Settlement 5 in Osakarovka, where there is nothing but the flat steppe. There were fifty thousand people in the settlement. Militia on horseback guarded us all around to make sure that we would not escape. But where could you run to?

There is a stream there, the Ishim. That is where we got our drinking water and washed our clothes. We would gather tall weeds, and boil and eat them. On the steppe we dug a hole, similar to a grave, covered it over with whatever we could find, and we lived in it. That is how everyone lived the first year. There was one well for the whole of Settlement 5, eighty feet deep; it is there to this day. People used to stand in line day and night to get water. Mama would send you with a bucket, if only to fetch water for the sick children. There were no toilets, just a ditch a hundred feet long, that everyone used in common. And then people began to die from a dysentery epidemic. Every evening a cart would come. They would throw the corpses on it like logs, and then drive them off to the pits. It would happen that whole families would die. Our children too began to get sick with dysentery. They had high temperatures, and there were no doctors. Their lips became cracked, their pulses were rapid and we could only moisten their foreheads with water. On August 31 my little brother Zhenya died, Nadya died on September 11, and on the morning of September 17 Varya died. The sun had just risen halfway. Mama and I uncovered our hole, and as we lay there Varya died. And when the sun had risen so that the whole disk was showing, Grisha, the youngest, died. We had no coffins—people had to dig holes themselves and throw the corpses in them. Thankfully, we had a relative from our farm, Uncle Peter. God grant him the Heavenly Kingdom!

He said to Mama, "Dasha, don't be upset, we'll weave baskets for your children." There was some brushwood there. So Mama put all of her children in baskets. Then Mama asked the young men from the farm, "Dig out a little more under the side of the grave, so we can push the baskets in there." And they buried more and more and more on top, and then they filled it in. Out of fifty thousand, were there half left? Out of our family Paul, Vanya, I were left, along with Mama.

Later we started working. Some dug sod, while we youngsters, twelve of us, were harnessed to a carriage and had to haul the sod to the construction sites. Houses were being constructed, and they built walls out of sod. But we did not wind up in those first houses. Then my mother fell sick with typhus and lay unconscious for two weeks, while we sat there.

Winter began, and we started to be covered by a little snow. After the snow fell Papa came to us; he went through a lot of trouble to get permission to be reunited with us. Papa began to work, and things became a little easier for us. Papa made a corner out of sod in our burrow, and covered the top of the hole with sod. He had brought a sheepskin coat with him which we had been able to pass on to him when he was in solitary confinement. I lay under that sheepskin coat with my little brother all winter, because we were poorly clothed—they brought us here in whatever clothes they found us when they took us. Forgive me, of course, for saying it, but we figured that more fleas crawled all over us than we could ever catch and kill. We had to eat dry rations since there was no place to cook there. They would bring us dry lentils and we would chew on that. That winter was the hardest. Paul and Vanya didn't live through it, and of all the children, I was the only one left with Papa and Mama. By the second year they had already built houses and partitioned them off into five apartments each, and then we made our own stove.

What we lived through! God forbid that it should happen again!

> *If you've not been in Kazakhstan,*
> *Then you've not sorrow undergone.*
> *But if you've been there, then I'll bet—*
> *Until your grave you won't forget!*

Where there used to be graves in Settlement 5, there is now level ground. I can't imagine now where they're buried—it's a large village. There used to be so many holes there, but I wouldn't know how to find them now. Who would remember where those holes were? It seems to me that nobody would. Now only a few old people remain. If Mama were still alive, maybe she would remember.

2. NINA "KHOKHLUSHKA"

My name is Nina "Khokhlushka."* Well—I could tell you my last name, but no one knows me by my last name. I'm from the Sumsk Province, from the Zernovo station. In 1941, when the war began, I was in Ternopol. We were evacuated from Ternopol to Kiev. When we reached Kiev they told us, "Save yourselves however you can." Somehow I made it back home to my father and mother. I had just gotten there when the Germans came. I worked for them—I cleaned their boots. Two of my sisters were immediately sent off to Germany, but they ordered me to sign some sort of paper and left me to clean boots. But when our forces arrived, I let slip that I had signed something, but to this day I don't know what. On the basis of that signed document they pronounced me guilty. Only afterwards did they explain to me that I was a German agent. They sentenced me to

*Khokhlushka is a slang term for a Ukrainian woman.—TRANS.

Some spiritual daughters of Elder Sebastian (from right to left):
Olga Fyodorovna Orlova, Nina "Khokhlushka"
and Lydia Vladimirovna Zhukova.
Photograph taken in 1997.

ten years. I spent four years at the tree-felling operations in the Kirov Province, and then they sent me off to Karaganda. I served in Karaganda for six years. What did I see there? Only suffering and torment. I have three numbers tattooed on me—here's a number, here's a number, and here's a number—I was printed all over.

Later, when they released me, they wrote: "Permanent exile to Akmolinsk." They brought me from Karaganda to Akmolinsk, and I immediately got sick with jaundice. When I recovered, I left the hospital and thought, "Where am I to go?" I stood outside, wearing prisoners' clothes, and everyone was avoiding me. I stood there and wept bitterly. Then some people walked up to me and asked, "What's wrong? Why are you crying like that?" I told them about my situation. "Well, my dear, you're from the camps, and we're exiles here. We'll take you in." Now there's God's providence! They took me in and found work for me in a hospital, and I worked there for four years. Just then they freed everyone from permanent exile status. I returned home from Akmolinsk, and everyone disdained me, since I had just come from prison. But there, in the Bryansk Province, in the village of Brasovo, there lived an elder, Fr. Matthew from the Ploschansk Monastery. I came to him and said, "Batiushka! There's no life for me here!" And this is what Fr. Matthew told me: "You should go back where you came from. You'll find all your own people there, and you'll be granted unexpected joy!" Ai-Ai! I started trembling! What could be there?! What kind of joy is there?! I had gone through so much suffering there and shed so many tears, and I had served a prison term there! In Aktas! In Karabas! I had been freed from Dolinka, and he says, "Go back where you came from!"

I returned to Akmolinsk, where I started to go to church all the time. The priest, Fr. Nicholas Moiseyev told me, "You know, Nina, you should go to Karaganda—there's a Batiushka

Sebastian there. You're all alone; maybe he'll take you in." And so for the first time I came to see the Elder. When I went in to see him, he was standing there, like the father of a large family, and was quietly blessing everyone. I had just opened the door when Mother Anastasia cried out: "She's one of ours! One of ours!" Later, when Fr. Sebastian summoned me and I entered his cell, I fell to his feet and kissed his boots. I didn't know what to say, and wept bitterly: "Dear Batiushka! Dear Batiushka! Not only did I not want to come to Karaganda—I didn't even want to remember that it exists on earth! I served a prison term here, even though I was innocent; I served time in Aktas and Karabas, and I was released from Dolinka! And now I've come here to you!" I told him everything and wept bitterly. Tears welled up in his eyes, too. The mothers also began crying at the sight of our tears. The Elder called me a "passion bearer" for innocently serving a prison term—"for the sins of all humanity," as he said. He gave me a large icon of the Holy Trinity and a pile of candies: "Give these out, Nina, in Akmolinsk, to whomever you know."

I had been there for two days and I needed to return. They escorted me and put me on the train, and then Fr. Sebastian said to me, "Come to see me again." Then I started to travel to see him regularly. I traveled thus for three years, and then he blessed me to stay in Karaganda. This was around 1960. I came here and the Elder sent me to work at the hospital. He used to send all of his people to work in the hospital. I worked in the children's section, and we baptized many unfortunate children with the Elder's blessing. And then the enemy rose up against me. Once I began to feel sick and I said to a child, "Ooh-ooh! I wish you would choke, I'm so fed up with you!" I came to my senses and ran to Fr. Sebastian: "Batiushka! Look what I did today!" He didn't scold me, he just said right away, "Could that really have been you? That was the devil! Leave the Childrens' Section, because the enemy is angry that we've baptized many children. Go to the first section—there aren't any of our people there." From then on I worked in the Botkin (1st) Section.

For fifteen years I hadn't received any news at all from my sister Maria, who had been taken to Germany. "Batiushka," I said, "we don't know how to pray for Maria—she hasn't returned from Germany." And he said, "She's alive!"

"How can this be? We haven't heard about her for fifteen years?"

"Well, she's alive, and you'll hear about her soon." And, in fact, we soon received a letter from Maria—she was in France.

Once I went over to the pannikhida table, and the Elder said right away, "Nina! Your parents gave me a bun!" What was he talking about? I left, and couldn't understand—what kind of bun did my relatives give him? When I arrived at home, there was a letter in the mailbox from my parents. They wrote, "How we've been praying for Batiushka! We baked a nice cake and passed it out in his name in church." Then I understood.

I had by this time already stopped thinking of that elder, Matthew; I had forgotten him. And then suddenly I started recalling him in my thoughts. I told Elder Sebastian all about him and about what he had said to me. The Elder said, "No, you shouldn't forget him like that. Go there and give him a prosphoron from me and have him pray for me."

I stood there in church and thought about the trip to my home town. I went up to Fr. Sebastian for a blessing, and he asked, "Where have you been? You've been traveling to your homeland, haven't you?" He blessed me to go home to see my mother and father.

"Batiushka, how long should I spend there?"

"Stay there for as long as your mother blesses you to. Buy them some sugar." In their letter, my parents had written, "Bring us some sugar." He had foreseen all of this. When I arrived in my homeland, I went to Elder Matthew and gave him the prosphoron and showed him a photograph of Fr. Sebastian. He said, "Ah! Now this is a great Elder!" Then he kissed the photograph. "But he'll die soon, five years early, since you're not obedient to him." And he prayed for him. That was Elder Matthew from the Ploshchansk Monastery. I wept—Aktas ... Karabas ... Dolinka.... And now I had found my "unexpected joy"—I had found Fr. Sebastian!

3. ANASTASIA PETROVNA PARSHINA

Schema-nun Eupraxia was the same age as Fr. Sebastian. She told me that she often used to travel to see the Elders in Optina Monastery. Fr. Sebastian was then a young novice. Once she came, and he walked up to her and said to her affectionately, "My little child, my little child!" She thought, "A novice—and that's how he addresses me—'little child!' I've come to see the Elders; who is he to call me that?" Later she came to Karaganda to see him and Fr. Sebastian kept her here. And so she became his "little child."

Mother Eupraxia also used to tell us the following: she was sent into exile, and Hieromonk Hierotheus was in the same settlement. There a young girl, Seraphima, lived with him, who was very ill with tuberculosis. Then Fr. Hierotheus received a letter from Fr. Sebastian. He wrote, "Tonsure Seraphima with the name Sophia. Don't delay." The letter had been received on the eve of some great feast. "What should we do?" they thought. "We can't abandon the feast." So they decided to go to her right after the All-night Vigil. They gathered quickly after the service. When they came, Seraphima was all flushed. Fr. Hierotheus performed the tonsure; Mother Eupraxia was present, along with another nun, who became her "monastic godmother" at the tonsure. Nun Sophia asked her godmother to read the monastic Rule of prayer to her for the first time. Her godmother stayed to read the Rule. Then nun Sophia began tossing about in her bed. Her godmother asked her, "What's the matter?"

"Demons are all around me and they're gnashing their teeth. My soul is troubled by this horrible gnashing of teeth."

"Are you afraid of them?"

"No, I'm not afraid, but it's unpleasant to my soul." By the end of the Rule, when the sun had begun to dawn, the young nun Sophia gave her soul into God's hands.

4. PRIEST JOHN TIMAKOV
Auxiliary Priest, Karaganda

In the middle of the summer of 1931 they brought us from the Samara Province to the steppe, to the spot of the future settlement of New Tikhonovka. I was young, and with me were my wife and our small child. We dug a hole three feet deep and covered it with a roof made of horse-cloths and put a bag containing all of our belongings at out heads. Our baby lasted for a month in that hole, and then died. During the winter, when they transferred us to incompletely constructed barracks, another child was born to us.

That first winter raged with typhus and was very cold. It was hard to live on the rations, and everyone grew weak. In 1931 and 1932 all the children and the elderly died. By 1933 only the young were left; you would rarely see an old person. And then even the younger people began to die. In Tikhonovka up to two hundred people would die each day. Three work brigades dug graves (ten feet wide and sixteen feet long). They would sew a person up in a dirty horse-cloth and toss him in the hole. They didn't succeed in digging graves in the winter. They laid the corpses in piles as large as a house; five to seven hundred people

Mineshafts in Karaganda. At the left are miners' hovels.
Photograph from the 1950s.

in each pile would lay stacked on top of each other, like firewood. Our second child also died. My wife and I survived
thanks to the fact that we sold her fox-fur coat that she had inherited from her mother. We bought a sheep, slaughtered it, ate
it, and remained barely alive.

I, along with other exiles, worked in the Kirov Mine. It was
five miles from the mine to our settlement. Every day we had to
walk across the steppe, both there and back. When you work in
the mine, subsoil water drips from the ceiling, like rain. You
leave the mine soaking wet, with water in your galoshes and wet
foot-cloths. You'd put on a dry undershirt and run back to the
settlement through the -20° cold. By the time you'd get there,
your clothes would be frozen to your body. Some miners would
fall dead while returning from work, and then they would lie
there on the road all winter. It happened that during snow
storms the road wouldn't be visible, and the dead bodies would

lie there in place of landmarks across the steppe. They would gather them on small carts in the spring. I too reached the point of exhaustion. I would barely make it home alive because of fatigue. I got very sick with anemia and fits of vomiting. For a long time I begged the commandant of the settlement to allow us to move to a dugout near the mine, and with great difficulty we got permission. When we moved there we began to live as though in heaven. I didn't have to walk the ten miles. I would leave the mine, walk across the road and right into the dugout. There I revived a little.

We didn't have any priests until 1934. Only one Old-believer priest, Fr. Sergius, used to come to baptize children. In 1934, Fr. James Penkov was released from the Karlag. Among the older inhabitants of the village of Bud-Gora, they had preserved an antimension, a cross, and a set of priest's vestments. They gave all this to Fr. James, and he began to secretly perform the Divine Services, going from house to house. Members of the Komsomol caught him many times and brought him to the commandant's office. They forbade him to serve and threatened to arrest him again, but Fr. James would reply, "I gave a vow to God, and I'm going to serve." He would say to his elderly acquaintances, "I want to suffer for the Faith." In 1937 they came for him and took him, and to this day we have had no news of him.

Until 1938 we used to travel to Akmolinsk to receive Communion. In 1938 Fr. Vladimir Kholodkov was released from the Karlag, and again we, fifteen or twenty of us, began to secretly gather in the dugouts. We would celebrate the Liturgy on feast days and receive Communion.

When the war began and Stalin gave a decree allowing prayer to God, Fr. Vladimir went to the mining council and secured permission to serve openly. Then people started coming to us. The prayer house was in a dugout near the Kirov mine, where we lived and worked. We had literally been serving "underground"; our windows were in the ceiling. When we began to serve publicly, around five hundred people began to gather for the services. We widened the dugout, built sheds, and served in this way until 1950, when we built the church dedicated to Archangel Michael.

I first heard about Fr. Sebastian in 1943, and I began to visit him. Then, with his blessing I moved to Melkombinat, built myself a house, and helped to build and purchase houses for widows with children for whom the Elder had arranged living accommodations in Melkombinat. Time moved along, and life gradually fell into place. Already in 1955 they had opened up a church in Mikhailovka. Then, at the end of 1955 my sister wrote to me from Kuibyshev: "Vanya, come see us; we miss you." I said to Fr. Sebastian, "Bless me to go to my home town." But he said, "You don't need to—don't go." But after three weeks had gone by, on New Year's Day, 1956, I came up to kiss the cross after the service, and the Elder said to me suddenly, "Ivan Semyonovich, you wanted to go to Kuibyshev; go there, only get ready to go quickly. Quickly!" And so that very evening I got on the train and left. I arrived in Kuibyshev, and there was something wondrous—Zoya was standing there.* The city was in a commotion. Crowds of people were at Zoya's house, and people were openly going to church, crossing themselves and

---

*In 1956 an event occurred in Kuibyshev (now Samara) which turned many peoples' attention to God. During the Nativity Fast, a girl named Zoya committed a blasphemous act on New Year's Eve: instead of dancing with her fiancee Nicholas, she decided to dance with an icon of St. Nicholas. While dancing, she suddenly turned to stone, and remained standing there, still alive. At night Zoya would cry out terribly, calling people to repentance. She remained in this state for 128 days. On the night of Pascha her body revived, and on the third day of Bright Week she departed to the Lord, passing through this terrible path for the expiation of her sins. (See *The Orthodox Word*, 1965, no. 6, pp. 226-227.)

repenting. I went to try to see Zoya, but the police were no longer letting anyone into the house. I stayed in Kuibyshev for a week, and upon returning I informed the inhabitants of Kara-ganda about Zoya, and about God's Providence for the world, which is perishing in sin.

Some more about Elder Sebastian's clairvoyance:

My eight-year-old daughter fell ill with tuberculosis. I brought her to the doctors, but they said, "We can't treat her here; take her to the health resort in Borovoe, or else she'll die." We went to see the Elder and asked him, "Batiushka, bless us to take her to the resort, or my daughter will die."

"Yes," he said, "it would be better to bury her here than to go there." My wife and I grieved—we felt so sorry for our daughter! She was such a nice little girl; she was clever, obedi-ent, and meek, like an angel. And so I took her to Borovoe. There, it's true, they healed her, but after she came back from the health resort she changed and became like a stranger to us. Later she entered the Pioneers, then the Komsomol, and then she became a member of the party. To this day she has not come to the Faith.

My other daughter, having grown up, became acquainted with a young man, a German by nationality, who asked her to marry him. To this my daughter replied, "My father is a be-liever, and he won't give me to you because you're not bap-tized." The young man, whose name was Volodya, agreed to first be baptized and then be married to my daughter. Then I went to Fr. Sebastian for a blessing, but he said, "I'll marry them, but he doesn't need to be baptized." If it had been some other priest who told me that I would have objected, since it's forbid-den to marry someone who is not baptized. But in this case I said nothing, since I knew that he didn't make mistakes. When we spoke with Volodya's mother, she told us that in 1942 a priest had come to their exile settlement and baptized all the children, including Volodya. Fr. Sebastian knew all this, even though he had not seen Volodya with his own eyes.

5. Vera Afanasievna Tkachenko
Elder Sebastian's Cell-Attendant

I became acquainted with Fr. Sebastian in 1939. I was eight years old, and he had just been released from prison. I was then living at my aunt's house on Lower Street. My aunt was a believer, and we often went together with the Elder from house to house and prayed. When my mother died I became extremely close to him, since he felt sorry for orphans. He would say, "If I had not been an orphan myself, I would not have had such compassion for others." Then Fr. Sebastian said, "I'd like to take you in." I was then eleven years old. He settled me with a nun, where I lived under the Elder's supervision. When I turned sixteen, he took me on as his cell-attendant, and I constantly lived by him and took care of him.

When we lived on Lower Street, we used to all eat from one dish. Five or six people would sit at the table and Fr. Sebastian would sit with us. It would happen that we would all be very hungry, but they could only set one dish for all of us. "No," I'd think, "I won't get my fill." And a miracle would happen! There would be food left over in the dish, and everyone would be full. How was he able to do that? I don't know.

Our church was still unregistered at that time, so for ten years we went from house to house to pray. For example, it would be necessary to go to Fyodorovka to pray, and the Elder would say, "Let's get up at half past four and go to Fyodorovka." And we'd all get up and go on foot to Fyodorovka. I'd carry the books at my shoulder, Fr. Sebastian would take a stick and bundle, and Mothers Varya and Grusha would be there—they

Fr. Sebastian's cell-attendants: Vera Afanasievna
Tkachenko (left) and Maria Nikitichna Obraztsova.

were the Elder's choir. There we would pray, and at half past seven he would bless me to go to work. (It was forbidden to not work—all who did not work were investigated.) When I would come back from work—again I had to go and pray. We used to go from one end of Karaganda to the other, because it was impossible to serve continuously in one place.

Fr. Sebastian was an exceptional person. He would weep with those who wept and rejoice with those who rejoiced. He always practiced mental prayer, and the prayer had descended into his heart. But the life of his soul was concealed from us. It's difficult to explain in what sense it was closed—it was only possible to sense it. I remember how I once recounted my trip to Moscow to the Elder and told him about the Moscow churches, and about how I had gone up to the Patriarch for a blessing. He listened and was silent, but something was going on inside of him. His eyes changed—they turned from brown to gray. I told him about this, but he didn't answer; he only lowered his eyes. He was, of course, very wise—he did not always speak openly. And, after all, I was still a child, and it wasn't so easy to grasp what he was speaking about. Sometimes he would slap you on the forehead, lovingly of course, to knock out any foolishness. All sorts of thoughts come up, after all. Well, for example, I once thought, "What kind of life have I got? In the morning I leave for work—they're praying. In the evening I come back from work—they're praying; I can't take it any longer! It is better to live in the world and not worry." Then the Elder came up and slapped me gently on the forehead with the back of his hand.

This is the kind of thing I was concerned about: I would look into the altar from the cliros—aha! The Elder's taking off his vestments! I'd have to go quickly to his cell and get it ready so that everything would be on the table when he came. When Fr. Sebastian had finished eating, I'd have to see to it that he lay down quickly to rest. People would come in, first one, then another, but when he was tired he would sometimes say, "I can't receive them." Once I asked him, "What I should say to them?"

"Just tell them—don't offend them; just find a way to say it. If it's really necessary, let them wait."

I went. "Fr. Sebastian's resting," I said. After he had rested, he started reading a book. Again I said, "Batiushka, a woman has come."

"Let her wait." And he kept reading. Again I went to explain. Then the people started murmuring, "Eh, you yourself don't want to let us see him!" I went back to him. He said, "No, let them wait—it's not time yet."

"Batiushka," I said, "they're saying that I'm the one who's not letting them in to see you."

He said, "If you like sledding, you should like carrying the sled, too. You know, I also lived with an Elder in Optina."

Sometimes I wouldn't let people in to see him at all, because he would say, "I can't receive anyone today—I feel very poorly." And the people would say, "Vera's really strict—she could give you a whipping!"

Once the following incident happened: The Elder had sent me to Moscow, and Mother Julia and Maria Obraztsova (his other cell-attendant) stayed behind with him. They wrote to me, "Vera, come back—it's hard without you." And the Elder also said, "Ech, you dunces! Vera wouldn't have allowed such disorder." Everybody acted as though they were just passing through. When Fr. Sebastian had already fallen ill, the two "policemen" were stationed there—Shurik and Alyosha. Since even they couldn't cope with things, they had to call me. I had to come and "make short work of things." The young men, of course, were easier to deal with, and I was already used to defending the Elder. They complained to him, "Batiushka, why is Vera so angry, and won't let us in to see you?" He said, "That kind of people are needed in a monastery too."

Once Fr. Sebastian asked Bishop Pitirim to send him two typewriters. When they were brought, the Elder said, "Here's one for you, Vera, and one for Maria Obraztsova." I wondered, "What do I need this for? What am I going to do with it?" After the Elder's death, however, I found it quite useful. I learned to type and for twenty-five years I have taught classes in typewriting and clerical work. Maria also thought, "What do I need this for? That was in the evening. In the morning the Elder said to Maria, "No, you don't need it—you're going to be a church reader." And he gave the typewriter to Elena Agafonova.*

6. Maria Obraztsova
Elder Sebastian's Cell-Attendant

I came to Fr. Sebastian for the first time in 1948, from Tikhonovka. It was the Feast of the Nativity of Christ. When I arrived they were serving in a small residential house, guarded by a fence and barbed wire—that's how our church looked. They served Great Vespers and Liturgy. The service made such an impression on me that it's impossible to convey it; I forgot where I was. When the service was over, at four o'clock in the morning, they arranged for my friend and me to rest at the nuns' house on Lower Street. We arrived, and it was a tiny peasant hut, yet so tidy—there were gauze curtains, and strips of carpet were laid out. We rested, ate, and then it was time for us to go home. But the mothers asked, "Have you seen Fr. Sebastian?"

"No, we haven't." Suddenly the Elder knocked on the window with his finger, from outside the house. Fear fell upon me, but Nicholas, our friend from Tikhonovka, said "Here's what we'll do; we'll take a blessing, and you—since it's your first time,

---

*Elena Alexandrovna Agafonova presently works as chief clerk in the Alma-Ata and Semipalatinsk Diocesan Administration.

bow before him." Fr. Sebastian entered, took off his coat, and greeted us with the Feast. We fell at his feet, but he said, "You don't need to do that, this is a great Feast. Then he left everyone and took me and my friend to his room. I was quite frightened, but he began to question us: "Where do you live? With whom do you live? Which of your relatives are alive?" My whole being was trembling within me. Then he blessed me to come visit him.

After that talk I was beside myself with joy for two months. Why was I so happy? Because now I knew the Elder. And so I visited him for two years. Then he said, "You should move here; have your mother come see me." She came. He asked, "How many children do you have?"

"Four daughters and a son."

"Well, I'm taking one of your daughters from you."

"Take her."

"Now don't you be sad—you'll come here to visit her."

He bought for us, three girls, a small house in Melkombinat. This was in 1950. He bought us the house, gave us a rule of prayer, and we began to live there. We came to Mikhailovka for feasts, and the Elder often came to our place in Melkombinat. What a joy that was! The minute he would arrive, all the people would rush over; the news would spread as though carried by the breeze. And he would serve Molebens and Pannikhidas at our place. When he would leave Melkombinat, it was as if day had turned to night. "Batiushka, I'll go with you!"

"No, of course I can't take you; there's no room." But as a consolation he would give me a photograph or some kind of picture. "Batiushka, will you sign it?"

"Oh, you! I'll do that the next time that I don't take you."

When we had settled in Melkombinat (this was in the autumn), the Elder said, "Now build a large room here, sixteen feet square." We started building it. There were three of us girls, and he sent us an older man, a real loser, and some timber was brought. Already by Nativity the Elder had blessed the room with holy water and served the Liturgy in it. At that time he was serving secretly on feasts, Saturdays and Sundays. Nearby in Stakhanov, a young woman lived in a small house, and he also used to serve Liturgy at her place. Then he would serve Liturgy at a Mordvinian's house, which had crooked windows and doors. That's how it was until 1955, when we received the documents to register our community.

Melkombinat was his offspring, like Diveyevo was for St. Seraphim. He noticed everything—if someone's house was falling apart, if someone's shed was in bad condition, or if someone's well was collapsing. He would arrive, we'd pray, and then we would quickly set the table. Wherever Fr. Sebastian was, everyone followed. There would sit the Elder, Shurik, and Petya; and there would be all types, all ages—everyone! It was a large family, and their loving mother was with them. You couldn't call the Elder "father." He was a loving mother.

Let me tell you about the following incident. Once a woman came from Tikhonovka and said, "Batiushka, Shura (Alexandra Sofronovna, his spiritual daughter) is sick. It's a heart ailment." He told her, "All right then, we'll go see her tomorrow." On that day there was a blizzard; it was pitch dark, and all the roads were covered. By morning the blizzard had let up, but the cold was severe. But we left all the same. Fr. Sebastian took along me and Nicholas, a deacon who served with us. We were going along, when the taxi driver, who took us as far as the Second Mine, said, "I'm not going any further—there's no road." Well, what were we to do? We kept going on foot. But the cold was impossible! Right then a horse came by, pulling a small sled. We asked if we could put the Elder on the sled, while Nicholas and I stood on the back runners. We finally arrived at the sick woman's house by one o'clock in the afternoon. No sooner had Fr. Sebastian come through the door, then her husband fell right at his feet and sobbed, "Batiushka, Shura's in the hospital! An ambulance took her away!" The Elder shook his head: "Well, that's all right, it's pleasing to God that way." And the husband cried, "Shura's been tormenting me! She kept saying, 'Look under what conditions we've asked Fr. Sebastian to come here, and I won't even be at home!'" The Elder said to me, "You know, Maria, you should go this evening to the hospital to see her and tell her that I didn't come; otherwise she'll really worry...." Now, who could do such a thing? Only one's own mother.

I came to the hospital in the evening and said, "Alexandra Sofronovna, Fr. Sebastian sent me to tell you that he can't come; the road is untravelable." She said, "Glory to Thee, O Lord! I couldn't sleep all night, thinking that he would arrive and I'd be in the hospital." But the woman who was taking care of her came in and said, "Shura, the Elder did come, after all." Of course, she was very upset, but she greatly appreciated all this. "O Lord!" she said, "But who am I? I'm so unworthy! And yet he came anyway!"

Later, Fr. Sebastian appointed me as his cell-attendant. We lived well. Mother Julia and I slept on the floor, on a large piece of felt, and Vera slept on a fold-out cot. When it was very cold, the Elder would open his cell, come out, and cover us with his podrasnik as we slept. Sometimes he would send me off to Lower Street where the nuns lived. I would say to them, "This room is warm and clean, and the dinner is wonderful. But Mother Barbara would say, "You should have to be chased over here with a stick! It's better to sleep on a piece of felt, as long as it's near the Elder."

Fr. Sebastian had the type of personality that you couldn't describe in words. He would come after services and if, for example, it was cool, he would say, "Vera, put a vest over my shoulders." But he would never say, "Why is it so cold?" He was strict with himself but kind to his neighbors. He would never complain if something wasn't just so. But once the following thing happened—it was even funny. It was Tuesday evening, and the Feast of Archangel Michael. I gave him dinner: "Batiushka, would you like tea with milk?"

"No, without milk."

I came to the kitchen and told Mother Anastasia, "Matushka, Fr. Sebastian wants tea without milk."

"No," she said. "Here, bring it with milk!"

"No, Matushka, I won't take it to him."

"Take it, I tell you!"

I took it. The Elder looked at me and said, "I asked for tea without milk."

"Batiushka, that's what Mother Anastasia told me to do—'Take it, and that's that!'"

He got up, took the cup of tea and milk, brought it to the kitchen, went up to Mother Anastasia, and poured the whole cup over her. She scolded me, saying, "You loafer, why did you bring him the tea with milk?!"

"But Matushka, you poured it for me!"

"Oh! Vera would have fought with me, but she wouldn't have brought it to him. But you went right ahead! See what happened!"

But all of this was, of course, a game. They had their own way of talking with the Elder, which was incomprehensible to us. He would sometimes say to her, "Nastya, now's not the time," meaning for foolishness. She acted as a fool-for-Christ's-sake, but not to the degree that she would have liked. Mother Anastasia was a great one, too.

Once she fell ill on my mother's nameday. She cooked pancakes at our place all day, but only towards the end of the day did she ask for some antidoron. That's how abstinent she was. Fr. Sebastian also ate very little. Mother Barbara would say, "Even when not fasting, he fasted." They would bring him food "hot off the griddle," as they say, but he would swallow three spoonfuls and say, "Take it away." Or, another example would be the first day of Great Lent. Usually on the first day no one is allowed to eat. After the Great Canon they would be given a piece of prosphoron each. Then the Elder would order potatoes to be cooked at twelve o'clock, and at three o'clock, when they were already cool, he would eat a half of a small potato and say, "Well, my fathers are fasting (meaning the serving priests) but I'm not." In this way he would humble himself. "I'm sick, after all," he would say, "and so I've broken the fast."

He was exceptionally full of love. Once, for instance, it was the Feast of Alexander Nevsky, August 30. I said, "Batiushka, I'm going home to dig potatoes."

"Go, go; otherwise your mother will be waiting for you." I left. We were digging potatoes in the field, when rain began to fall. We needed to have everything done in time and to make it to church by five o'clock for the Feast of the Placing of the Cincture of the Most Holy Theotokos. I was as if on pins and needles. Meanwhile the Elder rested, then got up, opened the curtains and said, "It's raining, and someone's out digging potatoes. Vera, go and call Maria, and tell her not to come to the Vigil."

"But who should I call? They're out in the field."

"Just go and call." Vera went and called us at home. My sister had just that moment opened the door—she had come home for her lunch break. She opened the door and the phone rang. She lifted the receiver and Vera said, "Tell your abbess to stay home and not come to the Vigil." My sister left a note on the table: "You don't have to go to the Vigil." Well, of course, when I came home all wet and tired and read the note, I had a good cry. What a Batiushka! How he knew the soul and could see right through it!

Once the following thing happened. The Elder told Natasha, "Go to the Obraztsovs and tell them to slaughter their cow. This was in March. We had fed the cow all winter and now we had to butcher it! My mother said, "My God, what a pity!" Some time passed and Fr. Sebastian called Natasha: "Did you go?"

"I went."

"Go right now and tell them to slaughter the cow." Natasha came and said, "What's going on, are you mocking him?"

Mother said, "Well, I guess we have to butcher it, but it's too bad." Again time dragged on, and by this time it was April. The Elder sternly, simply full of exasperation, said, "How long are they going to torture the beast?" Natalia came and said, "Slaughter it right this instant! I'm not leaving until you slaughter it!" We butchered the cow and it had a rusty nail in its stomach. It had been suffering from this and would have died anyway, and the Elder knew this.

Once, when we were still in our first year in Melkombinat, during the first week of Great Lent at one o'clock in the afternoon we were eating kissel* with fruit, and a piece of apple core got stuck in my throat—I couldn't breath in or out. We went to see Fr. Sebastian, but he had gone to prayers, and the service ended at nine in the evening. We went home to Lower Street together with the Elder. We sat down to dinner, but I couldn't eat; I couldn't even swallow my saliva. The Elder questioned Natalia: "What did you eat, and when did you eat?" Then he tore off a piece of bread and gave it to me: "Here, take this and eat it." I thought, "But how am I going to eat it?" I ate a small piece—no problem, it went down. Then I tried a bigger piece, and it was as though nothing had happened to me. I was silent. When they had finished reading Evening Prayers, I bowed at the Elder's feet: "Batiushka! The Lord save you! It's as though

*A starchy, pudding-like fruit desert.—ED.

nothing happened"! But he replied, "Well then, glory be to God."

Once Fr. Sebastian said to me, "Do you want to know how the Patriarch signs his name?" and handed me a sheet of paper, written by Mother Agnia (I knew her handwriting). On the top at a slant a resolution was written in red crayon. "Here" he said, "read what's at a slant, but don't read anything else." He gave me the paper and went out into the corridor. I was burning with curiosity—what had Mother Agnia written, and what had His Holiness signed? And then I thought to myself: "Oh, you have no conscience! Aren't you ashamed of yourself? The Elder forbade you to read it." I placed the paper on the table and stepped away from it. The Elder was nowhere to be found. But I was still interested—just what had Mother Agnia written? Again I went up to the table, and again, "No, I won't do it," and I walked away. Three times I was seized with curiosity. Then Fr. Sebastian entered and smiled: "Well, read it then!" It was Mother Agnia's request for the monastic tonsure. He soon tonsured her into the mantia.

Of course, it was hard for us to take Fr. Sebastian's repose. Everyone grieved and wept. After half a year I had a dream that will never be erased from my memory. I dreamt that I had entered a church, and the Elder was in the altar, taking out particles from prosphora; but the altar was not like ours, it was narrow. I was standing at the door and had my hands held out to receive a blessing, and I called out in a whisper, "Batiushka!" He turned around, came up to me, and blessed me. I was silent and didn't know what to say—should I say a lot? Perhaps he wouldn't have time. Should I say a little? But I didn't know how to formulate it, in order to say that which was essential—so I was silent. But he came up close to me and said, "I'm praying for you!" And then I woke up. Oh! How I ran about for joy! He had seemed alive, and again he had comforted me.

A year after his death the Feast of Annunciation fell on the same day as Palm Sunday. The service was very complicated. I was the reader, and I didn't know how to correctly combine both Feasts. Fr. Sebastian appeared to me in a dream and laid out everything in order: "Look; look very closely," he said. "This is for Palm Sunday, this is for the Feast (that is, the Annunciation). Six stichera for the Feast, and four for Palm Sunday. Glory: of Palm Sunday; Both now: of the Feast." Again he seemed as though alive. When he had explained everything I woke up and remembered it all, and that's how I led the service.

I remember how, before he reposed, we had been waiting for Bishop Pitirim. It was night-time. Fr. Sebastian was sitting in his cell, by the stove. Vera was cooking something and changing the bedsheets, Olga Fyodorovna was undoing the Elder's hair (which was tied in back), and I was washing him behind his ears. There was a deathly silence.... He was sitting there, looking at the icon corner. It seemed as though you could have asked him anything you wanted, but all of us were as if frozen. He himself broke the silence. He said, "When I die, remember how you followed me." And now this memory has stayed with us as a consolation for our whole lives. The Elder has left us. Of course, we don't have it so bad here in Mikhailovka, and we're trying with all our might to keep things together, but it's far from perfect, since he's not here. Well, the priests we have are, incidentally, his, the Elder's; yes, yes. Therefore everyone is trying.

7. Tatiana Artemovna Izyumova

My parents were special-status exiles. They were exiled from the Volgograd Province in 1931. There were my mother, father, and three children. They were brought to the barren steppe, to Settlement 13, which is almost ten miles from Temirtau. There were twenty-five thousand people in that settlement, and everyone made dugouts in the steppe. By winter they had erected something like a shed out of brushwood, and ten families lived in that totally unheated shed. There were no windows, the roof barely covered the shed, and everyone lay on plank beds with practically no clothing. Sometimes my father would come home from work, and my mother and all the children would be lying there covered with snow. He would brush off the snow and ask, "Are you alive in there?"

"Yes, we're alive." There was nothing to eat or drink. My older brother once found a block of wood, brought it to my father, and said, "Papa, chop up this block and heat some tea up for us." At that moment the commandant walked up, took our father by the collar, and held him under arrest for three months because of that piece of wood.

By spring practically no people were left in Settlement 13; everyone had died off. Our family was spared by a miracle—even the children and my mother. Then they were moved to Tikhonovka, where there were five-apartment dugouts, made from clay and elm wood. That's where I was born, in 1939. In 1940 Mama was run over while she was waiting in line for bread. She was pregnant and died. In 1941 they took my older brother to the Front, where he was killed. My father labored for the war effort by working two or three shifts in the mine. This was the "second Front," and every day people were killed in the mines. Every day, when he was leaving for work, he would bid me farewell: "Well, my little daughter, whether I'll return from the mine or not, God knows."

And so we grew up. I remember they used to call us "kulaks." I didn't understand the meaning of this word, and asked my father, "Papa, why do they call us kulaks?" He said: "They call us that, my child, because when we used to live in Russia we never had a pillow to lay our heads on, and we used to sleep in the fields on our fists.* They called us that because we labored and worked the land, and fed Russia with our labors."

In 1955, when I was sixteen years old, I met Fr. Sebastian. That was the first time I had come to church. There was a service in progress, and Fr. Sebastian was serving. I stood there quietly and listened. Such a rebirth took place in my youthful soul, and an unearthly feeling of joy and enthusiasm took my breath away. Then I began to go to church. I became better acquainted with the Elder, and he began to draw me in. He was so handsome, exceptionally kind, and very affectionate. He associated very simply and in a kindly way with people, and met everyone with heartfelt warmth, especially when a person would come to him for the first time. I started to become familiar with choral singing. The Elder especially loved the Optina chants, and he would sometimes come to the cliros himself and sing. It was a women's choir, like a monastic one. The nuns sang, as well as young girls. There wasn't anything like a monastery here then, but there was a monastic spirit present. The community was not large; there were only ten or twelve nuns, but there were also secret nuns. Fr. Sebastian loved long services very much. In our church nothing was left out, and nothing was shortened. He tried to install the spirit of Optina Monastery in this church, in which he had expended much labor. He would say, "I've poured out a lot of sweat here, to found this church."

When I came for the first time, the Elder asked me, "Where is your mother?"

I answered, "Batiushka, my mother died; I don't remember her."

"Did she have a funeral?"

"No."

"Well then, let's serve a funeral for your mother." And he immediately began to serve a funeral for my mother.

---

*Kulak in Russian literally means "fist."—TRANS.

The following thing happened to me. My eight-year-old nephew got into a fight while playing with some boys outside. Afraid that he would be scolded at home, he ran away from home with his friends. They got on a train headed towards Tashkent. The whole family, of course, was very worried. I came to the Elder with bitter tears, fell at his feet and said, "Batiushka! Such terrible grief has befallen me! My nephew has disappeared, and there's been no news of him for a month." He stroked my head and said, "Don't worry, Tanyushka, God will grant it, he'll be found." Time passed, and we received a telegram which said that my nephew was being held in Alma-Ata. My sister went and got him. In my joy I brought the Elder a large cluster of grapes and a big watermelon as a token of gratitude. He stroked my head and said, "Well, I told you your nephew would turn up, and you see—he's been found." Yes, thanks to his prayers.

He was a great, a great God-pleaser; he worked great miracles, but secretly, hidden from peoples' gaze. He would express his clairvoyance very modestly. When the girls, his spiritual children, were around him, looking at them all he would sometimes say, "I know you better than you know yourselves." That's how great his clairvoyance was. Sometimes you'd go to confession with a great load, with pain of soul; you'd be carrying so many woes, so much care and sorrow. But when you had confessed, when you had spoken to the Elder, you would leave as if on wings—everything would be left behind. That's what kind of feeling you would have. He could heal human souls by his word or by his touch. He would pat your head, or say a certain word which would immediately open your soul and bring peace and calm. But when a person would go against God's will or when the Elder wanted to steer a person away from trouble, then he would be strict. He could reproach someone strictly, but then he would say, "Ach, I didn't sleep all night; I was worrying about you and praying to God." He suffered through everything very painfully, and every human sorrow was close to him, as though it were his own. He would say, "I myself grew up as an orphan, and I take the grief of orphanhood as my own; the grief of others is close to my heart."

Once the following thing happened after Fr. Sebastian's death: a woman arrived from Novosibirsk, by the name of Nadezhda. She had cancer. She fell on his grave and sobbed bitterly. Then she prayed, as well as she could, and asked him for help. She took some earth from his grave when she left. Upon arriving home, she placed the earth in a clean dish, poured in some water and began to drink the water. Gradually her sickness disappeared, and afterwards she would testify to her healing.

Once our cliros was left without a choir director and they offered the position to me. This was after the Elder's repose. I was very troubled as to whether or not I would be able to direct the choir, and I beseeched the Elder: "Batiushka, is it the will of God that I do this? Will I be able to cope with this?" I prayed thus mentally, and during the night I had a dream about him. He was in Melkombinat—his favorite place, his skete. There is a small dugout there, and I opened the door, entered, and saw the Elder serving, fully vested, with a cross and a censer in his hands. I opened the door and, with the thought of whether or not he would agree to have me direct the choir, I fell at his feet and said, "Bless me!" He made a large sign of the Cross over me. I kissed his hand and woke up at that moment with the sensation of his warm hand in my palms. I understood that God's consent was upon this. I accepted the offer and began to direct the choir and, glory be to God, I still direct it to this day.

8. Anna Vasilievna Zaikova

I used to live in Mordovia. My parents died, and I came to Elder James to ask him to perform their funeral. The clairvoyant elder, Elder James, lived in Barkie. I came for the funeral service, and he said to me, "Oh, if you knew where you are going! And what a nice road it will be! And if you knew who will meet you there! A pillar from earth to heaven!" I was thinking to myself, "What?! A pillar from earth to heaven will meet me?" Well, in 1959 my daughter left for Temirtau and wrote, "Mama, come immediately!" And so I sold everything and came here. But there was such a weight on my soul. You see, back in the village I'd been singing in the choir. So I came right here to the church. I came and saw two boys leading Fr. Sebastian by the hand. People were crowding around him but he walked straight to me and blessed me right there, in the middle of the church. From that time on I started coming here. I've been coming here for thirty years, and it's such a joy! You won't find a greater joy anywhere else!

When I came, I had no place to live, so then—forgive me, Lord!—I went up to the Elder: "Batiushka, I've gotten married!" I had gotten married to an old man—I had no place to live. He said, "You got married? If you don't go through the church ceremony, then leave here." I came home and said, "Grandpa, I'm leaving."

"What do you mean, leaving?"

"Well, you won't have a proper ceremony, will you?"

"I'll do it!" And we came right here and got married. From that time on I've been coming here without stop.

As soon as I came here Mother Anastasia—she didn't even know me—called me by name right away: "Anna! why aren't you praying for your godmother, for Anastasia? She brought you to church for the third day after her repose! And you're not praying for her! She's dead, you know!" But I didn't know that my godmother had died. How could I have known? She was in Russia. I stood there, looking at Mother Anastasia and wondered—what else was she going to tell me? She gave me a prosphoron: "Here, take it—eat it with Grandpa!" Right then Grandpa became ill. Maybe she'd seen that he was going to die soon. Yes, the elders were wondrous....

And Elder James in Barkie—how wonderful he was! He's a saint; people are healed on his grave. I once came to see him—I was eighteen years old. Lord, I was nothing but sin! But I didn't understand it at all! I was living with my grandmother. Once my grandmother was out of matches. I took some eggs from the nest without asking my grandmother. "Well," I thought, "after all, it's not a sin." I took them from the nest, ran to the store, bought some matches and brought them to my grandmother. Then I went to see Elder James, and he said, "You bought matches with eggs." How he knew a man's sins—you couldn't hide anything! I looked at him and thought, "Who's he talking to?" And he tapped me on the forehead: "I'm talking to you." Then I said, "Ah, Batiushka, forgive me! It was I who did it!" He saw a person in the light, as though he could see right through him.

Elder Sebastian was a really sincere person, and he loved everyone. All people for him were like children. We would come from Temirtau, and he would want so much to indulge us, so that we wouldn't be angry. He received us as though we were made of gold, and we're such sinners!

Yes, I also once saw the following: there were a lot of people, and Fr. Sebastian cried out, "Stay where you are—don't come in!" Some man had come, evidently with bad intentions, and wanted to go in to see him. But the Elder only raised his hand, and the man couldn't move. It was as if he were rooted to the spot—he couldn't move one way or another. May God grant the Heavenly Kingdom to Fr. Sebastian!

And how could I not remember Mother Agnia! I was supposed to receive my pension, but I couldn't get it no matter how I tried. I came to see her, sat down at the threshold, and there I sat. Everyone kept pushing to see her, and then she said to me, "Come over here." She sat me down by her feet and blessed me: "You'll receive your pension." Then she asked me, "Do you make icons?" I used to set icons in frames. "Yes, Matushka, I do. Forgive me, I've photographed icons (there were no copies available anywhere); I've even photographed them myself." She said, "You've come too late—otherwise you would have learned to paint them. Well, go with God. If that's what you're doing, then keep working."

Now in Temirtau they've finished building the church. I've been going to Temirtau to sing every day for five years now. But Fr. Sebastian is always in my heart, so we come here from Temirtau. The road has gotten better, so we're never late. We arrive before they've started, when the doors aren't yet open; through the Elder's prayers we visit his church. Here all are brothers and sisters no matter where we've been and my soul aches to be here. My whole soul is here—you know what I mean? And why is it like that? My soul is drawn here, of course. I stand there [in Temirtau] in the choir and sing, but my heart is here.

9. MARIA VASILIEVNA ANDRIEVSKAYA

In 1931 we were exiled from the Saratov province. They brought us to Osarovka in cattle cars and then they tossed us to the ground like cattle. I remember it all now as if it had been yesterday—rain was pouring down in buckets, and we collected the rainwater and drank it. I was then five years old, my brother was two years older than I, my little sister was three years old, and there were two infants—five children in all, plus my mother, father, grandmother, and grandfather. In the Saratov Province we were farmers and had always gone to church. They brought us to Osakarovka in a special train, to the barren steppe where we didn't sleep for two whole days. We sat on the ground next to our father and mother and held tightly to their legs. After two days, some Kazaks came in wagons, seated us in them and brought us to Settlement 5. As they were bringing us, we asked our father, "Papa, Papa—where will our house be?" He said, "Soon, we'll be there soon, wait a little." They brought us to Settlement 5, and we asked, "But where's the house? Where's our house?" There was nothing there, just a pole with the inscription "Settlement 5," and soldiers on guard, so that we wouldn't run off. They brought us to the river Ishim, and again they tossed us to the ground. We children were bawling. Our father went and chopped down some poplar trees, and then we dug out a square hole and arranged the sticks in rows on the ground to make a shelter. We lived on the ground in that dugout until the Feast of the Protection of the Theotokos [October 1]. On the Feast of the Protection, one and a half feet of snow fell. In the morning my brother woke up and said, "Mama, Grandpa's freezing and I'm freezing from him." We rushed over, but Grandpa was already finished, dead.

We built barracks. The teenagers and adults carried sod on their backs for three and a half miles. After the Feast of the Protection we were settled in these barracks—there was no glass for the windows, nor were there doors. Our father was still alive then, and he would pour water in a washtub. The water would freeze, and he would take the ice and set it in the windows in place of glass. Two hundred people were sent to these barracks. In the morning you'd get up, and over here there would be ten dead people, and over there would be another five. We would carry off the corpses. I can't forget that. A Mordvinian family of twenty people lived with us, and only two of them escaped to Russia. The rest died off. They brought eighteen thousand people to Settlement 5, and by spring five thousand were left. Our father died in 1932, and a month later our mother gave birth, and the six of us children were left, together with our blind grandmother. And how did we live? By begging. Our mother forbade us to steal: "No, daughter, never fill yourself on someone else's food. It's better for you to go out there with your hand out." And so I went. Someone might give something, while someone else wouldn't, and would kick you out.

Then our newborn brother, younger sister, and grandmother all died. We began to grow to adolescence, and we went to work in a childrens' brigade. In 1937 they tried to force our mother to go to a collective farm, but she didn't want to go. They said to her, "You know what you are? You're a kulak." They sentenced her to three years and sent her to the Far East. We children were left alone. My brother was fourteen years old, I was twelve, my sister was ten, and my younger brother was eight. We worked in the children's brigade, begged, worked as nurses for children, and spun yarn. We would bring and feed each other with whatever they would give us. That's how we lived for three years. Then our mother was freed, and soon the war began. They took my brother and he was killed at the Front. That's how our luck was; that's how our life went on in tears, poverty and sorrow.

In 1955 we became acquainted with Elder Sebastian. He blessed our whole family to move to Mikhailovka. Yes ... then we began to live as though in Paradise. A year after his blessing we had built a house. We were always near him and brought all our needs or sorrows to him. "It's all right," the Elder would say. "Put your hope in God; He won't abandon you." He always helped us by his holy prayers, of which we sinners were, of course, unworthy.

10. Matrona Tikhonovna Frolova

When I returned to the homeland from the Front in 1945, I wanted very much to set my life in order. Therefore I enthusiastically socialized with young people in order to find myself a man. I was working as a nurse and one day, while coming to a sick woman to treat her with cupping glasses, I saw a photograph on the wall of a priest surrounded by many sisters in white kerchiefs. I was a believer, and prayed constantly. "Who is that?" I asked. "Why, that's Elder Sebastian," they replied. "He lives in Karaganda." My heart was so sorrowful, and from all the carousing it had become filled with a feeling of sadness. I thought, "My God, what failures I've had since the Front! I can in no way put my life in order, and the years are going by." "Why don't you write him a letter?" I was told. I wrote one, and Fr. Sebastian invited me to come to Karaganda. I came for a short time and began telling him about all the failures I had had after the Front. He said, "The Lord has not appointed family life for you, and you won't get married." And I thought, "What's this? He has appointed it for everyone else, but for me alone He hasn't?" The Elder spoke up again: "Go back to Russia, settle your accounts there, and come back here. You have God's blessing to live in Karaganda." I went back but wasn't able to leave Russia for Karaganda for a long time. The world had its grip on me, as though it had shackled me with chains. Fr. Sebastian had been praying earnestly, but it took me four months to return.

My baptismal name is Matrona. When they registered me to go to the Front, they wrote in my documents the name Maria. And so that's what everyone called me—Maria. I sent the Elder a telegram with the words, "Meet me. Maria." But he told his household, "Matrona's coming to us; go and meet her." He accepted me into his house. He wouldn't take in just anyone like that; he was protecting me strongly against satan. But I couldn't get used to living in Karaganda, and I kept wanting to get out of there. I packed my suitcase and said, "I've got to go; I can't live here." The Elder put the suitcase in his car and brought me back to his house. And I again began to live with them. I lived there for close to a year, and all the nuns that were with the Elder were always dissatisfied with me because I talked too much. They didn't like that; they were used to living in silence, not using any superfluous words, while I would say whatever nonsense came to mind, Lord forgive me! When he would appear in the evening after the service, they would bring him complaints about me, but he would try to persuade them, saying, "Matushkas, there are so many of you, and I endure all of you. But you don't want to put up with one Matrona." That's how he would always admonish them. As long as I lived there, people would always complain about me, because I really was badly behaved. But the Elder would say, "She was at the Front; she's endured a lot, and the Lord has preserved her. Don't cause misfortunes for her; she came to me, not to you."

Later he bought me a small house. Sometimes he would come and visit me, look at the vegetable garden and say, "Ah! Matrona's little garden! Her garden is just like her soul!" I had such tall weeds in my garden; they were practically up to my waist. And the Elder made such efforts to bring me to my senses. I would kneel down before him and cry; my heart was so bitter, because satan was tempting me very intensely. Fr. Sebastian would look, not at me, but next to me, and would say, "Satan, satan, why do you torment her soul?"

I was a nurse, and I would often treat the Elder with cupping glasses. He would say, "Matrona—you treat me, and I'll treat you." And everything became easier and easier for me.

How he labored over us, and how valuable we all were to him. And now, as I live I have no needs. I have no one, neither a husband nor children; I have spent my entire life alone. And I've never had any needs—not for food, drink or firewood—not for anything, as though someone were carrying me on his wings.

11. Lydia Vladimirovna Zhukova

Our family was brought from the Samara Province to Karaganda in 1931. There were four of us children plus our mother and father. They brought us by train in freight cars. First they brought us to Akmolinsk, where we lived in crude huts made of branches. But I don't remember it; my mother told me about it. I don't remember, either, how long we lived in those huts. I don't even remember how my three-year-old infant sister Nadezhda died. I was five years old at the time and had two older brothers. From Akmolinsk they moved us to Kompaneisk, to the steppe. When I was eleven years old and we moved to Greater Mikhailovka, for some reason I thought that the village of Mikhailovka was the village of Pushkinskoye.

We all survived and lived through the exile; only our baby Nadezhda died. Then my parents met Fr. Sebastian. I remember how when I would finish school there would be water spilled around the room when I came home after classes. Only now do I understand that they used to baptize people in our house, but they hid that from me then. I saw the Elder for the first time in 1952, after I had graduated from the institute. With his blessing my parents had by then moved to Melkombinat, and the Elder used to go there often and serve the Liturgy or Vespers. People would come immediately from all over Melkombinat, so we built a large house in order to fit everyone. Fr. Sebastian loved each and every one of us. I remember how once after we had prayed, eaten dinner, and everyone had left, he slept over at our place. Matrona the nurse wouldn't leave, no matter what. She wanted to see the Elder and hear him every minute. She used to come before everyone else and would be the last to leave. I had already poured water into a basin and with my looks told her, "Go away!" but she wouldn't go. I sat the Elder down on his bed, took off his shoes, brought over the water, and began to wash his feet. Then he saw that Matrona was looking in, and said, "Lydia Vladimirovna, all right then, let Matrona wash the other foot!"

At the age of seventy my father became a deacon and later a priest. He served in the Mikhailovka church with Fr. Sebastian. My mother and father used to say, "What a good thing it was that they exiled us! If we hadn't been exiled we would never have seen such an elder!" That's how they thanked God.

12. THE SAMARTSEV FAMILY

Basil Ivanovich Samartsev

We used to live in the Orenburg Province. Our parents were deeply religious people. In 1931 the authorities accused my father of being a kulak and sent him to prison. In May of 1931 they took us—six children and our mother—to the open steppe of Settlement 9 near Karaganda. My older brother was eleven years old, then came Genochka. I was four years old. Then there was Ivan, who was three, Eugene, who was two, and the youngest, Paul, who was a babe at the breast. We had a large piece of felt with us and a trunk. We dug a hole in the ground, laid down the felt, broke apart the trunk and set it up in place of a roof. This was our house. When it would rain or snow, we covered the hole with the felt. The six of us children used to huddle up against our mother like little chicks.

Then they began building adobe houses, and they drove everyone out to knead the clay. The overseer would ride on horseback and drive people to the clay with a lash. We cut sod and all sorts of grasses and bushes—we had to build the barracks by winter, so we wouldn't perish. That's how the Tikhonovka settlement at the Second Mine grew up. They gave us children very meager rations. There was a small stream which would dry up, and there wouldn't be enough water. By winter we had put up walls, windows, doors, and two stoves for each barrack. Twenty families lived in each barrack, and during the winter everyone lay on plank beds. One family would be lying there, then another, and a third—it was a solid mass of planks and a tiny passage between them.

The winter of 1932 was very severe. I saw with my own eyes how whole families were lying there, dead. People died of hunger and from the cold, and from all sorts of diseases. There was dysentery and diarrhea, but there wasn't anything with which to treat them. There was very little bread. It was a famine. Those who were from Orenburg or Siberia were stronger. But those who were from more productive areas, such as Tambov, Voronezh, or Penza were weaker, and whole families died off. How were they buried? They dug pits ten feet wide. They dragged the dead families from the barracks, tossed them onto a cart, brought them to the pits and dropped them in like logs. That winter, in one week my brothers Paul, Ivan, and Eugene died. And we didn't even notice when Genochka died. We began calling him to come eat, but Genochka was dead. They made boxes for small children, but they wrapped baby Paul in a rag, placed him in an iron pipe, dug out a little grave, and buried him. That's how it was. After two years there were five thousand people left in Tikhonovka. Twenty thousand lay there, under Old Tikhonovka. Of us, two brothers and our mother survived.

In 1933 our father arrived, but soon our mother died of hunger.

The special-status exiles who were believers used to gather in groups for prayer. When the nuns Martha and Maria were released from Dolinka and sent to Tikhonovka, they told us that the Optina Elder, Fr. Sebastian, would soon be released from Dolinka as well. We began waiting for him.

Before the War began, we received bread by ration cards. In Tikhonovka there were long lines, so I would walk to the city for bread. When Fr. Sebastian was released and he moved to Mikhailovka, he also went to the city for bread. I wanted very much to meet him in the city, and when I did see him I went up to him and started talking with him. What a joy it was when he invited me to his home on Lower Street. From that time on our acquaintance was established.

Nina Petrovna Samartseva

I had difficulty giving birth, after which I caught a cold, which turned into pneumonia. They discharged me from the maternity ward as a hopeless case, to die at home. Fr. Sebastian began coming to see me. He would come and say, "Here, I've brought you some fruit, and here's some fish." This was during Great Lent, and he was bringing me carp: "Cook this carp!" But I wasn't eating anything; I was already dying. The doctor came from the hospital and said, "Why treat her? Nothing will help her." Our doctors, Olga Fyodorovna and Thaisia Grigorievna, came and gave me injections twice a day. The Elder felt very sorry for me. "A man is stronger," he said, "but a woman is defenseless." At first boys were born to us, and then girls. "Batiushka," we'd say, "we have a little girl."

"Oh, a little girl," he would say, "I love little girls." He would sit at my bedside for a little while and talk with me. His head tilted a little to one side and shook slightly. And so he came to see me every day for a month, and by spring I recovered by his prayers.

13. Valentina Sergeyevna Popova

We used to work in the Karaganda confection factory. The factory was a communist establishment, and all the workers were members of the trade union, but we never became members. In the factory they used to look down on us because we were believers. But we loved to work and we worked well. Once a television crew came to shoot a documentary about exemplary workers. They wanted to film us, but the foreman forbade it and said, "You can't—they're believers." Of course, the other workers later swore at us for a long time and laughed: "You've lost a lot—you're such young people and yet you believe in God!" We came to see Elder Sebastian and told him, and he comforted us. There's not a single mother who can comfort like he could. "It's all right," he would say, "you can endure a little. You'll enter into their trust yet; they'll even trust you with the keys and put you in charge of the warehouse."

Of course, they persecuted us at work, and that winter they kicked us out of the factory workshop to do outdoor construction work. We unloaded freight cars full of coal, loaded it onto trucks, and did anything else that was needed. Later we became friends with the director and the chief engineer, Ivan Semyonovich. Ivan Semyonovich came to our place as a guest, where he saw that we were fasting, and he liked that. He kept asking us all about the fasts and about Christian celebrations and said, "How well you live! I'd like to live that way, too!" Then they put us in charge of the warehouse and entrusted us with the keys. The director trusted us with the use of his apartment when he would leave town.

14. Nun Nina
(Nina Prokopievna Korshunova †1997)

When we were doing outdoor construction work, my health was severely undermined. Then Fr. Sebastian didn't bless me to go to work any more. For half a year I received workers' compensation. Then the Elder said, "You need to work in the church." I was placed in the "second category" of disability. I began work in the church and work there to this day.

Once a large tumor grew on my hand. With us, if we had any sorrow or needs, we'd run to Fr. Sebastian. I went to him and said, "Batiushka, there's a lump on my hand that keeps growing and growing. My mother says that I should have an operation." He was looking out the window, and patted my hand and said, "Yes, it's a large lump, but no, it's not necessary to operate." And I don't know if the lump disappeared that minute or a little later, but when I arrived home there was no lump on my hand.

When we were still fifteen or sixteen years old, we bought tickets to the cinema—of course, without asking for the Elder's blessing. He foresaw this and took us with him to Melkombinat. There he visited with someone, sat with him for a while, walked through his garden, and then visited other people. "Well," he said, "we're in no hurry." *We*, of course, were in a hurry, but we kept quiet. Mother Barbara was with us and said, "But the girls are in a hurry to get somewhere." He smiled and kept walking, and time was dragging on. Seven o'clock passed, and then eight o'clock.... Then the Elder said, "Well, now we can go home." So we never wound up at the movies. That was our youth.

Once before Nativity the Elder blessed me and my sister to whitewash Fr. Peter's room. We came in the morning, and before beginning work we wanted to get the Elder's blessing, but his cell-attendant said, "Fr. Sebastian's very sick; it's impossible." We were upset by this, but we went to work. When we had whitewashed everything and were getting ready to go home, we went again to get the Elder's blessing, but his cell-attendant again said, "He's sick, you can't go in to see him." It was already late and it was dark outside. As we walked past the Elder's window we saw that his light was on and that the blinds were open. We could see him sitting in his cell, and that Anatole Prosvirnin was sitting at his feet. (At that time he was still studying at the Academy and had come to see the Elder on his Christmas vacation.) I told my sister, "Oh, the Elder's sitting there, and Vera didn't let us get his blessing!" Well, I thought, I'll get it at a distance. We went up to the window and I said, "Batiushka, bless!" But my sister said, "What are you doing, peeping into windows? Fr. Sebastian would say that this isn't good."

"Well," I replied, "he won't think it's us—he'll think it's Glafira running around out here." And we went home.

The next day when we went to church the Elder was serving a Pannikhida, and Glafira was standing beside him. When I got his blessing, he held on to my hand and said to Glafira, "What have you been doing, peeping in windows?" Really! Glafira burst into tears; she didn't understand what this was about. I went to see Mother Anastasia. (With us, when the Elder was unapproachable we'd go to Mother Anastasia, and she'd absolve everything.) "Matushka," I said, "Glafira didn't understand anything and she's crying; should I explain it to her?" "No," she said, "you don't need to say anything, it'll be all right."

Fr. Sebastian wanted all four of us sisters to live together in Karaganda. He said, "I'm buying you a house and you'll live there. But Eugenia, one of my sisters who lived with our parents in Zhaltyr, in the Tselinograd Province, wrote me a letter saying that she intended to get married. When I told the Elder about

Eugenia's intent to get married, he asked, "Who else is there in your family?"

"An older brother," I said.

"Where does he work?"

"For the police."

"Well, he'll help out." But I thought, "How can he help?" And then my brother went to Zhaltyr and began scolding our parents: "What are you thinking of? She's only eighteen years old, and you're giving her up to be married! I won't allow it! I'll take her to my place; I'll teach her—she's going to be a doctor!" The wedding was cancelled and my brother brought Eugenia to Karaganda. Later, of course, he regretted what he had done: "I brought her here to no purpose," he said. "There at least she would have gotten married, but here she's started going to church." And our sister stayed here to live with us under the Elder.

Occasionally Fr. Sebastian would spend the night at our place. Who would get to braid his hair? It's impossible to describe what a joy that was for us! Mother Barbara would say: "Girls! There's a little piece of the Lord in the Elder. How sweet must the Lord Himself be!" We used to comb out his hair and collect the hair. Even now I have some of his hair.

When Fr. Sebastian had already become extremely weak and they had to carry him to church in their arms, his cell-attendant Vera wouldn't let anyone in to see him. But I really wanted to be at his side. And once Petya and Shurik were carrying him from the church, and the Elder said to me, "Well, let's go; I'll lead you through the toll-houses." I thought, "What is he talking about?" And I walked behind him. He said, "Come in, come in!" I went in. He crossed himself and we all crossed ourselves. I looked and he smiled, went over to the table, and then he gave me an orange and an apple and said, "Well then, go." But I was afraid to go, since Vera was rather strict with us. I wanted to leave through another door, but it was closed and latched so I had to leave through the hall. As I was leaving Vera flew at me and let me have it. She beat me and thrashed me: "How could you?! The Elder's sick and you're coming here?!" At this point Petya came to my defence, and my mother ran in and began to grapple with her, saying: "What do you think you're doing?" And then my father ran up and said, "You nasty thing! What are you doing? The Elder himself blessed her!" So these were my "toll-houses," until I reached the door. And the Elder had smiled and said, "Well then, go!"

When Fr. Sebastian was sick we wouldn't go home to spend the night. We slept on plank beds in the lodge. We were afraid that he would die and we wouldn't be there at his repose. On Radonitsa, at 4:45 in the morning I saw the Elder in a dream. He was standing by the pannikhida table and giving his cell-attendant Barbara candles. He said, "Here, give everyone a candle," and then he lit one himself. I woke up and said: "Tanya, Fr. Sebastian has died!" I had just said that when they knocked at the door: "The Elder's doing poorly!" They didn't say that he was dead, but that he was "doing poorly." We ran to his cell and saw him lying there (he had not been covered up yet), wearing his epitrachelion. The Bishop was standing in front. Vera, Olga Fyodorovna, and Glafira all stood there forsaken—the Elder had died. And he had been the first to tell us.

15. Thaisia Grigorievna Fomina

Hilarion Vasilievich Fomin was my grandfather. Fr. Sebastian was also like a grandfather to me. Grandpa Hilarion became a widower at the age of forty-seven. He was left with four children, from the age of seven on up. His daughter Maria, my godmother, was then nineteen years old. She took upon herself the responsibility of raising all of the children and taking care of our grandfather. Our family came to Karaganda on the first of August, 1955, at the Elder's blessing. We settled in Melkombinat. Grandpa Hilarion was a layman but deeply religious. He was always praying and reading spiritual books, and from his early years until his death he never shaved his beard. He honored the Elder greatly and they were never on unfriendly terms. I was always around my grandfather. When he died, Fr. Sebastian served his funeral.

The Elder had spiritual wisdom and love for orphans and widows. He always tried to help them with at least a piece of bread. But sometimes he was quite strict. Even though I was a relative, I felt a sort of fear around him, and I couldn't behave freely or loosely in front of him. Once, when the Elder was already weak, I escorted him from the street into his cell. When we entered the cell his cell-attendant wasn't around to help him undress. And so I decided that I would help him myself. He turned and said: "And what do you think, that I can't take care of myself?" I stayed right where I was, while he undressed by himself and hung up his clothes. "I myself am still helping people." In this way he put me in my place.

A great many people came to Mikhailovka to see the Elder. The sisters received everyone and served them. At first I considered this as their obligation, until I understood how strangers can be a burden, and how difficult it was to endure everything, all their infirmities, and to take care of them. One should give all the sisters credit for their hospitality. They were spiritual people and they lived spiritually.

When Fr. Sebastian died, Archbishop Joseph didn't come to the funeral. But there was wisdom in this—Bishop Pitirim came, and Archbishop Joseph knew about this. Bishop Pitirim was the Elder's spiritual son, and therefore he had been blessed by the Patriarch to perform the funeral. Vladika Pitirim was a bishop, while Vladika Joseph was an archbishop. In order to not cause an uncomfortable situation, Archbishop Joseph did not come.

After the Elder's death, there was no lack of peace among us. If any conflicts did occur, they were trivial. The Lord preserves us. It's true that his spiritual children didn't always obey him—that sort of thing has always happened and always will. That's the way people are. We're pleased when people speak well of us, but when they speak against us we don't like it. But we would ask for forgiveness afterwards.

16. Antonina Ivanova

I worked in the mines for ten years. When they issued the decree for all women to leave the mines I was left without work. Then Fr. Sebastian sent for me, and I came. "There," he said, "see that woman sitting there? She has a sick child, a little boy. Go with her and look after him."

The next day I went to see the boy at the hospital. He was in his seventh year. He was so nice and had been raised well, but he couldn't walk—he was paralyzed. I slept at his side in the hospital, fed him, and took him on walks. Then they sent the boy home as a hopeless case. Fr. Sebastian immediately predicted that Volodya wouldn't live, and gradually prepared the parents for this. But the parents couldn't resign themselves to this; he was their only child. The parents were prepared to do anything; they took all measures. They called in many doctors and brought in some Chinese person who stuck needles in his spine and did cauterizations. They also brought a sorceress home, but the boy didn't get better.

Before the boy fell ill his father drank a lot, and when he got drunk he used to shout and swear terribly. Once he and his neighbor were swearing at each other in the yard in the sight of his little boy. One of them grabbed an axe to strike the other, and the six-year-old boy climbed up a six foot fence out of fright and couldn't get down; they had to come and get him. This immediately paralyzed him, and then he became blind and unable to speak. The boy's mother went to the Elder and wept, and he comforted her. The boy was sick for seven months. Fr. Sebastian came often, gave him Communion, and said that the boy was like a martyr. When Volodya died, the Elder sent Mother Anastasia to their house with some of the other nuns. They washed the boy, prayed, and made all the preparations for the funeral. Mother Anastasia sat for a long time and then said: "Zhenya (the boy's father) is not here. Come now! Petya, Kolya—go look in the sheds, or in another minute we'll have one more coffin." And in the farthest shed they found Zhenya—he had already put a noose around his neck. That's how Mother Anastasia saved him. She too was a great one; the Elder had sent her there on purpose. Mother Anastasia didn't go anywhere until they had buried the boy.

17. Valentina Petrovna Panova

Our family was living in Tselinograd* when we heard in a local church that there was an unusual priest in Karaganda. In the winter of 1955 we went with our parents to Karaganda to have a look at Fr. Sebastian. I was in school then, in the ninth grade. We came, we confessed, we received Communion, had a look at the Elder, and left. He really did make an unusual impression. Even though outwardly he was a normal person, when I approached him for a blessing, my heart stopped beating from a feeling of reverent trembling. I was stunned by this feeling.

---

*Tselinograd is the previous name for Akmolinsk.—Trans.

In 1956 I graduated from school, and since I had a penchant for painting I decided to go to Moscow and enroll in the Stroganov School. Then one of our relatives came to us from Fr. Sebastian and told us that the Elder hadn't blessed me to enroll in the school. But since I had already bought a ticket, I went but did not enroll in the school. My father brought me to Karaganda. The Elder blessed me to stay there and said, "You'll live with Mother Agnia and help her." I lived with mother Agnia for four years. She too was an unusual person. We deeply respected her and we accepted all that she said without any doubts. There were always people coming to see her from morning till night, and we fed them all, even though I don't know how we afforded it. Mother Agnia was exceptionally hospitable. People would leave and others would come, and I'd have to gather everyone at the table again. During the breaks between seeing people, she would paint icons. Sometimes I'd say: "Matushka, when are you going to work? I'll close the gates!"

"How can you?" she would respond. "People are coming, and we should see the people first of all." She placed love of people above all and could drop everything if even a child came. People came from other cities just to see her, because they sensed her warmth, hospitality, and kindness. She treated everyone solely with affection, with love. A person cannot have so much warmth and kindness just on one's own. This was a gift from above; her kindness was spiritual. When Mother Agnia died, people wept: "Our benefactress has died. To whom can we now come whenever we want? Who will receive us at any old time?" She used to spoil me. She never demanded anything from me; she would only feed me tasty things. I'd come home from work and she would ask, "Are you hungry?"

"No, Matushka, we've just eaten."

"No, you're hungry; I"ll prepare something for you." And she, sick, leaning on a stand, would go to the stove and cook some exceptionally tasty pancakes.

I can't relate anything special about Mother Agnia. It seems to me that every day was special then. It was as though everything was mundane, yet there was was a daily struggle. From morning to night our doors would not be shut. Sometimes our boys would come—Petya and Alyosha—and she would greet them with reverence. We would look at them and think, "They'll probably be priests, since she greeted them like that." I remember how Fr. Alexander came when he was still a teenager, and she regarded him so respectfully that she practically asked him for a blessing. He hadn't even thought of the priesthood, but everything progressed along the course which had already been prepared.

Mother Anastasia was harsher. She could look you in the eye and speak sternly. She had a look about her which gave the impression that she could see right through you, and see everything within you. I was a little afraid of her, even though she was very kind. She loved to treat everyone to her own homemade kvass. You'd pass by on your way to church, and Mother Anastasia would be right there on the road: "Can I treat you to some kvass?"

"Please do, Matushka."

We also respected Mother Anastasia, but sometimes she would say things that we couldn't quite believe. She used to say that Fr. Sebastian would be canonized and would be taken away from here. She would say that times would change and the Soviet Union would fall apart. But for me this was all a fantasy, because everything was so solid then. She would tell us to not forget her when they take the Elder away from here. I heard this myself, but at that time I couldn't believe that it could be so.

I didn't even believe Fr. Sebastian's prophesies about our family. When he said that our family would move from Tselinograd to

Karaganda, I objected: "No, that will never happen. All our relatives are there. My older sister and her husband are there, and Papa will never leave my sister." But the Elder smiled: "You'll come and buy a house, plant a garden, and you'll have everything." That was in 1959, and by 1960 our family was already in Karaganda. We greeted the new year sitting on our suitcases.

The Elder prophesied that my mother would die while on the road, and when my mother would leave to visit one of our relatives, we were cautious about letting her go. Her death actually did happen on the road, but not in the way we thought it would. My mother and father died together in an automobile accident here in Karaganda in 1976, as they were driving across a bridge.

I had wonderful parents. They were very pious and kind. But our Elder and Eldresses were even warmer. Fr. Sebastian could say just one word and you would fly away from him as though on wings. A worldly person cannot love and give as much as the spiritual ones can love and spread warmth.

18. THE KHMYROV FAMILY

Monk Sebastian (Alexander Alexeyevich Khmyrov)

In 1931 we were accused as kulaks and sent from the Tambov Province to Karaganda. They sent our mother, three of us brothers and another eleven families from our village in one railroad car. At first they brought us to Petropavlovsk on the Feast of the Apostles Peter and Paul.* As I remember now, they fed us nettle soup in Petropavlovsk. Then from Petropavlosk we traveled for two weeks to Kompaneisk.

---

*The name of the village, "Petropavlovsk," means "of Peter and Paul."—TRANS.

There it was—the open, burnt steppe. They set us there at night, and it was raining. We stole boards from the railroad cars—the planks we had lain on. We broke them into four pieces, and made supports. Then we chopped down some elm trees, covered the supports with them, and the result was a hut. We lived in those huts. They forced everyone to work, to make adobe. I was a young adolescent, but I also worked, turning the clay bricks so that they would dry out in the sun. Then they would bring the bricks to the construction site and make houses out of them. They cut sod and also made houses out of that. We had only just managed to put up the walls when winter began, and there were no ceilings in the houses. In December there was a typhus outbreak because everything was dirty. The food was insipid; the soup was tasteless, and bread was given out in four-hundred-gram rations. People were dying. On the Feast of the Meeting of the Lord my two brothers died. They were in the hospital in the Old City— Karaganda-1, as it was then called. They informed my mother, and she went to the hospital to look for them. There they asked her, "What do you want?"

"Well, we've been informed that our reposed sons are here; we're looking for them."

"And when did they inform you?"

"Yesterday."

"Oh! Don't even look for them. Those people aren't here anymore, they've sent them off. Five carts came and took them away, and they were dropped into a common grave. That's where yours are now. But these fresh corpses are lying right over here." My mother identified one of my brothers. They took him, placed him on a sled, and brought him to Kompaneisk. There was already a cemetery there, and they dug a hole, sort of like a grave, wrapped my brother in a light jacket, and buried him. Cartloads of people were brought to Kompaneisk in this manner. It was a great tragedy. It was terrible, and impossible to relate in all its details. The houses didn't have ceilings, and snow would pile up. People would get up in the morning from under the snow—those who were alive. And those who weren't alive would lie there under the snow. They would drag them out and put them on a wagon. These totally worn out men would cart them along; they'd haul those wheelbarrows. They were forcibly compelled to collect and haul off the dead bodies. It would happen that they would be pulling the wagon, and the one who was pulling it would fall dead. They'd pick him up, put him on the wagon, and go on pulling it further. This was a very difficult life; everyone felt it in those years.

Then I grew up, and in 1936 I was already sixteen years old. There was no term of imprisonment there, and people got out of there however they could. I left for Russia. When the war was already over and I had gotten married, my wife and my little daughter Lyubov and I came to live in Karaganda in 1951.

We happened to find out that Fr. Sebastian was here and we became good friends with him. Our family grew larger and the children grew up. How many sorrows there were—you'd never be able to recount them all. I'd go to see the Elder and have a word with him; he'd give me advice and alleviate my grief. When my wife fell sick, and meanwhile my youngest daughter was no more than a year old, he came to our home. I wept and he wept along with me. He said, "I know how hard an orphan's life is."

Nun Eunice (Alexandra Florovna Khmyrova)

In the winter of 1964 I fell seriously ill. After a lengthy liver treatment which gave no results, my bile ducts became inflamed and bile was released into my bloodstream. The doctors concluded that if they didn't operate, I wouldn't live more than three days, but they couldn't guarantee that I would live after the operation. My husband went to see Fr. Sebastian, and he immediately blessed the operation, handing him two kerchiefs for me—one for a handkerchief and one for a head-covering.

I knew that I was hopelessly ill. It was hard for me to go to the operation. I had left eight small children at home knowing that I wouldn't return to them again. Not long before this I had a dream, that I had walked away from my house towards the East with a small child in my arms. (I had lost a five-month-old daughter.) I told the Elder about this dream and said, "Batiushka, I'm going to die!" He answered, "Why?" and shed tears, saying sadly, "This is because of your sickness."

The operation lasted several hours. At the same time in the church they were serving Liturgy. Fr. Sebastian came out to the ambo and with tears began to implore, "Brothers and sisters! Let's pray! At this moment a woman who has many children is being operated on…. " He couldn't finish speaking; he began to weep and left for the altar. Following him, Fr. Alexander Krivonosov came out to the people with the same request, but he couldn't finish either and burst into tears. Then the Elder came out again, served a Moleben with an Akathist, and all the people (the church was always full when Fr. Sebastian was present) knelt and prayed together with him. The operation was successful.

When they released me from the hospital, my eldest daughter went to the church. Mother Anastasia asked her: "How does your mother feel?" My daughter replied, "We've already taken her out of the hospital." "There!" she said, gazing at an icon, "They prayed it out of God!" That's how great the love and prayers of the Elder were.

In 1962, during Great Lent, I was greatly tormented by headaches. At that time the Elder came to our place to give Communion to my sick mother-in-law. Right then I asked for his blessing to go to the grave of Blessed Xenia of St. Petersburg during the summer, but he replied, "I bless you to go, without putting it off, to the grave of Righteous Simeon of Verkhoturye." But I had a six-month-old infant in my arms; how could I leave him? But the Elder's prayers were so powerful that on that very night the child stopped nursing—he refused it himself. When my husband and I went to ask the Elder what day we should get the ticket for, he answered, "On the third day of Pascha—May 2." We immediately went to get the tickets, but there were no more tickets for that day at the ticket office. We returned to the Elder: "Batiushka, there are no tickets." He replied, "Go there and ask for only two tickets." We returned to the ticket office and asked for two tickets. The ticket seller said, "Here—two tickets for Verkhoturye have been turned in," and she gave them to us.

Before our departure Fr. Sebastian blessed us and kissed us both on the head. Already on the road I felt relief from the pain. And when we venerated the relics of Righteous Simeon, I was completely healed.

When we went to Verkhoturye, the Elder gave us a letter to pass on to Fr. Leonid, a priest in Verkhoturye. Here's what happened: Fr. Sebastian came to our house with nuns Anastasia and Irina. We all sat at one table, but my husband and I couldn't understand what the Elder was speaking about with the nuns. It was concealed from us by God, even though they were speaking Russian. And when Mother Irina asked, "Batiushka, should I write it all down?" he replied, "All of it; write all of it." From those words on we could understand everything. The Elder blessed Mother Irina to dictate while I wrote the letter to Fr. Leonid. From this letter I understood that Fr. Leonid was in a state of *prelest*. When we arrived in Verkhoturye we handed the letter to Fr. Leonid. Fr. Sebastian had never seen him, but wrote to him in his letter, "I've known you since you were ordained by Vladyka John," and he indicated when and where it had taken place. Fr. Leonid, having read the letter, said, "Truly this is a great man! He told the whole truth about me, without ever having seen me."

This Fr. Leonid was a good priest. He had spent nineteen years in prison, but had now fallen. Our Elder, having spiritually foreseen his fall, extended a helping hand to him, although he was far away.

Seventeen years after Fr. Sebastian's death, in 1983, my headaches began again, and they were just as unbearable as they had been in 1962. Once in the daytime I begged, "Batiushka, help me!" and I fell asleep. I saw the Elder in a dream. He was telling me something, I don't remember what, and he touched my head with his hand. I woke up and felt that the pain had ceased.

My son Misha (now Abbot Aristarchus) was very ill at the age of three and, lying in bed, begged, "Mother of God, tell Batiushka to come; I'm so sick!"

At that time Fr. Sebastian was going somewhere in a car with nun Iraida. He said suddenly, "Let's drop in on a sick person right now, he's waiting for me." He arrived and said, "Who's sick here?" He went to the room where Misha lay, blessed him, gave him a big red apple, and left. Then the child got up immediately, as though he hadn't been sick. The Elder heard the pleas of his spiritual children, and he fulfilled them.

When my son Alexei was nine months old, he fell very ill with dyspepsia. Medicines weren't helping him. The doctors said that the child would die and insisted that he be put in a hospital. We went to the Elder and asked, "Should we put Alexis in the hospital, or not?" He replied, "Give him Holy Communion three days in a row." That's just what we did. When he had received Communion for the third time, the child immediately fell asleep. After his sleep he became completely healthy. Now Alexei serves as a deacon in the Moscow region.

Monk Sebastian (Khmyrov)

One day I came to the church in the evening, when suddenly during the service I was seized by a fever and my nose began to feel very painful. I decided to wait for the anointing and then leave—I felt that bad. I stepped up to be anointed, and Fr. Sebastian anointed me and touched my nose as if by accident. It was so painful! I was walking towards the exit and felt that I was getting better, and I understood that he had sensed my illness and had healed me.

Once he invited my sixteen-year-old daughter Lyuba, my eldest, to see him in his cell. He spoke with her, and during their conversation he was suddenly transfigured—he became young, beardless, and bright as an angel, and the whole cell was covered by an unusual light. In this manner the Lord revealed the spiritual greatness and purity of the Elder, even while he was still alive.

The following incident occurred. My child's godfather was a truck driver, and he had to drive through a shallow stream. The bank was steep, and the truck suddenly started to fall over the embankment. At that moment he cried out, "Batiushka, help me!"—and right then he safely drove back onto the road. It's amazing how he heard everyone who called out to him for help, even when they were far away.

19. Olga Sergeyevna Martynova

Our family lived in the Astrakhan Province. There were my father, mother, and seven children. We had a windmill, three cows, and some bulls and horses—our father was a good manager. Our family was religious and God-fearing. In 1930 they pressured my father to join a collective farm, but he refused. I remember how three women and two men entered our house and said, "Good day and how do you do, Sergei Petrovich! You are subject to dispossession for being a kulak!" "Well, if that's how it is," said father, "then go ahead." All night they made an inventory of our house; they made note of every rag and every pot. They arrested both of my older brothers, and they served out their sentences separately from us. They did not place my father under arrest as he was an invalid. They brought a cart and took my mother, father, and five children plus our infant niece, Klavochka, and brought us to Astrakhan, to a desert region of the steppe. In addition to us they brought seventy other families there. We made a shed out of boards and for half a year we lived in it. On August 1, 1931, they took all of us who lived on the steppe and transported us in freight cars, like cattle. We didn't have bread or water, and all of us—men and women, elderly and children—went mixed together in these freight cars, and the toilet was there, too. The cars rocked from side to side as though drunk, and people began to die on the way.

After eighteen days they brought us to the area near Karaganda where the village Maikunduk is now located, and they unloaded everyone onto the ground. We were exhausted and barely alive. Klavochka would open her little mouth and point with her finger—she was thirsty and hungry. There were some Kazak yurts there on the steppe. Our father went over to them. "Give us a little water," he asked. "Give us your boots," they responded, "then you'll get some." Our father knew the Kazak language (some Kazaks lived in Astrakhan), so he persuaded them and they gave him a bucket of water. There was our family, but other families were asking for the water, so they divided it up right there. Late in the evening they loaded us back into the freight cars and brought us to Prishakhtinsk. There was a field there, and a tall Siberian pea tree. They put up tents for the overseers and did nothing for us—we could have died, for all they cared. Some sort of supervisor went and paced out a plot for each family: "Thirteen feet this way and thirteen feet that way. Your address is Reconstruction Street no. 12. You have permission to write home." We didn't have anything to chop down the pea tree with. We climbed up to our thirteen by thirteen plot and began digging a hole. After we had dug it out, we got some sticks from somewhere and placed them over the hole, like a little hut, and covered it with parts of the pea tree. Then we spread out grass on the floor—and that was our shelter. All nine of us lay on top of one another. In a week our little Klavochka died, and then adults started to die.

By winter people began to build dugouts by cutting slices from the roots of the pea trees. We built the dugouts out of these slices. There were no windows or doors. For example, your blanket would be in the doorway, and mine would be covering the window-opening. A person would have nothing to cover himself with. Our family didn't even have anything to cover the windows and doorway with. We didn't have anything to eat either, only a little kasha which we had managed to take along with us. But one has to eat. Our father built a small stove out of earth. He used to put a pot on the stove and cook something out of herbs and grasses, and we would sit next to the stove. It would smoke, snow would fly in through the window, and there we'd sit.

On the 18th of March, 1932, our father fell ill with typhus. We weren't allowed to take him to the hospital because the police wouldn't release him. But I was a young girl and the police didn't beat me. (Then they used to beat everyone, but they didn't touch me.) My mother said, "Take Papa to the hospital." I went and found a small cart, and took him there. But the hospital was in such a state—there were no windows or doors, and snow and ice lay on the floor inside the building. My father had a high fever, and they set him down on the ice. I came in the morning and my father had already died; he had frozen on the ice.

In the spring they started to force everyone to work, to make adobe. They made the children guard the bricks, so that the Kazaks' cattle wouldn't trample on them. Children, even little ones, went, so as to receive their ration of six hundred grams of bread. Adults received eight hundred grams. You'd look at the steppe, in the direction of the cemetery, and see that they'd be carrying a countless multitude of corpses. They wouldn't even carry them, but they'd find a small board, tie some rope on it, put the corpse on the board, and drag it across the ground by the rope. How else could they have done it? The people had no strength. In Prishakhtinsk, Tikhonovka, and Kompaneisk the common graves were sixty-five feet long and twelve feet wide, so that they could stack them in there foot to foot. There were no coffins. They would cover them up with some sort of rag or towel. Next they would stack and stack them in rows, until the grave would be full. Then they would cover them over.

In our family my sister, my mother, and my two brothers who had been sent to prison in Astrakhan remained alive.

I became acquainted with Elder Sebastian in 1946. By that time I had already gotten married, and in February of 1946 my father-in-law died. One old woman brought Fr. Sebastian to perform the funeral for him. At that time I didn't even dare to ask the Elder's name, but he came up to me himself and asked me my name. He asked me to cook him some lenten piroshki, as it was a fast day, and for the funeral meal everything was prepared very modestly. When my father-in-law's funeral was over they placed his coffin on a sled, and a horse pulled him to the cemetery. It was a long way to the cemetery; the wind was blowing and it was very cold. We were all bundled up from head to toe, but the Elder came out practically uncovered, in a poor ryassa, his head covered in an old scarf. He was carrying an iron cross before him with his bare hands. In this manner we went on foot for seven miles in the bitter cold.

After the burial I still hadn't asked the Elder what his name was, but on the way back he sat me down on the sled. I asked him, "Batiushka, how could you hold an iron cross in your bare hands in such freezing weather?" He replied, "Well, let me tell you! Once I went through the following ordeal: When they were trying to force me to deny the Orthodox faith, they put me outside in the cold for a whole night dressed in a single ryassa and posted a guard. The guard was changed every two hours while I stood continuously in the same place. But the Mother of God placed upon me such a nice 'fur coat' that I was warm inside it. In the morning they brought me to be interrogated and said, 'If you don't renounce Christ, then go to prison.' And so they sentenced me to seven years."

This was my first acquaintance with Fr. Sebastian, which in essence wasn't an acquaintance, since I didn't attach any significance to this meeting. I fed him the piroshki and that was the end of it.

A year later the nun Evdokia died. I came to cook for the funeral feast, and the Elder arrived. He came up to me and said, "And here is my dear Olga cooking piroshki. But dear Olga's eyeballs still don't work, no matter what." He handed me four hundred rubles and said, "Take care of all of the funeral meals for this nun." This was my second meeting with Batiushka, but again it was without anything being cleared up. We remained as distant as we had been previously.

A few more years went by, and the year 1950 began. I started to have terrible headaches. I was tormented for many days, and once during the night I grabbed my head and pulled my hair, which came out on one side. I became completely bald on one side. No remedies helped at all. Not even one little hair would grow back, and the doctors refused to treat me, since I was as

Elder Sebastian serving the funeral of Nun Vera. The priest on the left is Fr. Alexander Krivonosov. On the Elder's other side is the young Alexander Kiselev, Fr. Sebastian's future successor as rector of the Mikhailovka church.

bald as an onion. My acquaintances began to advise me: "Go to Mikhailovka, to Fr. Sebastian—he'll cure you." Again I didn't pay any attention. I thought, "What's that supposed to mean—go to Fr. Sebastian for treatment; how could that be?" But more people started to advise me, and others told me to go to Batiushka. I finally packed and came to see him. When I opened the door to the church and saw him (he was standing on the ambo), I barely recognized him. In 1946 he still had some dark hair, but by now it had become completely white. I approached him after the service, and he said, "Stay here and spend the night; go to Mother Cornelia's place." They brought me to her and the Elder came over, and he and I conversed all night. He questioned me about where I was from, where I was born, how we had been dispossessed, how we had suffered, whom I was now living with, how many children I had, if my mother was alive, and if she was a believer. "And you?" he asked. "Me? I'm neither here nor there."

"Batiushka," I said, "I saw in a dream that I need to serve twenty Molebens. Take some money from me, serve them all for me right away, and I won't bother you any more."

"No," he replied. "We'll serve twenty Molebens for you, but you have to come to church for twenty Sundays in a row. I'll read the Akathists for you myself." He would take me into the vestry and we would kneel there, and every Sunday he would read the Akathists for me. In this way I became accustomed to the Elder, to the church, the choir, and to the customs here. I began to believe, and began to confess and receive Communion. I dragged my husband along, and he began to go to church with me. By then all my children had started to grow up. We would go and take them along with us, and Fr. Sebastian knew them all by name. Soon I felt better, and by the Elder's prayers my hair began to grow back. Through my sickness, belief was born in us, and we became closer to the Elder.

After a little time had gone by my six-year-old nephew fell ill. He had fallen from his bicycle and had begun to limp. His parents didn't pay any attention to this. I decided to take him to a doctor. A surgeon examined him and said, "His hip is infected." They operated and it was unsuccessful. They opened it up a second time and cleaned the bone, but again it was unsuccessful. Then I went to church and suddenly the Elder asked me himself, "Olga, is someone sick at your place?"

"Yes," I replied, "my nephew."

"Transfer him to the Mikhailovka hospital—you know, an acquaintance of yours is a surgeon there." I made arrangements and transferred my nephew to that hospital. The doctors saw right then that the boy was barely alive, and he was quickly under the knife again. They performed an emergency operation, already his third one. Sunday arrived. I came to the church, and the Elder asked, "Did you bring the boy? Why aren't you seeing this thing through? Why don't you bring him to me? People come to me from Moscow and Petersburg, and you're right here but you don't bring him to me. Go right now, straight to the hospital, and bring him to me in your arms!"

I went to the hospital, and the boy's mother was with him. We picked up Misha and took turns carrying him to the church in our arms. This was before Vespers. We brought him into the church and carried him to the Elder, who called to him: "Mishenka, Mish-enka!" But he only raised his eyes and lay there like a rag, all dried out and lifeless. Fr. Sebastian said, "Take him over to the icon of the Holy Trinity, where confessions are heard." I brought him there. He commanded that a chair be placed there and said, "Stand Mishenka on the chair!" I was horrified! The child's hands and feet were like rags—how would he stand? After all, he was half dead! Then the Elder called for his mother and said, "Hold him from both sides and keep him there. Courage, courage!" We set him there, with his feet touching the chair, and we held him up from both sides, stretching him out to his full height. Then Fr. Sebastian called over two nuns and said, "Pray to God!" and he himself began praying. We held Misha, and as I watched he became firmer and firmer and stood more and more upright. Then he straightened up completely and stood on his own feet! The Elder said, "Take him off the chair and lead him; he'll walk on his own two feet. And so Michael began to walk. Everyone was terrified! Fr. Sebastian rubbed him with holy oil and told his mother: "Stay here with him and spend the night. I'll give him Holy Communion tomorrow and he'll never limp." But his mother didn't stay; she went home with Misha in joy. The Elder had also asked her to bring a sack of flour in gratitude to God, but she brought only a little bag. Our Mishenka became such a nice boy, but he limped on one leg. After all, his mother was disobedient and didn't leave him there to receive Communion.

During the Paschal period of 1954 I had an attack of appendicitis and didn't think to get a blessing for the operation—I went on my own will. During the service the Elder saw that I wasn't there and said to one of my friends, "Here's some prosphora. Go quickly to the hospital, and catch Olga before the operation. Have her eat the prosphora, or else the operation will be difficult and painful." When she came they were already calling me. I ate the prosphora and went in for the operation, which lasted four and a half hours.

Some time later I became pregnant. The doctors said that I shouldn't give birth but should have an abortion. I went to see Fr. Sebastian: "What should I do? Please bless me to have an abortion." He said, "You'll crawl into hell and drag me in with you! There'll be no 'pleases!'" Then he gave me a beautiful bouquet of flowers from the altar: "Toss out the dry ones and leave only the fresh ones, and steep one a day in tea and drink it, so that this delivery won't be as difficult as your previous ones." He gave me an icon of the Annunciation and said, "You'll give birth to a son who'll be handsome and wise and loved by all. Don't kill him. He'll be a help to you in your old age. And name him Seraphim, since nobody glorifies St. Seraphim and nobody is given that name anymore." And, in fact, on the Feast of the Annunciation I successfully gave birth to a son, and now he's a doctor.

In 1957 I became pregnant, and went to the Elder to confess and receive Communion. He said, "I'll give you a little present." At that time people had brought him many apples. He looked through them for a long time and finally handed me an apple which was red on one side and green on the other, and he said, "Eat the whole thing yourself; don't give any to anyone else. You'll give birth to a little girl, but you won't come to see me very soon. You'll have complications after childbirth." I gave birth to a little girl, Masha. She was healthy for fifteen years and sick for fifteen years; then she died at the age of thirty. And that apple was half red, half green.

Once I came to services and the Elder said, "As soon as I bless you from the altar, go home." Then, suddenly during services he walked up to me and said, "Well, go home. Only as soon as you enter the house say immediately, 'I want to buy a cow.'" But I responded, "Batiushka, the day's over already. I'm certainly not going to buy a cow now."

"Buy it!" he said. "Just as soon as you enter say, 'I want to buy a cow!' and then buy it. There will be a red one, a spotted one, and one with a star on its forehead. Take the red one—that's your cow. In two days you'll bring me fresh cream."

As I went home I thought, "What does all this mean?" When I came home, I saw that my brother and his wife were sitting there; they had come on a visit. I said: "Greetings! I want to buy a cow!" My brother answered, "What's the problem? If there's money in your pocket, there'll be a cow in your yard. Let's go—my friends are selling three cows." We arrived and three cows were standing there, just as Fr. Sebastian had described. I chose the red one, and two days later I sent some fresh milk for the Elder. I couldn't go myself, so I asked my neighbor to do it. She declined, saying, "How could I go to the Elder with somebody else's alms?" But she brought it anyway. She had barely entered when he said, "Let's have Olga's cream!"

Time passed, and my children grew up. The time came for my daughter Lydia to enter the institute. We came to see Fr. Sebastian: "Batiushka, bless Lydia to enter the institute."

But he said, "Lidochka, where are you planning to go?"

"To the judicial faculty at KazGU."*

"Oh," he said, "she wants to eat apples in Alma-Ata. But I'll bless you to eat a Karaganda potato— it'll be good for you. Do you want to convict people? Will you convict me, too? No, no. Sit at home this year and learn how to sew from your mother; this will come in handy for you. Next year enter the medical institute. They'll open a new department there; go to that department." My daughter decided to try anyway to enroll in the medical institute that very year, but she was not accepted. That year she learned how to sew and was accepted the next year without a problem.

Then it came time for Sasha to enter an institute. I asked Sasha, "Which institute are you going to?" He said, "Given the kind of blessing Lydia got, I'm not going to make any plans. Wherever the Elder tells me to go, that's where I'm going." And my other son, Anatole, finished the eighth grade and decided to get a blessing to enroll in the technical high school. We came to see the Elder: "Batiushka, Sasha needs to enter an institute."

"Well then, Sasha, which institute do you want to go to?"

"Batiushka, I'll go to whichever one you tell me to."

*Kazakh State University, in Alma-Ata.—ED.

"Go to the polytechnical institute, to the construction faculty, and you'll be our much-needed engineer. God bless you." (Now that son is the senior construction superintendent of the city. The new church of the Nativity of the Most Holy Theotokos in Karaganda is being built with his assistance.)

Then he asked Anatole, "Where do you want to go?"

"I want to go to the technical school."

"To the technical school? Your mother teaches you and teaches you. You've only finished the eighth grade and want to go to a technical school? You have no blessing at all for that. When you've finished the tenth grade, then come see me."

And what did my Anatole do? "Mama," he said, "what does the Elder's blessing mean, anyway?" His uncle worked at that time in the admissions commission. "Let's go to my uncle," he said. "He'll help me get in and I'll study there." I agreed: "Let's go, if that's what you want." They gave Anatole an entrance examination. He took it and failed. "Mama," he pleaded, "go to my uncle and have him give me another examination." I went. "Let the boy have his fun," I thought. He took it a second time, and again he failed. The third time his uncle even petitioned on his behalf, but he failed again. So, without a blessing even relatives didn't help. And my Anatole entered the trade school.

In 1962 he had to take part in a Mayday demonstration together with his college. That year May 1 fell during Bright Week. He left for the demonstration in the morning, and by evening he hadn't come home yet. "Oh well," I thought, "he probably went to see my brother." The next morning I went to church and Fr. Sebastian called me over and said, "Go home; you need to be at home. Here are some eggs for you." And he gave me some cracked and damaged eggs. "What's this about?" I thought, and somehow I didn't feel good about it. I came home. "Has Anatole been here?" I asked. "No, he hasn't." In the evening I again went to the church and again the Elder came up to me and said, "Go home—go home right now." And again he gave me cracked eggs. Mother Anastasia also gave me some eggs which were cracked and said, "You'd better get home quickly," and she hurried me along. I went. I had just turned the corner, when I saw Lydia, my daughter, running to meet us. "Mama," she said, "something awful has happened to us! They've stabbed Anatole, and he's lying unconscious in the hospital!" It turned out that some hooligans had stabbed him in the stomach at the demonstration. They operated on him. Anatole lay unconscious for nine days, but Fr. Sebastian and Mother Anastasia prayed him out. He was near death, in a hopeless condition. No one had to tell the Elder or the Eldress anything; they knew themselves what happened to people. Anatole lay in the hospital for eight months and recovered, and he's alive now.

20. MARIA FYODOROVNA AND OLGA FYODOROVNA ORLOVA

Maria Fyodorovna

My parents were deeply religious people. When our family was accused of being kulaks and was dispossessed in 1931, my father said, "This is what God has sent us. We have to drink this cup." They arrested my father and detained him separately from us, and many years passed before we were reunited. They brought my mother and the four of us children to Kompaneisk, to a bare hillside where there was neither water or bread. We dug a burrow in the ground and Peter, Olga, Alexandra and I lived in it. Our mother was pregnant and gave birth prematurely. Mother suffered greatly. Our hole was covered with blood; there was blood splattered on our clothes, and there was nowhere to wash them—the steppe was all around. "Daughter," my mother implored, "find a small stone and throw the clothes over it. Wet them with a little water and scrape them with a knife." I was little, and I still didn't know how to wash clothes.

Then they began building dugouts. They would dig clay, pour water on it, knead it with their feet and make bricks. They made barracks that had neither windows nor doors. In the barracks were plank beds, and people would lie on them, covering themselves with whatever they could find. In the morning they'd get up and drag off the dead bodies. We didn't mourn over the dead there. It was beyond us. Our mother would only pray and read Akathists, and we would sit beside her: "Mama, we want to eat! Mama, let's eat!"

"Wait—I'm almost done reading the Akathist."

"Mama!"

"Hold on, there's just one page left." She would drag out the time. "I'm finishing up right now, and then God will help us." She would finish reading, take a piece of bread, and cut off pieces from it. And we'd point with our fingers: "Who's that for?"

"That's for Peter."

"And who's that for?"

"That's for Maria, that's for Olga, and that's for Alexandra." That's just how it was. We'd scrape up all the crumbs, and our mother always tried to give us some of her ration. How did we survive—how?! It's unbelievable, since it was impossible to survive there! I was very susceptible to colds, and lay there with rheumatism. My legs were covered with infected sores. My mother would sit and weep. The flies flew in clouds, and she covered my legs with a cheesecloth.

But how God helped us! We all grew up and received a higher education. Peter graduated from the academy. Olga and Alexandra are doctors, and I'm a teacher. God preserved us through our mother's prayers; it's a miracle that we remained alive.

Olga Fyodorovna Orlova (left) and Eldress Anastasia.

Olga Fyodorovna (Elder Sebastian's Physician)

In 1949 my sister Alexandra and I graduated from the Alma-Ata Medical Institute. The time came to decide where we would settle permanently to work. After talking to our parents, we decided to take assignments in Kokchetav. Our brother Peter lived there with his family, and we all decided to move there and live with him. But suddenly a telegram came unexpectedly from our father. In it he informed us that we should take an assignment only in Karaganda, and that he would tell us the reason in a letter. Before long we received this letter. My father wrote that, following the advice of a believer who was a friend of his, he had gone to the Mikhailovka church to see Fr. Sebastian and get his blessing for the departure. The Elder questioned him in detail about the purpose of our move, listened to everything attentively, and then said, "No, Fyodor Ivanovich, I don't bless your departure—a son is a son, a daughter-in-law is a daughter-in-law, but daughters are daughters. Today your son lives there, but tomorrow he might move somewhere else." (In fact, my brother and his family soon left Kokchetav.) "Let your daughters take a job assignment only in Karaganda." Our father told the Elder that he had already sold everything and asked him what he was supposed to do now. To this the Elder replied, "Don't be afraid, Fyodor Ivanovich. God will help, and everything will be fine."

My sister and I did as the Elder told us. Arriving in Karaganda, we immediately hurried to the Mikhailovka church. Fr. Sebastian met us with a radiant smile. When we entered he was standing by the window. Wearing bright vestments, lit up by the sun's rays, he seemed to be radiating light himself. Having received his blessing, we had no difficulty finding work in the regional hospital.

When we had settled in Karaganda, I began to attend the Mikhailovka church in the evenings after work. Fr. Sebastian served daily in the morning and in the evening. I very much liked how he served and how the church choir sang. I began to pay close attention to the Elder. I was always amazed at his God-fearing, reverent, and touching attitude towards the services, as well as his great patience with regard to the parishioners, whom he tried to help in everything.

He was very modest, meek, and charitable. There isn't anyone who would not love him with his whole soul after meeting him even once. Being a doctor, I noticed that he was very fatigued and sick. During services he would often cough and have difficulty breathing. In conversations with him I asked him in detail about the condition of his health and offered him my services as a doctor. From that time on I began to look after him constantly.

When I started to go to church, I had no understanding about spiritual life, about eldership, or in general about the essence of Christianity. When I came into contact for the first time with an instance of the spiritual clairvoyance of Fr. Sebastian, I thought that it was a chance coincidence of my thoughts with his. But then the following thing happened: once during Vespers I stood and thought, "How nice it is here! I don't even feel like going home. I'd like to stay and spend the night with Anfisa Ivanovna, who lives at the church." The service ended, and I began to prepare to go home. Suddenly Fr. Sebastian came up to me and said, "Olga Fyodorovna, stay here and spend the night at the church with Anfisa Ivanovna." I was overjoyed and exclaimed, "Batiushka! I was just daydreaming about that. Isn't it amazing that we had the same thought?" He smiled but didn't answer, and went to his cell.

Soon after that he blessed me to confess and receive Christ's Holy Mysteries. In the morning I came to the church and saw that there were many people who wanted to confess. I became distressed and thought that it obviously wouldn't work out for me to confess, since I had to go to work soon. Suddenly the door to the confessional room opened and the Elder appeared at the threshold. He extended his hand to me and said: "Come, Olga Fyodorovna, let's go to Confession." I didn't know how to confess or what to say. My head was full of confusion and I was overcome by various thoughts. Suddenly he said, "Well, Olga Fyodorovna, I have various thoughts in my head." Then he began to enumerate all my thoughts which had been affecting me and especially bothering me. I said, "Batiushka, but I also have such thoughts. Are they really sinful?" He replied, "Yes, you have to flee from them and chase them away, since they're sinful."

Another time, as I was standing in the church and praying, the subdeacon came up to me and said, "Olga Fyodorovna, the Elder's calling for you." I quickly went over to the pannikhida table, as I thought he was ill, since that happened often. But he was sitting on a small chair before an icon of the Holy Trinity and holding something in his lap. There were many people around him, but I tried to get through and saw that he was holding a small plate on his lap, on which lay some small loaves of blessed bread which had wine poured over them. It was the first time I had seen such loaves. "Well, this is something," I thought, "they themselves eat bread soaked with wine, but they give us plain bread!" This thought pierced through my mind suddenly, like a flash of lightning. Then Fr. Sebastian turned in my direction, dismissed those standing near him and said, "Olga Fyodorovna, take some blessed bread and eat it," and he handed me a piece of bread, soaked with wine. He didn't give any more to anyone else. I was again amazed at how all my thoughts were revealed to him. I was ashamed and frightened.

No less amazing were other incidents which testify to the Elder's holy clairvoyance.

It was the Feast of the Holy Trinity.* The service was very festive, and Fr. Sebastian was joyful, lively, and in a peaceful state. The choir sang especially well. When after the ninth ode of the canon they began to sing the Praises, I couldn't make out the combination of the words at the place where they sang "Svet, i Sveta Podatel." I didn't know which way was correct: "Svet iz Sveta Podatel'," or "Svet, i Sveta Podatel."**

This disturbed me and I wanted to find out how it was exactly, but it wasn't the appropriate moment to ask. Soon after the Feast I came to an evening service. The Elder wasn't serving,

---

*That is, the Feast of Pentecost.—ED.

**In the first case it would mean "Light from the Light-giver," and in the second, it would mean "Light and Light-giver."—TRANS.

but he was listening to the service from his cell. I went in to see him and ask for a blessing. When I extended my hands towards him, he put his palm on them and smiled, but he didn't bless me. Then he said, "Olga Fyodorovna, 'Svet, i Sveta Podatel'!" I was amazed, and said, "But Batiushka, that was very part that I didn't understand!" He again smiled and blessed me. Once more his clairvoyance amazed me.

When I was thirty-two years old I became seriously ill with a woman's illness. I thought that I had cancer and was very worried. What's more, I was worried because with this type of illness I could not receive the Holy Mysteries, venerate the icons, be anointed with oil, eat prosphora and blessed bread, or light candles.

Once during a service I was especially sorrowful and turned to the Lord mentally: " O Lord, I'm like a leper and haven't been able to venerate holy objects for so long. I probably have cancer. What a sorrow this is!"—and I burst out crying. At that moment the subdeacon left the pannikhida area, quickly came up to me and said, "Olga Fyodorovna, the Elder's calling for you." I forgot about my illness and hurried to him, thinking that he was sick. When I entered he was sitting happily on a chair and, smiling, he said to me, "Olga Fyodorovna, it will go away. Sometimes this even happens to young people. It's forbidden to venerate the icons, and to eat prosphora and drink holy water is also forbidden, but the blessed bread—that you can eat. You can have people light candles for you, but you yourself should not place them before the icons," and he blessed me, giving me half of a small loaf of blessed bread.

I left him encouraged and full of joy, with hope for my recovery. And in the next few days I actually became completely well.

When my mother was seriously ill, Fr. Sebastian would come to us to give her Communion. During one of his visits, as we came up to venerate the cross after Communion, the Elder said to my sister Catherine, "Katenka, don't get married."

"Why?" my sister asked.

"Don't get married, Katenka, or you'll bitterly, bitterly weep," said the Elder, although he had never even seen her fiance and Catherine had said nothing to him about her intentions. As he was leaving us, Fr. Sebastian told me that they wouldn't live together but would get divorced. Catherine didn't obey him, and soon after the wedding his prediction came true.

I knew that the Elder didn't like it when on his nameday people would pay special attention to him and give him presents. But for a long time I had wanted to give him some material to make vestments with, and I was afraid to even mention this. Once, while returning from work I went into the church. Walking past Fr. Sebastian's cell, I glanced in the window and saw that he was standing at the window, beckoning me with his finger. I went into the cell, and he opened the door and said, "How glad I am to see you, Olga Fyodorovna. Come in. I'm in great need of some vestments made of this type of material," and he showed me some cuffs of a bluish-white color. "I have cuffs, but I don't have vestments. The vestments would be useful during the Feasts of the Theotokos and of the Lord." I understood that he was finally responding to my long-standing secret wishes, and said, "Batiushka, bless me to buy the fabric."

Being near Fr. Sebastian for a period of many years, we were repeatedly convinced of the power of the Elder's blessings. The following incident can serve as an example which confirms the power of his blessings.

In the beginning of the 1960s a decree was issued demanding the sale of privately owned cattle. We had a cow and now we were forced to sell it. On Saturday our father went to church.

After the service he went up to the Elder and explained to him that it was no longer possible for us to keep our cow, and that the next day, Sunday, it would be necessary to sell it. The latter replied, "That's fine, Fyodor Ivanovich, I bless you. Tomorrow come to the Liturgy, and after 'Our Father,' go sell the cow."

My father said, "But Batiushka, how is that possible? After all, it'll be late. I'll need to travel a long way, to the Old City, and there won't be anyone at the market by then."

The Elder replied, "That's all right, Fyodor Ivanovich, God will help, and you'll sell it." And that's how it turned out. He went from the church to the horseyard in the New City, then he went home for the cow. Only then did he go to the market in the Old City, which was six miles away. My father rode on a cart with the cow tied to it. On the way he met people who were already returning from the market who laughed at him, saying that he was going in vain, since there was nobody left at the market. But my father decided to go there anyway and try to do his business. When he had driven up to the market, he saw that in fact there was hardly anyone there, and that those who were there were getting ready to go home. At that point a person walked up to him and said, "Well, old man, have you come to sell your cow?"

My father responded, "Yes, I'd like to sell it."

The buyer offered his price: "Let's not bargain. If you're in agreement, then let's shake on it." After a little haggling they agreed on a price; and in this manner, to everyone's surprise, my father sold the cow successfully and for a desirable price.

Here's how Fr. Sebastian taught me humility on my nameday.

Once, in the middle of July, I dropped in to see the Elder in his cell. At that time he was examining a small rug with his cell-attendant Maria Obraztsova. "Ah, Olga Fyodorovna," he said, "come in, come in, you're always welcome."

"What are you doing, Batiushka?" I asked.

"We're looking at a rug, but there are crosses on it, and that means that we can't walk on it. Maria," he turned to his cell-attendant, "maybe we'll present it to Olga Fyodorovna on her nameday."

"Yes, Batiushka, that would be fine."

"Your nameday is in a few days isn't it, Olga?" the Elder continued. "Will you invite me to your nameday party?" My heart stopped. I loved the Elder so much, but I feared him just as much, and I had never invited him to my place; he always used to come on his own. Of course I said, "Certainly you should come, Batiushka."

Three days before my nameday he summoned me, gave me some instruction, an Akathist, and a large prosphora. After receiving all these presents, as well as his promise to come on my nameday, I became a bit conceited.

Then came the Feast of St. Olga, Equal-to-the-Apostles. At home they transformed the whole upstairs during the day. Everyone washed, cleaned, and prepared a large amount of various milk and fruit dishes. I received Communion at the church. After Liturgy everyone went up for the Elder's blessing. I walked up as well, but he turned away and blessed others, as though he didn't see me. I stood there, waiting for his blessing. "Ach, what an ordeal!" he said. "Is that you, Olga Fyodorovna?" And he blessed me half turned-away. (He would usually bless with a large sign of the Cross.) In my heart I felt a sort of grating. "What's happened?" I thought. My mood immediately became gloomy, as though it wasn't my nameday. "Batiushka," I said, "they're waiting; let's go."

But he said, "Vera, get ready. I'll eat now and then rest in my cell." I stayed and waited while he ate, rested, got up, and went to his church-cell. I sat there as if I were in an electric chair and waited for him. In his cell he spoke with someone for a long time and then called for Peter: "Peter, get the car started, we're going soon."

"Batiushka," I asked, "are you going to our place?"

But he said, "Oh, what is she thinking—to your place. No, no, no; we're going to Melkombinat, to Olga Stepanovna."

"But Batiushka, they're waiting for us!" But he seemed to not hear me, and we left for Melkombinat. There we served a Pannikhida and a Moleben, and ate in the trapeza. Then we went to see the Zhukovs, and the Elder said, "Peter, let's go!" Well, I thought, now we're going to my place. Even though it would be late, at least we'd get there. We drove up to our house, stopped at the gate, and Fr. Sebastian said, "Olga Fyodorovna, get out."

"Batiushka," I said, "how can this be?! How will they receive me at home?! What will I say?! Why won't you come in?!" He said nothing and left. But he had often said to me, "Olga Fyodorovna, in the future you'll have humility before everything." That's how he could humble one down.

At our next meeting he said, "Olga Fyodorovna, you must excuse me that I didn't come ... there was something I ... I don't even remember why.... I was either in a hurry ... or felt poorly ... I no longer remember."

"Oh Batiushka," I said, "I really caught it at home!" Well, that's the way it goes.

When I was working as a district doctor in the Mikhailovka polyclinic, one of my duties was to make house calls and to visit the sick in my district. I wound up seeing a variety of circumstances—both decent and indecent. Once, after having seen plenty of all sorts of things, I came to the church with the intention of preparing for Communion on the following day. After praying, I was getting ready to go home, when suddenly the Elder's cell door opened. He came out and said: "Olga Fyodorovna, let's go to Confession." I grew numb. Why had he decided to confess me today? I went into his cell. He blessed me and immediately began to speak: "Olga Fyodorovna, you go around the district and treat the sick. This is, of course, a good work. But you observe various scenes of life—both decent and indecent, beneficial for the soul and not beneficial. Don't allow anything indecent to soak into you." Ah! My ears were burning—I had just gotten an eyeful of everything. "Batiushka," I said, "forgive me!" He confessed me and I left. He didn't confess anyone else that evening, but had stayed for my sake, so that we would both not put off until tomorrow dealing with that which is not beneficial for the soul.

Fr. Sebastian often gave me money to distribute to the sick and the poor. I would say, "Batiushka, how am I supposed to do this?"

"Don't be embarrassed, Olga Fyodorovna. If, let's say, you're on duty at the hospital, walk up to a patient, look at the history of his illness and speak a little with him. If you find that he's from somewhere else or is poor, place the money under his pillow without his noticing. And if during an appointment in the polyclinic you see that a patient is poor, you can write him a prescription, explain everything and tuck the money into the prescription, using your own discretion, depending on the cost of the medicine." In this way he cared for everyone, and I did what he blessed me to.

I'll mention an example of a miraculous healing by the Elder's prayers. In 1960 Pelagia Melnik came from the city of Izhevsk to see Fr. Sebastian. For the past half year she couldn't eat bread, kasha, potatoes, or other foods. She fed herself entirely on milk and raw eggs. She had become weak and moved only with great difficulty. When Pelagia tried to go into the Elder's cell, they wouldn't let her through, since there were so many who wanted to see him. She asked them to let her through without waiting in line, but it was futile. Suddenly the door opened and Fr. Sebastian came out and said, "Let this woman through to see me, she's very sick." Having entered his cell, Pelagia fell on her knees before him, and without pronouncing a single word she began weeping bitterly. He told her, "Don't cry, Pelagia; it'll all pass and you'll be healed." He gave her some fresh prosphora, a glass of water, a large apple, and said, "Eat this." She replied that for half a year she hadn't eaten bread, that her throat was sore and food would not pass through it. The Elder said, "I bless you. Go to the baptistry, sit on the wide bench, and eat it up." She went to the baptistry, sat on the bench and ate the Elder's gifts easily and freely. After this she immediately fell asleep and slept for a whole day and night. Fr. Sebastian went up to her several times, but forbade anyone to wake her up. Pelagia awoke in perfect health. The Elder told her, "You have a difficult job, but everything will soon change." And, in fact, half a month after her return to Izhevsk, Pelagia was transferred to another, easier job, without her even having submitted a request.

P. I. Kosinova recounted the following: She came to see the Elder with complaints of pain in the rectum and in the lumbar area. After an examination at the oncological clinic she was diagnosed with rectal cancer and an operation was suggested. Before the operation she decided to go to Fr. Sebastian for a blessing, and to place candles in the church and have a Moleben served. But the Elder said, "Don't be in such a hurry, or you'll be in time to die under the knife. Stay alive for a while; after all, you have children." She approached him three times, but he had only one answer—not to have the operation. He advised her to buy some aloe, make a solution out of it and drink it. He also suggested that she have a Moleben served with the blessing of water to the Savior, the Mother of God, her Guardian Angel, and all the Saints. Three months later she went to the oncological clinic for a follow-up examination. The examination showed that the tumor had almost completely disappeared. Soon she was completely well.

She related the following about her son Michael: on the first day of Great Lent, Michael went to see off one of his friends. His mother was opposed to this and was worried, seeing her son's disobedience. Being offended at him, she had the thought, "Punish him, O Lord!" For a long time she waited for her son's return, but in vain. Finally at midnight she received a call that her son was in the hospital with a compound fracture of his shin bones. Michael lay in the hospital for about three months, but the break would not heal. They operated on him three times, but the bone wound up healing in the wrong way. They suggested a fourth operation, but Michael had himself released from the hospital and went home in a cast. He didn't work for over a year. His mother suggested to Michael that he receive Communion, but he wouldn't consent to it. Then his mother went to see Fr. Sebastian and told him everything. After hearing her out, he told her to bring her son to church. With difficulty they talked him into it and brought him. The Elder gave Michael Holy Communion and told him to have a Moleben served. After the Moleben the Elder went over to Michael, who was sitting in a chair, and commanded him to stand with his crutches. He made the sign of the Cross over him from the front and back and said, "Go with God. God bless you. Now you can have an operation, or not have one." And he walked away from him. In two weeks our neighbor, who is a doctor, brought Michael to the hospital for an examination in order to resolve the question concerning the operation. In the x-rays there were clearly visible signs of healing—bone tissue had formed, and the bone had begun to heal. The operation turned out to be unnecessary.

The same woman's granddaughter Tanya was run over by a car and had her legs and hip bones broken. This happened on the eve of the Dormition of the Mother of God.

The breaks did not heal for a long time. Mother Anastasia was told about this, and she told Fr. Sebastian. He sent the girl a prosphoron and offered to give her Communion, which was done. The Elder asked Tanya if she had been wearing a cross.

"She's suffering because of her sins," he said, "but it's all right, she'll gradually get better." And that's what happened.

Maria Fyodorovna

My husband was an unbeliever, a communist, and he often got drunk. Life was hard, both morally and materially. When he was sober, my husband was very kind, but when he was drunk he would oppress me for my faith and make terrible scenes. He used to shout at the icons: "Hah! These idols! I'll throw them out!" But my mother would say, "It wasn't you who put them there, so don't you throw them out." My father had given me the icon "Unexpected Joy," and placed it on the shelf, in a secluded place, so that it wouldn't be noticeable. I used to pray there secretly.

Once Fr. Sebastian asked me how life was. I told him about everything and said, "I'll probably divorce him." He didn't say anything to me, but handed me an apple and some cookies. And time passed.

Then once I came home, and the house was quiet. I opened the door to the hall and saw my husband kneeling by the opened shelf before the icon, half-drunk. He was praying "O Good Mother of the Good King… " He didn't know any more, just that one thing, and he kept repeating it. I asked, "What are you kneeling for?" He replied, "Don't you see that I'm praying? I knew you had an icon there." So, by the Elder's prayers, fear had gripped him and he had started praying. However, he would pray only when he drank, while he was ashamed to do it when he was sober. Then he stopped making scenes and no longer wanted to throw away the icons. Some time later he suddenly said, "Masha, let's get married in the church." I was amazed and didn't believe him, and said, "You're making fun of the Faith." But he responded, "Come on, let's get married, and we'll live better. Sew yourself a dress." He got all the children to agree to it. I went to see the Elder and told him, and he said: "Well, that's good! Come."

Fr. Alexander Krivonosov performed the marriage ceremony for us and my husband began to change. He noticed that I ate modestly on Wednesday and Friday, and he started coming home from work before me to prepare something suitable for the fast. The children asked him why he was cooking lenten food, and he answered, "What do you mean? Your mother doesn't eat, so we'll fast too."

Time passed. My husband fell ill with the flu and said, "In our family everyone dies suddenly." We put him in the hospital and they found a darkening of his lungs which had turned into cancer. Before his operation he confessed with fear and received the sacraments of Unction and Holy Communion. They operated on him, and he died. After his death I had a dream. My husband had come home, and I said to him, "Here, Petya, have a drink!" and I handed him a shot of vodka. He took it, walked over to the sink, poured it out, and said, "At our place we don't drink." And so, by the Elder's prayers, the Lord brought my husband to salvation.

Olga Fyodorovna

Fr. Sebastian always blessed us to take our vacation in such a way that the first two weeks of it would coincide with the last two weeks of Great Lent, and the two last weeks would coincide with the first two weeks of Pascha. In 1966 I took my vacation beginning on April 1. During the night, on April 1, Julia called me from the church: "Olga Fyodorovna, the Elder is feeling poorly. Peter's coming to pick you up, so get ready." I gathered my medicines and went. I came home only after the Elder's death.

Fr. Sebastian prayed for everyone during his lifetime, and he continues to pray and help after his death. In confirmation of this I will describe two dreams.

On the twentieth day after the Elder's repose I was on a business trip in Moscow. At 1:30 in the morning according to Moscow time (in Karaganda it was already 4:30, which was the time of the Elder's death) I had a dream about him. He was cheerful and smiling, and said, "Olga Fyodorovna, may the Lord save you for everything—for everything," and he waved his hand at me. I wanted to say something, but I didn't have time before I woke up. In my soul I felt such joy—it was just as if I had seen him alive.

In January, 1994, I again dreamt about the Elder. It was as if I were in church, the service had finished, and everyone was leaving. Many, myself included, headed for the lodge to receive the Elder's blessing. Here I met his cell-attendant Vera and I said, "Vera, go to Fr. Sebastian, do what you need to do, and then ask permission for me to enter." Vera said, "Very well, Olga Fyodorovna," and went into the cell. After some time she came out and said, "Go in, Olga Fyodorovna, the Elder gave permission." I thanked her and went in to see him. He sat in the front corner of the cell before the icon of the Savior, leaning his elbows on a small table. He was dressed in a beautiful new riassa, the hem of which fell to the floor, and a klobuk with a veil, which was also new. It gave the impression that he had just come from somewhere but had not changed his clothes yet. (He usually used to take off his riassa and klobuk right away.) He had a festive appearance. I went up to him, fell on my knees, and said, "Bless, Batiushka." He blessed me and I kissed his hand and felt that it was warm and soft, as though alive. I pressed against his hand and said, "Dear Batiushka, it's been so long since I've seen you; how I miss you." I suddenly felt a spasm in my throat and felt like I would burst out crying. He said affectionately, "But you know, I'm here every day." I thought, "How can that be, when he's 'there'?" I began to say, "How can it be, Batiushka, when you're.... " But he interrupted me and said, "Yes, yes. I'm both here and there, but I visit here every day." He said these phrases distinctly and earnestly. Then I woke up.

In this manner Fr. Sebastian made me and others understand that he doesn't forsake us, that he watches carefully over his flock, that he comes to us on the earth, and that by prayer we can always appeal to him for help and instruction.

21. Raisa Ivanovna Kuzmicheva

Our family was exiled from the Kursk Province in 1931. There was our mother and father, two small children and my father's mother. They brought us to the barren steppe at Kompaneisk. As far as the eye could see, to the horizon itself, there wasn't even so much as a bush or a small tree. At first the exiles constructed grass and brush huts and then they built dugouts. It was terribly unsanitary—there were no clothes, no food, and there was one well for the whole settlement from which we drew water in a jar. People died off in whole families. My parents buried the two children and my father's mother. They wrapped them in rags and placed them in a mass grave. My parents were left by themselves. What they lived through is impossible to describe. The most difficult years were 1931, 1932, and 1933. Then things became easier. People began to dig vegetable gardens next to their dugouts, and they began to receive bread by ration cards. I was born in 1935, and my brother Nicholas was born in 1938. In 1939 my mother heard about Fr. Sebastian and brought my brother to Greater Mikhailovka, where the Elder baptized him. She was immediately permeated with great respect for Fr. Sebastian, and from that time on began to go to see him there. The Elder was very weak. He had just been freed from Dolinka at that time and had settled in Mikhailovka with the nuns who had also been freed, Mother Aggripina, Mother Barbara and Mother Thekla. She went to see him there to pray to God and to receive the Elder's blessing, along with Maria Kuzminichna Polyakova and Alexandra Mikhailovna Syomina. Like my mother, they were also deeply religious and had likewise been victims of repression and been exiled to Karaganda.

Alexandra Syomina had lived in the same monastery as Mother Aggripina. When the monasteries were closed and persecutions began against the monastic inhabitants, Mother Agrippina wound up in a camp and Alexandra got married. Sometime later she also was exiled to Karaganda. Here they met again.

We had time to eat just a little bread before the war began. Our father was killed near Stalingrad in 1942. When our mother (she was a strong believer) received the death notification, she wept very much, of course, and immediately made a vow to God that she would eat no meat. And to the end of her life she did not eat meat.

Fr. Sebastian, having learned about our losses, being a very good man and not indifferent to the sufferings of others, tried to help us as much as possible—and not only us—although at that time he lived poorly and had no personal resourses.

During the war years the Elder began coming to see us in Kompaneisk. He gathered all the widows and orphans together and he tried to help them, even though he himself lived in poverty. On the day of his arrival my mother would ask me to get up on the roof and watch for when he would start walking to our house from the railroad station. I remember how he walked—he had a white beard, white hair, a light-colored raincoat and a gray hat, and he walked with a stick. Mother Barbara and Mother Agrippina would be with him, and everyone would run up to him for his blessing. I would run headlong to my mother, and she would send me to Settlement 15 to tell the people there that he had arrived. Every arrival of his was a real feast day for those who knew him, especially for me and my brother. In the first place this was because he always came with treats, and also because there always emanated from him a kind of bright joy, which even I could sense. More often than not he would leave the same day on the evening train; but before this, on the way to the train station he would visit the gravely ill, immobile nun Eupraxia, the sister of Mother Olympiada. Both sisters were huddled together at their brother's house in a tiny room, where there were no arrangements for a sick person. Fr. Sebastian helped the sick woman with money and three years later moved her to Mikhailovka, having bought a small house for the two sisters with his own means.

Our family lived constantly in a state of semi-starvation. Day and night our mother worked at a sewing machine by the light of a kerosene lamp in order to feed me and my brother. The Elder knew this. From 1942 on he began inviting me to his house on Lower Street as a guest during school vacation. He probably did this in order to feed a half-starved child and to strengthen the belief in God which my mother had instilled in me. Those were the happiest days of my childhood. Even when I was on my way there in the train my heart would stand still with joy in expectation of the meeting ahead. When I would step over the threshold of his small, clean house, where the earthen floors were covered with tarpaper and multicolored braided rugs, it seemed to me to be the most wonderful place on earth, and its inhabitants were like angels in the flesh. I felt reverence before them. Mother Agrippina, Mother Barbara, and Mother Thekla would be dressed in long, neat dresses, with white aprons tied around their waists and white kerchiefs on their heads. They were polite and amiable. They always spoke quietly and never raised their voices. In the kitchen stood Fr. Sebastian's bed, under a clean, perfectly white bedspread, while in another room were three more beds, pushed flush against each other, on which the nuns would sleep. What a generous soul one would need to have to invite someone else's child as a guest while living in such close quarters, and a child who would bring nothing but inconvenience and cares! And it was evident that I wasn't the only one that the Elder invited. There were always people in his house, including children. When some people left, others would come.

All three nuns—Mother Agrippina, Mother Barbara and Mother Thekla—were then working in the hospital. Mother Agrippina was a nurse, Mother Barbara was in management, and Mother Thekla was a cook. They were still relatively young (forty-four to forty-six years old) and pretty, especially Mothers Agrippina and Barbara. Mother Agrippina had a rosy-white, clear face, large blue eyes and a very charming smile. Mother Barbara had a noble, intelligent face, a nice figure, a smooth, graceful step and a pleasant, soft voice. It was later related that all the medical personnel and the patients in the polyclinic were delighted with Mother Barbara and considered her to be a model of intelligence, orderliness and thoroughness.

There was no church yet at that time, and they prayed in homes, wherever they were invited. Therefore Fr. Sebastian did not always spend the night at Lower St. He generally stayed wherever there was to be a service in the morning.

They would feed me well and take me to the bathhouse. We often walked to Zelenstroi with Fr. Sebastian. They met him warmly there. Pointing at me, he would smile affectionately and say, "Look at what a little girl she is, and she's already in the third grade!"

Elder Sebastian, whom I knew for twenty-three years, was an outstanding individual. Up to the point when the monasteries were closed, he was a novice of the last Optina Elder

(Nektary). And as his true successor, he was just such a man of prayer, a man of righteous, ascetic life and a true elder. But he was not withdrawn into himself and did not go off into his inner world, but, being gifted by God with unusual kindness and generosity of soul, he lived for others or, more accurately, for God and his neighbor.

Even I, who knew the Elder while I was still a child, unconsciously noticed how he was not like other priests. At that time in our region there lived other hieromonks who had been released from Dolinka: Fr. Cephas, Fr. Macarius, Fr. Parthenius, Fr. Caesarius, and Fr. Parmenas. All of them were good priests, but not one of them called forth such reverent feelings as did Fr. Sebastian. Streams of grace emanated from him, and everyone sensed this. He even had an unusual outward appearance: he was a bit taller than average and had a handsome, inspired face; young, dark, penetrating eyes and silky hair, like a child's. He had a smooth gait and unhurried, measured movements. He even gave blessings in a somewhat special way. At first he would carefully, with love, sign one with the sign of the Cross, and would then give him his soft, warm hand. The Elder had very beautiful, gentle hands. The expression on his face was almost always kind, smiling lightly, and very rarely strict. Fr. Sebastian was respected even by unbelievers and representatives of the soviet authority, whose relationship towards the Church and those who served it was arrogantly scornful and occasionally even hostile.

The Elder was very neat in his way of life and loved cleanliness and order in everything. He was always collected and poised, both inwardly and outwardly. No one ever saw him carelessly dressed or uncombed. He had very beautiful manners, but they were not merely outward—they proceeded from the depths of his soul and were dictated by his care for others.

The Elder ate very little and wouln't even eat a whole egg right away. He liked very simple, basically vegetarian, foods. He also slept very little—not more than four or five hours a day.

He was very delicate and tactful, and would never humiliate, grieve, or snub anyone, and he never emphasized a person's physical defects. In Fr. Sebastian's presence it would never occur to anyone to say that someone was deaf, blind, lame, etc. If you found yourself within the highly moral field which surrounded him, it was impossible to act in a mean way or speak rudely. He did not have special favorites, but would behave the same towards everyone, and by so doing he drew even more people into his circle. Everywhere, always, and in everything he was quiet and modest, and he even strove to do his good deeds in such a way as to be unnoticed by others. Sometimes you'd go to see him for a blessing and he would very carefully stuff some money into your hand which had been folded four times. Often, after his visits to our house and after we'd prepared the beds in the evening, we'd find a little money under the bedspread. Mother Agrippina would leave it there by the Elder's orders. It seems clear that he did it that way because of his sensitivity to others, in order to not embarrass a person or force him to thank the Elder in public. In the twenty-three years of my acquaintance with him I never once heard him praise himself or set himself as an example before others. He was completely devoid of self-love and self-satisfaction. On the contrary, he would often say, "I'm an ignorant person—I only finished the fourth grade. I have no gift for words and I have no voice." He would often read sermons from a book, without adding anything himself. While sitting at the table with his spiritual children he would sometimes tell a story about something, but in a quiet, modest manner, without making a show of himself. Despite his lack of a higher education, the Elder spoke quite correctly and expressed his ideas well on paper, having a very beautiful handwriting.

The Elder's kind heart especially ached over poor widows and orphans. Our family as well fell within the sphere of his kindness. In the summer of 1951 Maria Kuzminichna and Fr. Parmenas, by Fr. Sebastian's blessing, moved to Melkombinat (three miles from Mikhailovka). At first they lived with the Samartsevs (a mother and two grown, unmarried sons), and then they bought a small adobe house for two owners—for themselves and for us. We didn't have a kopeck for even a poor little house, and thus Fr. Parmenas and Fr. Sebastian split the cost of our half.

By that time many believers had already moved, by Fr. Sebastian's blessing, to Melkombinat from various corners of Karaganda: from Maikuduk, Tikhonovka, Prishakhtinsk, and Kompaneisk. For the most part these were families or, to be more precise, the remnants of families, which remained alive after the tragedy which they had endured of being special-status exiles in the early 1930s. The inhabitants of Melkombinat were people whose hearts were worn by suffering, who were broken by fate, and they included widows and orphaned children. Each one had his own pain, his own wounds in his soul. There were people with difficult characters: capricious ones, suspicious ones, aggressive ones, and those who were withdrawn. But Fr. Sebastian would find an approach to every suffering soul. Also among the people who surrounded the Elder were many monastics who had been exiled to Karaganda during the years of persecution or who had come later to him from Central Russia. They were the backbone of the Karaganda church. Among them were unique, talented people, ascetics of lofty spiritual life. On the whole it was a strong Christian community, a "skete" of the steppes of Kazakhstan, which the Optina Elder was able to organize and make to grow on the sanctified land of the Karaganda work camps, even during the time of the godless communist regime.

Maria Kuzminichna and Fr. Parmenas (who by that time had become extremely weak, having already suffered one stroke), performed the divine services at home both morning and evening. People would attend them, myself among them. Here I became aquainted with Valya and Nina Patrina. Tall, slender and black-eyed, with a thick, dark braid, Valya immediately struck me by her appearance. She seemed to me to be a real beauty. They lived in a small, cozy home, not far from us. Their mother, Aunt Nastya, was a remarkable, deeply religious woman, and a great admirer of Elder Sebastian. She raised her daughters in a true Christian spirit. In their home were many icons and church books, and a lampada was always burning. In addition, Aunt Nastya also knew many religious songs, which their family trio sang harmoniously and beautifully. Of all the many songs, I liked two the most: "I Am Drowning in the Sea like Peter," and "I Am on the Bank of the Sea of Galilee." Materially, they did not live too poorly, since they received a good pension in recompense for their father, who had perished in the mines. In addition, Aunt Nastya also quickly and nicely knitted shawls. Fr. Sebastian greatly respected this family and sometimes stayed with them when he came to Melkombinat.

I went to school on foot (it was two-and-a-half or three miles away). Once in the spring I got up very early and left for school. It was dark, and there were streams flowing all around. In the dark I fell into some kind of puddle and walked through the water up to my knees singing the song, "I Am Drowning in the Sea like Peter."

When I graduated from ninth grade I began to go to church regularly on Saturdays and Sundays (it was not yet registered then) along with the Patrinas. I would stop by at their place and we would all (Valya, Nina and Aunt Nastya) go on foot across the dam. At that time there were almost no buses, and everyone went on foot. I came to like church services, the singing, and the

Some of the Elder's spiritual daughters. Standing, from left to right: Nina Patrina, Raisa Kuzmicheva, Valentina Patrina and Raisa Voshchinnikova. Seated: Nina Plotnikova and Mother Agrippina.

voices of Mother Agrippina, Mother Barbara and Xenia Ivanovna more and more.

By autumn of 1952, my love for church services had become so strong that I already had the thought—shouldn't I quit the tenth grade so I can constantly be in church? But Fr. Sebastian would in no way approve of my decision, and therefore I had to finish the tenth grade no matter what. Of course, I studied without any desire to do so, while church became the main meaning and joy of my life. I counted all the days, minutes and hours and couldn't wait for Saturday. And although the time dragged on endlessly, Saturday would come anyway, and I would be unable to hide my joy from those around me any longer. I would look at my classmates and would think with compassion and pity, "You poor things! You don't know anything; you don't even experience one thousandth of the joy that I'm experiencing. You're going home now, but I'm going on wings to church, where everything is solemn, extraordinary and beautiful!"

I liked everything in church—the cleanliness, the coziness, the subtle fragrance of the burning candles, the harmonious, quiet, prayerful singing, the very kind, friendly people and, of course, more than anything, the Elder himself, all aglow with kindness and heavenly grace. I liked very much the beautiful voices of Mother Agrippina, Mother Barbara, Xenia Ivanovna, and Agafya Ivanovna. They didn't just have beautiful voices—the way that they sang was very prayerful and monastic. I revered them, I took delight in their singing, while I seemed to myself to be a nothing and a pitiful one. When the service was over, everyone would go to the cloakroom and Mother Agrippina would say to me, "Rayushka, get ready to spend the night with us." From these words my heart would stop from happiness. Five seconds later I would be ready and joyfully waiting for Mother Agrippina and the others. I must say that I wasn't the only one who liked Mother Agrippina. Everyone in Melkombinat, especially the young, loved her.

Here I became acquainted with yet another pretty girl—Raisa Voshchinnikova, whom I had noticed in the church a year earlier. Now I came to know her more closely, and I liked not only her outward appearance, but also her sweet, affectionate character and her intelligence. We often went together with Raisa to spend the night at Lower Street. Raisa also liked Mother Agrippina, and all three of us usually walked together—the two Raisas on either side, and Mother Agrippina in the middle.

Since the old house on Lower Street was cramped and was already becoming unsuitable, they began to build a new house after Pentecost in 1953. The construction was supervised by Mother Agrippina. She gathered the workers, paid them, and organized their feeding. The construction went very quickly—by the Feast of the Exaltation of the Cross* of that year the house was ready. Excepting Saturdays, Sundays, and the greater and lesser church feasts, the house was built in forty to forty-five days. I worked from the first to the last day of construction. We were fed well, and the assistant workers were paid three rubles a day, which at that time was not bad money. It was quite interesting and enjoyable to work, and there were always a lot of people. The table was set right out in the street. In addition to giving them seconds, Mother Agrippina pampered the workers—one with a pie, one with an apple, another with candy. Those were still poor years, and even I, for example, was never really full; candy and pies meant something back then. Everyone worked with great enthusiasm and inspiration, and an unusual flow of spiritual and physical strength could be felt. The mood of all was tranquil and benevolent towards one another.

The Elder would often come to the construction site and would occasionally come on foot. What a joy it was for all of us! Everyone would instantly stop their work and rush to take a blessing from him. He would bless everyone with love and thank the workers with warm, sincere words. He almost always smiled and would sometimes tell an amusing story from his own life. Fr. Sebastian had a great sense of humor and a subtle understanding, and he valued this in others. Mother Agrippina usually asked him for advice, and he would listen to her attentively, sometimes intently thinking over what was said to him, and he always gave wise, professional advice. He was always well-informed in all spheres of human activity and was able to give wise advice to anyone.

After such visits our souls were even more joyful, and the work would proceed even better. In the evening, after work, everyone except me went off to their homes. There would be

*September 14 (o.s.).—ED.

279

four of us left—Mother Agrippina, Mother Barbara, Mother Thekla and I. We would have some tea and then sit on a bench and sing songs: Mother Barbara sang alto, Mother Agrippina sang first soprano, and I would quietly join in. We especially liked the song, "Across the Heavens at Midnight, an Angel Flew." The nights were warm and moonlit, and the multicolored lights of the brilliant stars played and winked at us. My soul, overflowing with unearthly joy, would be carried away somewhere distant, beyond the clouds. One would think only of that which was sublimely beautiful and radiant. These were unforgettable moments.

In the daytime I often had to knead straw into the clay, and it was amazing that I liked this work. Once, as usual, the three of us were sitting and singing songs. I looked at my boots, covered with clay, and said, "Such nice boots—what a shame it is to wash them off. After all, tomorrow I'm going to knead clay anyway!" Everyone laughed at my suggestion, but advised me to wash my feet anyway. I (and not only I) felt happy all the time, and there always flickered in my soul a feeling of gratitude towards Fr. Sebastian, who had so abruptly changed my lot for the better. I constantly thought, "My God! Why am I so happy?! Why, I'm associating with and walking on the same ground with such extraordinary people!" I wanted to somehow thank these people, to be at my best before them; I wanted them to notice me, too. I constantly felt within myself a spiritual enthusiasm; I worked with zest, not knowing fatigue. I usually woke up very early and couldn't sleep any more due to my excitedly happy state. Therefore I would immediately get down to work: I would tidy up the henhouse, sweep the courtyard, and carry over the sand and water. Mothers Agrippina, Barbara and Thekla would say to me, "Well, what a worker this little girl is!"

They noticed in me an ability to draw, and Fr. Sebastian blessed me to learn to paint icons from Mother Agnia.

Therefore, after I finished the tenth grade, for a year I didn't study anywhere or work, but would disappear for whole days in the church and would also run errands. I liked this work better than painting, since there were no conditions at all for studying. Mother Agnia was huddled in a tiny room, was not healthy and was overloaded with work, and therefore she had no time for disciples.

That year was not wasted for me—I studied quite a bit and learned much. Being in church every day, I gradually learned to sing and became acquainted with the church rubrics, mastered the singing of church hymns and could already sing, with one other person, Pannikhidas, Molebens and funerals. On weekdays the Elder sometimes took me along with him to funerals, commemorative dinners, and house blessings. Despite the fact that he was enormously busy, Fr. Sebastian always remembered others; he knew that there was a little girl spinning around there somewhere, whom he needed to make happy for a while and take along with him. At the beginning of the 1950s, when the church was not yet registered, we often served in another church house, located a hundred steps from the main building, in which a very religious Mordvinian woman, Pelagia, had lived earlier.

I remember how in 1954 I heard the All-night Vigil for the Nativity of Christ for the first time. As I entered the Mordvinian's house at five in the afternoon, I saw Mothers Barbara, Agrippina, Mother Parasceva, and Xenia Ivanovna standing in the front corner of the large room in black festal dresses and snow-white kerchiefs, beautiful and majestic. They joined in the singing with harmonious and reverent angelic voices: "God is with us, understand O ye nations, and submit yourselves, for God is with us!"* It was such wonderful singing that I was stunned; chills went through my body, and my soul exulted

---

*From the service of Great Compline.—ED.

from the joy and light that overflowed within it. I stood there quietly, forgetting everything in the world, and wept softly from happiness. Later, every time I would hear a church choral song for the first time, my reaction would always be the same. Music always penetrated to the very bottom of my soul and overturned everything there....

Valya Patrina now stood on the cliros and sang alto beside Mother Barbara. She didn't have a loud voice, but a gentle, pleasant one; and she herself was a very good girl—pretty, modest, and neat. She would stand through the whole service just like a candle, without stirring, not shifting from one foot to the other, not sitting for a minute, and not looking off to the side. She would stand through the whole long service, with her arms crossed on her chest, and would look only at the icons, the book and the notes. I always admired her and envied her with a radiant envy.

Of all the nuns who were there then, each of whom was remarkable in her own way, the friendliest, the most sociable and kindest was Mother Agrippina. Besides the fact that she helped Fr. Sebastian with the management of the household, she still devoted much attention to the young women. She nursed them, just like a sitting-hen would nurse her chicks. They in their turn would reach out for her, and therefore Agrippina Dimitrievna was always surrounded by young people. The first thing she did with a new girl was to check her singing abilities, and if she discovered even a little potential, she would take her under her wing. She would place one who possessed talent near the cliros, right beside her, since the cliros was not enormous then, and she would begin to work with her: here she would have to reprimand her, and there she would have to praise her. She would constantly say to me, "Louder, more boldly; sing!" After services she would solicitously gather all her chicks for practice and seat them conveniently and correctly, usually in such a way that the new girls sat in front of those who were more experienced. I most often sat in front of Raisa Voshchinnikova and was amazed at how, with her pretty, gentle voice, she could precisely and correctly sing from sheet music.

Mother Barbara, Xenia Ivanovna, and Agafya Ivanovna also regarded us attentively, for which we not only respected them, but even revered them. They, of course, earned such a reverently trembling regard. They were all devoid of even a hint of jealousy towards their future replacements. They were not afraid that the young ones, having learned to sing, would overshadow the older ones. None of them suffered from this human weakness. After their departure there was no one on the cliros like them.

In the autumn of 1954, at the Elder's blessing, I enrolled in medical school. He basically sent all the young women to study to be nurses. Also graduating medical school, besides me, were Raisa Voshchinnikova, Alla Nesterova, Thaisia Fomina,* Zhenya Korshunova, Valya Dolgova, Ludmilla Sadovikova and others. Some of them worked in the hospitals as nurses. There were also doctors among the Elder's admirers, as well as other specialists with a higher education.

Right up until his repose he occupied himself with the outfitting of the church. He was constantly concerned with how, out of a simple house, he could make a comfortable, beautiful, cozy and inexpensive church. This was done under Fr. Sebastian's auspices with all kinds of resourceful additions and reconstructions. The first major reconstruction was done in 1955. At that time they tore down the main exterior wall and pushed it back two or three yards. The work that was done was enormous and complicated, but on the other hand, the church became more spacious. When they demolished the interior partitions, it became even more roomy.

In 1959 they did the second major reconstruction. This time the work that was done was even more labor intensive.

---

*Elder Sebastian's grand-niece.

First, they took out the old floors, along with the joists and the brick pilings. A layer of earth was removed to a depth of two-and-a-half feet, and along the whole perimeter they laid a new stone foundation and a new floor. Now the church had become almost a yard taller. Then they built a new narthex, replaced the roof, and erected two small domes on it. They built several household accomodations, a baptistry, a room for serving Pannikhidas, and a prosphora bakery.

During the Elder's time there was always cleanliness and order in the church. Fr. Sebastian was an assiduous manager and saw to it that the money was spent economically, that nothing was lost, and that nothing was thrown out. The work force lacked nothing. In the middle of the 1950s, having heard about the Elder's God-pleasing life, people began to come to him from all ends of the country. Some, with his blessing, moved to Karaganda permanently. Fr. Sebastian received them all with love, helped them all with advice, and gave some material assistance. Being gifted with an exceptional memory, he knew by name and patronymic not only his own spiritual children, but even their relatives, and he knew their needs, anxieties and cares. Since Fr. Sebastian was endowed by God with the gift of foresight, all of his spiritual children (at first there were dozens, but later hundreds) would not make a single serious step without his blessing; and if someone did, he would repent deeply of it later. All the believing parishioners who knew and respected the Elder lived as one harmonious family, helping and coming to one another's aid.

In the spring of 1955 my family was robbed, although we had nothing to steal. They broke the window, tied up my brother, and hit my mother over the head so hard that she lost consciousness. When I was informed of this and came running home, a pile of things, and even money, already lay in the corner of the room. This had all been brought to us by believers.

They all responded to our misfortune and shared with us, down to their last things.

The Elder had a beneficial influence on people; when near him they became nobler, kinder. Around him there was a constant, highly moral field; and finding oneself in it, it was impossible to commit a mean or improper deed. Many were simply afraid of Fr. Sebastian's all-seeing eye. Remembering and knowing everything about each member of the community, he not only helped those in need himself, but instructed others to do this. He constantly reminded them—this one needs to be taken to the hospital; this one needs to be helped with labor; that one needs material assistance. And no one ever dared to refuse him. Without complaining of tiredness or lack of time, people did good with joy. Therefore God helped them, and the work went successfully. Everyone almost always had joy in their souls.

Fr. Sebastian was an affectionate spiritual father for his flock. Even while censing the church he cast his attentive gaze over all the worshipers and would commit to memory who was in church and who wasn't. He even noticed what frame of mind they were in. Once my mother was complaining about my brother, that he didn't go to church, but Fr. Sebastian said to her, "What do you mean, he doesn't go? He was there recently—I saw him!"

He especially kept his eye on the singers. If one of the beginners in the choir didn't stand in her place due to a feeling of inhibition or depression, the Elder would without fail notice this and sometimes, during the censing, would take the "modest one" by the hand and lead her to the cliros. Any grievance or inhibition would instantly pass.

As a wise, far-seeing organizer, he took great care for the church personnel. He considered the main ones to be the singers, the readers, and the psalmists. He tried to introduce all the young people to singing and to place them on the cliros. In such instances he would say, "Grusha, see if she's got a good ear!" But sometimes, without any verification, he would place someone on the cliros. And he was never mistaken. Everyone that the Elder assigned to the cliros later became a good singer. Everyone knew how to read. During the Elder's time there was no lack of church singers and readers, and even on minor feasts the cliros would be full of singers. Fr. Sebastian was a refined expert in and a great lover of church singing. He greatly valued singers, and he gathered them and helped them. For a good singer he would spare nothing. Mother Agrippina would often distribute from three to ten rubles apiece to the singers from the Elder's personal money, and on great feasts the singers were given presents. Even two years before his death, being quite sick, the Elder organized a left cliros, which later played a large role in the life of the church. After Fr. Sebastian no one took such care of the choir members. Those who later served in the church, who laid claim to being his followers, were indifferent to church singing. "The left cliros is singing itself hoarse!" they would say. But the Elder, even during the last years of his life, would look at the cliros several times during the service to see if everything was all right there. His heart really ached for the choir.

In 1959 three spiritual sisters, Katya, Kania, and Tanya, at the blessing and advice of Fr. Sebastian, took into their home from the hospital a gravely ill, immobile girl, Margarita, who had no relatives. They surrounded her with exceptional care, attention and love. They looked after her as their closest, dearest one. The Elder cared for her, often visiting her. He would talk with her, comforting her and giving her money. Believers from the whole settlement of Melkombinat, in an uninterrupted flood, went to visit and console the sick girl. She was quite touched by this extraordinary care and was endlessly grateful to Fr. Sebastian and all the believers. She did not wish to die as much as she dreamed of recovering. But, unfortunately, she died in the arms of those loving, good people.

There were many young people in our community—mostly girls, but there were a few boys, too. Fr. Sebastian, being a refined psychologist and an expert on human souls, knew the latent desire of youth for new impressions and strove to do much for them. Several times, using his own means, he organized trips for young people to the cities of Balkhash and Borovoye. For instance, in 1956 several people (Raisa Voshchinnikova, Maria Obraztsova, Vera Afanasievna, Nadezhda Vladimirovna and the author of these lines) went to Balkhash. The Elder prudently and wisely always put a group together in such a way that there were those that were young and those that were not so young in it. We went to the local church there and were the guests of the priest, Fr. Athanasius, whom we liked a great deal. We bathed in the river, strolled through the city, and admired the lake, which was then clean and full of water. We spent the time quite well and were supplied with fresh impressions, being very thankful to the Elder for this.... He used any opportunity to make young people happy. He had no particular favorites; he basically regarded all equally, and by this he united people even more around him.

Fr. Sebastian greatly loved to come to Melkombinat and did so often, as long as he had the strength. He frequently stayed with the Zhukovs or with Natalia Andreyevna, who at that time was living with Maria Obraztsova and Marusya Berezhnova. They always awaited him with great expectation and made preparations for his arrival, especially in the summer, since he liked to walk in the garden. Therefore they would bring everything in the garden into an orderly state, since the Elder might reprimand them if he saw disarray. No one wanted to receive such reprimands, so they tried hard. I especially liked it when he would stay with Natalia Andreyevna. They had a large, well-tended garden, and in their cozy home there was even a special room for church services. After services at home, no one wanted to leave. They would feed everyone lunch, and would receive the Elder's blessing. Then they would sing songs, which he greatly loved. He especially liked the song, "O Terrible Death!" At this point he would rest for a little while, and then everyone would walk together to see Zoya Shmoilova, Shura Kopylova, the Zhukovs, the Patrinas and others. No one would go home before the Elder left.

Even on lesser church feasts there were always many people in church. For the most part, all the parishioners were from Melkombinat. For morning services, especially during Great Lent, they would get up at five o'clock and go on foot across the dam. I remember once, on the first day of the Fast, there were three of us walking: Maria Obraztsova, Alla Nesterova and I. We left at 4:30 in the morning and we were already at the church by 5:30.

I also remember how in the beginning of the 1960s, on the evening of Great Thursday, after the reading of the Twelve Gospels, all of Melkombinat left the church with lit candles, going on foot across the dam. The night was quiet, and we walked like that for a long time, while the candles burned brightly and evenly. This was a touching and majestic sight. But the main grandeur of that procession was in the spiritual unity of the people. This unity was present in all deeds and events, large and small, joyful and sorrowful. The funerals of all the members of the community were also crowded. Nobody was asked to go or talked into it; they all came on their own, knowing that it was the sacred duty of each of them. I remember how when back in 1960 Xenia Ivanovna Dolgova died, they carried her in their arms and sang the whole way from her house to the church, about one and a half miles. There were a great many people.

Everyone strove to spend more time near the Elder, and thus after the end of the Liturgy, the Moleben and the Pannikhida, they didn't want to go home. If there was an All-night Vigil that evening they would remain until evening, and sometimes even until morning, since they again did not want to go home in the evening after the Vigil.

Vera Afanasievna and Maria Obraztsova became the Elder's cell-attendants from the beginning of the 1960s until the end [of his life], and were always there. Valya Dolgova, Alla Nesterova, Zhenya Korshunova and the author of these lines worked as nurses in the clinical hospital, located not far from the church. Even on those days when we were at home, we would drop by the church in the morning before work to take a blessing from Fr. Sebastian. And in the evening, after the change of shift, we would drop by again to stand for a while at services and to take a blessing from the Elder once again.

In the church courtyard was the Elder's cell and the lodge, where the sole, kind mistress was Mother Anastasia. Half of the lodge, where long plank beds stood, was closed off with a curtain in the daytime, while in the second half there stood the stove and a table which was never empty, since there were always people there being fed. The plank beds were likewise never empty. Several people slept on them each night, and on great feasts the beds would be totally occupied. After a Vigil everyone would go to the lodge to have dinner. Then Fr. Sebastian would bless everyone, and sometimes they would sing songs. The cell-attendant at that time, Maria Obraztsova, a very good and kind woman, would sometimes make a suggestion to the Elder if one of those spending the night was in a bad frame of mind. He would invite that person to plait his hair into a braid. While doing it she would relate her woes to him, the reasons for her bad state, and he would calm her down. To plait the Elder's braid was the cherished dream of each of us. Usually after doing this, all grief and sorrow would vanish as if by magic.

Fr. Sebastian knew the church rubrics quite well. With him church services were conducted strictly according to the rule—nothing was either changed or shortened. After the conclusion of services, he almost always went to the cliros and thanked the singers. Sometimes, in a delicate way, he would reprove them. He greatly loved quiet, harmonious, prayerful singing. At the table and in his free time he would often hold conversations about singing and singers, relating interesting incidents from his monastery life. He constantly reminded us that one need not take pride in talent if there is any, since all is in God's hands. God gives talent, but due to pride He can also take it back.

There weren't only angels gathered under Fr. Sebastian's wing. There were also capricious people with difficult personalities, and opinionated and agressive people. But the Elder found an approach to everyone—he would find a key to fit every sullen, reserved soul. People constantly went to him with complaints, with social squabbles, and asked his help in unravelling their complex tangle of problems. He always helped, heard them out attentively, and tried to thoroughly investigate the essence of the problem. When he did this he would gaze with such love and kindness straight into the eyes of the one with whom he was speaking that gradually the truth would be revealed to him; and if these problems had been created by the complainer himself, the latter would become ashamed. There were some that the Elder had to convince for a long time, bringing forth examples from his own life in the monastery. Everyone would leave him in a totally different state—calm and at peace.

He considered patience and humility to be the chief virtues. During his time there was no open enmity, hatred or gossip in our community. He was condescending towards people, forgiving their weaknesses and shortcomings, and did not demand too much from them. For instance, he permitted the weak and the sick to eat milk products during fasts, and would some-times say, "It's better to eat meat than one another." He didn't like it when certain people would begin, with excessive zeal, to pray or to fast at an inappropriate time. He would even scold people for this. Fr. Sebastian did not like any kind of extremes or anything excessive.

He did not advise young women to marry. But when Raisa Voshchinnikova once openly admitted to the Elder that she loved children and wanted to have her own little girl, he smiled and said, "Well, all right! Then come with a little girl! Only don't forget the church!"

What is there to say about myself? Now I'm already sixty-one years old. By the Elder's blessing I've worked my whole life as a nurse and have sung in the church choir. In my soul there constantly glimmers a feeling of gratitude towards Fr. Sebastian. In a fatherly way he carefully directed my life to the path of Christian love of God and neighbor.

22. Archdeacon Basil Denezhkin

In 1937 my older sister and I were sentenced to ten years in labor camps, according to article 58 of the penal code.* We were in the Karlag for the whole period of the sentence. It was when I was in the 19th Dolinka division during Pascha of 1943 that I heard about Elder Sebastian for the first time. Someone had sent us some prosphora from Karaganda with a note: "Eat this and have no doubts. Hieromonk Sebastian from Optina Monastery was serving." We were very happy to break the fast on the holy day of Pascha with the prosphora. After eating the prosphora, which we shared with other believers, our hearts felt joy; and we

---

*This section dealt with "counter-revolutionary sabotage" and could be applied to any action judged to have negative economic impact.—Ed.

ОБЫКНОВЕННЫЙ РАЗВОД.

THE USUAL CHANGE OF SHIFT
[*See p. 182 for information on these drawings.*]

Ночь.

NIGHT

were inspired with the hope of seeing the Elder with our own eyes and receiving from him the spiritual sustenance that we needed.

The long years of waiting went by. In 1947 I was released from the camp and exiled to the Uspensk mine. My sister was also released. With great effort we received permission for us to be in exile together at the Uspensk mine. In 1951 our younger sister Olga came from our home town to live with us. It had been difficult for her to live alone in the rural environment. Our friends advised Olga to go to Fr. Sebastian in Karaganda. She went, and the Elder blessed her to stay in Karaganda and work in Melkombinat. From that time on we became closer to Fr. Sebastian through our correspondence with our sister.

The Elder was well known not only in Karaganda, but also in various parts of Russia. Whoever had visited him and received his blessing and had partaken of his spiritual councils and consolations would preserve very kind memories of him. One archdeacon whom we knew, James, with whom I had spent my term in the Karlag, wrote us from the Vladimir diocese: "You write that your sister Olga has begun living in Melkombinat, which is where I lived in 1945 and 1947, and where Fr. Sebastian often visits; to see and converse with him was for me an absolute delight." In another letter he wrote: "*A new commandment I give unto you, that ye love one another* (John 13:34). Love—this is a true miracle. Fr. Sebastian is important precisely because of his love, and because he has strengthened our lives by his own life, showing himself to be a true apostle of the teaching of love." Further on he included the following poem:

> *In days of doubt, of sacrilege and lies,*
> *When the fallen world is bathed in blood, demented,*
> *For brotherhood among all men he cries,*
> *And his speech with evangelic love is scented.*

Not given to debate, both vain and unavailing,
This true disciple of Christ crucified goes straight
To all those broken, filled with sorrow, and the ailing,
To all grown weak under their crosses' heavy weight.

With spiritual sight, he pierces to our inmost soul
With those who grieve he mourns, and hastes to help the ill,
He is for us a prophet, with ascetic self-control,
And beacon-like, this dismal night with light does fill.

This letter roused in me an even greater desire to see the Elder. In 1953, during Holy Week, I received a week's vacation at the factory in order to have tests for a contusion which I received in an accident in the mine. I got ready for the trip in a great hurry and left on the first train to Karaganda. When I arrived, I tracked down house number 59 on Lower Street. It was Great Thursday. The Elder wasn't at home, but he walked up soon, and behind him an infant was being brought for baptism. I missed the rites of the Church so much that I dared to ask him to permit me to be present at the baptism. He gave his permission. After the baptism he lay down to rest a bit, and the nuns began preparing the trapeza. They gave me the *Lives of Saints* of St. Dimitry of Rostov and asked me to read it aloud. Just as, after a prolonged illness, a recovering organism greedily takes and assimilates food, so did I, who had been starving for spiritual food, zealously take up the reading of the book.

Before long, the Elder came out of his room, said a prayer, and we sat down at trapeza. I entered into conversation with him and reminded him of Archdeacon James, whom we both knew, and with whom we corresponded. Right there at the table I told him by heart the contents of the letter. The nuns liked the poetry very much, and they asked me to write it down. I glanced at the Elder and said, "Of course I'll write it down, if Fr. Sebastian blesses it." He was silent for a moment and replied with a smile,

"They'll throw you in prison for this." He did not seek praise for himself, and we were convinced of this more than once afterwards.

After we had eaten lunch we began to prepare for the service, which was the reading of the Twelve Passion Gospels. The Elder suggested that I go with him, and we went to to the prayer house on West Street. There we entered a small room where there were three nuns. One of them, Mother Anastasia, lay on the bed moaning. The Elder asked, "What's wrong with you, Mother?"

"My head aches, Batiushka."

"Then why did you lie down near the stove? It's hot here." Then he went into the altar and began to prepare everything he would need for the service. He didn't have permission [from the authorities] to serve in the prayer house, so on that day they served in the house of Polya the Mordvinian. The singers came, and the three-room house was stuffed full of worshipers. I stood near the singers, praying and forgetting myself out of joy. Occasionally I posed the question to myself: "Isn't this all a dream?"

The service ended at eleven o'clock and Mother Agrippina came over to me and said, "The Elder has blessed you to spend the night at our place on Lower St. Will you be coming with us?" The sisters hastily got ready and we set out on foot for Lower St. Fr. Sebastian remained at Polya's. Buses were not running there at that time, but they weren't particularly needed. Conversing about spiritual topics we unnoticeably arrived at the house, and old Mother Catherine met us. We had dinner and read the Prayers Before Sleep. Mother Agrippina led me to the Elder's room and said, "Here—you'll sleep on the Elder's bed." I don't remember whether I felt fear, but what a joyful feeling filled my whole being.

The next day, after the Burial Service with the Winding Sheet, I confessed to the Elder. I had been used to confessing from my childhood, and now I sensed that Fr. Sebastian's

Confession was special; it breathed with more love than grief. When I had set forth everything that had accumulated on my soul for the past few years, he covered me with his epitrachileon and read the prayer of absolution; tears ran involuntarily down my cheeks. I felt such relief in my soul, as though I had been born again into the world.

On the evening of Great Saturday my sister Olga and I came to the prayer house. There were many people gathered there—everyone had brought *kulich* and *pascha** to be blessed. They were waiting for Fr. Sebastian; he was going from house to house in Mikhailovka, blessing the *paschas*. The people were worried, because the police had come and said, "What's the priest going from house to house for? Let him serve in the prayer house." Soon the Elder arrived, and he was told that the police had come and ordered him to serve in the prayer house. The Elder also became concerned and asked, "But did they give permission in writing?"

"No."

"Well, in that case we can't serve. Go to your homes. Those who are from Melkombinat should come to us at Lower Street in small groups, and I'll bless your *paschas* there." We went in, the Elder blessed the *paschas*, and those from Melkombinat went home straight across the dam, singing Paschal *irmoi* the whole way. When we arrived at Melkombinat at two in the morning, my sister and I, together with some other believers, sang the Paschal Matins, read the Typica service and prepared for Holy Communion.

In the morning after a short rest we gathered in a group and walked around Melkombinat, singing the praises of the Resurrected Lord. In the evening we went to Mikhailovka, where the

---

*Traditional Russian confections served at Pascha. *Kulich* is a sweet egg-bread made with candied fruit, and *pascha* is a sweet cheese mixture formed in a pyramidal shape.—ED.

Elder served Vespers and Matins at home. After the service he informed us that the next day we would serve Liturgy at number 8 Stakhanov Street. The nuns again invited me to spend the night at their house on Lower St. The Elder did not come home for the night and they again had me sleep in his bed. Under the impressions from the Paschal services and the furnishings of the Elder's room, I felt as though I were in paradise.

In the morning the service proceeded festively and prayerfully, despite the fact that the large house was quite crowded, full of worshipers. After the service everyone gathered at the common trapeza, where I recognized Mother Anastasia. She was so joyful; she treated me with paschal food, and I exulted in soul together with her.

On the third and fourth days of Pascha, the services were celebrated at the same place, the house on Stakhanov Street. What patience was needed to serve from one day to the next for many years under such conditions!

My vacation was over, and I had to return home. After receiving Fr. Sebastian's blessing and saying goodbye to my younger sister, I returned safely to the Uspensk mine where my older sister awaited me. I didn't know how to thank God for sending me this spiritual consolation, especially for my meeting with the Elder. A person who has tasted spiritual food will feel for a long time the calming effect of God's grace in his soul and will strive more and more to acquire this precious spiritual pearl.

In 1954 we had to go through a great trial. Some proxies came from Moscow to the mine and declared that, by official decree, we were to remain in exile at the mine for life; and if we were to leave of our own will, we would face a large prison sentence. This was a blow for us—we had been hoping to move to Karaganda in two or three years. Only one consolation remained for us: to go to Fr. Sebastian and pour out our sorrows to him. During Nativity in 1955, having gotten permission from my supervisors, I came to Karaganda for three days. The Elder attentively heard me out, and after being silent for a moment, he said, "Don't be afraid. This will all gradually pass, and you'll come to live in Karaganda." It was as if a great weight had fallen from my shoulders.

In that same year, when it was once more my turn for a vacation from the factory, I again spent some time at the Elder's. He blessed me to stay with my sister in Melkombinat, where three more young women were living. My sister had great faith in the Elder and was devoted to him. She told me many stories about his visits to Melkombinat, about his spiritual instructions, and about the material support that he had given to many people. "Once," she related, "all of our potatoes were used up by spring. We were sitting and talking about how we needed to go to the market and buy at least a few potatoes. Then we looked out the window and saw that someone was bringing us a sack of potatoes on a sled, and from behind the Elder was helping with his staff."

It would happen that Olga and I would be talking, and she would say, "When I attend a funeral performed by Fr. Sebastian for his spiritual children, I get the desire to have him perform my funeral as well. It seems to me that those souls are blessed for whom he performs funerals and for whom he prays." That's what she said, and the Lord heeded her desire. Soon our Olga was diagnosed with liver cancer. My sister showed amazing patience during her illness. She refused to lie in the hospital and would not take any medication, submitting herself completely to God's will. The Elder often called on her. Three weeks before Olga's death my older sister had a dream: it was as though she were in Olga's room and Olga was saying to her, "Look at what the Elder prepared for me." She opened her wardrobe, and inside were clothes glowing with a golden light, and a golden crown. After seeing that dream, my older sister went the next day to Karaganda and told the Elder about it. He said, "It's not I who prepared these things, but the Lord, Who, for her long suffering, blessed her to prepare monastic garb." And he tonsured Olga. When Olga died, Fr. Sebastian served her funeral. This was on April 1, 1956.

The Elder like to serve funerals for the reposed, especially for those who died in a state of full Christian preparedness. When someone had died without having received Holy Communion, he would turn to their relatives and ask, "Did the reposed receive Communion?"

"No, and it's been a long time; we don't remember." And the Elder would begin to explain: "Listen when we read the prayer of absolution. We refer to their sins and say that the person has repented of all this with a contrite heart. But when we don't know when he or she has repented, we are speaking an untruth before God."

Returning to the Uspensk mine after the funeral, I wondered sadly, "Now when will I be able come to Karaganda again? When will I pray in the church, and see the Elder and all who have become dear to my heart?" God's Providence, however, decided otherwise. Two weeks later a special package was received from Moscow. The contents were as follows: "On April 10, 1956, by the order of the General Prosecutor of the USSR, your exile status is revoked. You have full rights, as a citizen, to free travel throughout the Soviet Union." Not only did it fall to my lot to experience this joy personally, I also took part in the happiness of others, since I was a postal worker. Telegrams flew to relatives and loved ones in all corners of Russia. Applications to resign from jobs due to a desire to depart the area began to come in, and the industry did not hold people back. I also handed in an application for release. The postal supervisor shook my hand in a friendly manner and signed my petition. Our cherished dream of moving to Karaganda was fulfilled. Quickly gathering our modest belongings, I brought our things with my older sister by car to Olga's apartment in Melkombinat. This was on Wednesday of Bright Week. The next day was the fortieth day after Olga's death. Fr. Sebastian and all the Melkombinat believers gathered at her house for it.

The Paschal days flew by, and after them Radonitsa, and I had to arrange my work situation. The Elder blessed me to work as the custodian of the church storeroom. Paul Alexandrovich Kovalenko was then the church warden and he was satisfied with me, since I successfully carried out all the duties which were placed on me. But it would happen that through ignorance I would go against the Elder's blessing. Once in the autumn, on the eve of the Feast of the Apostle and Evangelist John the Theologian, the warden sent me to the village of Dubovka, where our workers had been repairing the house in which the Elder usually served. I saw that the work was nearly finished, and when the workers asked me how long they should work, I told them to work until five o'clock, thinking that they would have the job finished by then. And that's what they did. By the time they arrived in Mikhailovka for the All-night Vigil, which also began at five o'clock, half of the service had gone by. As the Elder especially revered John the Theologian, he summoned me and gave me a stern reprimand. I begged his forgiveness, but this incident remained in my memory for a long time.

Fr. Sebastian did not like to bless his children to go on vacation to other regions, to relatives or acquaintances, and he would often say, "In twenty-five years I haven't gone anywhere and I don't have any desire to travel. The Holy Fathers say, 'You won't be the same when you return to the monastery as you were when you left.' On the way and while resting, while associating with different types of people, you'll scatter everything spiritual that you gathered with difficulty and over much time." One parishioner related the following: "A few years after the end of the war, my relatives began to invite me to come and see them. I went to the Elder for a blessing, but he wouldn't bless it, saying, 'But you have a cow. Go to the state farm and earn feed for her for the winter.' I came home and told my family that Fr. Sebastian wouldn't bless me to go to see my relatives. They began to object, 'You weren't able to explain yourself properly; we'll go and ask him ourselves.' My wife and daughter went and began to try to talk him into it, saying that it had been so many years since we'd seen each other, and they succeeded and got his blessing. I went and visited my relatives, and during our gatherings there the drinking bouts went on at full tilt, a habit which I had broken earlier. I returned home by fall and the cattle were left without feed. But the main thing was that my old illness had returned." From this one could conclude that it was necessary to listen to the Elder from the first word.

Fr. Sebastian took care of everyone who turned to him for help. Once he heard that in Odessa there was a paralyzed priest in a difficult situation. He had been acquainted with the Elder in Optina, and he asked him to bring him to Karaganda. The Elder did not refuse. The priest was brought and settled in his own little house, where he was well taken care of and often brought to church for services. The priest thanked Fr. Sebastian with tears, and died two years later, having made the proper preparations.

Sometimes the Elder bore tribulations caused by those whom he had helped. Once in the beginning of the 1950s a hieromonk Anthony appealed to him for help, and he took him in and blessed him to serve together with him. This hieromonk had an impressive outward appearance and a beautiful voice. He attracted to his side many of the Elder's spiritual children, including some of the closest ones. Eventually Fr. Anthony conceived the desire to send Fr. Sebastian into retirement and serve his parish himself. With this aim he went to Alma-Ata to see His

Eminence Metropolitan Nicholas. The Elder blessed the sexton and a member of the inspection commission, Paul Kuzmich, to go together with him.

"When we entered Metropolitan Nicholas's reception room," Paul Kuzmich later related, "Fr. Anthony began saying that Fr. Sebastian was old and weak, and that Mother Agrippina was giving orders to everyone in the parish. 'Very well,' said the hierarch, 'we'll retire Fr. Sebastian and appoint you in his place.' When I heard these words I began to cry. I fell at the Metropolitan's feet and began to ask him for Christ's sake not to retire Fr. Sebastian. 'After all, he supports so many people, among whom are the ill and paralyzed, such as Hieromonk Parmenus, who has been freed from Dolinka and whom the Elder also took in and provides for. They'll perish without his help.' In this manner I tearfully implored the Metropolitan. He understood that Fr. Anthony had misled him, and he rose from his chair, came over to me and raised me from my knees with the words, 'Brother, don't cry like that. We'll leave Fr. Sebastian in his place; let him serve as he has been. Calm down.'" That is how Paul Kuzmich defended the Elder.

In 1957 the diocese of Petropavlosk and Kustanai was formed, and Karaganda was included in it. Archbishop Joseph (Chernov), who had been released from the Karlag, was appointed as head of the diocese. He began to visit us often. In Karaganda there were three parishes—at the Second Mine, in Tikhonovka, and in Mikhailovka. The Archbishop was attracted to our parish for its prayerful spirit, and, after serving in various churches of Karaganda, he always came to spend the night at the Elder's and would often converse with him.

In 1958 our church warden Paul Alexandrovich Kovalenko was ordained to the priesthood. Fr. Sebastian summoned me and offered me the position of church warden. No matter how much I declined, citing my lack of experience in management

Archbishop Joseph (Chernov) of Alma-Ata in Mikhailovka.

and construction work, I had to accept this job as an obedience and labored in this field for twenty years.

Once a mother and daughter came from Uzbekistan. After services the Elder went to his cell, since he needed to eat. The young woman came up to him for a blessing and said to him, "Is it possible to have a talk with you?" Those close to the Elder thought that he would not bless her right then, but Fr. Sebastian replied that they could, and received them in his cell. They spoke for about an hour; the young woman was worried about her job. She worked as a topographer in the steppe with other young people. The Elder calmed her down and said that this work would be replaced by other work, but that she would have a little difficulty with her apartment, and it soon turned out that way. He blessed them to stay for a few days to pray. During that time she went to see the Elder several times. She related, "I wanted so much to have a small piece of the Elder's podrasnik as a remembrance. I kept this only in my thoughts, but Fr. Sebastian took his summer podrasnik and gave it to me: 'Take this as a remembrance.' I was so amazed at his clairvoyance and at the gift. We reverently preserve it as a dear relic."

Fr. Sebastian's health noticeably weakened, but he did not miss services. Once he had a strangulated hernia. He lay on his back during this tormenting illness, pallid, for half a day. Doctors were called, who suggested an operation, but he did not consent. They themselves were not even certain that he would survive one, due to his weak heart. What patience he had during this affliction—not a groan was heard, not a complaint about the intensity of it. All the worshippers in the church earnestly prayed for his recovery. A day later the strangulation relaxed. The Elder got up from his bed and was again in church to offer up prayers of gratitude.

The Elder accepted his being raised to the rank of archimandrite with profound humility. After the service was over, holding his mitre in his hands, he said, "Here is a mitre. You think it can save you? Only good works according to faith can save." The Elder indeed fulfilled the words of the Gospel: *If any man desire to be first, the same shall be last of all, and servant of all* (Mark 9:35). The Elder prayed for the living, but he especially loved to pray for the dead. This love marked his repose. He greeted Pascha with the living and on Radonitsa passed over to the celestial world to share the Paschal joy with the deceased.

Why did believers love and revere their dear Elder so much? For his selfless pastoral Christian love. If one were to more deeply scrutinize his whole life and activity in the parish and compare it with that of a parish priest, there would be a great difference. A parish priest, if he is of the white [married] clergy, has a family; and his first care is for his family, while his care for the parish is secondary. If the priest is a monastic, which is often encountered these days, he is more immersed within himself; and with cautious apprehension guards himself from the female sex, not entering into close association with them. And this is understandable according to logic and according to the monastic rule.

Fr. Sebastian took upon himself a podvig that not everyone would have the strength for—he sacrificed his monastic repose, and would often receive reproaches instead of gratitude, even from monastics, who did not understand the essence of the matter, but looked at the surface of things. They would make remarks about him: "Fr. Sebastian's always fraternizing with girls." In such cases he would never explain or justify himself. He considered it his sacred duty to save Christian souls. He had in his pastor's heart selfless Christian love. He would send up fervent prayers to God for those whom the Lord had entrusted to him, and for the whole world, tossed by the waves of the sea of life.

How many people Elder Sebastian saved from eternal destruction is known to God alone. This is why his flock and all his spiritual children wept bitterly, accompanying their dear Batiushka into eternity. One's heart felt as if it were bearing an irreplaceable loss. He left us one consolation—to pray in the holy church in which he zealously performed the divine services, offering up fervent prayer to God for his flock and for the whole world, and to visit his dear grave.

When Metropolitan Joseph of Alma-Ata visited Karaganda after the Elder's death, he wished to visit his grave. The parish clergy met him as always. He served a Vigil and Divine Liturgy, and then served Vigil and Liturgy in the second church. He promised to serve a Parastasis for Fr. Sebastian, but then his situation changed and he did not fulfill his promise. This was at the end of winter. He quickly prepared for his departure by plane, but the weather changed and they would not recieve the plane in Alma-Ata due to the weather. The Metropolitan then returned to us from the airport, but still did not serve the Parastasis. The next day the weather calmed down somewhat and His Eminence prepared for his departure. He was brought to the airport, seated on the plane, and flew off for Alma-Ata. What was our astonishment when, after a little more than three hours, he again came to Karaganda! It turned out that they had reached Alma-Ata and circled it, but had to return to Karaganda, since the Alma-Ata airport wouldn't let them in because of the weather. It was only on the third day that he was able to go home. This was a lesson for him not to give a promise to his spiritual father without fulfilling it.

While writing these lines, I have often felt the fatherly love and the power of the Elder's prayers, and in a simple narrative I have set down that which has been preserved in my memory so as not to commit to oblivion his words and deeds, which were so dear to us.

23. ARCHPRIEST EUSTATHIUS PROKOPCHUK
(Church of the Nativity of the Theotokos, Karaganda)

I had known about eldership and elders from my childhood years. I was born in the Ukraine, in a religious family. In our family group there were people of a religious calling as well as monastics, and therefore we often had talks on religious themes, including eldership. In the midst of these talks a desire was imprinted upon my soul—to find an elder during my lifetime. But the way the Lord granted it to me was that, against my will, I was brought to Karaganda in 1945 to work in the mines. On the way I thought that here, in this remote steppe, only atheists could live. But it turned out that aside from civilians, many special-status exiles lived among the mines, the majority of whom were believers. From them I heard that here in the steppe, in the village of Greater Mikhailovka, there was an Elder, Fr. Sebastian. After I heard this, I began trying to see him.

Greater Mikhailovka is located at a distance of six miles from the Kirov mine. The only transport at that time was by cart, and I did not own a horse. I somehow got hold of a bicycle and rode to Mikhailovka. There I found Lower Street and located the Elder's dugout by number. I got off the bicycle and stopped at the door.... I was gripped by fear—how could I, such a sinner, enter the Elder's cell? I squatted down and began to weep.... Nevertheless, plucking up my courage, I decided to go in. I knocked and a nun opened the door, let me into the room, and offered me a seat. Fr. Sebastian wasn't home, but when he arrived I stood up to get his blessing. But he walked past me to the icon corner, crossed himself, made three bows, and then came up to me and blessed me. I looked at him and thought, "Well, the Lord has led me to an elder."

That was in 1948. I had a question for him concerning my private life. I had met a girl and wanted to marry her. The Elder heard me out and blessed me to come to see him together with her. We came, and he performed the marriage ceremony for us and instructed us. From that time we began coming to see him regularly and became "Batiushka-ites." But in conversations the Elder would, from time to time, call me "Fr. Eustathius." I didn't attach any meaning to this, thinking that "father" meant the father of our family. But Mother Alexandra said, "You'll probably serve as a priest, since the Elder calls you "Fr. Eustathius." Within me was born the desire to study in a seminary. I told Fr. Sebastian about this. He blessed me, and I began to prepare myself. But all the same I couldn't make up my mind to leave. A year went by, then another…. I had already decided that it was not my fate to study, when once, while I was busy at home with some construction work, with amazing force the thought was suddenly aroused in my consciousness: "I'm going to the seminary!" I immediately dropped everything, sat down on a bench, and again: "I've got to go!" I stood up went over to my wife and told her with determination, "I'm going to study." And that was it. The Elder blessed me. I went, enrolled, and began my studies.

When I finished school I had offers to stay and serve in Russia. I wrote about this to Fr. Sebastian, but he replied, "Write to him and tell him to come here." And so I returned to Karaganda. I needed to be ordained. The Elder told me about this and further said that I would have to dedicate my life entirely to God and the Church. He did not insist, however. His words were, "Whatever you do, that's how it will be." Again I tarried and put it off. I wanted to be a priest, but I can't explain exactly why I didn't get ordained. Perhaps it was the will of God that things happened the way they did. But I had to feed my family, and so again I went to work in the mines, and in my free time I went to see the Elder at the church and sang on the cliros. In the church the nuns would say to me, "An elder's blessing doesn't just pass away. You'll have to be a priest all the same." I should mention that I liked working as a miner, and that I was considered one of the better workers. I would undertake very complex jobs, where it would be difficult to stay alive. The work was attractive to me. I went to church less and less often, while Fr. Sebastian grew weaker.

Then once I got up at five in the morning to go to my shift, and I walked out onto the street. It was warm outside, but it was overcast and a light rain was falling. I looked at the sky and suddenly knew—the Elder had died! Immediately there arose a feeling in me as though something had suddenly come to an end. I went to the room and told my family, "Fr. Sebastian has died." They said, "How? What? How do you know?" And then our neighbor knocked on the window; she had been informed by telephone that the Elder had died. I went to the mine, asked for a leave of absence, and left for Mikhailovka.

The next day we buried the Elder. As I returned from the cemetery, I came to the conclusion that since he had died, everything I had done was lost. My aspirations, my studies in the seminary—all had been in vain. Fr. Sebastian had died, and all was lost, myself included. I came to such a state that nothing gave me joy—neither my family, my work, nor my life. I reached such a point that I decided that I had lost myself hopelessly and that there was no longer a place for me in this world, nor would there be in the age to come, either. There was only hell for me, and that was all. This is what I concluded after Fr. Sebastian's funeral, but I didn't say a word to anyone about it. I figured that nobody could help me any more, so I didn't turn to anyone.

The first night after the funeral I dreamt about a garden. But I can't convey in words what a garden it was! Neither an end nor a border could be seen. There were very tall trees standing there, and beyond the trees, even higher than them, huge golden domes were visible, with shining golden crosses. I looked and was amazed—what churches! What cathedrals! And in the garden, in this abode, there was no sun—rather light was emanating from it. I stood at the very edge of the garden. I looked ahead and saw Fr. Sebastian walking along. He was wearing a black riassa and a skufia, and in his hand was a staff—as he always used to walk. But he was glowing, he had grown younger, and the power in him could be sensed. A monk was accompanying him. It seemed as though someone said to me, "This monk is showing the Elder his heavenly abode." I went up to him for a blessing, and he blessed me, and said, "You, Eustathius, come to me!" He said this twice, and I kissed his hand—it was warm, as usual.

This dream, this vision, and the Elder's words and blessing kept me from total despair.

Nonetheless, I stopped going to his church. My friends from work invited me to sing with them in the church at the Second Mine, and I began to go there.

Ten years went by. I continued singing in the choir and working in the mine. In 1976, in one mine operation we had to take the blower of a local ventilation system out into the passageway. The blower was suspended from the roof of a twenty-foot-high connecting passage. For safety, a rack made of beams was placed under the blower, which would support it in case it fell. I began the job. First I disconnected everything from the blower which had to do with the electrical part, and the blower was left hanging from its suspension bracket. Now, in order to remove it from the bracket, it was necessary to hit the pin by which it was held to the bracket and knock the pin out. Then the blower would fall onto the rack. I examined the rack and determined that if I were to stand on the neighboring platform and strike the pin, the blower would fall on the rack. If the rack would not support its weight and break (the blower weighed 660 pounds), I would be safe on the neighboring platform. And I began the job: I struck the pin, it began to give and was holding on by just a little bit. I hit it one more time; the ventilator fell on the racks and they held its weight. But everything under me broke, and I fell down. While everything was collapsing below me, the first thought that came to me was, "All this is because of my disobedience to the Elder!"

I fell from the twenty-foot height on my back in the mud and mire. My helmet with its light went off to the side, and the light illumined the space above in such a way that I saw that the edge of the rack was breaking and the blower was sliding across the beams right towards me. When I saw this, another thought shot through my consciousness: "Turn on your left side!" This all happened in a fraction of a second. By some miracle I managed to turn on my side and the blower flew past me, only slightly wounding my pelvis. The frightened workers ran towards me and I tried to stand, but my legs didn't work. An ambulance was lowered into the passage, and I was brought up to the surface and taken to the hospital.

On the first night I spent in the hospital I again had an amazing dream. I was in a hospital; only this hospital was not on earth, but in the air. It was very quiet and bright there, but the light was somehow unearthly. I was lying there, as were other patients, and I saw Fr. Alexander Krivonosov, who by that time had already reposed, coming straight through the air. He entered the hospital ward through an open window, came up to me and gave me some very white linen and two white prosphora. I awoke. I became full of joy, and my spirit revived after this dream.

I spent three months in the hospital. When I was released, I could already walk without crutches. I said to myself, "What must be, must be!" and I went slowly, leaning on a cane, to the Mikhailovka Church. As I walked I thought, "If they accept me in the choir, I'll sing. And if they don't accept me, then I'll come here anyway, like the rest of the parishioners." As I came up to the church they were singing the Cherubic Hymn. I went in, and my tears began to flow. I crossed myself, bowed, and mentally addressed the Elder: "Batiushka, forgive your son who has gone astray!" Then the singers saw me and called me to the cliros. After the service, at the cliros Mother Anastasia said to me, "You'll be offered ordination. See that you don't refuse. This will be your last offer." Then I replied, now with determination, "Matushka, I'm ready."

But time passed; I waited and waited, but no offer was made to me, and they ordained others. They passed me over once, and then again. Mother Anastasia had died and they kept passing me by, but I kept silent.

Again I had a dream: Liturgy was being served. Fr. Sebastian was serving, but he was wearing a bishop's vestments—sakkos, omophorion and mitre. They were all golden, and of such beauty as I have never in my life seen. I was standing at the cliros preparing for Holy Communion. In the church there were only children. The Elder came out onto the ambo with the chalice and the children surrounded him and waited for Communion. Suddenly the children parted and made way for me: "Go on through!" I went through and approached the Elder, and he communed me with two pieces of Christ's Body. After receiving Communion I awoke.

That very year, on the Sunday of the Triumph of Orthodoxy, I was ordained to the diaconate, and on the next day to the priesthood.

And so, for thirty years, as if it had been one day, I worked in the mines, and it is now eighteen years that I have been serving as a priest in the Church of the Nativity of the Theotokos, founded and built by Elder Sebastian. I believe that the Lord was attentive to my heart's desire, back in my childhood, to find an elder. And to this day, pardoning and chastising me, he preserves my soul under the protection of the Elder's prayers.

24. Elena Alexandrovna Agafonova

I came from Alma-Ata to Karaganda in 1960. I was twenty years old. Fr. Sebastian was not in Mikhailovka on the day of my arrival; he had gone to Melkombinat. Mother Anastasia greeted me cordially, fed me borscht and brought me to see the Elder in Melkombinat. She and I stood at a bus stop next to a four-story paneled house, and she turned to me: "Lena, it would be nice to live on the first floor of such a house!" At the time I didn't attach any meaning to her words, but now I live precisely on the first floor of such a house.

When we arrived in Melkombinat, Fr. Sebastian had just finished praying and was leaving the house. Peter, his driver, came out after him. The Elder looked very kindly at me and blessed me. Mother Anastasia said to Peter, "Peter, take Lena in your arms and carry her to the car!" He replied, "But Matushka, she's so big!"

Fr. Sebastian died long ago, and Mother Anastasia has died as well, but Abbot Peter is alive and his prayers support me greatly.

Fr. Sebastian blessed me to stay with Mother Agnia. Later, my mother came to be with me, and the Elder bought us a small house of our own. I lived in Karaganda until the Elder's repose. The time I spent near him was the happiest time of my life. At that time I didn't have any cares or worries, and all of my problems were resolved very simply by the Elder's prayers.

Fr. Sebastian had many young women in Mikhailovka. They were nuns, and the Elder's prayers united us in such a way that we lived like a single family. For example, he would be hearing confessions and we'd all be standing there, holding our breath. He would give someone some instruction, would say something, and then the prayer of absolution. At that moment it seemed as though we were one person standing there, and one person confessing. Everyone was bound in a single union of love by the Elder's care. He greatly valued this unity and would often tell us, "Eat, drink, and sleep as much as you like, girls; only live more peacefully." He saw a person's difficult life and would try to ease it by his attention and the warmth of his soul. But if a person would approach him trying to test him, or hiding something unkind in his heart, then the Elder would be very strict. Once, after a service, coming out of the altar and walking through the church, he abruptly stopped by a woman we didn't know and suddenly he practically yelled, "What do I know?! Eh?! I know what day it is and the date, and I don't know anything else!" This was said so sternly that we were stupefied. It turned out that the woman had come to test him.

I nevertheless missed Alma-Ata. We were once sitting at the table and I was thinking about Alma-Ata. The Elder said, "Lenushka, do you miss Alma-Ata?" And he blessed me to go to Alma-Ata on my vacation. As I was getting ready to go he gave me a great deal of money and said, "Here, take this, Lenushka; make change and give it to the poor who sit at either side of the stairs at the St. Nicholas Cathedral. Let those who know me and know about me in Alma-Ata pray for me." He also used to give me a lot of bread to give out to my acquaintances in Alma-Ata. Mother Anastasia also sent bread to Alma-Ata. Mother Agnia once gave me a letter to pass on to Archbishop Joseph. When I came to see him and we were talking about Fr. Sebastian, the Archbishop said, "Love him, take pity on him, and carry him in your arms." And before long we made an armchair for the Elder and began carrying him in our arms.

Once, not long before Fr. Sebastian's repose, many girls were gathered in his cell, and he led a discussion about eternity—about eternal life and the infinite blessedness of the saints. They posed a question about holy relics: How does the Lord glorify the body? He conversed with us about everything and at the end of the talk he glanced at us, smiled, and said quietly, "In thirty years my body will be raised from the earth."

In the summer of 1968 there was an attempt made by the Republic of China to cross the Soviet border in the region of Lake Zholanoshkol, in the Semipalatinsk Province. China was laying claim to a part of the territory of Kazakhstan. At the time I was living in Alma-Ata. During that period there was an uneasiness felt in the atmosphere of the city; the faces of the city dwellers were sorrowful and everyone was worried. The believers hurried to the St. Nicholas Cathedral in the morning. After the Liturgy the priest of the St. Nicholas Cathedral, Fr. Paul Milovanov,* came out onto the ambo and addressed all the worshippers: "Brothers and sisters! Let us pray to the Lord and entreat the Heavenly Queen and all the holy God-pleasers that the Lord would have mercy on us and stave off disaster from us." Fr. Paul and all the worshippers dropped to their knees. He read the prayers with tears, and everyone prayed and wept. Then they all venerated the cross. Fr. Paul blessed everyone, and they began slowly to disperse.

That night I had the following dream: the service in the St. Nicholas Cathedral had ended, and everyone was slowly dispersing. I was the last to exit the high porch of the cathedral, and I turned to cross myself. I had just raised my hand to make the sign of the Cross, when I saw that Fr. Sebastian was stepping out of the church onto the porch. Then he stopped at the top of the steps. He was wearing a white linen podrasnik, and his head was uncovered. Light was radiating from him; his eyes were turned towards the heavens, streams of tears were flowing down his cheeks, and these were the words of his prayer: "O Lord, forgive them! O Lord have mercy on them!" I heard his prayerful voice very distinctly. Then I woke up. It was three in the morning. I immediately remembered how, upon sending me to Alma-Ata,

---

*In monasticism Hieromonk Isaac (†1991).

the Elder used to give me bread and money, that they might remember him there.

25. ARCHPRIEST VALERY ZAKHAROV
(Rector of the Saint Nicholas Cathedral in Alma-Ata)

During the 1970s Metropolitan Joseph (Chernov) of Alma-Ata and Kazakhstan said the following words in one of his sermons: "We, the residents of Alma-Ata, live at the foot of the Tyan Shan Mountains. On the one hand we're fortunate because of the beauty of these mountains which brings joy to the human eye, but on the other hand the mountains harbor the danger of earthquakes and sudden floods from mountain runoff. But Alma-Ata will never be carried off by floods, and will never be destroyed by an earthquake, because we have great men of prayer in Metropolitan Nicholas* and Schema-Archimandrite Sebastian." This is what Metropolitan Joseph said; I remember it exactly.

26. METROPOLITAN PITIRIM OF VOLOKOLAMSK AND YURIEV

In 1966 I was included in a group of pilgrims bound for the Holy Land. The head of our group was the then-chairman of the Department of External Church Relations, the now-reposed Metropolitan Nikodim of Leningrad and Ladoga. The trip was intended to be rather crucial—we were to decide a multitude of questions regarding our Ecclesiastical Mission in Jerusalem.

---

*Metropolitan of Alma-Ata and Kazakhstan Nicholas (Mogilevsky), 1878-1955. After spending ten years in labor camps and exile, he directed the Alma-Ata and Kazakhstan dioceses from 1945 to 1955. He is buried in the Central Municipal Cemetery.

On the eve of our departure, during the first days of April, I called Archimandrite Sebastian in Karaganda and asked his holy prayers and a blessing for the journey. But, unexpectedly for me, the Elder advised me to turn down this trip. "That's how it has to be; you'll understand it later," he told me on the phone. His answer simply stunned me—I was in a state of total confusion and bewilderment. On the one hand, I had always believed in and complied with the Elder's blessing; but on the other hand, I thought, how would I explain my refusal to the Metropolitan?

The decision came in an entirely unexpected way. Right before the departure, literally on the eve of it, I came down with an intense fever—my temperature went up to 104°. It was obvious that I would be unable to go. I called Metropolitan Nikodim and informed him of what had happened. Apparently, the Metropolitan was quite upset that my trip would not take place. I spoke with him over the telephone, we discussed our business, and he wished me a speedy recovery.

Several days went by and suddenly there was a call from Karaganda, from Fr. Sebastian. They begged me to fly out immediately to see him. How surprised I was then—the Elder had literally talked me out of such a crucial trip to the Holy Land, and now all of a sudden, "Fly out quickly." But I hastened to fulfill the blessing of Fr. Sebastian, and I was already feeling much better.

On April 3/16, a Saturday, I flew in to Karaganda and drove straight from the airport to the Elder. He looked very bad and was totally weak. I had certainly never seen him like that during any of his other illnesses. He asked me to tonsure him into the schema. The preparations were begun immediately. It was impossible to put it off any longer—the Elder was very weak.

Thanks be to the Lord, everything turned out quite successfully. Despite his exhaustion and weakness, Fr. Sebastian was fully conscious and we succeeded in performing his tonsure into the great angelic schema.

27. ARCHPRIEST ALEXANDER KISELEV
(Rector of the Church of the Nativity of
the Most Holy Theotokos in Karaganda)

I was fifteen years old when, in 1956, I moved from the Tambov Province to Karaganda at Fr. Sebastian's blessing. I had finished school and was living with my parents. On the Feast of the Exaltation of the Cross of the Lord the Elder blessed me to enter the altar and to wear a sticharion. From that time on I began to serve in the altar on feast days.

The time came for me to enter the army. On the day when my notification was being brought before the first commission, the Elder came to Melkombinat where we were living. I went up to him to receive a blessing to go before the commission, and he immediately uttered these prophetic words: "God will grant it—they won't take you, Shura." And, in fact, when I came to see the therapeutist and he took my blood pressure, it turned out to be high. The doctor sent me for tests and gave me a deferment for a month, then for a year, then for two years. Then I had to see the commission annually, but my pressure remained high. Several years later they issued me a military identification card. Thus I never entered the army. But the first words were the Elder's: "God will grant it—they won't take you."

Our family lived for the first four years in a small two-room dugout. In 1961, with Fr. Sebastian's blessing, we bought a somewhat larger house. When he came to bless it, he stayed to spend the night. It must be said that whenever he would come to Melkombinat, people would immediately gather—even sixty or more. It wasn't necessary to invite anyone—everyone would drop what they were doing and come to pray and sit at table with him. If there was a nameday or some other family festivity, then the festivity would be held in common, for all.

Elder Sebastian with the young sub-deacon Alexander Kiselev.

After the Elder had blessed our home and the people had dispersed, we were sitting with him at evening tea and he said, "Shura, make shutters for the windows." I said, "Batiushka, there are all sorts of things needed here." I didn't pay much attention to his words, since there was a lot of work to do around the house. And look what happened: two months later, in the evening, some hooligans threw a brick through the window of the room in which my grandfather lived, and it flew past his head and fell in the corner. Then I remembered that I had to make shutters, and my uncle and I quickly fulfilled this blessing.

There were no empty words with Fr. Sebastian. If he said something, you had to get a blessing and carry it out.

Another incident happened with my grandfather. He was quite old and suffered from senility, and would sometimes rise early, quietly open the door and run off. Then I would get on my bicycle and look for him all over Melkombinat. Once in the late autumn, when snow had already fallen, my grandfather walked out of the house. We looked for him all evening, and in the morning went to Fr. Sebastian: "Batiushka, Grandpa's disappeared; we can't find him." His words were, "Well, that's all right—God will grant it, he'll come back." We didn't see our grandfather for two weeks. We looked for him everywhere—in the hospitals and morgues; and we reported him to the police. We no longer knew what to think. We came to the Elder: "Batiushka, could it be that he was murdered?"

He made as if to agree: "Maybe he was murdered."

"Or maybe something else was done to him?"

"Maybe that's what it was." But the Elder's first words were, "God will grant it, he'll be found." And after two weeks our neighbor brought our grandfather home. He had met him at a bus stop. To this day it remains a mystery where our grandfather had been for two weeks.

There was yet another very interesting incident. One year in Karaganda there was a poor harvest of potatoes, and in the autumn Fr. Sebastian gave a sack or two of potatoes to each of the families of his spiritual children. Among them he gave a sack to my uncle, whose family consisted of three people. Winter went by, and before Pascha our uncle came home and told his wife, "Shura, our neighbors' potatoes which were given to them by the Elder's blessing don't diminish. They were given a sack-full; the whole family has been eating them, and the potatoes haven't decreased."

"And we too," said his wife, "have not been buying potatoes. We've been cooking them all winter, and look—we still have some left." Now that was a miracle. It was unnoticeable, but what was blessed by the Elder didn't diminish.

Here is how I went to the seminary. I was not intending to become a priest, and Fr. Sebastian had never spoken to me about this. By his blessing, I graduated from FZU and acquired the trade of a cabinet and furniture-maker. I worked in a furniture factory, and in my spare time helped out at the church. Two months after the Elder's death, when Fr. Alexander Krivonosov became senior priest, he summoned me and asked, "Sasha, don't you want to go and study at the seminary?" This question was unexpected for me; I hadn't thought about this. I didn't give Fr. Alexander a definite answer, but said, "I'll go and ask my mother's advice."

In the evening my mother and I read the Evening Prayers. Above my bed hung the Elder's portrait, and I asked him to show me in some way what I should do. I went to sleep and had an interesting dream: it was as though Fr. Sebastian was at Fr. Peter's house and was getting ready to go somewhere. I wanted to go up to him with the intention of asking about what I should do, but a woman got ahead of me with her own question. The woman conversed with him and walked off, but for some reason I didn't approach the Elder. At that moment he opened the fence-gate, walked out, and began walking down Spring Lane towards the house where the nuns lived. He walked up to their gate, opened it, and disappeared. I returned to Fr. Peter's house. Mother Anastasia was sitting there, and I posed my question to her: "Matushka, Fr. Alexander asked me if I wouldn't like to go and study at a theological seminary." She looked me intently in the eye and said, "Well, what do you want—to be happy here or there?"

After that dream, which took place at four in the morning, I woke up everyone in the house and recounted it to them—it had made such an impression on me. In the morning I went to Mikhailovka and, this time fully awake, I told everything to Mother Anastasia. She in turn replied to me, "Well, here's what—go to Mother Agnia," and she sent me to the other Eldress. She heard me out and said, "No, I don't know anything—whatever

Mother Anastasia decides." You understand, it's the humility of these great people, when they push you away from themselves. That's how our reposed Elder was. Often, we would accompany him from the church to his cell, and someone would ask him along the way, "Batiushka, my little girl is sick," or, "My husband is sick," the Elder would reply, "You should go to the doctor. Olga Fyodorovna is there, she'll advise you." He himself would pray, and it would help, but he as it were pushed people away from himself. In the same way these eldresses would pass a person back and forth like a soccer ball. I came to Mother Anastasia again: "Matushka," I said, "Mother Agnia sent me back to you."

"Well, good," she said. As it turned out, Fr. Innocent (Prosvirnin), who was then still a student of the theological academy, happened to be right there; he had come to pray at the Elder's grave. "Here's what you two should do—go to Fr. Sebastian's grave, cast lots, and pray. You put them there, and let him pick one up." And early in the morning, even before dawn, we went to the grave, prayed quietly, made prostrations, and Fr. Innocent (he was then still Anatole Ivanovich) picked the lot and—it was God's blessing that I go to the seminary. That's how I ended up at the seminary.

When I was already a student, I interpreted the dream: While I was near the Elder, I didn't have to think about anything; all was well with me. As the Apostles said on the day of Transfiguration: *Lord, it is good for us to be here: if thou wilt, let us make here three tabernacles; one for Thee, and one for Moses, and one for Elias* (Matt. 17:4). But we don't need anything, it's so good for us to be with Thee. In the same way I felt well, and I didn't give much thought to anything. I don't know how to express this in words—one can only experience it. My soul simply felt well, and you didn't have to prompt the heart. I hadn't asked anything of the Elder, and therefore he didn't tell

Alexander Kiselev and Anatole Prosvirnin (right)
at the grave of Elder Sebastian.

me anything. When I was already a student at the seminary,
there were many celebrations in the Lavra and various forums.
There was a Synod—the select people of Patriarch Pimen—and
I was a direct participant, the special courier of the Synod. But I
did not sense that spiritual disposition, that spiritual grace, that
tranquility of soul, that I sensed in the Elder's presence while I
was still a young man. It seemed that the multitude of bishops
and everything that was celebrative and festive … all of this was,
without a doubt, good, but that other … that quietness, that
peace of soul that I felt around Fr. Sebastian; that was no longer
there.

In our church there are certain traditions which were
brought here by the Elder according to the customs he inherited

from Optina. For example, throughout Russia the clergy performs the services for Pentecost in green vestments, but in our church we use white vestments. The Elder explained that the green color on that Feast symbolizes the abundant green of nature, while white symbolizes the Holy Spirit. That is, the spiritual side of the celebration is emphasized. Then on our main Feast of the Nativity of the Most Holy Theotokos we don't have blue vestments, but gold vestments, based on the greatness of the Feast. This was also his blessing. "Thy birth, O Theotokos Virgin, has brought joy to all the inhabited earth; for from thee has shone forth the Sun of Righteousness, Christ our God.... "* That is, here the beginning of our salvation is revealed, and this day reveals to the world the Mother of the Light. This is precisely how Fr. Sebastian theologically understood this celebration.

I remember how once the late Metropolitan Joseph came with Fr. Stephen Teodorovich, who was then his secretary. Fr. Stephen, seeing that they were preparing yellow vestments, objected, "What's this you're preparing? Why? It's a celebration of the Theotokos. His Eminence has blue vestments, and you're preparing yellow ones?" They reported this to the Metropolitan, but he didn't object. "Let it be as they have it," he said. He served in blue, and everyone else was in gold vestments. The altar and the whole church were decorated in gold.

And the Ascension of the Lord is the crown of God's Economy for the salvation of mankind. At Ascension we always have a procession and a common meal. This is because it was on the Feast of Ascension in 1955 that we received permission to open the church. On Ascension we always place a table in the yard, and all who desire, up to five hundred parishioners, partake of the common meal. But on the day of Fr. Sebastian's memory we always serve a Parastasis, a Liturgy for the reposed and a

---

*From the Troparion of the Feast of the Nativity of the Most Holy Theotokos.—ED.

Pannikhida at his grave. On that day there is also a meal for everyone. And just as our Elder always used to help everyone—he would give money and give away everything he had—we too now try to give something to others on the Elder's memorial day. As Batiushka was charitable towards us, so are we trying, to the measure of our capabilities.

Then, during the meat-fare period, on Sundays, when everyone has either gold or yellow vestments, we have dark maroon. Not red, like at Pascha, but dark maroon. This was also the Elder's blessing. And when during the fasts in Moscow they have violet or gold vestments on Sundays, we always have green.

We used to sing Optina melodies at the cliros. But there are few of the older singers left. Little of the earlier chant has been preserved, but we're trying to keep what there is.

There are other customs as well. For example, with us on Saturdays during the All-night Vigil, the Gospel remains before the ambo until the Great Doxology, and only at "Most Blessed art Thou, O Virgin Theotokos..." do we take the Gospel into the altar.

Fr. Sebastian used to read Small Compline in the evenings, and in the mornings before Liturgy the Morning Prayers and two Akathists would be read. Also, during forefeasts and afterfeasts, three-ode Canons would be read during Small Compline, and the verses from the sixth ode of the Canon to the martyrs were always read at the Beatitudes during the Liturgy. The Elder tried to serve correctly and according to the typicon.

Now, through the efforts of our parish, the construction of a new cathedral with three altars is being completed. Like the Elder's church, the main altar will be consecrated in honor of the Nativity of the Most Holy Theotokos. The right altar, like the Optina Skete, will be consecrated in honor of St. John the Forerunner; and the left altar, by the blessing of Archbishop Alexei of

Rector and builder of the new Karaganda church, Archpriest
Alexander Kiselev, at the grave of Elder Sebastian in 1997.

Alma-Ata and Semipalatinsk, will be in honor of St. Sebastian the Confessor, Elder of Karaganda, recipient of the grace of Optina eldership. In this section will be located a shrine containing the relics of St. Sebastian. The cathedral is being built according to classical canons, and its foundation is in the form of Noah's Ark. It has a capacity of twelve hundred people. Its height will be fifty feet, and the highest point of the dome will be ninety-eight feet. They say that Fr. Sebastian had foretold this cathedral, but I didn't hear anything myself. The laying of the cornerstone took place on July 1/14, 1991, on the day of the Holy Unmercenaries Cosmas and Damian.

Exactly four years later, in July of 1995, at the time of the visit of His Holiness Patriarch Alexei II of Moscow and all Russia (this was the first visit of a Russian Patriarch to the land of Kazakhstan in the history of the Russian Church), His Holiness celebrated a Pannikhida for the repose of the innumerable victims of the Karlag, on the square by walls of the already erected cathedral. After the Pannikhida, he unexpectedly drove out to the quiet Mikhailovka cemetery to the grave of the Elder, so dear to everyone as the focal point of the spiritual depths of the unbounded Kazakhstan steppe. There is no doubt that it was by the action of God's Providence that there were representatives of all levels of society and all levels of the spiritual hierarchy gathered at the Elder's grave. The Patriarch, bishops, the clergy, the heads of all the regional and municipal administrations, the Elder's spiritual children, and all of Orthodox Karaganda offered up a prayer before the Lord's throne for the repose in the abodes of the righteous for the Elder—dear and unforgettable to some, little known to others. Fr. Sebastian had gathered everyone together as a heavenly intercessor with a deeply loving heart, as one who sorrows and prays for the race of man.

28. An Anonymous Witness

Saint Stephen the Sabbaite and holy Martyr Sebastian, pray to Christ our God to help us unworthy ones recall in detail Fr. Sebastian's labors of prayer and write trustworthy accounts of them.

People treasure and read with faith—"for their health," as it were—tales about podvigs for Christ.

I heard the following story several years ago, once when I was standing in a line. The conversation dealt with the subject of believers. Someone said that in stories about people of God there are a lot of things out of the ordinary and that these can be assumed to be the inventions of self-aggrandizers. Then one woman standing in line said that, although she personally did not pray to God, for the sake of fairness she had to recount the fate of her daughter.

Unfortunately, I can no longer relate the story as I heard it in the mother's own words. It will be, essentially, a short rendition of her narrative. May the truth be preserved for the sake of Christ.

The daughter of the woman who told the story went to a bathhouse. In the bathhouse a certain woman washing herself next to her asked her to beat her back with bast (bark) strips. When the daughter had carried out the request of this stranger, a misfortune happened to the daughter—she became paralyzed. (She had failed to cross herself.) In such a condition the daughter was taken from the bathhouse to the hospital by ambulance. The daughter lay in the hospital for a year. She was sent home incapable of movement. One old woman advised her mother to turn to the Elder from Mikhailovka.

"When I heard this advice," the mother said, "I thought: How can this old, ignorant man be of any help? After all, they couldn't even help her in the hospital!" But nevertheless maternal love led her, dubious as she was, to the church at Mikhailovka. When the mother of the bedridden girl addressed Fr. Sebastian, he said, "How can an old, ignorant man be of any help?" These words struck the petitioner as a miracle—this had been precisely her thought. The mother began to weep. Fr. Sebastian prayed for a long time at the bedside of her ailing daughter. When he left he said, "Little daughter, when you've learned to walk again, take your children; you'll be living in Mikhailovka near the church." The daughter began to learn to walk the very next day, as if by the word of the Savior, "Arise and walk…."

Some time went by, and the recovered daughter went to work. At home there was much joy. But she didn't move to Mikhailovka to live near the church. They often entertained guests. Imperceptibly a year or a year and a half passed by. Once while out walking, the husband of the formerly sick woman, being jealous of her and a certain guest, struck her with an axe and killed her. Give rest, O God, to thy slave who was slain (due to the sin of disobedience to the Elder).

*   *   *

It is certainly a sin to know about and yet remain silent concerning the prayerful podvigs of Fr. Sebastian, for it is a sin to bury a talent in the ground. For this reason I must speak about myself. I smoked for more than thirty years. And for almost thirty years I had tried to break this pernicious habit, since I suffered from tuberculosis, but I could not refrain from smoking. And then in 1974, if my memory has not deceived me, on the eve of the 31st of December,* there was an Unction service. After Fr. Paul traced the sign of the Cross on my forehead with oil, my first thought was this: "Fr. Sebastian, pray to God that I might quit smoking." Glory be to Christ our God—after this

---

*The day of the commemoration of Martyr Sebastian, and Elder Sebastian's nameday.—ED.

anointing with oil I didn't smoke once, and three years have already passed since I have had the desire to smoke....

*　　*　　*

In the church of the Holy Archangel of God, Michael, I wrote down the names of reposed-in-Christ Tikhon, Joseph, Sebastian and Agnia to be commemorated at a Pannikhida. This was in 1976, on Victory Day [a soviet World War II holiday]. After the end of the Pannikhida I went out to the church courtyard, and my attention was drawn to an old man who was complaining about the pain in his legs. When I asked his name, the old man answered, "Tikhon."

"Did you know Fr. Sebastian?"

"Of course I knew him," said Tikhon, "The Elder blessed me three times; and when he blessed me the third and last time, he explained that he would not say what he was blessing me for. People from all regions and from all kinds of places came to see him."

"And how did people respond to his advice?"

Tikhon related the following: One of his acquaintances, evidently from Saran, came to see Fr. Sebastian for a blessing to buy a cow. The Elder said, "Go to the market. On the way you'll meet a man leading a cow. Ask the price of the cow and give him the money for it, without examining it or haggling." The next day everything happened just as Fr. Sebastian had said. And the cow he bought wound up setting records for milk production.

Further, Tikhon recounted his pilgrimage to the Kiev Caves Lavra in the 1930s. (At that time, those who came to such places were not permitted to stay more than three days, but Tikhon prayed at the Lavra for three months.) During this pilgrimage he visited all the monasteries in Kiev and the other holy places of that city which were prophesied by the Apostle of Christ, Andrew the First-called. In the course of this pilgrimage Tikhon was vouchsafed to see holy relics in a silver coffin that had remained incorrupt for five hundred years. The silver coffin was opened for "doctors" who "took a sample." Tikhon related that after a number of years, during World War II, the Germans were tempted by the silver coffin, but Something forced the armed marauders to put the coffin back in its place. In the Lavra, recalled Tikhon, a priest described the spiritual podvigs for Christ's sake of a worthy individual of the Voronezh Province. (Pray for us, O unknown ascetic of Christ!) This priest said, "When he will have accomplished three hundred podvigs, he will be numbered with the choir of the saints."

"What was done by Elder Sebastian to the glory of Christ will, in time, be gathered together," Tikhon said in conclusion.

*   *   *

On the feast day of St. Nicholas, the slave of God Arsenius spoke about his acquaintance from Termitau. This acquaintance was preparing to go to Alma-Ata to help his son buy a house there. The son already had an agreement with the owner of the house regarding the purchase. The acquaintance came to Fr. Sebastian for a blessing. The Elder refused. He wound up asking him again. He again did not bless. And then he tried yet a third time. "Go ahead, only the business won't work out," said Fr. Sebastian. Having arrived in Alma-Ata, the father busied himself with the processing of the purchase of the house. It turned out that the house that his son wished to buy was due to be demolished. The "business" did not come about.

*   *   *

One Sunday, slave of Christ Theodore related the following: A woman was preparing herself for surgery to remove a malignant tumor. Before entering the hospital reception office, she remembered that she had not received a blessing. She left to see the Elder for a blessing. "Don't rush to the knife," said Fr. Sebastian. This woman is still alive (1975), without having had the operation....

*   *   *

Fr. Sebastian sometimes would say that at Liturgy so many people received Communion, but only a certain number were deemed worthy of Communion. O seer of mysteries, Elder Sebastian, pray to Christ God for us!...

People who often saw Fr. Sebastian amidst his daily circumstances relate that sometimes, without any evident cause, he would say, "Let's rise and pray; such-and-such a person is having a hard time." Later, this "hard time" would always be confirmed. He truly was a "good shepherd."

Fr. Sebastian blessed people to arise at 5:30 a.m. (If you get up at 5:30 a.m., then at 6 a.m. you'll be praying to God.) Apparently, according to medical statistics, the majority of people at the present time die at 6 a.m.

*   *   *

Once Fr. Sebastian suddenly said, "Let's pray. Schema-monk Sabbas just reposed." Mother Evdokia, who was present at the time, guessed or felt that he was speaking about her brother Schema-monk Sabbas and could not keep from sobbing.

"Don't cry," said Fr. Sebastian, "his soul is saved." As we were later informed, the brother of Nun Evdokia, Schema-monk Sabbas, reposed in Jerusalem. His obedience, upon his arrival from Mount Athos, had been to read commemoration lists [for the living and the dead] at the Sepulchre of the Lord. Schema-monk Sabbas testified in his letters to his sister about the mystery of the Divine Fire which descends upon the Lord's Sepulchre from heaven on Great Saturday, and likewise about the mystery of the generation of material fire from the Holy Fire, which ignites a multitude of candles in the Church almost immediately. "The Divine Fire," wrote Schema-monk Sabbas, "only warms but does not burn." He was buried on the Mount of Olives in Jerusalem.

The great slave of God Parasceva, who came from Temirtau (half an hour northwest of Karaganda), asked Fr. Sebastian to make the sign of the Cross over her, "at least over her heart." The Elder made the sign of the the Cross over her heart, the upper part of her abdomen and on her side. In fact, it was true that it was the aged Parasceva's heart, stomach and appendix that hurt. But how could the Elder have known about this without questioning her?

*   *   *

Fr. Sebastian was requested to come to Temirtau to see some extremely ill people. He promised to come the next day and sent Mother Anna to prepare the sick for their meeting.

"I don't know the address; I only know the last name," said Mother Anna when she came for a blessing. In reply, Fr. Sebastian only repeated several times, "You must know it." Toward evening, Mother Anna left for Temirtau on a bus on which there were only six people. She conversed with a fellow traveller and the latter's husband. It turned out that this couple knew the exact address which Mother Anna "had to know."

The next day Fr. Sebastian came to see the sick ones. The bedridden slave of God Michael, who was "rotting alive," asked, "Batiushka, will I be able to walk again?"

"You will. You'll even come to my grave," replied Fr. Sebastian. And turning to the man's relatives, the Elder said, "He'll even work to support himself." A few days later Michael's body began to be cleansed of scales, which turned into scabs covering his skin. Soon Michael began to walk, and recovered his health. He also worked "for himself," and even traveled to the Pskov Caves Monastery.

*   *   *

By God's mercy one can encounter striking examples of foresight into the future even in our own time. Here are cases of clairvoyance related to me by people whose names cannot yet be disclosed.

An elderly couple came to the Elder for a blessing to journey to their home town. Fr. Sebastian said to them, "Wait one week." Six days later the husband reposed. (This is what one slave of God related on the holy eve of the feast of the Bogoliubsk Icon of the Theotokos.)

From the age of eight the slave of God Alexandra was persistently visited, at first in dreams and later in broad daylight, by two figures: an elder and an eldress. When Alexandra was already a young maiden, she moved with her family to live in Karaganda. There at the church she met, in the flesh, the bearers of the images known to her from childhood. These were Elder Sebastian and Eldress Anastasia.

A certain Elder Irinarchus foretold the martyric death of Evdokia, Alexandra's mother, on a "Great Day."

Fr. Sebastian advised Evdokia's family to move to Melkombinat. The move was not an easy matter, and they procrastinated. On Pascha, Evdokia was returning from church on an overcrowded bus; she was squeezed against something made of iron, which ruptured her intestines. The slave of God Eudocia reposed in the hospital. Alexandra personally related this to me at her mother's grave on the Feast of the Holy Trinity.

Fr. Sebastian sometimes refused to bless marriages. "Children aren't needed for hell," he would thus explain his refusal in such cases. However, the Elder was condescending towards those who had gone astray. If someone out of disobedience clearly stood on a path fraught with peril, then he would not leave such a one without pastoral aid.

Holy Elder Sebastian, pray to God for us!

The reliquary of St. Sebastian in the new cathedral.

PART III

The Teachings of Elder Sebastian

Но, о Господи,
щедротами Твоея об
личи нас, ниже гневом
Твоим накажи нас,
Сам даждь нам пре
преже конца покаяти
ся Тебе, Аминь,

A note in the Elder's own hand.

The Teachings of Elder Sebastian

1. On Prayer

The Elder used to say about prayer: "One can pray in any place and at any time—standing, sitting, lying down, during work or while traveling. But to converse in church is sinful."

He would sternly reprimand those who talked in church during the service, especially monastics. Sometimes he would even come out of the altar in his vestments and reprimand them.

He reminded us repeatedly that, upon entering a bus, an airplane, a car, etc., it is essential to silently cross oneself, not paying attention to anyone, even to the laughter of others. Because of one, two, or three believers others can also be saved from terrible misfortunes. An example of this was the following: A few women from a distant place got together in the evening after services to ride home by bus. After Fr. Sebastian blessed them, he prayed for a long time in front of the icon of the Holy Trinity, and everyone noticed this. And what happened? While the bus was descending from a bridge, the driver noticed something black on the road ahead and hit the brakes so hard that the bus flipped over off the bridge and landed on the ground, again standing on its wheels. This all happened so quickly that the passengers hadn't had time to understand what was going on and what had happened to them. All were alive and unharmed except for one girl and the conductor, who received slight injuries.

The sisters who lived with the Elder noticed more than once that he would suddenly walk over to the icon corner and begin silently praying. This was a sign that a prayer for help had come to him from somewhere far off. This would be revealed subsequently. Once, for example, in the city of Tambov, 2,500 miles from Karaganda, a young woman who was walking home late from work began to be pursued by a man. She cried out, "Batiushka, save me!" and was rescued by some kind people.

The Elder used to remark about the sign of the Cross, "One must make the sign of the Cross correctly, with fear of God, with faith, and not just by waving one's hand. And then bow—then it has power."

2. On Humility, Pride, and Faith

Fr. Sebastian would often remind people to forgive one another's offenses and not to harbor remembrance of evil, saying that *God resisteth the proud, but giveth grace unto the humble* (James 4:6). And about the proud: "A raging stallion ends up in a deep pit." There were occasions when due to pride, disobedience and self-opinion people would fall and would endure temptations.

Once one of the members of the choir in the Elder's church, Alexandra by name, all of a sudden, abruptly and strikingly, manifested a strong and beautiful voice. And she began to be proud—she became haughty and began to strut around with her voice and look down on others. Our nuns, especially Mother Barbara, reproved her delicately, but Shura didn't listen to them. Once, on the night of Pascha, Fr. Sebastian sent her, together with some others, to sing Paschal Matins in the chapel, since the people did not all fit into the church, and Matins was also served in the chapel in the courtyard. But Shura flatly refused to go. Everyone was amazed at her refusal and advised her to be obedient to the Elder. But Shura didn't obey. Then he said very sternly, "Shura, don't be proud; God will take your voice away and you won't sing!" He certainly saw it coming! She soon became sick and wound up in the hospital, and when she came back, she could no longer sing—she had lost her voice. The Elder and those around him felt great pity for Shura, but her health and her voice just never returned to her.

The Lord worked miracles among the simple and humble, through the Elder's prayers. One girl still in her childhood had an illness in her eyes. (They became swollen and seemed to be skinned over.) The doctors declined to treat her. Then she turned to Fr. Sebastian, who blessed her to have a Moleben served with the blessing of water before the icon of the Mother of God "Joy of All Who Sorrow," and to wash her eyes with holy water. To the joy of all, the swelling disappeared, her eyes opened and she began to see as she had before.

Those who came with humility and faith that God, through Fr. Sebastian's prayers, would help them in their affairs, he would receive more promptly and would tell them something profitable. But he would not receive anyone who came without the fear of God and without faith, but simply for the sake of curiosity or idle talk. He would say sternly, "I don't know anything; I'm a sinful, sick and ignorant person, like everyone else. What do you think I am, some kind of clairvoyant?" If these people were from another, nearby parish, he would say, "You have your own priests."

Once, during a conversation about human temperaments, the Elder said, and even pointed out to us, "Those people one shouldn't touch; out of pride they can't bear reproofs or reprimands. But others, according to their humility, one can become acquainted with."

Sometimes he would scold one person in front of everyone (he might even be guiltless, but humble and patient), in order to bring to their senses those who could not be spoken to directly about their faults and shortcomings. He would not reproach or expose such people himself and would forbid others to do so; but he would wait, be patient and pray until the person would realize it himself and turn with repentance to God and his spiritual father.

Those who were stronger in spirit he would humble down in front of everyone, delivering them from vainglory and spiritual pride (in the presence of which even good deeds do not bring benefit to the soul, and the person may perish for eternity). Those who understood this would rejoice at such a cleansing and would immediately beg forgiveness and ask for prayers for their correction.

There were occasions when Fr. Sebastian would force those who were older to ask forgiveness of the younger, or he would humble the offended while defending the offenders. There was spiritual wisdom concealed in this. Those who were experienced would understand this and not be offended.

He would appreciate it when a person gradually realized his shortcomings, infirmities, and vices on his own and when, not hoping in himself, he would ask God for help, for deliverance from them, and for mercy. Having repented, the person would receive from God that which he had asked for with humility and thankfulness.

When someone would come with a complaint against his neighbor, especially due to envy or jealousy, then he'd be done for. The Elder would give him such a trying and humiliating lesson and would offer him such a spiritual remedy as would cause him no rejoicing whatever, and he would have no desire to complain again. Fr. Sebastian strove to uproot such complaining from everyone as an infirmity of the soul.

With slanderers and calumniators he would act very wisely: he would punish the slandered one even more than the slanderer had expected him to be punished, thereby evoking shame in the slanderer and teaching him to not accuse his neighbor.

When someone came to the Elder with secret anger against his neighbor, wishing to find in him a defense for himself and to justify himself while accusing his neighbor, then instead of defending him, the Elder would scold him in front of everyone and humble him for his prideful thoughts and deeds.

In the case of offense or misunderstanding he taught people to ask forgiveness of one another and not to remember evil, especially before Communion. And he would give the example of the story of two close friends, Titus and Evagrius, which is known to everyone.*

Another time he would reveal in whom and in what way pride (the beginning of all sins) was appearing. For some it would be in the way they walked, for others it would be in their voice, and for a third type their spiritual pride would be concealed, which is the most dangerous and harmful for a person and which it is necessary to recognize and reveal to one's spiritual father. Only the Lord, through the prayers of one's spiritual father, will lay bare all the innermost recesses of the human soul with all its nuances, and all the serpents hiding in it will crawl out to the surface to the surprise and horror of oneself and others.

---

*The hieromonk Titus and the hierodeacon Evagrius were monks of the Kiev Caves Lavra during the twelfth century. At first they were the closest of friends, but later, through the instigation of the enemy of mankind, there arose such enmity between them that they could not stand even to look at one another. Then Titus fell seriously ill and, coming to his senses, attempted to make peace with his brother before his death. But Evagrius cursed him, saying that he would not be reconciled, either in this life or in the next. An angel then struck Evagrius dead and raised Titus up healthy from his sickbed.

"Every person needs his own particular approach. Something that can be said to the benefit of one can be harmful to another." He often said, "Endure one another's infirmities and shortcomings—in this there is salvation. One does not fight fire with fire, but with water; and evil is conquered with love!"

When two young or old but well-to-do women would agree to live together without the Elder's blessing, he would say, "If only an old and well-off woman would take in a younger woman or a young widow, who would labor and take care of her, and be obedient, and school herself in everything good." He would in no way bless young people to live together. Those who made such agreements would not get along, because they would not yield to one other, and they would not learn anything good. But neither would he bless anyone to live alone, especially the proud and self-willed. He would point out the danger of such a life. As an example he would tell the story about the shiny nail, which would be rubbed by peoples' feet in the threshold. A second, rusty one lay in the far corner and nobody would touch it. To this he would add the saying, "Those who live together scour one another—and all are saved."

About pride, self-assurance, and self-confidence he would give the example of the parable told by the Optina Elders: "On a warm, summer day a beetle flew about and buzzed, 'these are my fields, my meadows, my forests.... ' But suddenly the wind arose, rain began to fall, and the beetle pressed himself under a tiny leaf and squeaked pitifully, 'Don't kick me out of here!'"

One mentally ill woman insulted Fr. Sebastian in front of everyone. She called him and his spiritual children names and also insulted those who looked after her. The Elder calmly responded, "Is that what you think I am? That's just how I really am! Well, go and find yourself someone better!"

He would often answer the question, "How should we live?" with the words of the Optina Elder Ambrose: "Live, don't grieve. Not a soul should you condemn, nor should you disquiet them, and to all my compliments."

To those who were not peaceful amongst themselves he would also say, in the words of the Optina Elders: "They scour one another and all are saved." "Patience and labor will wear everything down." He called resentment or misunderstanding in a family or between single people "spittle from the enemy." When those who had been at enmity made peace, they themselves would realize that this was the case.

3. ON ILLNESS

To those who complained about sickness he would some-times say, "One will pass, and another will find you!" "It is nec-essary for us to be ill; otherwise we won't be saved. Illnesses are gifts from heaven!"

For the consolation of the elderly and the infirm who were grieved that they could not go to God's church, he would say, "I bless you to silently and mentally pray 'Lord have mercy,' and 'O God be merciful unto me, a sinner.' The Lord will hear you. Endure illnesses without grumbling; illnesses cleanse the soul from sins."

To those getting on in years he would sometimes reply with the words of the prophet David: "… *threescore years and ten, and if we be in strength, mayhap fourscore years; and what is more than these is toil and travail* (Ps. 89:10-11). Young people become ill, and so how can the elderly not get ill, when the organism, like clothing, becomes dilapidated with age?"

Others think to improve their health and prolong their lives by drinking wine and eating meat. Fr. Sebastian would say, "No, meat is good for you if you have a healthy heart and stom-ach, but in the opposite case it's only harmful. Vegetarian food is easily assimilated by a sick organism and is therefore beneficial." He would use himself as an example: despite his many illnesses, he did not eat meat, and he lived to an advanced age. Then he would add, "Man does not live by food alone."

The Elder impressed upon us to take care of our health. When it was very cold he would have us dress up in warmer clothes and boots, even though it was not fashionable. "Preserve your health; it's a gift from God. To abuse one's health is sinful before God."

He would not bless certain young people to study past the tenth grade, in view of their poor health. "You'll learn much, but lose your health. And what kind of worker will you be without health? Plus, there will be spiritual devastation—the soul will lose the last spark of God!"

During winter, especially before the Feast of the Nativity of Christ, he would not bless people to whitewash the insides of their houses, protecting the health of his spiritual children and keeping their homes from dampness. He would only bless them to tidy up—that's all. Sometimes he would say, "In the monastery we would whitewash and clean up the rooms only for Pascha."

He did not recommend going to resorts or rest homes: "For that kind of money, undergo treatment at home, rest, and go to God's church more often." He would also say, "When you're sick, thank God!" To those complaining about sickness he would sometimes say: "How do you want to be saved? There's no other way!" "No one inherits two kingdoms, either. Whoever lives here for the flesh, for its pleasure, forgetting about the soul, will be deprived of the Heavenly Kingdom."

There were not a few instances when someone would come up to the Elder with a complaint about some sort of sickness. About this he would say to one person, "I'm sick, too; I have aches, too." He would add, "It will pass!" And everything would pass, and the person would became healthy. But to someone else he would say the same thing, but would not add the words, "It will pass." That meant that it would not go away.

In those cases when somebody was suffering with a headache, Fr Sebastian would advise him to take oil from the lampada before the icon of the Beheading of St. John the Baptist and rub it on his head, as well as to have Molebens served to St. John the Baptist.

There were occasions when someone would make a request: "Batiushka, pray for me—my teeth ache." He would reply, "Don't quarrel with your neighbor, live peacefully, and your teeth won't hurt!"

About certain psychologically or mentally ill people, or those who were possessed, the Elder would say, "This one will recover; this one will, from time to time, end up back in the hospital; this one will remain in such a condition until death." He would console some of the possessed and would persuade them to endure with God's help. "… you will become like the martyrs, and you'll enter the Heavenly Kingdom without going through the tollhouses."

It happened that someone would fall ill, lie at home and think, "If only the Elder would send something to me through somebody, if only a piece of dry bread! I would feel better right away." Soon thereafter someone would come and bring a gift from Fr. Sebastian to the great joy of the sick person. And he would immediately feel better.

He would sometimes say, "Why do some people suffer, become ill, endure sorrows and offenses, etc., almost all of their lives? Because of the sins of their parents and grandparents. These sufferers are like a living sacrifice offered up to atone for the sins of their parents and grandparents."

4. On Tending The Sick and Compassion

Fr. Sebastian impressed upon us to not forget the sick and suffering, especially those who are in the hospital, and to be sensitive and compassionate towards them—we ourselves could become one of them. He blessed many young girls to work in the hospital. "The cruelest heart, looking at such sufferers, may soften and become sympathetic and compassionate towards its neighbor. The soul's salvation depends on this."

Those who were jealous of people who lived in wealth he often took along with him when he went to perform home services for the poorest widows with children, living in earthen dugouts. He would say, "Now have a look at how people live! You love to look at nice houses and those who live in wealth, and you envy that in which there is no salvation. This is where salvation is! This is where the school of compassion and virtue is! To uproot envy you should look at those who live worse than you, and then there will be peace in your soul and not confusion. And you'll stop being envious."

Speaking about the benefit of non-acquisitiveness, the Elder would use as an example one acquaintance of his, a priest who left nothing behind at his death—neither money nor belongings. "How nice! How easy it is to die, when there's nothing superfluous! You'll have a refuge in the Heavenly Kingdom!"

Just as he himself was merciful and compassionate to the ill and infirm, he taught others to be likewise: "In this is our salvation. If you're not merciful towards your neighbors or, even worse, don't forgive them, then how will you ask for mercy and forgiveness for yourself from the Lord?"

But the Elder did not give alms without discernment, and he warned others about this. He especially avoided drunkards. He did not approve of stinginess or wastefulness without need. "Keep to the 'golden mean' in everything."

The following would happen: people who were caring for sick relatives would begin to feel burdened by them and would offend them to the point of tears. Even if they lived a long distance from the Elder, he would see this with his spiritual eyes and would suddenly show up at that family's home. He would calm the sick and offended person, reconcile everyone and pray that the Lord would grant patience and love both to the sick person and to the one taking care of him, unto the salvation of their souls.

5. On Holy Communion and Fasting

He sternly reprimanded those who, on their own initiative, would fast before Communion without a blessing (that is, not eat for one or two or even three days). He wouldn't even allow these people to receive Communion. Those who were weak and infirm he would bless to drink a cup of hot water and eat a piece of roll the night before, so that they would not feel ill by the morning.

Those who had weak or ailing stomachs or lungs he allowed to drink milk or tea with milk on fast days, as medicine, after partaking of the Divine Mysteries. But afterwards in Confession they were to tell the priest that he had allowed this because of sickness and infirmity, and ask God for forgiveness.

Fr. Sebastian would strictly remind the old nuns when they ate meat in the world, breaking the monastic rule (when at such an age even lenten foods should be taken in moderation). But he would not forbid the young ones to eat meat until they reached a certain age. Then he would gradually teach them to get used to breaking themselves of it. He valued moderation in everything.

He repeatedly said, "If you fail to observe the fasts without a good reason, the time will come when you'll be overtaken by sickness. Then you'll fast against your will. The Lord will allow this because of sins."

He would speak with pity of those who rarely came to church and who rarely if ever received Communion (especially the elderly). As an example, he would point out those who lived next door to the church: "They sit on the bench during the whole service but don't come to church, even though they call themselves Christians! And other people who live in distant places, even many miles away from the church, find time, for the sake of the salvation of their souls, to come to church on feast days to pray." He also deplored the fact that few men came to church: "It's almost only women that come; but where are the men?" Occasionally someone would say, "This year more people are coming to church!" However, he would respond, "They're not our people, but those who have come from elsewhere. But from our New City nobody comes, just as before, except for a few women."

Sometimes during Great Lent someone would say, "There were many communicants today." But he would reply, "There were many communicants, but there were not many who truly received Communion."

"Those who receive Communion opportunely should not become proud because of this, and those who are unable to do so due to circumstances should not despair. It happens that only just before a person's death is he vouchsafed to receive Communion for the salvation of his soul."

He often used to say, "The beginning is not valuable, nor is the middle, but the end is precious." He used many edifying examples to teach this, such as when someone at the beginning of the spiritual path would fervently take up prayer, fasting, and so on, even without a blessing, but would subsequently grow cold towards this path and abandon it. But others go forth moderately, with constancy and patience, and surpass everyone else. The Elder valued the middle way in all things, and would say, "All the Holy Fathers trod the royal path."

"Whoever proceeds gradually from the very beginning, without jumping from the first step across two or three others, but gradually passes across, one step after the other to the end, without hurrying, will be saved."

"Moderation, abstinence, discernment, timeliness, and a gradual approach are profitable for all and in everything."

There were occasions when, out of ignorance, some neophytes would approach the Holy Chalice without having confessed. Fr. Sebastian would ask sternly, "Did you confess?" And he would not allow them to receive Communion. After the service he would bring the person to the realization of how one should prepare oneself for partaking of the Holy Mysteries. He was especially upset with those who came late for services without a good reason and would insist on being confessed and communed without the required preparation, and would do so even when in good health. "Only the sick can receive Communion that way, but you're in good health and have a multitude of sins behind you. Is it really possible that you can't find the time to prepare yourself, to cleanse yourself through repentance, come to church on time, listen to the Rule [before Communion] and the service, and, having confessed, approach the Chalice with the fear of God?!" He would not allow such people to receive Communion, and would add, "Approaching the Chalice of the Holy Mysteries is not the same as stepping up to the table for a cup of soup or a cup of tea."

He would become very annoyed with someone who wase ill, or with his relatives, when they would wait to call a priest to give him Communion of the Holy Mysteries until the sick person's tongue could no longer move, or he had lost possession of his faculties. In some instances the relatives were guilty, and in other cases it was the sick person himself who, not having faith, would say reproachfully, "What do you want to do, bury me?" (There is a superstition that partaking of the Holy Mysteries will hasten a sick person's death.)

There was one case where a completely immobile young man received Unction. It seemed to him (as he later related himself) that when the Unction service was over, his wife and children came to him to say farewell, as to a dying man. But God granted that after receiving Unction and Holy Communion he began to get better. He was completely restored to health and began to work and to come to church.

Fr. Sebastian was displeased with those who did not want to receive Unction out of the conviction that only the dying receive Unction. Others believed in the superstition that one should not walk on the ground after receiving Unction, to which the Elder used to say with dissatisfaction, "Well fly then, if you can't walk." He even blessed young people to receive Unction, since almost all are sick in soul and body, and those who receive Unction with faith receive healing, strengthening, and forgiveness of their forgotten sins.

6. On Reverence for Feast Days and Saints

Fr. Sebastian often tried to persuade those in afflictions, illnesses and temptations to call upon the prayers of all the holy God-pleasers and to honor their memory. He likewise said to honor the day of the saint whose name we bear, but not our birthday.

The Elder was not pleased with those who would celebrate their birthdays but not their namedays. He would give the example of Herod, who, during a feast on his birthday, ordered the beheading of St. John the Baptist.

He would get very upset that people revered the feast days of miracle-working icons of the Mother of God more than the Feast of the Nativity of the Mother of God, one of the Twelve Great Feasts, on which day there would be few people at church.

In order to honor the Nativity of the Mother of God, the altar was consecrated in honor of this Feast, and the bishop would come on the Feast, when there would be a great celebration.

During the years that he served, Fr. Sebastian also brought to the awareness of the parishioners the significance and greatness of the holy Apostle John the Theologian and instructed them to come to church on the day of his memory. He would often say, "After all, in your families there is no peace and love among you. Who will help you, if not St. John the Theologian, the Apostle of love? 'Little children, love one another!'"

He often entreated people, and quite sternly warned them, against going to the market or to stores on feast days, that they might escape God's punishment. He taught people to value festal church services, and not to exchange them for anything worldly and harmful to the soul. "Only in church is a man renewed in soul and receives relief from his sorrows and illnesses."

He watched closely that on the Twelve Great Feasts everything would be triumphant and festive, and that the people would be dressed in festive clothes. Even if they were not new, they should at least be colorful. He also saw to it that people try to mark the feast day with food. But during a fast or on a week day he used to take note of those who were dressed in colorful clothes without a reason. He was attentive in everything—both in spiritual things and in earthly, mundane things.

He also used to make sure that the candles were made of pure beeswax, especially in the altar. "God's grace descends upon the aromatic fragrance of beeswax candles," the Elder would say, and he appreciated the labor-loving bee. He often used it as an example to us lazy and careless ones: "The bee offers so much that's useful—wax for God and medicinal honey for man." To children who did not respect their parents, and especially their mothers, he gave the example of how the bees guard their queen—they feel sorry for her, and in the event that she becomes ill they fly above her and fan her with their little wings to ease her condition.

The Elder often tried to persuade people that it's necessary to procure the very best items for the church and to leave the worse things for oneself. "But we do the opposite—we give ourselves that which is better, and give the church that which is worse." He also taught us to labor according to our conscience, to do the best that we can."

7. ON ICONS

Under no condition would the Elder bless us to accept distorted icons from the parishioners (that is, those painted not according to the canons, or carelessly, with distorted faces). But if someone gave old icons that were damaged in places, he would send them to be repaired and then give those icons to those who needed them. He especially valued ancient icons. When he would give someone an icon as a prayerful remembrance, he would sometimes say, "Now this is an ancient icon; it's done with paints." He did not allow people to adorn the icons with brightly-colored paper flowers.

Upon returning from performing services in people's homes, Fr. Sebastian was often distressed about the careless manner in which icons were kept in people's homes. Even if someone owned only one or two icons, they would be dirty, covered with dust, and hung somewhere in a far corner under a dirty curtain, so that no one would see them. But they would put photographs of themselves and their children practically in the icon corner itself.

8. On Order in Church

After services the Elder would bless us to immediately open the doors and vents to air out the room. There was even a schedule compiled for watchmen and guards as to how many hours they should open them before and after the service (taking into account the weather and time of year). He demanded that the cleaning women not raise dust while tidying up and that they protect the icons and gilding from dust and soot. He supervised the service staff and watched how each labored—who would work conscientiously, and who would work lazily and carelessly. During the nights he would observe the watchmen from the little window of his cell, and would sometimes say, "This watchman walked around the grounds all night; I saw it from my little window." About others he'd say, "But that one didn't leave his booth all night, which means he slept and wasn't keeping watch." He forbade such people to keep watch. He likewise observed all good and bad things that took place in the church and in the churchyard, and everything that required correction. Whenever someone walked through the church quickly and without the fear of God, or swung his arms, or shoved others, or even behaved that way outside in the courtyard, he would reprimand him in front of everyone, for the edification of all. He did this especially with those who allowed themselves to run, stamp their feet or make noise, imitating fools-for-Christ's-sake. Fr. Sebastian strictly forbade this. He saw a person's character and the inner condition of his soul by his walk and outward movements. "One should walk quietly and calmly, not taking big steps or stamping one's feet, especially in church, even when in a hurry. After all, the world watches us and takes an example from us." From the Cherubic Hymn until the end of the Liturgy all movement, the sale of candles and the writing of prayer-requests, etc., were forbidden. The Elder taught that one should stay in the church until the end of the Moleben, and therefore only after the Moleben would he bring the cross out to be venerated. He often repeated, "We are all old, weak, infirm, sick, clumsy, and we do everything slowly. That's why the service goes slowly. But when there are young priests, strong and healthy, then everything gets done quickly and the service is over sooner." (Unfortunately, everyone is now convinced of this.)

9. ON SINGING

He liked the singing of the choir to be prayerful and moving. "Shouting is not pleasing to God, nor especially is stamping one's feet. God is not deaf. He hears everything and knows our thoughts."

The Elder paid very close attention to reading and to the singing of the choir, that they be done with fear of God, reverently and prayerfully. He could not endure "shouting," when one person would drown others out. He appreciated the labor and patience of the singers, valued them, and devoted as much attention to them as possible. On feast days he would treat them to tea and give them gifts. He especially liked to give out handkerchiefs or head-scarves. Sometimes he gave out so many that there would be nothing left. Then he would give someone some money to buy more kerchiefs to give out.

10. ON CLOTHING

He scolded those nuns who liked to dress in the monastic garb for show, or those widows or girls living in the world who wore black. He would say, "It's best of all to dress modestly in blue or gray. Black won't save you and red won't cause you to perish." He advised young people to dress in various colors, so as not to be suspect at work and be reviled for no reason.

He also said, "Young people shouldn't devote a great deal of attention to their outward appearance. They shouldn't look after themselves excessively. They should not wash too often and should not dress fashionably, but more casually, not disturbing their own souls and consciences, and not becoming stumbling blocks for others. You want to save yourself and not bother others. But the elderly should be clean and tidy so that others would not have an aversion to them and turn away from them."

11. On Orphans

He regarded orphans with great sympathy and compassion. Upon meeting them he would first feed and comfort them, and then he would look them over from head to toe, to see who was dressed in what, and what sort of shoes they wore. He would question them about everything and would help in word, deed, and prayer. He cared for them as though he were their own mother and father.

12. On the Raising of Children

Fr. Sebastian occasionally spoke about marital ties and conjugal obligations—fidelity, trust, and patience in the event of the sickness of a spouse or of the children. He reproached ungrateful children, reminding them of their parents' cares—their labor, their love, the sleepless nights spent by their bedside during times of illness, and their fear for the life and health of their children. "The Lord deprives such children of happiness," said the Elder. "*Honour thy father and mother …*

that thou mayest live long on the earth (Eph. 6:2, 3)." He set as an example those children who honored their parents during their lives and prayed for them after their deaths.

He often warned parents who taught their children, virtually from their infancy, self-will and self-love: "Now children don't follow after their parents; parents follow their children." He observed how a little boy would tug his grandmother's or mother's hand, saying, "Let's go home; let's go outside!"—if only to leave the church. And the parents would obey and they would leave.

The Elder reproved parents many times for their excessive partiality for or attachment to their children, which reached the point that the parents were just about ready to pray to them instead of to God. "The simplest illiterate peasants dress however they can, in whatever they can find, and are undernourished so as to provide clothing and shoes for their children and educate them on an equal level with the city intelligentsia. But the children, having been educated, begin to despise the illiteracy and poor clothing of their parents and even become embarrassed by them."

Metropolitan Joseph (Chernov) prevailed upon parents to teach children from infancy to not kill living creatures, beginning with cockroaches, small insects, birds, cats, and dogs. Otherwise they will go on to people, and even their own parents will not be spared their cruelty. "Teach them to love and have pity on all of God's creation and not hurt them. This includes plants." But there were some mettlesome mothers who laughed at Metropolitan Joseph's sermon: "What good are cockroaches and little bugs?" They didn't even care to understand the meaning of it—that this wasn't what was beneficial to teach children. (Perhaps someone like that would understand later, when a son or grandson who had grown up hardened would teach her a lesson in childraising.)

13. On Obedience

There were occasions when people who came to see the Elder would hurry to leave as quickly as possible so as to avoid unpleasantness at work and at home. Against their wishes, however, he would detain them for one or two days. Those who were obedient and stayed would return safely, and everything would turn out well for them, both at home and at work. But those who were disobedient and left would encounter unpleasant situations on the way, at home or at work. And they would repent that they had disobeyed the Elder.

On the eve of a feast Fr. Sebastian would not bless anyone to travel, and those who left according to their own will would also not escape hardships and unpleasantness.

He did not approve of those who acted upon their own will, and the outcome of their actions was sad. One of the older girls conceived the idea of getting married without a blessing. Others told the Elder about this, and he answered, "What sort of husband is that? A hoodlum!" They begged and entreated her not to marry him: "If you marry him, you'll suffer!" That is exactly what happened later.

Occasionally the Elder would say in front of everyone, "He who does not learn to obey his parents, peers, elders, and even those younger than he will not obey anyone when he grows up, and no one will ever listen to him either."

14. On Death and Funerals

The Elder would grieve over people who, upon losing one dear to them, would reach the point of despair and hysteria and would cry and sob at the dead person's grave. He said that they were unbelievers. "It's hard for a person who has no faith to die, leaving family and riches; and it's difficult for unbelieving relatives to lose a loved one, in whom they had placed all their earthly happiness. The Lord cuts their hope to pieces, but they don't understand God's will. Though religious relatives also weep over their dead, they do so with reserve; though they grieve as well, it is with moderation. It's all dissolved by prayer and hope in God's help. A believer dies peacefully, as if falling asleep, and at his death his Guardian Angel's last kiss is imprinted on his face."

After the funeral of an unbeliever or of a person who had died unexpectedly, he would sometimes be unable to bear it and would say, "How hard it is to bury such people!" (He conducted funerals for those who had died without repentance and Communion of the Holy Mysteries only to console their loved ones.) And to those who read the Psalter over the bodies of unbelievers (to console the relatives) he would say the same thing: "How hard it is to read the Psalter for them!"

If the Elder was conducting a funeral for an elderly person who had led a pious life, then sometimes after the funeral he would comment, "A ripe ear has dropped into the eternal grainery!" He would speak differently about another person. The fate of the soul of the deceased was known to him.

He became especially distressed about those infants who would die without being given a funeral, in absentia or otherwise. "They still bring them to be baptized, but very rarely do they hold funerals for them. And do you think that few of them die?!"

Sometimes one of the singers, feeling sorry for the Elder, would offer to hold a funeral for a deceased person in absentia on the following day, but he would reply sternly, "And do you know how it is for him there? It can be postponed, but I myself might die, and then that soul will be left without a funeral."

Many times he prevailed on people not to not drink wine at funeral meals, and even more so, vodka. "During fasts serve fasting foods at memorial dinners, and on regular days also eat simply, without many dishes. The reposed have no need of this." He would bless the poor to feed three or four people with some kind of hot food and no more.

When one grieving woman, who had lost her only son, said, "I feel sorry for him—he was so good, obedient, polite to everyone, and a believer," Fr. Sebastian replied, "How good it is that for the rest of your life you'll have kind memories of him. If he had lived, in a year or two he would have become a drunkard with his friends, and his soul would have perished for eternity."

"If only the miners didn't swear and if they would have the fear of God, they would be like martyrs, descending to work underground, as if to their death. How would one know if he would come out of there alive or not?"

15. On Confession with the Elder

It sometimes happened that a person would come to Fr. Sebastian with a weight on his soul, being offended at someone, and his thoughts would be beating him like a hammer—should I tell him this, or something else? But he would have merely to see the Elder and receive his blessing, and everything would vanish like smoke, both the weight and the thoughts. From his affectionate, warm glance one's soul and heart would be warmed. Everything would become light and joyful. There would be nothing to say and no one to complain about; everyone would become good. Like the sun coming out from behind a dark cloud, he would warm and illumine everyone, both sinners and righteous ones. In the presence of the light from these rays a man would realize that he himself was worse than others.

When people talked about visions, he would give only one answer: "Well, I don't see anything!" And he would cite an example from the words of the Holy Fathers, that it is not he who sees angels that is greater, but he that sees his own sins.

16. ON VERBOSITY

He could not tolerate it when someone talked too much, with no point or benefit, and, God forbid, with the purpose of judging. Right then and there he would give him a piece of his mind and humble him down. But he himself would listen to people for the most part silently, and at the end would give an answer to everything in one or two words.

He would rebuke people for verbosity, and even more so for idle talk: "I know that you're capable of talking a lot," he would say to someone for the edification of all, "but I don't have any teeth and my throat hurts, and therefore it's hard for me to speak." In the wake of verbosity and idle talk, a nasty aftertaste would remain, as though someone had poured sand on your soul, even after soul-saving conversations.

The Elder would also say, "He who likes to speak a lot, to talk idly and joke, will have his speech taken away by the Lord at the end of his life." (This was actually observed in several cases.)

17. ON LAUGHTER AND FAMILIARITY OF ADDRESS

Fr. Sebastian could not endure laughter and over-familiarity of address, especially if someone was pushing or tugging, as well as joking, ridiculing and so forth. He gave as an example the Savior, Who never laughed, but wept, which His disciples were witness to. And no one ever saw the Mother of God laughing.

He did not approve of those who did not speak truthfully, even if they were joking. "Always tell the absolute truth and don't laugh. In laughter and familiarity is the beginning of fornication."

18. On God's Help and On Falls

The Elder would say, "Fear falls until your very death, and do not hope in your own strength but only in God's help, calling upon Him in prayer and with humility."

In connection with the fall of one virgin (not one of his close spiritual children), he gave a stern admonition to others: "An open, festering wound which is concealed from a bodily as well as a spiritual physician yields to treatment and healing with difficulty. At the very outset of a temptation, when I might be able to help, you conceal it and don't say anything to me. And now when you're up to your ears in trouble, you weep and beg me, 'Batiushka, save me!' But how can I save you, when it's already too late?!" And he added, "The most ferocious passion is fornication. It can war against a person on his sickbed and even on his deathbed, and especially against those who have spent their earthly life intemperately, until old age. This passion is in one's bones, and is the most shameless of all the passions. No one can be delivered from it on his own. Only the Lord can deliver you, when you turn to Him with tears and a contrite heart. One must keep this battle in mind until one's very death. All it takes is to forget yourself only a little, cease your prayers, lose the fear of God, and it will immediately make itself felt. Only unceasing prayer, the fear of God, the remembrance of death, and the remembrance of judgment, hell and Paradise will drive it off."

Sometimes when somebody would complain about his shortcomings and infirmities, he would reply, "Read books; you'll find everything there!" Some he blessed to read the Lives of Saints, and others he blessed to read the works of the Holy Fathers—each according to his need.

"In the work of your salvation do not forget to run to the help of the Holy Fathers and the holy martyrs. By their prayers the Lord delivers us from the passions. But don't think that any of you will be delivered from them by your own strength. In the war with the passions, place no hope in yourself until your very death. Only the Lord alone has the power to deliver those who ask for His help from the passions. And don't seek repose until your death."

Fr. Sebastian repeatedly told certain people who complained of being bothered by people, demons, passions, etc.: "There can only be repose when 'With the Saints give rest…' is sung. But do not seek repose until death. Man is born, not for rest, but to labor and endure for the sake of the life to come (repose). Here we are wanderers, strangers, guests. Wanderers find no rest in a foreign land, or in foreign matters. One step at a time they go on and on so as to reach their native fatherland, that is, the house of God, the Heavenly Kingdom, as soon as possible. And if here, in this earthly vale of sorrows, in the world of pleasures, one slows one's pace, then evening (that is, one's last days) will come unnoticed; and death will find his soul unprepared, without good works, and there will no longer be any time to do them. Death is inexorable! Neither a rich man, with all his wealth, nor a miser with all his money, nor a mighty hero with his strength, nor a Tsar, nor a soldier can buy off death, and no one can take with him anything which he has acquired. Man is born naked, and naked he departs. Only faith, good works, and almsgiving go with him to the future life, and no one can help, neither friends nor family."

19. On Judging

The Elder strictly forbade condemning and disparaging other priests (his own and others) and not taking their blessings. Such people he himself would not bless. "How do I know what type of person he is? Maybe he's better than all of us, and we censure him. How do we know his soul? If one judges according to outward appearance and actions, he can be mistaken, and this is a great sin."

"Why do you address my priests the way you address boys? I'll have you make prostrations!" That is what he would say to those who actually addressed priests (both young and old) as they would those inferior to or equal to themselves.

He could not endure it when someone praised, censured, or condemned others. He would find good qualities in the lowest, most feeble person, and would find negative sides to those who were praised. He humbled the proud and did away with empty glory.

He reprimanded certain "clairvoyants," saying, "I also see peoples' shortcomings, but I keep quiet; I don't expose them. It's better to pray for people silently, that they might recognize their shortcomings on their own, and not to expose them, as they say, 'straight from the shoulder,' or some people might lose heart and come to despair."

Sometimes he would say, "To teach others is like tossing stones from a belltower. But to carry out those teachings oneself is like dragging stones up a belltower."

20. On Abstinence

He also taught everyone to be thrifty and abstinent, especially in years with a poor harvest. One poor widow boasted that she had eaten fried potatoes at home. At this the Elder reproved her: "People don't have potatoes for their soup, while you treated yourself with that which someone gave you for Christ's sake."

There were instances when at lunch someone would set out buns with tea, and even butter. Although Fr. Sebastian would not object, he would not touch the butter. Looking at him, we would realize that butter was overindulgent and immoderate.

Another time his host invited him to sit at their table by himself. But he would not sit down until everyone else present was seated, and then he sat with them.

He did not approve of going to bed late and getting up late. "It's better to go to bed earlier and get up no later than five-thirty. That way you become accustomed to order and constancy."

The Elder did not approve of those who collected unnecessary things, and he did not praise those who squandered their goods without discernment, giving away every last thing, depriving themselves of what they needed. "You must keep to the golden mean, for extremes are destructive. Use the golden mean in everything earthly, and particularly in heavenly, spiritual things. He who runs ahead quickly should be stopped. And he who falls behind out of carelessness or infirmity and does not take care for the salvation of his soul should be helped to leap up from his slumber and to proceed on an equal footing with average people, neither running ahead nor falling behind."

Fr. Sebastian would say, "It's neither wine nor women nor money nor riches that are to blame for our sins and our passions, as some who wish to justify themselves say, but our own immoderacy. Drunkards blame wine, fornicators blame men or women, misers blame money, rich people blame wealth, and so on. That would mean that if there weren't wine, women, money, or riches, then sinners wouldn't sin. Everything is created very wisely and wonderfully by God. But due to unreasonable application and use of these things, evil is wrought."

He often said, "Find the evil in yourself, and not in other people or in things with which you have not been able to deal with rightly. That's how a child deals with fire or a sword—he burns himself or he cuts himself."

21. On Himself

Once to the question, "Why did you come here?" one woman replied in simplicity, "To have a look at you." The Elder replied, "To look at me? You have bad eyes."

He often appealed to the church council and in writing to the bishop about his desire to retire (to go into reclusion), with the words, "I've had enough of covering the roofs of others while my own is exposed." But there was only one answer: "Serve until your death."

Sensing that he would die soon, he often reminded us that our own people should be given priestly and leadership duties, even though they were weak and infirm. That way everything would be without change, as it was during his time.

He treated the singers to gifts on the great feasts. And after a Pannikhida he would give them out with his own hands to everyone present with the words, "This is how it is while I'm around; enjoy it, I have no family."

"What should I collect all this for? I don't need anything." But people would ask him tearfully to accept at least something from them. He would take something from someone, bless him, and then return it to that very person. From another he would take something and give it away to someone else right then. And from a third person he wouldn't take anything at all, despite that person's offence. If someone would leave something, he wouldn't touch it for a long time, and would then give it to someone needy.

He eagerly and lovingly presented prosphora to everyone, especially to those who had come from far away. During Bright Week, after services he would sit in the church or by the pannikhida table, and a basket-full of paschal eggs would be placed beside him. With a blessing he would hand everyone a paschal egg, to the joy and consolation of all.

22. On Monasticism and the World

He once said, "Between us, the monks, and the world there is a deep gulf. The world will never understand our life and we will never understand theirs. If monks knew beforehand how many temptations and afflictions awaited them on their narrow but salvific path, then no one would enter a monastery. And if the world knew of the future blessings of the monastics, they would all become monks."

"Why did they disperse the monasteries? Because monks began to ride around on troikas and wear soft cotton fabric. But in the past monastics wore canvas podrasniks and cotton-wool blend riassas, and labored conscientiously. Those were true monks. One abbess from the nobility, who did not come from among her own nuns, quickly drove her novices into the Kingdom of Heaven by her heartless treatment of them and by her cruelty. The poor nuns would break their fasts with cabbage while the abbess gave everything to the authorities to please them, depriving her nuns of what was needful."

He often repeated the words, "A servant who knew the will of his master and did not fulfill it, will be beaten more than a servant who did not know his master's will." And to some he would say directly, "After all, you know everything; you've traded God for the world." "The world promises gold, but gives you a quagmire." "He who is not married cares for God, and he who is married cares for his wife (cf. I Cor. 7:32-33)." "He who has not bound himself by the bonds of a family is always free. He has only one care—the salvation of his soul. The goal of life is purity; the end is the Kingdom of Heaven!"

When the Elder was somewhat younger and stronger in health, he refused to use transportation, saying, "I'm a monk; I should go on foot and not ride." And he would walk long distances, such as to the settlements of Fyodorovka, Melkombinat,

Zelentrest, Kirzavod, and so forth. He would say, "I used to love to walk with a teapot to the spring at the outskirts of Zelentrest for good water. And on the way I would sing, 'Having accomplished for us Thy mission....'"*

Two young women asked his novices to announce them to the Elder. He thought about this for a moment, then said, "One doesn't know how to act.... If you receive them well, they become attached to you, but if you don't receive them, they take offense!" By these words Fr. Sebastian helped the young novices (who later became priests) to understand that excessive attachment of young women to priests, as well as that of priests to young women, is not without danger. But rudeness is not safe either. Again, the praiseworthy golden mean. "He who can achieve it with God's help will avoid many temptations!"

Once in a house some girls sat in one room drinking tea while the older women sat in another room. (It would happen that when giving instruction it was necessary to tell the girls one thing and the women another.) Suddenly one of the women went to the room with the girls, where Elder Sebastian was also sitting. He looked at her sternly and said, "But here there are only girls, and the women are in the other room; go and sit there with them." She left displeased, crying and insulted, to which the Elder said, "What's there to be offended at? I told the truth, after all, that you're a woman and you should sit with the women. I didn't say that she was a man; what is she upset about?"

Once while at a table where both women and girls were sitting, one of the women made the remark that the Elder felt sorrier for girls than for women. To this, without looking at that individual, he said directly to her, "And how many times have you gotten married? You've seen all sorts of consolations, while the girls haven't seen anything! They're happy to finish off one

*The Kontakion for the Feast of the Lord's Ascension.—ED.

little spoonful of soup after Batiushka's done—for them that's a great consolation."

He often reminded us to watch over our thoughts and the purity of our hearts, and not to become like the foolish virgins, saying, "Virginity does not save one without good works and purity of heart." "The external is of no use if the interior is dirty and the passions have not been overcome." "Why did the Savior love St. John the Theologian, if not for his purity, chastity, love, faithfulness, tenderness and obedience!? All the disciples abandoned Jesus Christ on the Cross; St. John the Theologian alone stood fearlessly at the Cross." He would also often say: "Love is the highest of all the virtues." *"God is love* (I John 4:16)." *"Though I give my body to be burned, and have not love, it profiteth me nothing* (I Cor. 13:3)." "Where love is, there is God." "Where God is, there is peace, harmony and quiet. Where there is no love, there are contradiction, disruptions, disagreements, treachery, and slander." "Love is longsuffering, love remembers not evil, does not become angry, does not become irritated, and does not seek its own. Love seeks to benefit its neighbor and even its enemies." He gave as an example St. John the Theologian, who by love turned his disciple away from a band of thieves to the bosom of the Church.

He often liked to repeat the words of St. John the Theologian: "Little children, love one another!" By these words he reminded others of love for God and neighbor, without which labor, prayer, and fasting are of no use.

PART IV

*Selections from the Sermons
of Elder Sebastian*

Elder Sebastian at the royal doors of the Mikhailovka church.

Selections From Sermons

SERMON ON THE REPENTANT SINNER
(January 18/31, 1960)

Sinner, abandon your passions and sinful habits. Heaven, with more than ninety-nine righteous ones is calling you! The angels in heaven rejoice over a single repentant sinner. Heaven is seeking your salvation. Only repent and be converted, and break yourself of sin.

For your sake the Lord Himself was born in a manger of dumb beasts and suffered. He was insulted, spat upon, crowned with thorns, and was nailed to the Cross by the hand of his own creation. He suffered and died so as afterwards to be glorified and exalted. But you, O man, what can you be proud of? What do you possess that is truly yours, which is fit for eternity? You won't take your riches with you, and honor, glory, and health are temporal. Let us enrich ourselves for the future, and gather our wealth there through beggars, the poor, and the sick. You are a citizen of heaven, so why are you glued to the earth?! You are an heir of the Kingdom of Heaven and you possess an immortal soul, which the Only-begotten Son Himself redeemed by His death upon the Cross.

ON THE ACQUISITION OF A GUARDIAN ANGEL
(Undated. Cathedral of the Archangel Michael)

A Guardian Angel is present with a person who has a chaste heart and a pure conscience. If you listen to your heart and your conscience, you will always hear his voice, exhorting you to the truth. He who feels spiritual hunger, a spiritual feeling of the soul, will seek to be filled with the spiritual food of the word of God, in the same way that in the case of physical hunger a person looks for food in order to be filled. The person in whom this spiritual feeling is silenced or blinded by the passions will not feel any hunger except for physical hunger. But he who forgets bodily hunger will strive to appease his spiritual hunger. A passion blinds the soul through the gradual suggestion of a thought, and then by agreement and the carrying out of the deed: 1) the onset of the illness, 2) the state of illness, and 3) the death of the soul. Where a single passion is acting, the Holy Spirit and the Guardian Angel step away and the person dies in soul. O Lord! Save us from all these things! Holy Guardian Angels, pray to God for us!

On Love Towards One's Neighbors
(Undated)

How could one not love Him, the Founder and Creator of the Universe and of all things visible and invisible, the Creator of you as well, O man. The Lord created man and breathed into him the life-giving spirit. He gave him a will and reason, and a heart capable of delighting in the gifts of God. To love, not the Creator, but the creation, means to love not life, but death; to not love yourself, but to be your own enemy. To not love your neighbor as yourself means to set the Creator against yourself. You must love the Creator with all your soul, all your strength, and all your thoughts—to contemplate, think about and consider God and the blessings He has sent down to us. For He sees all our thoughts, desires, and intentions regarding Him and our neighbor, whom you should love for his salvation and not for yourself.

Homily in the Evening in the Lodge
(June 13/26, 1960)

He read an Akathist to the Mother of God "Unexpected Joy," and spoke for a long time.

"Three or four years have already gone by since I received the rank of archimandrite, and I still haven't acquired humility and patience. I'm impatient, lazy, careless, and I talk too much.... But one must go along the narrow path; there aren't two Heavenly Kingdoms. Bear your cross given you from baptism without murmuring to the end of your life, and endure all sorrows sent by God. The Lord Himself endured—He was born in a manger, in poverty, grew up in obscurity, and then He came out with his preaching and worked miracles, enlightening the simple people. But the Jews crucified Him on the Cross out of envy. All the apostles died martyric deaths, and all the first Christians poured out their blood, but we don't want to endure or bear the smallest thing. Lord have mercy! O Sweetest Jesus, forgive us.... One must always thank God for everything."

Commemoration of St. John the Theologian
(May 12/25, 1960)

In the beginning was the Word.... (John 1:1). The Savior entrusted His Mother to him, as to the most pure, most honorable and most gentle one. Blessed art thou, O son of thunder, who hath, like an eagle, soared higher than all, and roared forth thy teaching like thunder.

The Beginning of Great Lent
(January 25/February 7, 1960)

"Open unto me the doors of repentance, O Giver of life...."
With a profound awareness and sense of his own sinfulness, the

Publican repented. Not like the Pharisee, who addressed God with haughtiness and pride. The Publican cried to the Lord with a broken heart, not daring to lift his eyes up to heaven, smiting himself on the breast: "O Lord, be merciful to me, a sinner." Such was one who truly repented. He repented and no longer returned to his former sins, but began a new life in a renewed spirit.

SERMON
(Undated)

... Walk before the face of God, and bear Him in your heart. He enters into a pure heart, unoccupied by pride, licentiousness, impurity, and other vices and sins. O Lord, capture our hearts and cleanse them! The Lord descends into our hearts when we open the way for Him through humility, patience, purity, chastity, meekness, good works, love of one's neighbor and especially of God, obedience, prayer, and abstinence from spiritual and bodily sensations and thoughts. We block Him out through incontinence, impurity of feelings and thoughts, lack of endurance of griefs and sickness, grumbling, ingratitude, and the returning of evil for evil.

ARCHIMANDRITE SEBASTIAN'S NAMEDAY
(December 18/31, 1959)

Fr. Sebastian himself served. God has strengthened his weak health. Mother Maria, contrary to his wishes, forced someone to iron his phelonion. For her self-will and disobedience, he humbled her down right then. He vested, and during the service sat on the phelonion (usually in such a case he would lift it up) and creased it, so that it became even worse than it had been. There's a lesson for you! The Liturgy was festive as never before, as was the Moleben. And after everything were the congratulations for the nameday celebrant and a mass of the best thanks and good wishes. But the nameday celebrant, as always, the more they praised him, the more he humbled and diparaged himself. And he was even indignant with them for talking excessively and idly: "I don't need anything from you (either gifts, or praise or thankfulness); what gives me joy is peace, love, and harmony amongst you."

On the Samaritan Woman
(May 18/31, 1959)

The Lord God Himself is the true happiness of the soul, the true consolation and true blessing, which is what the Savior offered to the Samaritan woman. But others seek delight in the sensual pleasures of the coarse flesh, in riches, glory, and earthly power. The desires and pursuits of an infant are silly to a young boy; that which a boy desires is silly to a youth; that which a youth so passionately desires is silly to an adult; that which an adult desires is silly to the old man.... We fill our senses by the fulfillment of endless desires, while we devastate our soul. The senses are full, but the soul is empty. *Great is our Lord, and great is His strength, and of His understanding there is no measure* (Ps.146:5).

The Ascension of the Lord
(Undated)

Those who before were unworthy of earth, are now worthy of veneration in heaven. Less was lost before than is acquired now. God arranged all our former afflictions for our own good. Let us spend our time in holiness and our lives in purity, that we might be made worthy to inherit life in Heaven in the age to come. O ascended Jesus, raise up our souls and our thoughts from darkness, vanity, gloom, and bondage to the earth, the flesh, the world and their swiftly-passing seductions, to eternity and the future blessings prepared by the Lord Jesus Christ, Who has redeemed us with His blood.

COMMEMORATION OF THE HOLY APOSTLE ANDREW THE FIRST-CALLED
(November 30/December 13, 1958)

He was the first to erect a cross on the Kievan hills, and he said that that place and the whole country would one day blossom with Orthodoxy. While looking at the cross prepared for his crucifixion, he rejoiced and was gladdened in spirit with the hope that through the cross he would become united with Christ in the Heavenly Kingdom. Thus must we too attain spiritual joy and gladness for the blessings to come.

Holy love is the totality of perfection. The Mother of God had such love—'The heavenly wonder, the heavenly sanctity.'

"The Bridegroom of my soul is most jealous of all if I love something more than Him." (From the Patericon.) The Savior cried out from the Cross: *I thirst!* He was thirsting for our salvation....

ON GUARDIAN ANGELS
(November 8/21, 1958)

A Guardian Angel is given to each person at the moment of his baptism. How should one guard the union of the soul with its Guardian Angel? He carries out his activity through the conscience and the heart. When a person cares for the salvation of his soul, guards his conscience, and avoids all manner of sin, then he senses his Guardian Angel. The Guardian Angel instructs him in every good thing, sends him good thoughts, and warns him against evil. We will see our Guardian Angel on the day of our departure from this life. But what kind of meeting this will be will depend upon us and our deeds. Will our Guardian Angel rejoice or will he sorrow at our careless life? He steps away from those who do not acknowledge either him or their own souls; he steps away from those who do everything against their conscience, from those who have committed sin after sin, have become rooted in evil, and have deadened their consciences and hardened their hearts. From such a person a Guardian Angel steps away, and the spirit of darkness—the devil— steps in and makes that person his slave. And the soul of that person has perished. The Guardian Angel, having stepped away, weeps for that soul.

Let us be attentive towards our Guardian Angel, let us prayerfully beg his help in all good deeds and for deliverance from every sin. Let us entreat him to persistently lead us to the Lord, and let us not disgrace him by our actions.

Sermon
(January 1/14, 1959)

The Lord created the Universe in six days, and on the seventh day He rested. And He commanded the human race to labor for six days and on the seventh to rest and dedicate the time to God, to the glory of His name and the salvation of one's soul. But the enemy of the human race, out of envy, suggests to us that we not keep this commandment. Before the coming of Christ the Savior, when the Lord asked Pharaoh through Aaron to let the people go into the desert for three days to offer sacrifices, the Pharaoh instead of this made them labor and placed them under surveillance. And so that we would not go to the desert in soul, Pharaoh (or the evil one) says, "Go and trade, go about your business, please your boss, or get some bread and clothes for your children. What do you need time off for?" We steal time from God for our own business, but God curses us and does not grant us success. But when you leave your business to God's Providence, then God arranges it for the good and with abundance and sends a good outcome. Not only do we do a modest amount of work for six days, but on the seventh day we spend our time carelessly, in idleness and drinking, instead of going to church to offer up a sacrifice and thanksgiving to God for His blessings.

A Sunday Sermon
(November 25/December 8, 1958)

The heart is harder than a stone, harder than an anvil. An evil conscience and the hardening of the soul are from the sinful habit of fleshly and sensual sins, and from an absence of repentance. Such a person laughs at the sight of a corpse, and pays no attention to the reproaches and reproofs of others. He is ill and grieves with an embittered conscience. It's easier to break an anvil with a hammer than a human heart. The death of loved ones, the exhortations of other people, and the church teachings on the judgment, hell, illness, and sorrows—this is all a hammer beating against the heart. But the heart does not give in; it is incorrigible in its evil. Like one who has become drunk with wine, the mind has lost its senses and turns against everything good and human. O Lord, give us hearts of flesh and take away our stony ones, that we might feel the blows of the hammer! "They have mocked and beaten me, but I have felt no pain." *O altar, altar* (III Kings 13:2)—the prophet addressed the altar, and not the king and the people, whose hearts were harder than the stones of the altar.

Sermon
(August 27/September 9, 1958)

Blessed is he who does the will of God, and not his own personal, flesh-pleasing will. I entrust myself, from my whole soul, from my whole heart, to Thy will, O Lord. Do with me what is pleasing to Thee. He who does his own will has a slave's fear and an attachment to earthly things. He does not acquire the fear of God and cannot do the will of God.

THE BEHEADING OF JOHN THE BAPTIST
(August 29/September 11, 1958)

John the Baptist died ... as a martyr for the truth. The truth rejoices when people die for it. Now it's as though everyone thought that one can live lawlessly. If there were no truth, then there would not have been life on the earth, either. Everyone would have perished in their lawlessness. All of us must live according to truth, and by this to be an example to others. Truth, purity, love, and chastity are so beloved of the Lord. The holy martyrs went to martyrdom for the sake of truth, putting falsehood and lawlessness to shame.

A SERMON ON TIME
(August 26/September 8, 1958)

What is more precious than anything in the world? Time! And what do we waste uselessly and without being sorry? Time! What do we not value and what do we disregard more than anything? Time! When we waste time, we lose ourselves! We lose everything! When we have lost the most trivial item, we search for it. But when we lose time—we're not even aware of it. Time is given by God to use correctly for the salvation of the soul and the acquisition of the life to come. Time must be allocated in the same way that a good housekeeper allocates every coin—each one is used for something. Each one has its own purpose. In such a way let us also allocate time profitably, not for vain amusements and entertainments, conversations, feasts and parties. The Lord will call us to account for having stolen time for our own whims, and for not using it for God and our souls.

Synaxis of the Archangel Michael
(November 8/21, 1958)

There is not and cannot be equality, either on earth or in heaven. Equality exists only in the One Holy Trinity. The Archangel Michael conquered the Morning Star by humility, patience, and courage. The Archangel Gabriel is the messenger of the mysteries of God and of miracles. All of them have their particular duties.

A Sunday Sermon
(October 29/November 11, 1958)

Jairus' daughter died and the Lord resurrected her. In the same way, a person dies in his soul. He has sinful thoughts and wishes, he commits sin. Then grace departs and the soul dies. This is our negligence over our souls. We don't turn to a doctor when an illness had just begun and is easily healed. We don't seek help during the period of illness, either. But when one's daughter (soul) has already died, then we turn to the Physician of souls and bodies, the Lord: "My daughter has died." "She is not dead, but sleepeth," says the Lord.

You should offer yourself up as a sacrifice to the Lord from your youth, when you are in the prime of life, healthy, pure and strong in spirit—not when you've been deprived of all this, having worked for the devil.

Work while it is day (life) (cf. John 9:4)," said the Lord, for the night will come upon us—that is, old age and death, and then it will be too late. Thus, the foolish virgins did not have oil, because it was night when the Bridegroom came, and there was nowhere to buy oil. They had passed the day carelessly, negligently, and were left with their lamps empty, and the door to the bridal chamber was closed to them. In the same way we also offer the Lord not that which is lame, crooked, blind, or corrupt, but the healthy, the pure, the first-born. As the prophet says, I divided up the land, I have planted the field, I have tilled it, weeded it and watered it, but when I came for the fruits I found nothing. Here and there were ears in the field, and here and there were grapes on the vine. The enemies of the Lord had come, stolen, and carried everything away. In the same way, a person must also labor in the field of his soul, not uselessly; he must pay heed to himself so that the enemies—the world, the devil, the flesh, and death—do not come and steal everything. The world comes and takes its piece, attracting one to riches, luxury, and love of honor. Then the devil comes and takes away what is left—purity, chastity, innocence, and the fear of God. Old age and death come, and a man wants to reap something himself from his field, but he doesn't find anything. Only here and there is there an intention of doing a good deed, while still living a sinful life. And a man regrets that he has lived his life and has not acquired good deeds for the future life. Now death has come, and there is no longer any time for repentance, for tears and prayers. Sudden death is particularly dangerous. Therefore you should not put off repentance and the acquisition of good works until old age, when you will no longer have either physical or spiritual strength. Everything will have been stolen by the enemies, and there will be nothing for yourself; the lamps will be empty.

Pray with love to God, and begin every activity with prayer. Without prayer there are only vain works. In prayer ask that God's will be done, as well as his commandments, and not that which we desire. One must love God without ceasing, and pray without ceasing. Love truly and pray with faith, and the Lord will not hold back His mercy. "Upon whom shall I look, if not upon the meek and humble of heart?" Abase yourself, and acknowledge your insignificance before the Lord, the Creator of everyone and everything. "If he doesn't love me, then I won't love him"—these are demonic words. Let him not love you, and conquer his hate with love. With true love and the fear of God, conquer the passion of hate.

"Man looks at the face, but the Lord looks at the heart." "God speaks to the mind with instruction and to the heart with inspiration."

APODOSIS OF PASCHA
(Undated)

Ask of God purity of heart and forgiveness of sins, grieving in repentance over what you have done and considering yourself worse than all others. And the Lord Himself will come to you, and you will feel such a joy in your heart, which the world does not know. Do everything according to God and for God, and not for people, whom you should love, but from whom you should flee. "Seek after God and thy soul shall live" (cf. Jer. 38:20). You must preserve purity of conscience and acquire a chaste heart. Hence both our deeds and our actions must correspond to Christ's commandments, that others might not say about us, "They even call themselves Christians and pray, but what do they do?" One must preserve purity and a chaste heart, that the enemy might not profit from us, even in the smallest thing, and that our conscience might not reproach us for our lives. Then there will be peace and joy in our heart.

SERMON
(Undated)

O Holy Spirit, receive us like a mother in Thine embrace. Come and abide in us, and make an abode in our hearts. We will cleanse our minds, hearts, and souls from impure thoughts, feelings, and desires—from all that defiles us. Help us, O Lord, by Thy grace, for without it we cannot be saved on our own and be preserved. O Most Holy Trinity, our God, glory to Thee! Strengthen my struggling heart on the rock of Thy commandments.

PART V

The Eldresses of Karaganda

Schema-nun Agnia.

I

Schema-nun Agnia

Schema-nun Agnia (Alexandra Vasilievna Starodubtseva) was born on April 15, 1884. She was born blind, and her parents brought her to Voronezh, to the relics of St. Mitrofan. At his relics the little girl was healed—she received her sight.

Her parents died early. First her father died, and when Alexandra was fourteen years old her mother died. Alexandra was left with her older sister and younger brother. Her sister began raising her brother, and Alexandra left the gymnasium and begged her relatives to bring her to the Sukhotinsk Convent of the Sign, where there was a famous school of iconography. She spent twenty-one years in this convent, was tonsured a riassaphore-nun with the name Agnia, and learned the art of iconography there.

Mother Agnia was the spiritual daughter of Elder Barsanuphius, and every year, when she was given leave, she would go to see him at Optina Monastery. She painted his portrait, which the Tretyakov Gallery later requested from her. Not long before his death, Fr. Barsanuphius gave the portrait, which he greatly valued, back to her. It always hung in Mother Agnia's cell in Karaganda. She used to say: "It wasn't I who painted the portrait; Fr. Barsanuphius painted it with my hand."

She knew Fr. Sebastian well through Optina Monastery, and visited him also every year until the closure of the monastery. She said that Fr. Sebastian was very handsome in his youth, with an especially radiant face. He was affable and kind with visitors, and strove to do everything for everyone. Elder Barsanuphius called him a grace-filled one. Elder Joseph loved him very much and said that he was "tender of soul."

Once the following incident occurred: Mother Agnia had come to see the Elders and was standing in the reception room of the "hut." The novice Stephen came up to her and lightly touched her hand with his hand. At the time she was disturbed in soul at what seemed to her to be a liberty on the part of the novice. But life showed her that the future Elder even then foresaw in her his spiritual child, and that her hand would labor much in the beautiful adornment of churches with holy icons.

In November of 1919 the Sukhotinsk Monastery was dissolved by the bolsheviks, and Mother Agnia settled in the city of Novokhopersk, in the Voronezh Province. At this period Mother Agnia wrote in her diary: "O Lord, help me to live through everything here, and give me strength and patience. Now I need wisdom to resolve serious questions for myself, being left alone in an unfamiliar place. February 18, 1929."

She had to endure many sorrows, poverty, and humiliations. But she never said a word about this.

In 1952, Fr. Sebastian summoned her to Karaganda to paint icons for the prayer house. And on January 4, 1952, express train no. 32 brought Mother Agnia to Karaganda. It was hard for her to get used to living in Karaganda; at first she had the intention of returning to Novokhopersk, but through the Elder's prayers she stayed. At first she lived in the church lodge, where she also painted icons. The first icon that she painted was an icon of the Savior holding the Gospel for the iconostasis. It was the same size as the Athonite icon [of the Theotokos], "Quick to

The young riassaphore nun Agnia at the
Convent of the Sign in Sukhotinsk.

Hear." When she was painting this icon, Fr. Sebastian often came up and stood beside her. When the icon was being finished, at a certain moment Fr. Sebastian said, "That's all; it's enough—not another stroke." Other icons were painted by her as well: the Most Holy Trinity, the Ascension of the Lord, the Flight into Egypt, Christ's Resurrection, and many others, which adorned the entire church. Her icons also adorned the church of the Archangel Michael in Karaganda, and churches in Shchuchinsk, Borovskoi, Osakarovka and in other cities and settlements. Many icons were painted by her for Archbishop Joseph in Alma-Ata, including an icon of St. John of Tobolsk.

In 1956 Mother Agnia was tonsured into the mantia, by the blessing of His Holiness Patriarch Alexei I.

Mother Agnia was not only a talented artist but a wise Eldress as well. She had the gift of clairvoyance, which she concealed from people, and to those who appealed to her with questions she would sometimes say, "What do you want? I'm an old lady; I don't know anything. I sit on the stove and don't go anywhere." But she knew everything and saw everything.

RAISA NIKOLAEVNA ANISIMOVA
(from Chelyabinsk)

In September of 1966 we came from Chelyabinsk to Verkhoturye for the celebration of the feast day of St. Simeon of Verkhoturye. The priest of the Verkhoturye church, Fr. Alexis, asked us, "Have you been to Karaganda? Fr. Sebastian is there, and it's only by his prayers that I'm alive. You must without fail go and visit him."

For a long time we intended to go, but kept putting off the trip. It was only in August of 1967, before Dormition, that five of us arrived in Karaganda, where we learned that it was already more than a year since the Elder had died. Mother Anastasia met us in the Mikhailovka church and told her novice, Anna Sidorovna, to take us to see Mother Agnia. We arrived at her house, and she came out into the yard, leaning on a stand that she used to help her walk. She looked at us with such a penetrating gaze that I thought, "Now she's going to see all of my sins!" and I stood behind everyone else. The Eldress said, "Come tomorrow. Receive Holy Communion and come."

The next day, after having received Communion, we came to see Mother Agnia. We learned from her novice Maria that the Eldress had spent the whole night preparing lunch for us. She seated us at the table and began to treat us. There was cabbage soup, kasha, watermelon, honeydew melon, and tea—what didn't she store up and cook for us! She fed us and fed us; we ate and ate. We were already stuffed, but we kept eating. She stood at the threshold of her cell and gazed at each of us. Then she took magazines and books, opened them to the necessary parts, and gave them to each of us to read. When we had finished reading them she began giving us gifts—to some she gave kerchiefs, and to others a piece of cloth for a dress. We declined: "You shouldn't—we already have everything we need." Why should we clean her out? But her novice Maria said, "Take it, since Matushka has blessed it."

We received a blessing to write letters to her, and I wrote, "Matushka, how well I remember your lunch; how tasty it was!" She replied, "Come for lunch again." And every year during our vacation we would come to Karaganda to see her.

I was attracted to the Eldress' goodness and kindness. I was young; I had only begun to become familiar with spiritual life, and at times I had met some cruel and coarse people amidst believers. But Mother Agnia immediately won us over by her benevolence. With time I understood that this kindness was the fruit of her lofty spiritual life.

She caused me to grow spiritually, and she taught me, "Without the Cross, without the sign of the Cross, one mustn't do anything; you must make the sign of the Cross over everything in the name of the Father, Son, and Holy Spirit.... The whole earth is ensnared in the nets of the demons; you should hold onto prayer at all times"—and everything she said was in the same spirit. But for me at that time the Cross and prayer meant little, and I continued to be unable to grasp it all; what did it mean that there were demons around us?

We left Karaganda for Chelyabinsk by the evening train. That day we had received Communion, and then they escorted us and saw us to our train car. Our tickets were for the upper bunks. We took our bedding and lay down in our places.

I was sleeping, but I heard Tselinograd being announced. A great many people got on and some young people with guitars came in and sat down in our compartment on the side seats. I looked and saw so many demons coming in with them—such little ones—and they were grabbing onto the berth with their nails. They had twisted tails, and they were turning their heads around and around, looking for a place to jump to. Below, on the floor, there were masses of them; there was no place to step! I was seeing all this in a dream; I wanted to open my eyes, but I couldn't. I was tense with fright. "God forbid that they should jump towards us!" I thought. One little demon came off the berth and was coming in my direction, crawling towards my legs. I drew in my legs and made the sign of the Cross over him: "In the name of the Father, Son, and Holy Spirit." Mother Agnia had said, after all, that one should guard oneself with the sign of the Cross. From this fear, that the demons were crawling towards me, I woke up and opened my eyes, but I still saw the demons. Then, just as if some kind of shroud fell from me, the demons disappeared; but I saw that people really had entered the train car. There were in fact very many of them, and young people with guitars were sitting in the side seats.

I lay there until morning and was afraid to straighten my legs. In the morning my travelling companions got up and were preparing to eat breakfast, but I was afraid to lower myself to the floor—after all, there had been so many demons there! The girls asked me what was wrong. I began to yell that I had seen demons after Communion. But there was one spiritual woman with us who calmed me down, saying that I had seen this vision because of my doubt; that by the Eldress' prayers the Lord had revealed to me how the world is ensnared by nets and how many fallen spirits surround us.

Mother Agnia nurtured faith, humility, and patience in me. But she did not always speak directly. It was more often like this: you would ask her about something, and she'd say, "I don't know." But later she would reveal everything through her novices, who were also spiritual people and who understood her. She would tell me, "Raisa Nikolaevna (she called everyone by their first name and patronymic, even young people), go lie down and rest; go and rest." I'd go to the room, lie down, and they would begin a conversation. And through this conversation I would receive answers to all my thoughts and perplexities. Or she would bless me to go to Fr. Sebastian's grave, and I'd go and pray there. And whatever I prayed about at the grave, she would gradually give me an answer, as if by chance.

At that time I didn't know anything about obedience or the significance of an Elder's blessing. Once Mother Agnia said to Maria, "If only we could buy a little milk." And I thought, "Oh, she wants some milk! I'll go and buy it for her, and do a good deed for her." I didn't think that I had to get her blessing, and I decided to do the good deed in secret. I went to the store—there wasn't any milk. I went to the central store, and there wasn't any there, either. I walked around half the city but I didn't find any milk, and I returned with nothing. Novice Maria asked, "Where have you been?"

"I've been looking for milk for Mother Agnia."

"How did you dare," she said, "to leave without a blessing? You have to get a blessing." I went over to the Eldress: "Bless me to go to the store for milk." She said, "Go with God," and gave me some money. I arrived at the store and right then they were bringing in some dairy products. I bought them for exactly the sum which Mother Agnia had given me, to the kopeck. She had known how much money I would need.

There was another incident with me. On September 21, the Feast of the icon of the Mother of God "Of the Sign," I was told that this was the main Feast of the Sukhotinsk Convent, where the Eldress had spent many years and had became a monastic. For the occasion I bought a bouquet of flowers, brought them to her, and congratulated her. She said to her novice, "Maria, take the flowers and set them somewhere." Maria took them and set them in the icon corner by the large "Quick to Hear" icon. I left Mother Agnia and thought, "Well, none of the people from Karaganda congratulated her, but I congratulated her!" Then I heard Mother Agnia shout, "Manya! Take those flowers away! Take them and put them in the stove!"—and she said it so sternly. I went into the corridor and how I wept! How I reproached myself for my pride and vainglory! When I had cried myself out and calmed down, I heard Mother Agnia saying, tenderly, "Maria, bring the flowers over here." In this way she exposed and humbled me.

I came to see Mother Agnia for ten years. I saw her for the last time in the autumn of 1975. She was then ninety-two years old. She was very ill and was suffering from dropsy. From time to time she was given injections and had fluids pumped out of her. A lot of people were coming to see her, many of whom came from other cities, especially from Chelyabinsk. They would stay with her for months at a time. In the evening, when the last visitor would leave, she would call her novice: "Maria, lift my legs for me; I'm going to lie down." She could no longer lift them onto the bed by herself.

Once there were many visitors, and Mother Agnia had us sleep on the floor of her cell. During the night I woke up because of a strong knocking, and I was terrified. I looked at the Eldress' bed, and saw her sitting there, holding her staff in her hand and beating it on the floor. In the morning I asked, "Matushka, didn't you sleep? There was some kind of knocking going on." She said, "So many people come and tell me everything, and they leave the demons here, so I have to fight with them."

Once in the morning Mother Agnia called for Maria and said to her, "Go outside, there's a woman standing in the yard; tell her that I don't steal, but that I pray for people." That woman subsequently became a believer and greatly grieves now that during the Eldress' lifetime she did not go to see her.

Mother Agnia never kept any animals in her house, but in the last years of her life some cats turned up at her place. She fed them out of her own teacup, and petted them. The cats were obedient to her and unusually smart. When she acquired them, many began thinking that she had lost possession of her faculties due to old age. But this was not the case. Mother Agnia was a wise Eldress, and she exposed many human sins through the cats. Once two seminarians from Sergiev Posad came to Karaganda on their vacation. Before their arrival Mother Agnia said to Maria, "Bring the cats to my cell." Maria brought two cats, and they lay down on the table. Then the Eldress said, "Cover them with a new towel." Maria covered them, and they continued to lay there. The seminarians arrived and, crossing themselves, entered the cell. One of them went up to the table and said, "What an outrage—there are cats on the table!" And he wanted to throw them off. But the other one stopped him: "Don't touch them; they're exposing our sins and testing our humility." And the whole time the seminarians were with her the cats lay submissively on the table, but after they had left, the cats got up and left the cell.

In Mother Agnia's house things happened which at first glance might have been taken for chance occurrences, but which had a definite meaning. One young man by the name of George came from Chelyabinsk to see the Eldress. This was during the winter. He came into her cell, took a rabbit-fur hat off his head, and set it on the bed. Suddenly one of Mother Agnia's cats went up to the hat, began pushing it across the bed, and then tossed it on the floor. The cell-attendant picked up the hat and scolded the cat. George left the Eldress, went to the church, and hung his hat and coat on a hook in the narthex. But when he left the service and wanted to put on his things, he discovered that only his coat was on the hook. His hat had been stolen.

A twenty-year-old girl by the name of Tatiana came to see Mother Agnia from Dolinka. This story, of how the Eldress appointed Tatiana for the Heavenly Kingdom, the people of Karaganda tell in different ways. Some say that Tatiana had a fiancée who was a sailor, whom she had met and was planning to marry. Others maintain that Mother Agnia, in order to distract Tatiana's thoughts from the young men with whom she was acquainted, described a bridegroom to her who was now far away, who was serving as the captain of a ship and who would take her as his fiancée on a sailing voyage, as the abbess of his ship. And she gave her a prayer rope. Mother Agnia described the beauty of this bridegroom, the image of which, from her lips, corresponded to the image of our Lord Jesus Christ Himself.

In any case, the Eldress set the day of the "wedding," a year in advance, for August 2. Tatiana's father bought her a beautiful bridal veil, but Mother Agnia did not bless him to buy a wedding dress and shoes, saying, "It's not time yet." At the end of July, she ordered Tatiana to immediately go and buy a wax crown for the bridal veil. "The time is coming; there's no putting it off," and she gave her three candles "for the crowning." Tatiana didn't understand: "Why did she give me three candles for the crowning? What is she preparing me for? I don't think she's preparing me for marriage—but for what, I don't know."

On August 2 there was a car accident on the road. Novice Maria was then getting ready for church. "Manya! Manya!" the Eldress cried out to her, "Tanya's soul is rising up! Run quickly to church and tell them that they should commemorate the newly reposed, slain Tatiana!"

This is what had happened. Tatiana was riding on a bus which was passing a dump truck with a trailer that was carrying coal. As they were passing, the trailer tore loose from the dump truck and struck the bus. All the other passengers remained alive; Tatiana alone died.

They buried her in her white bridal veil with the wax crown, and Tatiana's wedding candles burned on three sides of her coffin.

ABBOT NICHOLAS (KARPOV)
(City of Shchuchinsk)

I became acquainted with Mother Agnia in 1973. At that time I was a totally worldly person, having nothing to do with the church, and I had come to yell at her (concerning my private life). It turned out that during my contact with her everything in my life was changed, and my soul became calm. Here was an old woman nearly ninety years old, but with such pure, clear blue eyes. Could it be that this old woman, who had lived in a monastery from the age of fourteen and had not been educated anywhere, would know anything and would be able to discuss life after the monastery? Nevertheless, she gave such answers to all my questions, that even an educated person wouldn't have been able to answer as she did.

When I came (this was still before I had served in the army), she chatted with me, gave me some tea, and sent me to the church: "Go to church and pray." How do you pray? Well, when I was a child my mother used to bring us to church and had us receive Communion, but aside from that I had never prayed in church. I came to the church, but there were few people there, and the old women looked around at me. I had the feeling that everyone was looking at me, and I wondered how to pray. I stood behind a column and prayed as well as I could. After I had prayed I came to see Mother Agnia. She gave me some tea, treated me to some food, and told me about her past, how she used to live, and how she entered the monastery. She said, "I used to know a gentleman, a very noble person, but when he would come to church, he always felt as though everyone were looking at him. He would go behind a column and stand there." At first I didn't understand, and I asked, "What was the man's surname?" thinking that it would be some well-known person from history. But she didn't answer me and began to speak further. Only afterwards did I understand that she had been speaking about me.

Mother Agnia wanted me to take a trip to Alma-Ata, to meet Metropolitan Joseph (Chernov). "We have a wonderful bishop," she said. She regarded him very warmly, and he greatly respected her. When he came to Karaganda he always visited her. But within me a great trust and liking for Mother Agnia had arisen, and I told her, "It's enough for me that I know you; I don't really need others.' Thus I did not succeed in making the acquaintance of Metropolitan Joseph before I joined the army.

I only served one year in the army, and when I was demobilized I decided to go to Zagorsk (Sergiev Posad) to enter the Seminary. Immediately, even before I received my passport, I went to Karaganda to receive the Eldress' blessing to study. At that time an acquaintance of Metropolitan Joseph's from Alma-Ata, Eustolia Ivanovna Leshcheva, was visiting her. Mother Agnia grabbed her: "She's going to Alma-Ata now; go along with her to see Metropolitan Joseph. Go, go!' There was nothing else for me to do. Since she was sending me there, I went.

The Metropolitan received me very kindly. I saw before me an old man in a common podrasnik and a padded jacket. I wasn't able to compare this Metropolitan with other Metropolitans, as I had never seen any before. I met the attentive gaze of His Eminence, who immediately wanted to understand who this person was who had come to see him. I had already heard much about him, and so I also looked attentively at the Elder whom Mother Agnia regarded so reverently. He was somewhat upset. (I later learned the reason for this—his cell-attendant was getting ready to leave him.) He questioned me about everything, and left me to stay there for a while. When I was leaving, he asked me, "Will you, perhaps, come visit me again?"

"As the Lord wills," I said. "Maybe I'll come again sometime."

I came home to Chelyabinsk, received my passport, and came again to Karaganda with the intention of leaving there immediately for Moscow. I had just arrived there (this was at ten o'clock in the morning), when Valya Veretennikova came in and looked at me quite oddly. She had been with Mother Agnia a short time before me, and then she had gone to the telephone station to call the Metropolitan about some sort of business, and he had asked, "Where is that person who's with Mother Agnia?"—he expressed this in a strange manner—"Where is that person? Let him come to see me; I need him greatly."

But Valya said, "He's not here; he left a long time ago for the Urals. I've just come from Mother Agnia; he's not there."

"But he's there, he's there. Tell Mother Agnia—have her send him to me." Then she came in and her eyes were wide open: I was sitting there with the Eldress, drinking tea. She told her that the Metropolitan had requested me to come. "Well, God's Providence is changing something," she said, "and you've got to go to Alma-Ata." I had made up my mind to go to Zagorsk, and now I was supposed to go to Alma-Ata; first one thing, and then another. "Well, whatever you bless me to do, Matushka, let it be that way," I said. In two days I was already in Alma-Ata with the Metropolitan.

He was very upset; his cell-attendant had left him. We hadn't seen each other for a little while, but he already looked like a worn-out old man. It was evident that he had gone through a great deal. He said, "Stay with me for a while." I lived with him for eight months, until the day of his repose.

Those people, Metropolitan Joseph and Mother Agnia, had a particular characteristic—they would simply take a person's soul into their hands, and that would be enough; either willingly or unwillingly he would change and be transformed. They were capable of having a grace-filled influence on the soul of another person. When a person who has spiritual burdens and is stirred up and is searching for something in life comes across such people, he is instantly calmed and immediately feels that he has found what he had been looking for. Both Mother Agnia and the Metropolitan had this quality, and it manifested itself quite vividly. That was the case with me as well. I hadn't known how to live or in which direction to go; then I saw Mother Agnia and her good deeds, and wanted to follow her example and imitate her in some way, even though at that time I was distant from the church. It was the same with Metropolitan Joseph—he took me into his own hands.

He was a very striking individual. Many impressions have remained after him, and not only with me. When he died, someone phoned and asked, "What, is it really true that Ivan Mikhailovich died?" (His name in the world was Ivan Mikhailovich.) "It's true," I said. "Ye-es.... " I heard with such sorrow in the receiver, "He was a lawful man!" He didn't say that he was highly cultured or anything like that. The expression seemed to me to be not entirely literary, and it was obviously a non-churchgoer who had called; maybe he had simply crossed the

Metropolitan's path somewhere in life. But he said it with such sorrow: "He was a lawful man."

Metropolitan Joseph and Mother Agnia were two people who very strongly respected each other. I can't even say who respected the other more—whether the Metropolitan respected Mother Agnia more, or whether Mother Agnia respected him more. Once I was preparing to leave him to go to Karaganda to visit the Eldress for a few days. But he was talking to me about monasticism at the time: "I'll tonsure you," he said. "I'll give you a document, but open it only after my repose." I refused, thinking that monasticism wasn't for me and that I didn't have the strength for it. But he probably thought that I just didn't want to be tonsured by him, and he said, "Well, all right; if you don't want it from me, then let Mother Agnia tonsure you. Go; she'll do it, and I'll certify it by my own hand." I declined this as well. Though I don't know to this day whether or not a nun has the right to tonsure a monk, this is the blessing I had.

Mother Agnia predicted to Metropolitan Joseph that the office of patriarch would be offered to him. She spoke about this allegorically, but he immediately told her, "Matushka, be quiet, or else I'll excommunicate you." And, in fact, he was later chosen as a candidate for the patriarchal throne, but declined it.

Mother Agnia foresaw much in my life as well as in her own. My mother came to see Mother Agnia even before my acquaintance with her, and the Eldress gave her an icon of the Savior to give to me, foreseeing that my unbelief would pass and that I would even be ordained a priest.

Her clairvoyance manifested itself now and then as though by chance. I remember how once a very poor and sick woman arrived. Mother Agnia said, "Nicholas Mikhailovich (I was still young, twenty-two years old, but she called me by my first name and patronymic), Nicholas Mikhailovich, there are some eggs over there; give her some eggs."

"How many, Matushka?"

"Well, count how many there are; count them." I counted them—there were fifteen. "Well then, give them to her."

"But what about us?" I asked.

"We'll be brought some eggs; don't worry." After two hours had passed, another woman came, bringing eggs: "Matushka, please accept these eggs."

"Nicholas Mikhailovich," said Mother Agnia, "take them, and count how many of them there are; count them." I counted them and there were fifteen. It happened as though in passing, but when you begin to think about it.... Another time I was getting ready to go home to Chelyabinsk and I said, "Matushka, I need to go and make a phone call, to let my family members know."

"Well," she said, "go ahead and call at the train station. Go to services; don't worry, call at the train station." I prayed, I went to services and thought, "When am I going to call at the station? I don't even have a ticket yet. I'll go and call now." I went to the telephone station and it was closed. I got on a bus and went to another telephone station and called and called, but there was no connection. I remembered the Eldress' words, and I thought there was no use in what I was doing, so I went back to see Mother Agnia. When I arrived I was so cold that I didn't say anything to her; I drank some tea and began preparing for my departure. I arrived late at the train station, only fifteen minutes before the train was to leave. As I walked through the train station, I looked—there was a telephone station. The door was open, and nobody was there. I ran over, dialed the number, said two or three words, got on the train, and left for home. I literally needed just two or three minutes to make the call.

Mother Agnia and Metropolitan Joseph were two people who changed my life. Not only mine, but they changed many by their grace, humility, and their patience and prayers. As St. Seraphim said, "Acquire the spirit of peace and thousands around

Funeral of nuns Agnia and Thecla in Karaganda, 1976.

you will be saved." These were such people around whom truly thousands were saved.

Mother Agnia died on March 17, 1976, after being tonsured to the schema. When she came down with her terminal illness, she ate no food for forty days and, foreseeing her imminent repose, she predicted that there would be two coffins.

On March 17, after receiving the Holy Mysteries, Mother Agnia peacefully gave up her soul to the Lord. The sisters came to wash and vest her. With them came the last of the four nuns who had come to Fr. Sebastian in Karaganda during the years of his imprisonment, Mother Febronia (in monasticism Thekla). After vesting Mother Agnia, Mother Febronia also died suddenly. Mother Agnia took her along with her, from this vale of tears to the Heavenly bridal chamber of eternal joy—that's what the sisters decided. They were buried side by side in the Mikhailovka cemetery.

Schema-nun Anastasia.

2

Schema-nun Anastasia

Anastasia Ivanovna Shevelenko was born in 1888 in the Vityebsk Province, into a shoemaker's family.* She had a very difficult childhood. Her father drank and cursed, and his life ended when he was killed in a fistfight. Mother Anastasia remembered that not only did she herself not weep over her father, but she even convinced her mother to not cry, saying, "Now Papa won't curse." Her mother was left with eight children, all of them young. She remembered her mother quite well. Her mother was always calm and very religious. Her mother sent Anastasia to school, but she did not want to study: "When they called me to read for the first time," she recalled, "it happened to be a poem which I knew by heart—'There was a ringing frost outside.... ' I read it by the book very well and they immediately transferred me to the second grade. But when they called me to read the next time, it happened to be something unfamiliar. I wasn't able to read through it, and they transferred me back to the first grade. But I didn't want to study, and I gave it up."

About her childhood Mother Anastasia recalled, "Formerly, every family had its own elder—what the mother said was law."

*Taken down from Mother Anastasia's words by nun Julia.

"'Mama, what does the world rest on?'

"'Special people pray.'

"'But can I see them?'

"'No, they're special chosen people of God.' Suddenly Petya ran by.

"'Mama, Petya the idiot is running around.'

"'He's not an idiot.'

"'But the boys call him that and throw stones at him.'

"'They themselves are idiots,' said my mother, 'but Petya is a fool-for-Christ's-sake.' And I thought, 'Maybe I too can be an idiot for Christ's sake?' And glory be to God, I've lived as an idiot. (At that time the Lord took away a part of my mind.)"

When Anastasia was ten years old, her aunt (her father's sister) took her on to help in her trading business, and at the age of fourteen her brother arranged for her to wash dishes at a wine factory. She worked there for three years. Then Anastasia left home, but they found her and brought her home. From that time on she began to be considered insane. Soon she went, as usual, for some water, abandoned her bucket at the well and left for good to wander. The young eighteen-year-old girl began to roam, having no place to lay her head.

"Every night," she recalled, "I had to find a place to spend the night, and in the morning I'd go off again. It was very difficult, especially once. I remember that it was cold and muddy; rain was pouring down, and I was totally frozen. No matter where I went, I was turned down. The burden on my soul was unbearable. In a field I found a tiny shed. I put my head in the shed, but my torso was outside. That's how I spent the night. In the morning I went to church. I had just stepped on the church porch when I heard the priest reading *O sweetest and most generous Jesus....* I fell down, and streams of tears poured from my eyes. 'O Lord, I have forgotten Thee!' Immediately the deacon came up to me and invited me to his home. After this everyone began to invite me. Thus the Lord tests us and through afflictions teaches us to not place our trust *in princes, in sons of men,* but to place our trust in Him alone.

"Then I left for the city of Shuya in the Ivanov Province, to see my aunt. She assigned me to work as a maid for a factory owner. The work was easy, but I lived there for two weeks and left because of the pursuits of the man of the house. Then my aunt set me up to work for a landowner, who had been a spiritual son of Elder Ambrose. I was a housemaid there for six years. There was a great deal of work, but I managed it. I wanted to pray very much, but I had no time. The landowner's wife slept until noon. 'How can this be,' I thought, 'doesn't it bother her to waste the time?' And I would weep and run to church, and give out a little money to each of the beggars on the porch, so that there would be enough for everyone. That's how I worked it off—I hired people to pray for me.

"Later such a terrible sadness fell upon me, such despondency seized me, that it seemed impossible to go on living. 'Can it really be,' I thought, 'that I'll have to spend my whole life like this?' But the merciful Lord is very close to those who grieve. One nun, Rufina, advised me to go to Optina Monastery to see the Elders. I went. The enemy disturbed me with thoughts of returning, and I got there with difficulty. As soon as I reached the river Zhizdra and set one foot on the ferry, everything immediately became easy. Fr. Anatole blessed me to live in my old place. He wrote to the proprietor to receive me with love. The owner took me in, and I lived there for two more years. Then I went to the Polotsk Monastery, where I was tonsured. Once I had an argument there with one of the nuns. That nun was once carrying a teapot with boiling water. I rushed up to her, snatched the teapot from her and threw it aside. Everyone was shocked by this action. But some time went by, and this nun threw herself at my feet and admitted that she had wanted to scald me.

"I lived for two years in the Monastery and then left to wander. In Optina Monastery Elder Anatole blessed me to practice foolishness-for-Christ's-sake. He gave me two travelling companions and told us to go to the St. Tikhon [of Kaluga] Monastery. We had not gone far when I came down with a frightful case of dysentery. I couldn't walk; I lay there in the forest and saw my father coming towards me, without a hat, and he said, 'Don't stay here, go to the nearest village.' And we went on. We barely made it to the first hut. I sat down at the threshold, my eyes closed, and I lost consciousness. Suddenly some sort of invisible force touched me, and in place of my arms strong wings appeared and unfurled in both directions. My spiritual eyes were opened, and I saw a multitude of demons passing by me, ready to tear me to pieces. But I had recently received Communion, and I made the sign of the Cross across my torso and my wings, and the demons couldn't touch me. But the last one, the head demon, pulled out a deck of cards and wanted to hit me in the face with them, but he only nicked me. Then I remembered that I had played cards and not repented of it.

"We spent the night there. In the morning my companions set off for St. Tikhon's Monastery, but I couldn't get up. After a while I got up and wanted to go, but I again fell down in the shed, with my face in cow manure. I evidently lay there a long time, because it all dried on me. At that time I had a vision: I saw a woman dressed in black—it was the Mother of God—and under the manger was a monk, heirodeacon Paul (I was seeing him before he was even born.) Then they washed me and fed me, and I went to the village where the brother of Fr. George of Chekryakov lived. It grew dark. Where, I thought, would I spend the night? I went to the church and pushed on the door; it turned out to be unlocked. I was happy and entered the church and began to arrange a place to lie down for the night. I took off my outer layer of clothes and remained in a white undershirt

Eldress Anastasia in her youth.

with long sleeves. I didn't know how the night passed. In the morning the watchman came, saw me dressed only in white and was frightened, thinking that maybe I was a ghost. He ran off and returned with Fr. George's brother and his young wife. They grabbed me and led me to the police. On the way they asked for my passport. I told them that I didn't have a passport, but that I did have a scrap of paper. (When I had left the Polotsk Convent, one fool-for-Christ, a woman, told me to get a document from the Convent.) And when they had read my document, the young wife said, 'Oh, my dear blessed one!' (Mother Anastasia always wept at these words.) They brought me to their home and gave me borscht with meat. Seeing their zeal, I ate all of the borscht. Later they brought me to Fr. George of Chekryakov, to whom I revealed how difficult it had been for me to wander. He said, 'This is because you don't have a roof over your head. If you want, stay with us.' And what happened? Immediately everything felt better; I jumped up and again went off to wander. I went on and on and got lost in the forest. It was cold, there was already snow on the ground and I was lightly dressed, and so I began to freeze. I wanted to lie down, and I almost did. I saw a couple of men, ran away from them and came to a road. I ran to the first hut, where a shoemaker warmed me and fed me."

She lived at Optina when Elder Sebastian was a novice with Elder Nektary. There she went about in a torn red skirt. It would happen that the Lord would reveal to her some vice or another in someone, and then she would expose them in front of everyone, for which she would sometimes be beaten.* But Fr. Sebastian

---

*In particular, the following facts about Mother Anastasia are known from the accounts of residents of Karaganda: Once during an All-night Vigil she went up to a monk who was reading the Old Testament readings at Vespers, bared her chest, took him by the hand, and walked thus with him to the ambo. Likewise, during a procession on the Feast of the Transfiguration she climbed up a tree and began tossing apples at the clergy, thus foretelling the imminent closing of the monastery.

never hit her, he only stepped on her feet when she would get into the Elder's cell.

"And do you remember, Nastya," recalled Fr. Sebastian once, "how I once tossed you out in Optina, when you had hidden under the the Elder's bed? You flew head-over-heels down the stairs. Fr. Nektary said to me, 'Well, Stephen, toss her out, the disobedient one. Yeesh,' he said, 'She hid! Make short work of her! You'll be foolish all the same, there's no other road for you!'" At this point Fr. Sebastian was silent, then said, "How sorry I felt for you then! But—there's got to be obedience." But Mother Anastasia didn't want to be a fool-for-Christ's-sake, and she sobbed. (She was a beauty—her cheeks were rosy, and she had long braids.) But Elder Nektary said, "If you're not obedient to God, do you think it will be better in hell?"

"Once I went to the forest, and I was gathering berries. I sat down and ate, and then I was very thirsty. Suddenly I saw that a spring was pouring forth clear, tasty water from under ground. I took some water in a small dish and quenched my thirst. Then I walked through the forest and sang songs with all my might. From that time on I began to sing. I became thirsty again and went back to the same place, but the spring wasn't there any more.

"Once in Optina I was running across the ice without any shoes on. One of my friends came up to me and admonished me, telling me to put my shoes on, but I continued running around. Then I went to church to make three prostrations before each icon. My legs had become like wood, and they wouldn't bend. One elder noticed this. He came up to me and asked, 'Why don't your legs bend?' I told him that it was from prostrations, but he said, 'No, you let them get cold, and they're going to hurt.' I was greatly grieved, and afraid that I'd be left without legs and be made in one instant from a beauty into something gruesome—that's how affliction affects a person.

"I was twenty-six years old. In the autumn I got lost in the forest near Optina. It began snowing, and I was barefoot. I looked for the way back for a long time, arrived at the Skete at night, and sat down on a cast-iron slab. The monks saw me and invited me to the guard-hut. I didn't go with the monks, but went to the Monastery. When I knocked, they asked who was there. I didn't make myself known, but went off to the sawmill. The watchman's house there appeared to be empty, but it was unheated. I crawled up on top of the stove, but there was nothing to cover myself with. That's how it was until morning, when some acquaintances discovered me and took me home. There they warmed my legs, which had become like wood, especially the calves. But it was nothing; they weren't painful. They only began to hurt in Karaganda in 1964.

"When there were severe persecutions of Christians, I lived in Kaluga with a nun. I was very sick; they thought I wouldn't survive. Once in the morning my hostess left for church. I looked and it was as though I was reading my prayer-rule before an icon of the Mother of God, and the Mother of God began to move in the shrine. Then I saw her standing by the table in a white apostolnik looking at me, and the shrine was empty. I said to her, 'Mother of God, what is this happening for?' (I meant about the persecution of Christians.) But she said, 'Drink Theophany water with prosphora.' And she went back into the shrine."

"From that time on Mother Anastasia always stored a lot of water at Theophany. In Karaganda she froze water in round containers and all year she would give everyone Theophany water to drink with prosphora.

During the years of persecution Mother Anastasia was in the concentration camps.

After her release, she was brought to Kokchetav, to a settlement. "I went from hut to hut. I'd come to one house, and they'd say, 'We have no bread.' But they'd feed me potatoes and kvass. I came to another house, and there they immediately grabbed me and wanted to take me to the police—some of their linens had disappeared. But their neighbors interceded for me and they let me go. I kept going. At the third house they again grabbed me—a sack of their wheat had disappeared, and again I was blamed. It would have turned out badly for me if one man hadn't interceded for me, and they let me go. But after prison I really did look like a hooligan. And so it was already night; where was I going to spent the night? I went to some nuns, but I didn't dare to knock, and I lay in their yard. Snow fell and covered me with a thick layer, but I was warm."

In Karaganda she lived in the lodge. She loved to feed every-one, but ate very little herself. Whatever someone would give to her, she accepted happily, as though she needed it. Then she would give everything immediately to someone else. At first she slept in the bathhouse, where her odd and ends were kept. In the cold corner she piled up all kinds of mounds so that she wouldn't be able to lie on them for long. She slept in the evening and worked during the night, cleaning under the bunks and pre-paring kvass. She made very good kvass, and she gave it to every-one to drink. From time to time she would fly into a rage and would bring certain of the sisters to tears, for some reason or another. She would dress with a galosh on one foot and a felt boot on the other. It often happened that she would go about in galoshes and overshoes in the winter and in felt boots in the summer. Her dress was always dirty, and if she put on a clean one it wouldn't remain so for long. On her head would be a ker-chief or a rag, almost always disheveled. If you began tidying her up, she would chase you off: "Beat it!" Only before Communion did she dress cleanly and conduct herself properly.

Mother Anastasia possessed the gift of clairvoyance. Once some kind of burden was weighing heavily on me, and thoughts crowded my head so much that I couldn't pray. Suddenly some-one hit me hard on the shoulder from behind: "Have you turned up? I was looking for you all night!" Mother Anastasia said loudly. I immediately felt better. By hitting me with her hand and by her prayer she had chased off the evil one. More than once she answered my thoughts. Once I was having a hard time. "Even Mother Anastasia doesn't see it," I thought. Right then she walked up to me and silently looked at me straight in the eye. I said, "Pray for me; my soul is burdened."

"Well, Fr. Sebastian is alone in his room; run to him quickly." I came to the Elder, and he asked me, smiling, "What's wrong?"

"My soul is burdened." He ran his hand across my chest and said, "The evil one, my child, gives no rest. It will pass." And, in fact, it all passed.

During the Liturgy one old woman felt poorly, but it was impossible for her to go outside because of the multitude of peo-ple. Mother Anastasia was sitting in the left cliros and asked us to help the old woman to the cliros. Then she sat her down beside her and laid the old woman's head on her shoulder. Ten minutes hadn't gone by when the old woman stood up and thanked her—everything had passed. But Mother Anastasia became ill. She often took the illnesses of her close ones upon herself. This was difficult for her, and once she even admitted, "I felt sorry for someone who was very ill, so now I'll have to endure it."

In August, 1970, there was a plan to tear down the church lodge, something which Fr. Sebastian hadn't blessed while he was alive. The next day workers were supposed to come and be-gin the demolition. We all grieved that the Elder's blessing was being violated. That evening Mother Anastasia became very ill. She asked to be locked in and that no one be allowed in. She lay that way all night until three the next day. At three o'clock she jumped out of bed, ran from her room, and said, "Well, everything's all right; it's all better." At that moment the church warden arrived with the plenipotentiary, and the latter forbade the demolition of the lodge and the starting of the construction. Of course, this was by the Eldress' prayers.

In July, on the eve of the Feast of the translation of the relics of St. Sergius of Radonezh, Mother Anastasia told us, "Tomorrow, prepare yourselves to spend the Saint's day in the wilderness, in the village of Dolinka, where Fr. Sebastian served his imprisonment." We didn't receive this blessing very joyously, since we had been busy with heavy work—we had painted the church, and we were very tired. We began to refuse: "We're tired, we want to rest." But she said, "You can rest there. And you'll refresh your heads better than at home."

In the morning on the day of St. Sergius it was overcast and drizzling. When we started the Moleben, the rain began to fall in buckets. We were overjoyed: "Now we won't go; we'll rest." After the Moleben we went up to the Eldress with the hope that she wouldn't bless us for the trip. But barely had we opened the door when she immediately said, "Well, are you going?" We became flustered, looked at each other, and said, "However you bless." "Right now; don't waste a minute, be on your way. God be with you!" Without wanting to, we got ready and set out. Only we first went for a blessing to the grave of Elder Sebastian.

When we arrived in Dolinka, we went to the designated spot, to the division where Fr. Sebastian had been during the last years of his imprisonment. We walked for a long time until we reached the forest, and then we walked through the forest. The rain kept falling and falling. We walked and admired the beauty of nature and observed how skillfully and evenly planted were the rows of trees which had been planted by the prisoners, among whom was our Elder. Then we sat down under a tree, ate with a good appetite, rested, and went further. We forgot about the rain, which fell unceasingly. We felt superb, and our souls were overflowing with warmth and joy. We walked and reminisced about Fr. Sebastian. Under our feet were puddles and mud, but it was easy to walk. It even seemed to us that we weren't walking, but flying. By five in the evening we arrived at the division where the Elder had been. The rain immediately ceased and the sun peered out, and that place, surrounded by the forests planted by the prisoners, looked wonderful. When we began walking back, it began to rain again. But we, who had spent the whole day in the rain, were completely dry. We were very satisfied and joyful, our souls were light, and our heads were refreshed. We came home late in the evening, and when we told Mother Anastasia about the trip, she said, "The Elder himself was walking with you and sheltering you from the rain." We all thanked her greatly for such a feast day.

Once in the summer the sisters who had lived with Fr. Sebastian on Lower street were getting ready to go to the field to dig potatoes. Mother Anastasia also asked to go with them. She took a large sack and stuffed it full of galoshes, dresses, jackets, stockings, and so forth. She crammed the whole sack full. The sisters laughed: "What are you doing, Matushka? The sack will be heavy to carry."

"I'll get it there; let's go!" We arrived at the field and began working. Suddenly dark clouds appeared, the wind blew, rain came down in torrents, and it instantly became cold. Mother Anastasia began to dress and cover us, each one in something, and she gave out everything that was in the sack. We all thanked her.

THAISIA GRIGORIEVNA FOMINA

"I was very close to Mother Anastasia; she was even closer and dearer to me than Fr. Sebastian. Mother Anastasia was true love. She used to yell at some people, but she felt sorry for me my whole life. She walked the path of foolishness-for-Christ, and it was difficult to understand her. Even her brother by birth (who lived in Petersburg) considered her to be crazy. Her family loved her very much, but when she began to act strangely everyone wept over her. She felt sorry for her family; her sister Marina came here three times, back during the Elder's time. Some of our people visited her brother in Petersburg and saw him (he looked like her; she was very beautiful in her youth), and gave him Communion. But they couldn't understand that she was in her right mind.

"She did what she did in a concealed manner, without openly showing her wisdom, and occasionally in such a way that she was beaten, scolded, or considered to be harsh. I remember how she once yelled at one of our sisters because she had taken something without asking: 'You so-and-so—may your hands shrivel up!' I went up to her and said, 'Matushka, I also once took something from you without permission.' She turned and said, 'Here's my place, and here are my things; take anything you want and don't tell me about it.' She had needed to humble that sister in some way. And she didn't even have anything of her own. Whenever anything was brought to her—she needed it all and took it all. But five minutes later she would have nothing left; she had given everything away. Those in whom she foresaw great need or sorrow she would cater to more than the rest. Some would murmur that she was paying special attention to a particular person, but then such sorrow would befall that person that there would be nothing for him to be happy about.

"Or they would be sitting at the table. Mother Anastasia would give one person something, fill another's plate, and then a third. It would appear as though she herself were sitting and eating, but she would remain hungry. Once she even said to me, 'Thaisia, not once have I ever eaten bread to satiety.'

"From a young age, Mother Anastasia had been very sick with a woman's malady. An operation was suggested to her, but she refused, even though the disease caused her severe physical suffering. When she was still young, she went to an Elder in Optina Monastery regarding the issue, and he said, 'This is your set of chains.' She carried these 'chains' to the end. Besides this, her legs hurt; they were very swollen with varicose veins, and she had terrible cramps. She endured this and never used any sort of medicine. This was her labor, her podvig, which lasted all her life. Maybe she wore felt boots and galoshes because other foot-wear wouldn't fit her.

"Mother Anastasia sang at the cliros; she had a good voice. No one saw how she prayed, but everyone knew that she prayed for everyone.

"She worked at the church tirelessly. She washed and cleaned everything. She made very tasty kvass, and kissel out of oats. She would follow Fr. Sebastian everywhere, and would take kissel with her. The Elder would go to Melkombinat, and she would follow him. She could even go by foot, and she knew all the houses that he would visit. Once he went to see Alexandra Sofronovna in Melkombinat. Her husband had cancer of the esophagus, and he had gone to give him Communion and to serve a Moleben. While they were praying in the house, Mother Anastasia went to the garden to take care of things. When Sofronova went outside and took a look at her garden, she felt ill. The Eldress had pulled up all the cucumber plants, which were about to bloom, and had stuck them in the ground upside-down, with the roots sticking up. 'Mother! What have you done?! I should take a stick and thrash you!' But the next day such a hard frost hit that everything in the garden froze. Mother Anastasia had pulled up Sofronova's garden early, but she hadn't caused any loss.

"Sometimes she would come and work for a person, doing all that she could, and then, so they wouldn't praise her, she would put on somebody else's felt boots. 'Mother, why did you put on someone else's boots?'

"'Oh, so you're sorry to lose your boots?' Bang! She'd toss one boot one way and the other the other way, and then she'd leave, barefoot. Was one to thank her or scold her? Everyone was puzzled—a very complicated business.

"I'll tell you about one more incident. Mother Anastasia was walking through the church, pushing everyone out of her way. She went up to Mother Tamara and threw her off her chair: 'All right, get up! I'm going to give the seat to a sick person!' She drove away the elderly Mother Tamara and seated Aunt Liza, who was much younger. The sisters grumbled at her, 'What's with you, Mother, are you playing the fool!?' And what do you think? Soon Aunt Liza fell ill. She felt very poorly, and they put her in the hospital, and she felt sick there as well. Then they discovered that she had cancer. Mother Anastasia didn't bless her to have an operation; she foresaw that she was going to die. The young and healthy Aunt Liza died in a year and a half, while Mother Tamara lived another fifteen years. There you have it. It seems to us to be eccentricity, but she had her own law. She had such love; she was a kind of person that doesn't exist any more."

Antonina Ivanova

"Some guests came from Moscow to visit Fr. Sebastian. They took a taxi at the train station and before they arrived in Mikhailovka, the car got stuck in a pothole. (The roads were bad; they were full of potholes and the mud was knee-deep.) The car's wheels were spinning, and it couldn't get out.

"Some people came to Mother Anastasia and said, 'Matushka, guests are coming; they've gotten stuck in a pothole and can't get out.'

419

"'Well, let's go push them out,' said the Eldress. She got dressed and took a shovel on her shoulder. She came to the car, looked at it, tapped the body of the car from behind with the shovel, and said to the driver, 'Hey mister, sit down and drive; what are you dawdling for?' He looked at her very strangely, but was in no hurry to drive. Again she said, 'Drive the car!'—this time as an order. And when Mother Anastasia said something as an order, no one could resist her. Chills went up the driver's spine. He sat down in the car, began driving it, and the car flew out of the pothole. The driver was stunned. He brought the guests to the church and took off.

"The next day he came to thank Mother Anastasia. He brought her some gifts and asked, 'How were you able to push the car out? We would have needed a bulldozer.' She replied, 'The Lord helped!'"

Anna Shevchuk

"I came to Karaganda when Fr. Sebastian was no longer among the living, and Mothers Anastasia and Agnia had also reposed. I had come from the Ukraine to enter the correspondence course department of the Institute, and during examination time I stayed in Mikhailovka with the Elder's spiritual children. I began to come occasionally to the Mikhailovka church, even though at that time I was distant from religion.

"During my first visit to Karaganda (this was in December), I heard talk in the church that the following day would be the Elder's nameday, and that in the evening of this day they were going to serve a Parastasis. At that time I didn't know the rites of the Church, and I had no idea what a 'Parastasis' was. That night I had the following dream. A priest was leading me by hand through the church courtyard. People were crowded around us, but I saw him as though in a fog. I only heard the people calling out, 'Batiushka Sebastian, Batiushka Sebastian!' But the Elder seemed to be waving his hand, as if to say, 'Wait, I don't have time right now.' And he led me across the yard and showed me everything: 'This is our prosphora bakery; this is our refectory.' Where the gates are that lead up to the street, there seemed to be a lawn and a little running stream, and two nuns were sitting there and pouring out *zapivka*.* The people called them by name: Mother Agnia and Mother Anastasia. The Elder stopped, the nuns gave me some water to drink from the stream, and then I found myself in the church. In the middle of the church stood our priests—Fr. Peter, Fr. Alexander, Fr. Paul, and Fr. Vladimir. They were reading prayers and commemorating Fr. Sebastian. Then I woke up.

"In the house where I was living a portrait of a priest hung on the wall. When I woke up I asked, 'Whose portrait is that?'

"'Fr. Sebastian's,' replied my hosts.

"'Well, I just saw him in a dream.'

"'Well,' they said, 'that means that you're "one of ours."'

"And a few years later, when I graduated from the Institute, I remained in Karaganda, where I work to this day as an accountant in the Mikhailovka church.

"The first year I worked in the church I still was in the habit of using cosmetics. During Bright Week I went to a store and saw that French mascara was for sale there. I wanted to buy it, but it turned out that I didn't have any money with me. 'Oh well,' I thought, 'I'll come here some other time and buy it.' Then I had another dream: there was a church, and everyone was exchanging the triple Paschal kiss, and saying, 'Mother Anastasia, Mother Anastasia!' And Mother Anastasia was exchanging the triple kiss with everyone. 'But she doesn't know me,' I thought. Suddenly she came up to me: 'Christ is risen!'—and hit her Paschal egg

---

*A mixture of wine and hot water given to those who have just received Holy Communion.—TRANS.

421

against mine, cracking it. She was so joyful, and she hugged me. At that moment Fr. Alexander Kiselev walked up to us. He was holding my cosmetics in his hand, and he said, 'Matushka, how are you going to be saved with these?' I looked, and there was the mascara. I was so embarrassed. 'But Matushka,' I said, 'I didn't even buy it; I was only thinking about it!' And she hugged me: 'You don't need it; you don't need it,'—meaning that I didn't need to use makeup. And she kept feeding me something.

"This really amazed me; after all, I had only gone into the store in passing, but she knew everything and had been concerned.

"Mother Anastasia also placed me on the cliros in church. When I would come in to pray, I would stand and quietly sing along. At this time I had a dream that the church was full of people, with the priests standing in the middle of the church, as though they had come out for the magnification; and Mother Anastasia was on the cliros dressed in simple worldly attire (as she often was), standing there and calling for me. But I was terrified—how could I go over there with the priests standing here! Then Mother Anastasia took me by the hand, led me to the cliros, stood me before an icon of the Savior, and said, 'Read *Our Father*.' And she stood and waited for me to begin reading. I began to read loudly. After that dream the singers began to pull me to the cliros, telling me to sing. And to Fr. Alexander they said, 'What's that girl standing there for?' They put me on the cliros, and so I wound up there and got used to it.

Maria Fyodorovna Orlova

"I had been very sick with a skin disease. I was treated by university lecturers and professors, and it would get a little better, but then the huge sores would again appear on my hands. I hadn't been to church for a long time but when I came, Mother Anastasia asked, 'Why haven't you been here for so long?'

"'Matushka,' I said, 'I've been tormented. Take a look at what I've got on my hands! I can't even go to work—everyone avoids me.' And I showed her my hands. She said, 'Tfoo! What's this? This is nothing! Take your finger like this and spit on it, and spread the spit on your sore in the form of a cross.' I immediately began to do this in front of her. When I came home I spat and rubbed endlessly. And my sores went away immediately. It happened so quickly! They had been red and infected, and at first they darkened, then they turned blue. Then the wounds began to shrink and, glory be to God, everything went away. That's the story. But when I had been going to the hospital, they had set me on a chair so that all the students could see me as a rare example of an abundant exudative erythema."

Olga Sergeyevna Martynova

"My niece Irene worked as a warehouse worker. Once thirty imported shawls arrived at their warehouse. Either Irene wanted to engage in fraud with her co-workers, or God knows what; but when the store workers came to the warehouse to receive the shawls, they only signed for them. They brought the documents back to the store, and the shawls remained in the warehouse. There was an invoice but no shawls. But someone informed on them; the store was closed and sealed, and an auditing commision was placed in the store. During the night my niece didn't sleep, and in the morning she ran to me: 'Thus and thus,' she said, 'what am I going to do?' I couldn't suggest anything. 'Let's go to Mother Anastasia,' I said, 'and see what she says.' When we arrived, Mother Anastasia was at the cliros. We went up to her and explained that the documents were in the store, the shawls were in the warehouse, and that she was threatened with prison if the business were to come to light. What should we do? 'Nothing!' said the Eldress, and she turned to Irene: 'Go now, and find a vehicle that's used to pump out toilets, take the shawls, drive to the store, and park in front of it. A cleaning lady will come out of the store, carrying two buckets—don't approach this cleaning lady. A little while later another cleaning lady will come out, also carrying two buckets. Quickly go up to this one, hand her the shawls and say, "Toss these wherever there is room for them, just as long as it's on the premises."'

"That's what Irene did—she found the necessary vehicle and drove to the store, and they let her drive in front. Such a vehicle is not suspicious—after all, they had come to clean the toilets. Irene let the first cleaning lady pass by and ran up to the second one. She took the shawls and tossed them in the store—and that was it. With this the whole misfortune ended. Both the signatures and the shawls were there.

"There is another similar story. It came time for my son Stephen Stepanovich to enter the Institute. I came to see Mother Anastasia. 'Matushka,' I said, 'Stephen is entering the Institute; you've got to help him.' She said, 'Oh! That's very simple. Find out when he's going to take the examinations. Come to church on those days and bring forty ten-kopeck rolls here. We'll pray here, and he will get straight "fours."'* And that's what I did. He took his first examination, and I brought forty rolls. They were snatched up in an instant and handed out. My son came from the examination with a four. For the next examination it was the same way. There were four examinations in all, and I brought forty rolls for each examination; my son received fours for all the examinations. Thus, by Mother Anastasia's prayers, Stephen Stepanovich enrolled in the Institute.

---

*That is, perfect grades.—Trans.

Nina Khokhlushka

"Once on a Friday my co-workers from the hospital where I worked talked me into eating some sausage. The next day I came to church and stood through the Liturgy. After the Liturgy, Mother Anastasia began distributing holy water to everyone, and she said to me, 'Come over here.' I went over, and she started thrashing me, shouting to the whole church, 'Ach, you pig! Ach, you pig!' I was frightened—what did she mean by 'pig?' 'Matushka,' I shouted, 'give me some holy water!' But she didn't give me any, and continued to hit me. The people ran over: 'They're beating Khokhlushka!' But Mother Anastasia shouted, 'This is a pig!' That sausage was evidently pork.

"After she had given me a good thrashing, I calmed down and went to Fr. Sebastian for a blessing. I went up to him, and he said, 'Nina! You're a nameday child today!' That meant that I'd been clobbered. 'Well, here's some prosphora for you!' That's how they communicated in the spirit."

Monk Sebastian (Khmyrov)

"Once Mother Anastasia walked from the wing where the right choir stands, and walked through the church shouting, 'Who needs a kerchief? Who wants a black kerchief?' She walked up to the other wing, where Motya Minaeva said, 'Matushka, please give me the black kerchief; I don't have a black one.' But she said, 'Well, no; you don't need it.' And she kept going. And by the doors, by the entrance, our mother was standing and trembling: 'Uh oh, she'll probably give me the black kerchief; it probably foretells something terrible!' Mother Anastasia walked up to her and asked, 'Do you need a kerchief?'

"'No,' said our mother, 'I already have three black kerchiefs; I don't need it.'

"'Well, if you have three, then this is for you too.' And she gave the black kerchief to her. She had foreseen that our mother would become a nun."

Nun Eunice (Khmyrova)

"Mother Anastasia used to tell us, 'When I was blessed to be a fool-for-Christ's-sake, my first obedience was to take a bag and go begging. But I didn't want to. "Send me to do any sort of work," I said, "only not begging!" "No, no; don't go to work, go begging." I took a bag and I went on my way. But it was some sort of feast day; the young men had assembled, and I walked along with my little bag, dressed in a long loose dress. I heard the young men say, "What a pretty little lady!" I thought, "What do I do? It's me they're talking about." Then they said, "If we were to tidy her up—that would be something!" Then I crawled into a cellar and blew my nose all over myself. "Oh," they said, "she's cra-a-zy! She's crazy!" Then I felt better, and went on. "So!" I thought, "I'm already a fool! That means that now I'll have to be a fool." And that's what I've been all my life.'

"In Optina Monastery Fr. Sebastian once heated up the Elder's (Fr. Nektary's) cell and followed him to church. The Elder foresaw what Nastya was doing in the cell, and he didn't leave the church. She had opened the door and sat down on the threshold; she propped the door open and was sitting there. But the weather was coming in! The snow was flying right in! Fr. Sebastian came to throw some wood in the stove, but the cell was full of snow; and Nastya sat at the door without her coat, wearing only her dress and kerchief. She sat there with the door propped open, and wouldn't let him close it. He tried to persuade her: 'Come on, Nastya, let me close the door!' But she was silent. Then he carefully picked her up and carried her somewhere else, closed the door, and began to feed the stove. She used to be persecuted and beaten there, but Fr. Sebastian didn't beat her. He had already foreseen her life by then. By the time he had warmed up the cell, the Elder came back from the church.

"When she was already in Karaganda, Mother Anastasia would sometimes expose people's sins. One family that lives here in Melkombinat had a cow, and they used to sell everything from the cow at the market—sour cream and milk. They were a little greedy. Once they had made some sour cream to sell, and then they left to go somewhere. Mother Anastasia arrived, kneaded some dough using the sour cream, and baked a whole pile of buns—eat 'em up! She used up all the sour cream. The owners of the house grumbled at her, of course. Another time she came when they were at the market, pulled up all the cucumber plants in their garden, and laid them in a pile. When they arrived, they were quite upset: 'What's going on here?! How hard we worked, how much care we put into them!' This was in the evening. That night it all came to nothing—there was a frost that hit the gardens to such an extent that everything turned black. They had grumbled, but Mother Anastasia had given them to understand that 'I know what the Lord will grant, and what will happen tomorrow and the day after.'

"Sometimes Fr. Sebastian himself would expose people's sins through her. Once, when there was not yet a church, and the Elder used to pray in Melkombinat, after dinner he began to direct everyone to where they would spend the night. To Mother Anastasia he said, 'Go spend the night at Stephanida's place.' She went there, and knocked: 'Let me in to spend the night.'

"'We don't have any room,' they answered, and didn't let her in. This was during the wintertime. But since she had a blessing to spend the night at Stephanida's house, she might freeze—but she wouldn't leave. So she lay down on the threshold in the doorway. Of course, because of the Elder's prayers, she wouldn't freeze. In the morning the owners of the house got up and tried to open the door, but it wouldn't open—Mother Anastasia was lying on the threshold. Snow had fallen during the night and covered her. She jumped up and shook herself off: 'Oh, forgive me; I've bothered you.' The Elder had sent her deliberately in order to sting the cruel hearts of those people. Then they rushed to her: 'Mother Anastasia! But how can this be!? How can this be?' She was sick and practically uncovered, and it had been a cold winter night. Their hearts, of course, were pricked: 'We're the ones that treated her this way; after all, we did have room for her to spend the night.' And afterwards they went to Fr. Sebastian in repentance; they had sensed what this had been about.

"Another time, when the Elder had finished serving a Pannikhida in the church, Mother Anastasia ran up and took something from the pannikhida table. He began hitting her with a stick: 'Did you put there what you've taken?'

"'No, Batiushka, I didn't put it there.'

"'Then why do you take it? A Pannikhida is a fire. To take something from a Pannikhida, you have to pray. Do you know how to pray?' Mother Anastasia, of course, knew how. And she didn't need that bun. This was how the Elder, with Mother Anastasia, exposed those who would sneak up and take things from the pannikhida table. For them it was a lesson—they were reminded that a Pannikhida is a fire, and they long remembered how Fr. Sebastian had beaten Mother Anastasia with a stick.

"When we were burying our mother, after the funeral I and one slave of God, Nadezhda, who had helped at the funeral, both had dark blue spots appear on our right legs, which looked like anthrax. They burned, and we were nauseous and our heads ached. We suffered for nine days with this. Our legs became swollen, and both she and I felt poorly. On the ninth day

Mother Anastasia came for the funeral dinner. 'Matushka,' I said, 'after the funeral something appeared on our legs.' She said: 'Here are my boots. Here, put them on.' And she had one large rag boot, and another leather one from her left foot, which was smaller. She gave me the rag one: 'Here, put this on and let's go right now to Vespers.' But how was I supposed to walk in it? You could have fit three or four feet in it, it was so big. Nadya's was smaller, though, the one that was for the left foot. We gave Mother Anastasia my boots with snaps in exchange, and she said to Mother Irene,* 'Put walking sticks in their hands.' Mother Irene got some kind of twisted sticks from the yard. My stick was a little better, but Nadya's was outright curled. And so we walked to church with the sticks, and in those boots. I was wearing a black velvet dress and a new white batiste kerchief. But Mother Irene had covered her head with a dirty, torn shawl. I said, 'What did you cover yourself with such a rag for? That's what I was binding my leg with. Don't you have anything to cover yourself with?' 'No-o', said Mother Irene, 'this is fine, this is fine.' Well, if it was fine for her, then there was nothing for me to worry about. We arrived at the church. The medical student Motya saw us: 'Oho!' she shouted, 'they're being fools! They're acting like fools-for-Christ'! She didn't know that Mother Anastasia was healing us, and that our feet were terribly sore. Then I began lighting candles, and I caught my batiste kerchief on fire. Mother Irene ran up: 'Oh, oh, oh!'—and she snatched my kerchief off my head. 'Here, take mine'— and she covered me with her torn shawl. I had to go up for the anointing, and the church was full of people. I was a bit embarrassed, of course, and everyone said, 'Why aren't you dressed properly?' But what can you do? My foot was hurting. Oh, well. When we came home, Mother Anastasia said, 'Don't

---

*Abbess Irene (Koroleva) was born in 1916 and reposed on October 17, 1993. She is buried in the Mikhailovka cemetery.

go anywhere tomorrow; lie at home and don't eat anything all day. (It was the Feast of the Beheading of St. John the Forerunner.) Then your legs will go wherever you want, and your head won't ache.' Nadya and I came home from church and looked at our legs—there was nothing there! Everything had healed up, and the pain had subsided."

MARIA NIKITICHNA OBRAZTSOVA

"Mother Anastasia—now there was a mischief-maker! Once, when Fr. Sebastian was getting ready to go somewhere, he took a car full of girls with him. He gave seats to the nuns but he didn't take Mother Anastasia. She knocked on the car and yelled, 'Ooh! Give me a khlabuda,' that is, something to wear. For her it was unimportant whether it was winter or summer—she ran around practically undressed in front of the Elder. When he arrived, she was already there. She never lagged behind in her whole life. But she served him in faith and truth. And the Elder loved her."

LYDIA VLADIMIROVNA ZHUKOVA

"When Mother Julia was dying, she told me, 'Lida, when Mother Anastasia was feeling poorly, she said, "When they take Batiushka away to Optina Monastery, don't forget me."' That's what Mother Anastasia commanded Julia, then Julia likewise commanded me."

* * *

"In 1975 Metropolitan Joseph (Chernov) came on a routine visit to the Mikhailovka church. His Eminence often said about the Eldress, 'Mother Anastasia prophesies; she prophesies'. During this visit with him, Mother Anastasia began to say goodbye to him: 'Bless me, Vladyka, and forgive me; we won't see each other again.' But he didn't want to accept this prophecy. In

Alma-Ata in the summer, when some students of the Moscow seminary came to visit him, the Metropolitan addressed one of them—Peter Veretennikov—while they sitting at table: 'Petya, let's go to Tselinograd, and after Tselinograd we'll go to Karaganda and chastise Mother Anastasia.' But this did not come about. Circumstances arose in such a way that the Metropolitan flew immediately from Tselinograd to Alma-Ata; and on September 4, 1975, Metropolitan Joseph died in the hospital during an operation. Mother Anastasia had also said, 'If they don't put Vladyka in a hospital, he'll stay alive, but if he ends up in a hospital, then he'll die.'

"Mother Anastasia died on April 13, 1977. Before her death she was tonsured into the schema. She is buried in the Mikhailovka cemetery."

Archpriest Michael Neigum*

"I know for certain that Mother Anastasia was a holy person. She was saintly with the type of sanctity that doesn't catch your attention. The important thing is that she always hid her spirituality. Her spirituality only showed itself clearly when, for example, some predictions or prophecies would come to pass. Generally she was, I think, even intentionally a bit rude, and she walked with a waddle. She was always shuffling about and giving all sorts of little sermons to everyone. If one were to judge her by her outward appearance, by her behavior, then one wouldn't see any hints of a lofty spiritual life. Only after Fr. Sebastian's death did she begin to act 'normally,' but until then she was extremely difficult to take, and those who did not know her well considered her to be insane. But when the Elder died and the people who had been living right beside a saint suddenly began to have a lack of peace among themselves, Mother Anastasia acted in

---

*From the village of Shemetovo, in the Moscow province.

such a way that this became not so manifest. She calmed everyone down and set them at peace. The majority of the people around her sensed her love and kindness.

"I was born into a Lutheran family. I came to the Church several years after Fr. Sebastian's death. Then I left to serve in the army, and when I returned, my 'turbulent time' began: I didn't listen to anyone, and at one point I was totally uncontrollable. Many close friends seemed to distance themselves from me. But Mother Anastasia was able to force me to eat potatoes with lubricating oil, drink raw eggs (which I couldn't stand), or travel by bus in a woman's shawl, as if I were some kind of lunatic. And it was nothing to me; even though I was already a grown man, I rode in a woman's shawl through the whole city. She could say to me, "Go; run along the road on one leg," and I would go and run down the road around the church on one leg. Why did I do it? Because I had an inward disposition towards Mother Anastasia such as I had towards no one else on the earth—it's that simple. Also because, amidst all her simplicity and rudeness she was a very delicate person; it's difficult even to imagine such a person.

"I loved Mother Anastasia very much. Although, perhaps it was not her that I loved, but I liked her kind attitude towards me. It wasn't really her that I saw. I saw only her big felt boots in galoshes, that everyone respected her very much, and that she drew me closer to herself. I became vainglorious over the fact that she was well-disposed towards me.

"I spent a great deal of time in her company. Wherever she went, I was right behind her. They would go to see Mother Evdokia. There they would eat and read the Lives of the Saints, and I'd be with them the whole time. I was just unconsciously trying to be near holy people. Mother Anastasia didn't speak much, and she didn't tell stories. Everything was very, very quiet with them. I didn't care to go anywhere; I didn't even want to go home. I simply wanted to be at her side. That's all. I didn't need anything else.

"Later I enrolled for studies at the Theological Seminary. Once I had to return to Sergiev Posad from my school vacation, and I got a plane ticket to Moscow. But Mother Anastasia didn't let me go. She was forceful in not letting me go, as though she were making fun of me. She ordered me to her cell and began to speak with me. And I had been posing as an obedient person—I had been hopping around on one leg and drinking raw eggs. I had been making it appear that I was very obedient. And so, when she was speaking with me, I told her once and for all that I had a plane ticket, and that I had to hurry. But she paid no attention to that. I really wanted to go to Moscow then; I was bursting to go there. Therefore, when she detained me and I was going to be late, naturally it was unpleasant to my soul. I became angry; I gnashed my teeth. At that moment I even doubted her sanctity and her clairvoyance. I even insulted her in my thoughts. But she simply took away my ticket and didn't let me go.

"But when it turned out that the plane crashed upon landing and that everyone had died … yes … then it was a completely different matter. I didn't even tell her what had happened. And she didn't say a word to me…. I flew off a day later on the same flight number.

"From time to time I would visit Mother Agnia. I related a little differently to her, because I saw that she was very ill. All her fingers were crooked: she had polyarthritus, dropsy, and some other illnesses. She could barely move about with the help of a tall stand, but she would never show that she was in pain. This person too (I would later recall) touched me deeply. Usually the women liked to whisper about Mother Agnia and Mother Anastasia, that those nuns—oho! OHO! I didn't pay any particular attention to this but, all the same, Mother Agnia would touch my soul. Mother Agnia was like such a little child, a tender child, even though she was very old. Her little voice was like a little child's, and she spoke with me like a little child would.

"I can't say anything special about the nuns. I can only say that they were unusual in that they were truly clairvoyant and truly God-pleasing beings. But externally they conducted themselves like humble, quiet old women. It's true that Mother Anastasia sometimes got angry, that is, she could speak very harshly. But this never affected me. With me she was always like a loving grandmother. And one time I sensed that Mother Agnia could also speak harshly with a person. But that didn't affect me either. She was very loving to me ... so as not to scare me off. A boy had come from another religion, and she didn't want to scare me off.

"Now I recall my whole life, and it becomes clear that there was nothing in my life except sin, and that I was very guilty before the nuns. And I know with absolute certainty that it's by their prayers alone that I'm still living in this world. Great thanks be to God that there was a time in my life when I lived alongside such people. I have not spent a single day without turning to them, and I ask their help each day."

APPENDIX

This enormous field is a cemetery for fifteen thousand prisoners.
A contemporary photograph from the settlement of Spassk.

Historical Information on the "Karlag"

If one attempts to trace the historical origins of Karaganda, it will be found that the history of this city is nothing other than the history of the Karaganda labor camp and the history of the peasants who were resettled there in the 1930s. Up to the 1930s Karaganda, as such, did not exist. Only on the location of what is now the Old City,* on a hillock, did there stand a red-brick outbuilding with a dark red tin roof, built by Englishmen during the reign of the Tsar. It was by the English that the first opening was made on the spot of the future first mineshaft. The first coal that was mined was shipped out on camels. On that area of the steppe were several settlements of those who had moved there at the turn of the century—Old Tikhonovka, Greater Mikhailovka, Dubovka, Fyodorovka and Kreshchenovka, where Russian settlers lived. In several of them there stood Orthodox churches. This is all there was up to 1930, the year of the "great turning-point," when throughout all Russia there began the general collectivization, or the mass persecution, of the peasant class.

Included in the first "five-year-plan" was the task of opening up the virgin lands of Central Kazakhstan and the working of

---

*The name of one of the regions of present-day Karaganda.

the Karaganda coal basin. Since a cheap work force was needed for this, a commission was created for this in 1931 which, together with the GPU, set about the resolution of this question. The commission decided to deport to Central Kazakhstan 52,000 peasant families which, including children and the aged, came out to about half a million people. In February and March of 1931 there began the mass arrests of peasants and their deportation by convoy to the sultry steppe of Central Kazakhstan. At first, for the construction of the railroad from Akmolinsk to the future Karaganda, the fathers of the families and their oldest sons were sent to Akmolinsk. Four months later—that is, by May of 1931—it was already finished. After this they began to bring the families of the railroad workers to the Karaganda Province and the Osakarovka region. Tightly packed convoys of peasant families went under the strict guard of the GPU towards Karaganda. They came from the region along the Volga, beginning from the Province of Astrakhan and ending at the Chuvash and Mordovian Provinces. They came from the Penza, Tambov, Kursk, Voronezh and Orel Provinces; from Kharkov and Orenburg. They conveyed them across the hot steppe in tightly closed metal boxcars, in each one of which there was only one bucket for bodily needs. There travelled in such boxcars pregnant women, nursing mothers, children and the elderly. People began to die in the cars and they were brought, together with the living, to their designated locations. Again the stronger boys and girls were selected from the new arrivals to construct a road from Karaganda to Balkhash. The daily quota (even in winter) for each construction worker was eight tons of earth. The tools were wheelbarrows, crowbars, picks and spades. Those who did not fulfill their quota had their rations reduced. People would collapse. Graves were not dug for them; they were placed right on the railroad embankment and covered over with earth. Thus this railroad from Akmolinsk to Balkhash was literally built on bones.

ПИЩА.

FOOD

ГИГИЕНА!

HYGIENE

And so, 52,000 peasant families were brought during the summer and early autumn of 1931 to the territory of the future Karaganda and thrown under the open sky, left to the mercy of fate. They had no dwellings, nor was there a sufficiency of bread or water. People settled in hastily dug holes that they themselves dug, which were covered by old rags, that they might conceal themselves from the blazing sun and the arid winds of the steppe. During that unusually hot summer virtually all the children below the age of six perished from dysentery and hunger. Those who were left, from the age of ten to the elderly, were mobilized to erect earthen barracks. They did not manage to finish building the barracks by winter and in November, when snow was already falling and there were frosts, they began to settle in the unfinished, uninsulated and unheated barracks, which at times did not even have roofs. One hundred or more people would be lodged in a 540-square-foot area. During the winter of 1931-32 there was a wave of mass fatalities. The chief killers were cold, hunger, an epidemic of typhus, and scurvy. As a result, almost half of the peasants in the settlements died. However, no one made a count of those who died. There were only the burial crews sent by the commandants' offices, who collected the bodies on carts and piled them in ditches that were dug on the outskirts of the settlements.

In the late autumn of 1932 several columns of Kuban Cossacks were sent as replacements to the Osakarov region, where almost all of the peasants had frozen to death. In 1933, when famine struck almost the whole land, a new wave of deaths occurred.

During those terrible years, throughout the whole of the Karaganda Province there was not a single Orthodox church. The exiles met for prayer secretly, in the earthen huts. It was they who comprised what were later the first communities of the Karaganda churches. Beginning in 1942 they petitioned to have

Orthodox churches and prayer houses opened near the mine-shafts and the newly formed settlements.

What is there to say about the first five-year-plan? It was, of course, fulfilled. The first workers opened up thousands and thousands of acres of virgin land. By the middle of the 1930s twenty-five collective farms had been created in the Karaganda Province and the Osakarov region, and the first mines of the Karaganda coal basin were being worked.

But if one were to attempt to reckon the number of all the peasants who had perished here from 1931-33, it would turn out that only one out of four survived. In those hastily dug ditches on the outskirts of the exile settlements and under the railroad embankments from Akmolinsk to Balkhash, there repose the bones of approximately 400,000 peasants and their children.

As with the transportation of the "dispossessed kulaks," a similar problem was solved just as simply: where to obtain, for the development of the unpopulated steppe, a cheap and unde-manding work force—a work force which would be free from family and ready to be driven from place to place, which would not require the building of houses, hospitals or schools.

On December 19, 1931 the decision was made to form in Central Kazakhstan one of the branches of the Gulag—the Kar-lag.* The purpose of its organization was the creation of the ba-sis for agricultural production for the rapidly developing heavy industry of Central Kazakhstan. In one of the first directive documents it was said: "The Karaganda collective farm, organ-ized in 1931, has received an honorable and responsible task—to develop the vast region of Central Kazakhstan." This development began at the end of 1931 with the arrival, from all corners of Russia at the ancient steppe of Sari-Arka, transports

---

* A soviet abbreviation, meaning "Karaganda camp." It was, in fact, an enormous system of camps designed for agriculture.—ED.

The settlement of Dolinka. It was in this kind of supply hut made of clay that Elder Sebastian spent the final years of his imprisonment. Contemporary photograph.

of victims of political repression, along with people from the criminal world. The first transport, numbering 2,567 people, was quartered in a tent camp, ringed about on all four sides by barbed wire. The numbers in the camp grew from year to year, and the huge collective farm grew and developed along with it. Its sphere of influence spread from the Altai to Betpak-Dala, from "the Switzerland of Kazakhstan" to Ala-Tau. The territory of the Karlag was equal to the area of France. The capitol of the Karlag was the settlement of Dolinka (twenty miles from Karaganda). It was through its gates that prisoners arrived, at the Karabas station. The whole boundless steppe of Central Kazakhstan became a common grave for thousands upon thousands of its prisoners.

The Karlag had at its disposal electrical power, weapons, means of transportation, a post office and a telegraph. It consisted of twenty-six branches ("points"), located within a radius of from 2 to 250 miles from Dolinka. The branches were connected in a single farming plan, and there was not an instance when that plan was not fulfilled. There was a particular demand here. Around Dolinka, tightly girding it, there also grew the prison zone, equipped with all the conditions of camp regime—fences topped with barbed wire, watch towers, a ploughed and harrowed control zone, and circular posts of guard dogs. In the center of Dolinka there was placed another department—a prison within a prison, where additional terms were given to prisoners, where they were subject to torture, and where they were shot.

There functioned in the Karlag a board of the Karaganda provincial court that consisted of three persons, called the "Troika." Death sentences were carried out on the spot. Those sentenced were placed on their knees at the edge of a pit dug beforehand by other prisoners and shot in the back of the head. Those shot appeared on the roll lists with the stamp "died," and their personal files were destroyed.

The Karlag flourished. It had an abundance not only of cheap labor, but also possessed a mighty intellectual center. In it were detained world-famous scholars, military commanders, cultural figures, clergy and monastics. Behind the barbed wire of the steppe prisons were concentrated a large number of highly qualified agronomists of all kinds, livestock specialists, medical workers and economists. The living conditions for the prisoners of the Karlag were unbearable. A document drawn up by the investigating staff of the Gulag on February 4, 1941 testifies: "The prisoners are quartered in standard barracks. The walls of the barracks are adobe. They are equipped inside with double bunks. The floors are earthen and there are no winter window frames. It is dirty and damp, and the stove is not lit every day. In the men's barracks the air temperature is 39°, and in the women's it is 61°. Many prisoners do not have bedding. The bathhouse and the

ГДЕ ТЫ, ОДИНОЧЕСТВО ?!

WHERE ARE YOU, O SOLITUDE?!

„BCEX ПОЙМАЕМ!"

"WE'LL CATCH YOU ALL!"

washhouse, in view of the absence of heating, operate inter-mittantly. A tremendous number of lice were discovered, as well as an insufficiency of underwear, which is not changed and not washed. Less than fifty percent of the prisoners are provided with winter clothes. The majority are not dressed according to season, and are wearing summer shoes. Hot water is absent both in the barracks and at the work stations. At the work stations there is not even unboiled water. In place of water, the prisoners eat snow. The food does not contain the proper number of calo-ries. There are instances when they do not go out to work due to lack of shoes and clothing. Prisoners who do not go out to work for this reason are rated as those who refuse to work and are given the same rations as the latter. They are even sent to punish-ment isolation cells."

There were often escape attempts at the Karlag. They all ended with "liquidation." … It is no secret that the fatality rate in the Karlag was very great.

"In the end," as is said in one of the scientific accounts of the experimental stations, "the entire economic activity of the [Kar-lag] can be looked upon as an immense production experiment of the successful agricultural development of the extremely arid steppes and semi-deserts." And so it was. But it was all designed and built by the hands of prisoners, and on their own bones.

Troparion
Tone 3

O servant of the Holy Trinity, * earthly angel and heavenly man, * successor of the spiritual eldership of Optina, * initiate of the mysteries of Christ and confessor, * all-honorable abode of the Holy Spirit, * holy and venerable Father Sebastian, * ask for the world peace, * and for our souls great mercy.

Kontakion
Tone 3

Let us glorify, O ye faithful * him who hath entered into the joy of the Risen Lord, * the fellow-member of the choir of the Elders of Optina, * sharer in the lot of the martyrs and confessors, * co-celebrant with the initiates of God's mysteries, * earthly angel and heavenly man, * godly adornment of the city of Karaganda, * exceeding great intercessor for the land of Kazakhstan, * praise of the Church of Russia, * and let us cry out to him with gladness: * Rejoice O our all-honored and venerable Father Sebastian.

AKATHIST

TO OUR HOLY AND GOD-BEARING FATHER

Elder Sebastian of Optina and Karaganda

KONTAKION 1

Chosen one of the Chief Shepherd Christ Jesus in the time of cruel persecutions raised by the Godless authorities; * successor of the spiritual grace of Optina eldership; * meek sufferer for the Orthodox Faith and courageous confessor of Christ; * luminary of faith and piety granted by God to the city of Karaganda; * unsleeping protector of the whole country of Kazakhstan; * praise of the Church of Russia and joy of the people who bear the name of Christ; * O our holy Father Sebastian, we glorify thy podvigs and labors which thou didst take up for the sake of inheriting the Kingdom of Heaven, * and with fervent love we cry out to thee:

Rejoice, O holy Father Sebastian, pious confessor of faith and image of spiritual meekness!

IKOS 1

The Creator of angels, Who foreknew thee from the creation of the world, hast shown thee forth in these latter times, O holy Father Sebastian, to be an angel by thine immaterial life, an initiate of the mysteries and a harbinger of grace; a prophet, as one who foresaw the future; and a steadfast confessor, for thou didst endure persecution and torture for Christ. Do thou also teach us to sing to thee thus:

Rejoice, fragrant offshoot of pious parents;

Rejoice, thou who wast enlightened by the grace of the Holy Spirit in the fount of Baptism.

Rejoice, emulator of the piety of thy parents from thine infancy;

Rejoice, thou who wast brought by thy father and mother to St. Ambrose in Optina Monastery for a blessing.

Rejoice, thou who didst love the monastic life with all thy soul;

Rejoice, thou who didst establish thyself purely in the doing of the commandments of God from thy childhood.

Rejoice, thou who for the sake of God didst disdain all the beautiful things of this world from thy youth;

Rejoice, thou who, seeking the Kingdom of Heaven, didst settle in Optina Monastery under the protection of the spiritual Elders.

Rejoice, thou who didst perfectly renounce the fulfillment of thine own will;

Rejoice, thou who didst submit thyself with all thy
soul in obedience and humility.

Rejoice, meek disciple and novice of the holy Elder
Joseph;

Rejoice, co-ascetic and co-mystic of the God-
bearing Elder Nektary.

Rejoice, O holy Father Sebastian, pious confessor of
faith and image of spiritual meekness!

KONTAKION 2

St. Nektary, seeing how, for thy meekness and humility, the Heavenly Giver of Gifts would grant unto
thee the grace of spiritual foresight for thy spiritual children, indicated thee as his successor, naming thee
"Summer" for thy compassion and mercy towards the
suffering, and teaching thee to sing to God, the Provider
of all good things: Alleluia!

IKOS 2

Having thine understanding illuminated by the rays
of the Holy Spirit, thou didst evangelically love God,
glorified in Trinity of Hypostases. Having forsaken the
vain glory of the world, thou didst reach the salvific haven of Optina eldership and, taking up thy cross, didst
follow Christ with the spiritual elders, fasters and abste-
mious ones, maintaining thy life in humility. For this
reason are the faithful taught to sing to thee:

Rejoice, thou who didst love the narrow and most
sorrowful path more than the broad one;

Rejoice, thou who didst disdain the world, filled with many vain cares.

Rejoice, for thou didst preserve purity of body and soul, which is beloved of God;

Rejoice, for by fasting and prayer thou didst exchange the corruptible for the incorruptible.

Rejoice, for by abstinence in food thou didst subject the flesh to the spirit;

Rejoice, for by obedience and stillness thou didst mortify the passions of the soul.

Rejoice, for thou didst water the earth of thy heart with tears of repentance;

Rejoice, for having rejected the good things of earth thou didst lead thy mind up to the good things of heaven.

Rejoice, for thou didst ever enclose the sweetest name of Jesus in thy mind through prayer;

Rejoice, for through Him as through the Word, Holiest of the Holies, thou didst come to know God the Pre-eternal Father in the Holy Spirit.

Rejoice, for thou didst acquire the grace of the Comforter, the Spirit of Truth by the purity of thy heart;

Rejoice, for thou didst receive the power of spiritual foresight and eldership from God.

Rejoice, O holy Father Sebastian, pious confessor of faith and image of spiritual meekness!

KONTAKION 3

By the power of the grace of God, through the spiritual guidance of the Elders of Optina, thou wast led by the narrow way of monastic life to the reception of the destiny of pastoral service in the Holy Church and the podvig of confession of Christ, Crucified and Risen. Unto Him, O holy Father Sebastian, for the whole of thy life thou didst sing: Alleluia!

IKOS 3

Having in thy heart firm faith, undoubting hope, and true love for Christ our God Who was crucified for us, thou didst, at the time of the raising of persecutions by the God-fighting authorities against the Church of God, lean thy head upon the altar of Grace with humility and meekness, receiving the gift of the priesthood from hierarchical hands with trembling of heart, for the sake of the salvation of those perishing from the stench of atheism. Wherefore, from our zeal we render unto thee these praises:

Rejoice, thou who didst zealously serve Christ, the Good Shepherd;

Rejoice, receiver of revelations of the holy mysteries of Christ, shining forth with the gifts of the Holy Spirit.

Rejoice, thou who didst lay down thy life for the flock of Christ's rational sheep entrusted to thee;

Rejoice, preacher of the path of salvation to those seeking the Kingdom of Heaven.

Rejoice, divinely wise leader of those in search of the
Jerusalem on high;
Rejoice, divinely gifted instructor of those laboring
in piety.
Rejoice, good helmsman of those in the grip of sin-
ful passions;
Rejoice, patient teacher of the infirm and those of
little skill.
Rejoice, propitious consolation of those grown faint
from despondency and sorrow;
Rejoice, speedily defending helper of the helpless.
Rejoice, most wondrous father and clairvoyant
elder to monastics;
Rejoice, ardent preserver of the precepts of Optina.
Rejoice, O holy Father Sebastian, pious confessor of
faith and image of spiritual meekness!

KONTAKION 4

Not fearing the storm of fierce persecutions raised
by the Godless authorities, thou didst, with all the New
Martyrs and Confessors of Russia, take upon thyself the
easy yoke of Christ and, sorrowing in spirit, didst bear
His light burden. Thou didst reach the cold region of
Karaganda, where a numberless multitude of innocent
sufferers rendered up their souls to God. Thou, O
good-hearted father, didst zealously offer up thy prayers
to the Lamb of God for the repose of their souls, mourn-
ing over their graves with the song: Alleluia!

IKOS 4

Hearing how the children of the Church across the whole face of Holy Russia were receiving a brutal death and cruel persecutions for the Orthodox Faith, handed down to them by their fathers, thou wast not frightened, O blessed one, by the length of the cruel path, and didst humbly walk it, being exiled by the God-opposing persecutors. Thou didst overcome the fierce winter and the desert heat of summer and the fiery rage of the torments of the camps by thy patience, having acquired the spiritual warmth of eternal blessedness. For this we cry out to thee thus:

Rejoice, thou who didst inherit the blessedness of the Kingdom of Heaven by poverty of spirit;

Rejoice, thou who didst receive Christ's consolation by weeping over thy sins.

Rejoice, thou who wast sated by imperishable heavenly food through hunger and thirst for God's righteousness;

Rejoice, thou who didst receive the mercy of God by thy mercy of compassion for thy neighbor.

Rejoice, thou who, with a pure heart, didst see God in thy sufferings;

Rejoice, for in thy pacification of the embittered thou wast called a son of God.

Rejoice, thou who didst acquire the blessedness of the Kingdom of Heaven in being persecuted for righteousness' sake;

Rejoice, thou who in the midst of false revilement and malignant gossip wast clothed in Christ.

Rejoice, thou who didst entrust thyself to the Providence of God in the end;

Rejoice, emulator of Abraham, the father of the faithful, in thy banishment from thine earthly Fatherland.

Rejoice, thou who didst acquire the strength of Job in thine endurance of illnesses and afflictions;

Rejoice, thou who didst manifest the humility of David in thy meek endurance of persecutions.

Rejoice, O holy Father Sebastian, pious confessor of faith and image of spiritual meekness!

KONTAKION 5

Thou wast manifest as a divinely moving star, kindled by the Elders of Optina, O greatly esteemed Father Sebastian. Thou wast in truth placed by God to celebrate the Divine Services; and by thy pure mind, humble heart and meek soul thou didst offer up thy service to Him. Thou didst endure misfortunes, persecutions and illnesses, and confession for the sake of the Divine Truth, and thou wast shown to be His, by thy life and words, to all those in exile and imprisoned in prisons and camps. Thou didst strengthen the infirm and confirm the faithful to sing in thanksgiving to God: Alleluia!

IKOS 5

The people surrounding thee in the confines of the camps, seeing thy meekness and love, radiant with the purity of thy conscience, were amazed at thine extreme patience. And we, knowing of thine arduous suffering and pains, glorify thee, who didst evangelize the prisoners in apostolic manner, enlighten the darkened thoughts of men and lead the former spoils of the devil to Christ, and we cry out to thee in thanksgiving:

Rejoice, fragrant lily who blossomed forth in the steppe of Karaganda;

Rejoice, thou who didst heal withered souls with the myrrh of Christ-emulating virtues.

Rejoice, thou who didst languish long in prison in cruel hunger and great thirst;

Rejoice, for thou didst in these deprivations find Christ, Who came to thine aid.

Rejoice, thou who didst never abandon fasting and abstinence;

Rejoice, thou who didst ever blaze forth with prayer to God.

Rejoice, thou who wast strengthened invisibly by the grace of the Holy Spirit;

Rejoice, thou who didst by His power save from the snares of the devil those gone astray.

Rejoice, thou who didst lead them to one Holy Catholic and Apostolic Church;

Rejoice, thou who didst teach them true repentance and a pious way of life.

Rejoice, thou who didst in this way drive the evil spirits under heaven to inconsolable lamentation;

Rejoice, thou who didst turn to the Lord and save those formerly in the bonds of servitude to the demons.

Rejoice, O holy Father Sebastian, pious confessor of faith and image of spiritual meekness!

KONTAKION 6

The land of Kazakhstan, which received into its earth the drops of the blood of the New Martyrs of Russia, and the multitude of their suffering bodies which have reposed in its bosom for many years, preaches of the life, equal to that of the angels; the labors, equal to those of the Apostles; and the myriad of miracles of the Saint of Karaganda, Elder Schema-archimandrite Sebastian the Confessor, teaching the faithful to sing to Christ Jesus, the Setter of the contest: Alleluia!

IKOS 6

The light of thy perfect virtues shines forth through the vast expanse of Kazakhstan from the God-saved city of Karaganda, O holy Father Sebastian. Thou wast manifest as a bright and dew-bearing cloud, calming the flame of the anger of heaven, which was righteously moved against us for our sins, and didst cool the torrid heat of our passions of soul and body, reviving our withered hearts and helping to bring forth the fruits of the virtues of all those who sing to thee thus:

Rejoice, thou who didst make the fruitless Karaganda steppe fragrant with the fruit of thy virtues;

Rejoice, thou who didst come to love with thy heart the city of Karaganda as a Golgotha of the Church of Russia.

Rejoice, thou who didst establish in it a most wonderful church in the name of the Most Holy Theotokos in the image of Optina;

Rejoice, thou who didst raise up in it an altar in honor of Saint John the Baptist in memory of the Skete of the Forerunner.

Rejoice, thou who didst establish everything in this church resplendently as in a new Optina;

Rejoice, thou who didst undeceitfully labor in prayer, the priesthood, care for souls and eldership.

Rejoice, for thou didst keep vigil by day and gavest not sufficient sleep to thine eyes by night;

Rejoice, for many priests, monks and nuns, scattered by the evil persecutors, were gathered together in one place by thee.

Rejoice, for thou didst lead a multitude of layfolk under the protection of the Queen of Heaven;

Rejoice, for thou wast manifest as good guide to monastics.

Rejoice, for thou wast a most good shepherd and teacher for thy whole flock;

Rejoice, for thou didst live, not as a lord but as a servant for those who turned to thee.

Rejoice, O holy Father Sebastian, pious confessor of faith and image of spiritual meekness!

KONTAKION 7

Wishing to attain to the heavenly fatherland, though covered in a body of earth, thou didst give wing to thy spirit in prayer and, ascending in thy mind to God, thou didst see the good things on high, singing with all the heavenly powers to God: Alleluia!

IKOS 7

The Master of Heaven did show thee forth as a new citizen of the Jerusalem on high, and as one who would not exchange this for all the beautiful and corruptible things of the world. Thou didst prefer life with the angel-like Optina Elders and didst whiten thy priestly garments with the purity of thy life. Thou didst endure with joy abuse and persecution for the sake of Christ and wast adorned with diverse gifts of the Holy Spirit. For this reason the faithful are taught to sing to thee thus:

Rejoice, thou who didst labor from thy youth in the doing of the commandments of the Lord;

Rejoice, thou who in thy monastic life didst liken thyself to the bodiless angelic ranks.

Rejoice, fellow member of the choir of the spirit-bearing Optina Elders and of all the monastic fathers;

Rejoice, fellow partaker as a victorious martyr and confessor of Christ.

Rejoice, reverent co-celebrant with the receivers of the sacred mysteries of God;

Rejoice, confirmation of the Orthodox Faith.

Rejoice, unshakable pillar of the Church;

Rejoice, O shepherd who was ready to lay down thy life for thy flock.

Rejoice, thou who didst endure many torments and evil abuse in thy persecution for Christ;

Rejoice, thou who didst manifest thyself as a servant of the Heavenly King by thy firm confession of the faith.

Rejoice, thou who didst enter into the joy of the Lord through many sorrows;

Rejoice, thou who didst give it abundantly to all who came to thee in faith.

Rejoice, O holy Father Sebastian, pious confessor of faith and image of spiritual meekness!

KONTAKION 8

Terrifying to the demons, O holy Father Sebastian, was thy prayer, filled with meekness and humility. Thy prayer being ever illumined with light, thou didst acquire the mind of Christ, coming to know ineffable mysteries and contemplating the future as if present. Thou didst free all those who came to thee from demonic affliction and didst instruct them on the path of truth and salvation, crying out to God: Alleluia!

IKOS 8

Thou wast entirely enveloped with divine desire, O holy one, didst live on earth a life equal to that of the angels, and didst receive thine ultimate desire: during the radiant days of Paschal triumph thou didst fly off in soul to the heavenly treasures. Thou standest before the throne of the Most Holy Trinity in the joy of the Saints and hearest from us these praises:

Rejoice, thou who hast ascended from the earthly Paschal celebration to the joy of the eternal Pascha;

Rejoice, thou who hast died at last to sin on earth and acquired incorruptible immortality in Heaven.

Rejoice, for thou art standing before Sweetest Jesus, the Holy of Holies, in eternal glory;

Rejoice, for thou dost intercede before Him for all those who honor thy memory.

Rejoice, for thou hast received from Him a double portion of grace to help those seeking salvation;

Rejoice, thou who art glorified with the gift from Him of healing infirmities of soul and body.

Rejoice, unceasing stream of God's mercy;

Rejoice, inexhaustible source of spiritual joys, stillness and peace.

Rejoice, bright cloud, assuaging the heat of sinful passions;

Rejoice, grace-filled dew, watering and making glad the hearts of the faithful.

Rejoice, luminary, ever illumining us with the light of the virtues in the night of this world;

Rejoice, cluster of Christ's vineyard, feeding and gladdening us with the grace of the All-Holy Spirit.

Rejoice, O holy Father Sebastian, pious confessor of faith and image of spiritual meekness!

KONTAKION 9

All angelic nature is amazed at the great gifts bestowed upon thee from on high, O holy Father Sebastian, clairvoyant one, for the most radiant heavenly habitations have received thee as a new citizen with the Bodiless Powers; and thou hast been settled with the synaxis of the Holy and God-bearing Fathers, exulting with the Apostles, Prophets and holy Hierarchs, celebrating with the Martyrs and the Righteous, and crying out to God: Alleluia!

IKOS 9

Falsely philosophizing orators, blinded by pride, hearkening to the voice of the ancient murderer of mankind and father of lies, the devil, like wild beasts, breathing forth with the rage of Godlessness, raised up fierce persecutions against the Bride of God, the Holy Church. In the midst of them Christ the Lord, the Setter of the Contest, did manifest thee, O venerable one, as a luminary of Orthodoxy and an extraordinary confessor, teaching the faithful to sing to thee:

Rejoice, thou who wast not afraid of torture for the confession of the True God;

Rejoice, thou who didst not refuse to lay down thy life for the Orthodox Faith.

Rejoice, thou who didst not fear the menace of the Godless authorities;

Rejoice, thou who didst, in thy banishment, hasten to lead thy torturers to the knowledge of God.

Rejoice, thou who didst fertilize the withered barrenness of their hearts with thy tearful prayers;

Rejoice, thou who didst sow the seeds of the words of the Gospel in their souls by thy meek and silent endurance.

Rejoice, thou who didst scatter the storm clouds of their dark thoughts by the power of thy prayers;

Rejoice, thou who didst lead them to heartfelt repentance and contrition by the grace given thee by God.

Rejoice, thou who didst open in this way the gates of the Kingdom of Heaven;

Rejoice, thou who, when giving them spring water to drink, didst also give them the imperishable eternal water.

Rejoice, thou who, maintaining fasting and abstinence, didst give away thy food and clothing to the prisoners;

Rejoice, for even an ox, loving thee, warmed thee with its body in the time of winter frost.

Rejoice, O holy Father Sebastian, pious confessor of faith and image of spiritual meekness!

KONTAKION 10

Wishing to save the human race, He Who sits on the holy throne with the Father came to earth, was born of a Virgin who knew not wedlock, was crucified in the flesh, was buried and arose, and ascended back into the Heavens, saying, *If any man will come after me, let him deny himself, and take up his cross, and follow me.* Zealously following this, O holy Father Sebastian, thou didst receive the heights of Heaven, singing unto Christ: Alleluia!

IKOS 10

Orthodox people, not only in Kazakhstan, but in the whole world, obtained in thee an indestructible wall and an insuperable confirmation, O God-bearer Sebastian; for having ended thine angelic life during the radiant days of the Paschal celebration, O holy one, thou dost perform most powerful and glorious miracles throughout all the ends of the earth, standing before God, Who granted thee a Divine pledge, an imperishable crown and eternal glory. For this reason the faithful cry out to thee:

Rejoice, thou who didst steadfastly confess before men Christ, the Power of God and the Wisdom of God;

Rejoice, for the Lord doth confess thee before His Heavenly Father and His holy Angels.

Rejoice, thou who art now illumined by the brilliance of the Three-sunned Divine Light;

Rejoice, thou who hast left thy holy relics as a sign that thou abidest with us.

Rejoice, for thy relics heal every kind of affliction and illness;

Rejoice, for those who are in sorrow and confusion are made glad by them.

Rejoice, for the future General Resurrection is unceasingly preached by them;

Rejoice, for the demons tremble at thy relics.

Rejoice, thou cup pouring forth the precious gifts of God in great abundance;

Rejoice, vessel flowing forth with healing myrrh for the ailing.

Rejoice, candlestand shining with the light of Christ upon those in darkness and the shadow of death;

Rejoice, censer ever offering up for us as incense prayers pleasing to God.

Rejoice, O holy Father Sebastian, pious confessor of faith and image of spiritual meekness!

KONTAKION 11

All the Orthodox cry out a song of thanksgiving to the Fashioner of the Church, for He hath given thee to all who seek salvation as great helper and firm intercessor. Wherefore, O holy Father Sebastian, likewise give unto us, who revere thy holy memory, thy firm helping hand, and ever lead us, who are immersed in sin, out of the deadly deep, and help us to finish the remainder of our lives in true repentance, and vouchsafe us to be saved from everlasting anger, who sing: Alleluia!

IKOS 11

O brilliant lamp, aglow with the ever-shining light of the Most Holy Trinity, thou didst appear to the whole land of Kazakhstan, O venerable Father, and with the rays of thy Christ-like virtues dost scatter the darkness of sin, and with the warmth of thy God-pleasing prayers dost warm the hearts of the faithful, who with thanksgiving cry out to thee thus:

Rejoice, grace-filled treasure and adornment of the land of Kazakhstan;

Rejoice, joy and consolation of Russian Orthodoxy.

Rejoice, fruitful offshoot of Optina Monastery;

Rejoice, shelter, broader than a cloud, of the city of Karaganda.

Rejoice, abundantly flowing river, watering our hearts with salvific teachings;

Rejoice, hopeful harbor for those perishing in the sea of diverse attacks.

Rejoice, thou who dost drive away the stench of passions from those who come to thee;

Rejoice, thou who dost free them from temptations raised up by the world, the flesh and the devil through thine intercessions.

Rejoice, thou who dost impel impenitent sinners to perfect repentance;

Rejoice, banisher of evil spirits and conqueror of demonic hordes.

Rejoice, most skillful physician of sinful wounds;

Rejoice, thou who dost illumine our souls with the brightness of the grace of God.

Rejoice, O holy Father Sebastian, pious confessor of faith and image of spiritual meekness!

KONTAKION 12

We diligently ask of thee, O greatly adept one, for the grace given thee by God, our merciful and speedily attending Father. Send up thy bold prayer to the throne of the Life-creating Trinity for the benefit of our souls and for their unhindered passage from earth to Heaven. Entreat the All-good God, O holy one, for thy city, and for the holy church created by thy holy hands. Incline thine ear also to the magnificent cathedral church, erected in accordance with thy prophecy, wherein repose thy wonderworking relics, and move all who enter therein with faith, reverence and fear of God to sing to God: Alleluia!

IKOS 12

Hymning the wondrous works of God in the pathways of the Russian Church at Her completion of one thousand years of witness of the light of Holy Orthodoxy, we are amazed and we tremble, and yet we also rejoice. For what do we see?! The calm and still monastic Optina Hermitage, which was ravaged by the adversaries of God and lay in desecration and neglect for many years, now joyfully makes glad—for not only has it been returned again to its former beauty, but God has also revealed within it the healing relics of the spiritual Elders. Together with it the formerly unknown and fruitless city of Karaganda rejoices—for it treasures within itself the holy relics of one from the wondrous synaxis of the holy Fathers of Optina. Wondering at this, the Providence of God, with love we cry out to thee, O holy confessor:

Rejoice, forechosen servant of God the Unoriginate Father;

Rejoice, courageous confessor of the Lamb of God.

Rejoice, church, not made with hands, of God, the Most Holy Spirit;

Rejoice, O honorable bearer and praise of the Most Holy Trinity.

Rejoice, thou who dost repose in the unsetting day of the Kingdom of God;

Rejoice, thou who dost sing the thrice-holy Cherubic hymn with the Angels and all the Saints.

Rejoice, thou who dost shine forth with the fiery rays of the grace of God;

Rejoice, thou who dost beam like a radiant lamp in the Heavenly Kingdom of the Sun of Righteousness.

Rejoice, thou who dost enlighten all who honor thy memory with the light of thy grace;

Rejoice, tree of the Paradise of Jesus flowing with miracles bringing forth much fruit for the aid of the Orthodox.

Rejoice, fruitful branch of the vine of Christ that feeds us and gladdens us;

Rejoice, unshakable pillar and mighty confirmation of Holy Orthodoxy.

Rejoice, O holy Father Sebastian, pious confessor of faith and image of spiritual meekness!

KONTAKION 13

O holy Father Sebastian, pious confessor of faith and image of spiritual meekness! Accept our present thanksgiving offered up in praise of thee from our zeal, and by the boldness of thine intercession entreat that we might maintain our faith in purity; ask peace for the world, deliverance from hunger and destruction, remission of sins and the inheritance of the blessed eternal life. May we all joyfully sing with thee and with all the Saints: Alleluia! *Thrice.*

IKOS 1

The Creator of angels, Who foreknew thee from the creation of the world, hast shown thee forth in these latter times, O holy Father Sebastian, to be an angel by thine immaterial life, an initiate of the mysteries and a harbinger of grace; a prophet, as one who foresaw the future; and a steadfast confessor, for thou didst endure persecution and torture for Christ. Do thou also teach us to sing to thee thus:

Rejoice, fragrant offshoot of pious parents;

Rejoice, thou who wast enlightened by the grace of the Holy Spirit in the fount of Baptism.

Rejoice, emulator of the piety of thy parents from thine infancy;

Rejoice, thou who wast brought by thy father and mother to St. Ambrose in Optina Monastery for a blessing.

Rejoice, thou who didst love the monastic life with all thy soul;

Rejoice, thou who didst establish thyself purely in the doing of the commandments of God from thy childhood.

Rejoice, thou who, for the sake of God, didst disdain all the beautiful things of this world from thy youth;

Rejoice, thou who, seeking the Kingdom of Heaven, didst settle in Optina Monastery under the protection of the spiritual Elders.

Rejoice, thou who didst perfectly renounce the fulfillment of thine own will;

Rejoice, thou who didst submit thyself with all thy soul in obedience and humility.

Rejoice, meek disciple and novice of the holy Elder Joseph;

Rejoice, co-ascetic and co-mystic of the God-bearing Elder Nektary.

Rejoice, O holy Father Sebastian, pious confessor of faith and image of spiritual meekness!

KONTAKION 1

Chosen one of the Chief Shepherd Christ Jesus in the time of cruel persecutions raised by the Godless authorities; * successor of the spiritual grace of Optina eldership; * meek sufferer for the Orthodox Faith and courageous confessor of Christ; * luminary of faith and piety granted by God to the city of Karaganda; * unsleeping protector of the whole country of Kazakhstan; * praise of the Church of Russia and joy of the people who bear the name of Christ; * O our holy Father Sebastian, we glorify thy podvigs and labors which thou didst take up for the sake of inheriting the Kingdom of Heaven, * and with fervent love we cry out to thee:

Rejoice, O holy Father Sebastian, pious confessor of faith and image of spiritual meekness!

PRAYER

To our Holy Father Sebastian, Elder of Optina and Karaganda

O MOST HONORABLE AND HOLY ONE, filled with the grace of the Holy Spirit, dwelling place of the Savior and the Father, disciple and successor of the Elders of Optina, most radiant adornment of the city of Karaganda, God-given intercessor for the land of Kazakhstan, God-glorified shepherd of the Russian Church, protector of orphans and widows, unmercenary physician of the infirm, rule of faith and piety, codweller with the monastic Saints and fellow-participant with the martyrs, our God-bearing venerable Father Sebastian! Earnestly having recourse unto thee, we offer up a fervent entreaty: Give, even to our lowliness, from thy treasury; lay low our pride by thy humility; scorch our passions with thy passionlessness; banish from us the habit of sloth by thy wakefulness; arouse our insensitivity by the streams of thy tears; awaken us from negligence by thy vigilance; enkindle in us the flame of prayer by thy prayers; make us lovers of our brothers by thy love; grant unto us the spirit of meekness and humility, the spirit of chastity and piety; free us from the great infirmity of the passions and lead us to true repentance. Thou didst have in thy mind unceasingly the Son of God, Who was crucified for us. Teach us also to have His Sweetest Name unceasingly in our mind and heart, that being enflamed with love for Him we might be ready to meet the dread Day of Judgment and be vouchsafed to enter into the Kingdom of Heaven with thee and to glorify and hymn the Triunal power of our God: the Father, Son and Holy Spirit unto the ages. Amen.

Glossary

Akathist: a special service to Jesus Christ, the Mother of God, or a saint, during which one should stand; literally, "not sitting."

All-night Vigil: a service sung on the eve of a special feast; it is usually comprised of Vespers, Matins, and the First Hour.

altar: the part of an Orthodox church behind the iconostasis, where the preparation and consecration of the Body and Blood of Christ take place.

analogion: an icon stand or stand upon which the Book of the Holy Gospels is placed or read.

antimension: a cloth representing the Savior's shroud in which His Body was lain. This cloth contains a piece of relic and upon this the Divine Liturgy is celebrated.

antiphon: a Psalm, hymn or prayer sung in alternate parts. Also a verse or verses sung as a prelude or conclusion to some part of a service.

apostolnik: a head and shoulder covering worn by nuns, which leaves only the face exposed.

archimandrite: the highest rank conferred upon a priest-monk.

Batiushka: an endearing term for a priest or a monk. The first syllable is accented.

Canon: a set of hymns and verses sung to a particular saint or in honor of a feast; a rule or decree of a historic church council.

canonarch: the person who during Divine Services chants verses, one line at a time, which are then repeated by the choir.

catechumen: one undergoing training and instruction in preparation for Baptism.

catholicon: the main church of a monastery.

cell: room or dwelling place of a monastic.

cliros: the place in church where the services are read and sung.

coenobium: a monastery in which monastics live a common life under an abbot or abbess.

cuffs: wrist bands worn by priests during particular services when holy objects are to be handled.

ecclesiarch: in a monastery, one who is responsible for the good order of the church and the service books.

epitrachelion: a vestment that hangs from the neck of the priest and is the one indispensable vestment for all priestly ministrations.

hermitage: a monastic dwelling, traditionally of a solitary monastic, but often used interchangeably with the word "monastery."

hierodeacon: a monk who is in the rank of deacon.

hieromonk: a monk in priestly rank.

hieroschema-monk: a schema-monk in priestly rank.

iconostasis: a screen partitioning the altar area from the nave of the church on which icons are placed; the "Royal Doors" and deacons' doors allow the clergy and acolytes to enter or exit the altar.

irmos (pl. *irmoi*): the opening stanza of each canticle of a Canon.

kamilavka: head covering (without a veil) worn by monastics.

kathisma: (pl. *kathismata*): one of the twenty sections into which the Psalter is divided for use in Church services.

klobuk: head covering with a veil worn by monastics.

kontakion (pl. *kontakia*): a hymn used in the Divine services in honor of a particular saint or feast.

lampada: an oil lamp hanging before an icon.

lavra: a large coenobitic monastery.

Litia: a procession and solemn intercession at Vespers for special feasts, taking place in the narthex of the church. Also, the shortened Office of the Dead.

mantia: a mantle; the pleated, sleeveless outer robe worn by tonsured monks or nuns.

Matins: one of the daily services which takes place late at night or early in the morning. (According to the daily cycle it is scheduled at 3:00 a.m.) This service is comprised chiefly of psalms and a Canon of hymns which differ from day to day.

Matushka: an endearing term for a priest's wife or for a nun. Accented on the first syllable.

metochion (in Russian, *podvorye*): a dependency of a monastery, usually near or in a large city, for the economic needs of the monastery.

Moleben: a prayer service in which the faithful ask for heavenly help or give thanks to God.

nabedrennik (in Greek, *epigonation*): a diamond-shaped vestment worn at the thigh, given by bishops as an award to priests and hieromonks.

nameday: the feast day of the saint whose name one bears.

obedience: in addition to its ordinary meaning, it signifies a duty assigned and carried out as part of one's obedience to the superior or elder.

omophorion: outer stole used by Orthodox bishops.

Pannikhida: a service of prayer for those who have reposed.

paramon: a square piece of cloth worn by tonsured monastics on the back (under the clothing), upon which is depicted a cross and the words, "I bear on my body the wounds of Christ."

Parastasis: a special, longer service for the dead.

Pascha: the Feast of the Resurrection of our Lord Jesus Christ.

patristic: of or relating to the Holy Fathers of the Church.

phelonion: the large, stiff vestment worn over the shoulders by a priest at certain times during the Divine Services.

Philokalia: an anthology of classic ascetical writings compiled by St. Nikodimos of the Holy Mountain and St. Macarios of Corinth, inspired by and based upon the previous Patristic labors of St. Paisius Velichkovsky.

podrasnik: the basic robe worn by all monastics, including novices.

podvig: an ascetic feat, spiritual labor or, simply, Christian struggle.

prayer rope: a knotted rope commonly used by monastics and many Orthodox Christians in saying the Jesus Prayer.

prelest: spiritual deception or delusion.

Proskomedia: service of preparation for the Divine Liturgy.

prosphoron (pl. *prosphora):* a small round loaf of bread prepared especially for the Divine Liturgy.

relics: the body of a saint, or pieces of bone or objects associated with a saint or holy person, which are venerated by the faithful.

riassa: the outer cassock worn by tonsured monastics.

riassaphore: a monastic who wears a riassa but has yet to be fully tonsured a monk or nun.

riza: a metal covering used to adorn an icon.

royal doors: the central doors of the iconostasis that lead into the altar.

samovar: a metal urn used for heating water for tea.

schema-monk: one who has taken on the highest and strictest monastic discipline, leading a life of seclusion and prayer. He wears the "schema," a special cowl and stole.

schema-nun: a nun who is tonsured into the "schema."

semi-uncial script: mixed upper-lower case script which employs a half cursive style, used for centuries in copying liturgical and Patristic books.

Six Psalms: Psalms 3, 37, 62, 87, 102 and 142, intoned by a reader in the center of the church at the beginning of Matins.

skete: a small monastery; usually a close-knit "family" with an abbot or abbess as its head.

skufia: a soft cap worn by monastics.

sticharion: vestment worn by a deacon or an acolyte during Divine services. Also, the under-vestment worn by a priests when serving the Divine Liturgy.

sticheron (pl. *stichera):* verse of liturgical poetry which is sung in the Divine services.

Symbol of Faith: the credal statement of the Councils of Nicaea and Constantinople, also commonly referred to as the Nicene Creed.

synaxis: gathering, host or multitude, such as a gathering of saints.

Theotokos: the Greek word for the Mother of God; literally, "the God-birthgiver."

tonsure: the rite whereby a novice is clothed in the monastic habit and becomes a monk or nun.

trapeza: the monastery refectory; also the communal meal in the refectory.

trebnik: priest's service book.

troparion (pl. *troparia):* a hymn used in the daily cycle of services and also at Divine Liturgy in honor of a particular saint or feast.

Typica: a service usually chanted in place of the celebration of the Divine Liturgy, consisting of the "Typical Psalms" (Psalms 33, 102, and 145, and the Beatitudes), along with other hymns and prayers.

typicon: the order of Divine services. Also, the rules and ordinances of a particular monastery.

ukase: a decree made by a ruling bishop or a council of bishops.

verst: a Russian unit of length, equal approximately to two thirds of a mile.

Vespers: the daily evening service which begins the liturgical day. It consists of psalms, hymns and verses composed in honor of the feast or saint commemorated on any day.

Vladyka: an endearing term for a bishop, literally "Master." Accented on the second syllable.

Unction: the Sacrament of Anointing, usually for the sick or dying.

Select Bibliography

Agapit [Belovidov], Archimandrite. *Elder Ambrose of Optina* (in Russian). Moscow: Optina Monastery, 1900. Reprinted as *The Biography of Optina Elder Hieroschema-monk Ambrose.* Harbin, 1941.

Anatole, Elder of Optina. *A Collection of Letters to Nuns.* Trans. by Holy Nativity Convent. Jordanville, New York: Holy Trinity Monastery, 1993.

Andrew [Rymarenko], Archbishop. *The Restoration of the Orthodox Way of Life.* Platina, California: St. Herman of Alaska Brotherhood, 1976.

Bagdasarov, Roman V. and Fomin, Sergius V. *The Unknown Nilus* (in Russian—2 volumes). Moscow: Palomnik, 1995.

Benjamin [Fedchenkov], Metropolitan. *God's People: My Spiritual Encounters* (in Russian). Moscow: The Father's House Publishers, 1997.

Bykov, V. B. *Calm Havens for the Respite of a Suffering Soul* (in Russian). Moscow, 1913.

Chetverikov, Fr. Sergius. *Elder Ambrose of Optina.* Platina, California: St. Herman of Alaska Brotherhood, 1997.

Fomin, S. V. (ed.). *Little Flowers of Optina Monastery* (in Russian). Moscow: Palomnik, 1995.

The Glorification in the Choir of Saints of the Synaxis of Holy Fathers and Elders Who Shone Forth in Optina Monastery (in Russian). Kaluga: Optina Monastery of the Entrance of the Theotokos, 1996.

Kavelin, Fr. Leonid. *Elder Macarius of Optina.* Trans. by Valentina V. Lyovina. Platina, California: St. Herman of Alaska Brotherhood, 1995.

Kontzevitch, I. M. *The Acquisition of the Holy Spirit in Ancient Russia.* Platina, California: St. Herman of Alaska Brotherhood, 1988.

Kontzevitch, I. M. *Elder Nektary of Optina.* Platina, California: St. Herman of Alaska Brotherhood, 1998.

Kontzevitch, I. M. *Hieroschema-monk Nektary, The Last Optina Elder* (in Russian). Jordanville, New York: Holy Trinity Monastery, 1953.

Kontzevitch, I. M. *Optina Monastery and its Era* (in Russian). Jordanville, New York: Holy Trinity Monastery, 1970.

Koroleva, Vera (ed.). *The Karaganda Elder, St. Sebastian* (in Russian). Moscow: Pravoslavny Palomnik, 1998.

Lebedev, Mother Catherine. *Outline of the Life of the Elder of Optina Monastery Hieroschema-monk Joseph* (in Russian). Shamordino: Kazan Icon Convent of Elder Ambrose, 1911. Reprinted as *Optina Elder Joseph: Biography and Notes* (in Russian). Platina, California: St. Herman of Alaska Brotherhood, 1978. In English as *Elder Joseph of Optina.* Boston, Massachusetts: Holy Transfiguration Monastery, 1984.

Lemeshevsky, Metropolitan Manuel. *Russian Orthodox Bishops: 1893-1965* (in Russian and German). Vol. 5. Erlangen, Germany: Oikonomia, 1987.

The Life of Optina Elder Nektary (in Russian). Kaluga: Optina Monastery of the Entrance of the Theotokos into the Temple, 1996.

The Life and Writings of the Moldavian Elder Paisius Velichkovsky (in Russian). Moscow: Kozelsk Optina Monastery of the Entrance of the Theotokos, 1847. In English as [Metrophanes, Schema-monk]. *Blessed Paisius Velichkovsky: The Life and Ascetic Labors of Our Father, Elder*

Paisius, Archimandrite of the Holy Moldavian Monasteries of Niamets and Sekoul. Optina Version. Vol.1. Platina, California: St. Herman of Alaska Brotherhood, 1976.

The Lives of the Holy Elders of Optina Monastery (in Russian). Jordanville, New York: Holy Trinity Monastery, 1992.

Nikon [Belyaev], Hieromonk. *The Journal of the Last Elder of Optina Monastery* (in Russian). St. Petersburg: Satis, 1994.

Nilus, Sergius. *On the Bank of God's River: Notes of an Orthodox Man* (in Russian). Vol. 1. 2nd Ed. Moscow: Holy Trinity-St. Sergius Lavra, 1916. Reprint: Forestville, California: St. Elias Publications, 1975.

Nilus, Sergius. *On the Bank of God's River: Notes of an Orthodox Man* (in Russian). Vol. 2. San Francisco and Platina, California: Orthodox Christian Books and Icons, 1969.

The Optina Elders (in Russian). London, Canada: Zaria Publishers, 1990.

Polovinkin, Sergius. *Sergei Alexandrovich Nilus: A Biography* (in Russian). Moscow: Valaam Monastery, 1995.

Polovtsev, Archimandrite Juvenal, *Biography of the Abbot of the Kozelsk Optina Monastery of the Entrance, Archimandrite Moses* (in Russian). Moscow: Kozelsk Optina Monastery of the Entrance of the Theotokos, 1882. Reprinted as *Optina Elder Moses: Life and Writings* (in Russian). Platina, California: St. Herman of Alaska Brotherhood, 1976. In English as *Elder Moses of Optina.* Boston, Massachusetts: Holy Transfiguration Monastery, 1996.

Poselyanin, Eugene. *The Optina Hermitage* (in Russian). St. Petersburg, 1902.

Rymarenko, Evgenia G. *Recollections of Optina Elder Hieroschema-monk Nektary.* Spring Valley, New York: New Diveyevo Convent, 1974.

Sederholm, Hieromonk Clement. *Biography of the Superior of the Maloyaroslavits–St. Nicholas Monastery, Abbot Anthony* (in Russian). Moscow: Kozelsk Optina Monastery of the Entrance of the Theotokos, 1870. Reprinted as *Optina Elder Anthony: Life and Writings* (in Russian). Platina, California: St. Herman of Alaska Brotherhood, 1973. In English as *Elder Anthony of Optina.* Platina, California: St. Herman of Alaska Brotherhood, 1994.

Sederholm, Hieromonk Clement. *Biography of Optina Elder Hieromonk Leonid (in Schema Leo)* (in Russian). Moscow: Kozelsk Optina Monastery of the Entrance of the Theotokos, 1876. Reprinted as *Optina Elder Leonid (in Schema Leo): Life and Writings* (in Russian). Platina, California: St. Herman of Alaska Brotherhood, 1976. In English as *Elder Leonid of Optina.* Platina, California: St. Herman of Alaska Brotherhood, 1990.

Struve, N. (Ed.). *Russian Orthodox Hierarchs: Confessors and Martyrs* (in Russian). Paris: YMCA Press, 1986.

Torstensen, Tatiana Vladimirovna. *Recollections of Elder Sebastian of Karaganda* (in Russian). Moscow: Russky Khronograf, 1994.

Articles:

Alexei, Archbishop of Alma-Ata and Semipalatinsk. "Act of Canonization." *Light of Orthodoxy in Kazakhstan,* no. 46-47 (1997), pp. 2-6 (in Russian).

——. "The Translation of the Relics of the Holy Elder, Schema-archimandrite Sebastian in Karaganda." *Light of Orthodoxy in Kazakhstan,* no. 48 (1998), p. 27 (in Russian).

Andrew [Rymarenko], Archbishop. "The Restoration of the Orthodox Way of Life." *The Orthodox Word,* no. 63 (1975), pp. 138-43, 168-71.

"The Definition of Eldership—In Memorium, Ivan M. Kontzevitch, 1965-80." *The Orthodox Word,* no. 95 (1980), pp. 277-8.

Khodakovskaya, O. "Karaganda Elder." *Light of Orthodoxy in Kazakhstan,* no. 33 (1996), pp. 24-25 (in Russian).

Kontzevitch, I. M. "Optina Monastery and its Era." *The Orthodox Word,* no. 117 (1984), pp.156-62.

Koroleva, Vera (ed.). "The Life of Elder Schema-archimandrite Sebastian." *Prostor,* 1997, nos. 1-8 (in Russian).

Herman, Abbot. "Modern Links to Holy Russia: A Silent Giant For Modern America—The Life of Bishop Nektary Kontzevitch, Disciple of Elder Nektary of Optina." *The Orthodox Word,* no. 169 (1993), pp.55-89 and no. 170 (1993), pp.125-43.

Herman, Abbot. "The Optina Elders." *The Orthodox Word,* no. 117 (1984), pp.148-55.

Mikhailov, Valery. "Two New Names in the Constellation." *Kazakhstanskaya Pravda,* October 17, 1997, pp. 4-5 (in Russian).

"Monk-Martyr Vincent of Optina." *The Orthodox Word,* no. 98 (1981), pp.120-21.

"Optina Monastery in the Fate of N. A. Pavlovich." *Troitskoe Slovo,* no. 8 (1991), pp. 6-15 (in Russian).

Pavlovich, Nadezhda Alexandrovna. "Elder Nektary of Optina." *The Orthodox Word,* no. 129 (1986), pp.169-215.

"Recollections of Elder Nektary." *Nadezhda,* no. 15, pp. 93-164 (in Russian).

"Recollections of Sophia Alexandrovna Engelhardt." *Nadezhda,* no.16 (1993), pp. 208-224 (in Russian).

"St. Herman Summer Pilgrimage—Elder Nektary's Anniversary, 1928-1978." *The Orthodox Word,* no. 84 (1979), pp. 5-6.

T. V. (Tatiana Vladimirovna Torstensen). "Elder Sebastian of Karaganda." *Nadezhda,* no. 7, pp. 70-140 (in Russian).

Torstensen, Tatiana Vladimirovna. "Starets Sevastian of Karaganda." *Religion in Communist Lands* (Keston College), vol. 13, no. 2 (1985), pp.221-227.

Torstensen, Tatiana Vladimirovna. "Optina Elder Sebastian: Schema-archimandrite of Karaganda." *The Orthodox Word,* no. 152 (1990), pp. 132-47, 151-52; no. 153 (1990), pp. 235-50; no. 154 (1990), pp. 310-18; no 156 (1991), pp. 46-56; no. 157 (1991), pp. 108-12; no. 158 (1991), pp. 171-75; nos. 160-161 (1991), pp. 321-24.

Manuscripts:

Benjamin [Fedchenkov], Metropolitan. *Material on Hieroschema-monk Nektary.* Typescript, 180 pages (in Russian).

Denezhkin, Archdeacon Basil. *Recollections of the Grace-filled Elder, Schema-archimandrite Sebastian.* Manuscript, 90 pages (in Russian).

Kuzmicheva, Raisa Ivanovna. *Recollections of Batiushka Sebastian.* Manuscript (1996), 46 pages (in Russian).

On the Life of Optina Elder Sebastian. Unsigned manuscript, 21 pages (in Russian).

Torstensen, Tatiana Vladimirovna. *Elder Sebastian of Karaganda.* Typescript, 108 pages. Manuscript, 153 pages (in Russian).

Unsigned, untitled manuscript, 11 pages (in Russian).

Index

ELDER LEONID

OF OPTINA

by Fr. Clement Sederholm

Volume I in the Optina Elders Series:

Elder Leonid of Optina

by Fr. Clement Sederholm

Like a lion, Elder Leonid (†1841) introduced and firmly established in Optina the tradition of eldership as transmitted from St. Paisius Velichkovsky. Possessed with penetrating spiritual discernment, he was at the same time loving and fatherly. He could mystically see into human hearts, knowing when to rebuke, when to exhort, and when to console. Thousands came to him to be healed both in soul and body.

272 pages, paperback, illustrated, $10.00

ISBN 0-938635-50-6

ELDER ANTHONY

OF OPTINA

by Fr. Clement Sederholm

Volume II in the Optina Elders Series:

Elder Anthony of Optina

by Fr. Clement Sederholm

Through a life of terrible hardships and excruciating physical ailments, Elder Anthony (†1865) acquired perfect spiritual freedom through the careful guarding of his soul and the humble acceptance of God's providence. He remained joyful to the end, filled with tender compassion for all who came to him, and with an unconquerable inner peace.

269 pages, paperback, illustrated, $10.00

ISBN 0-938635-51-4

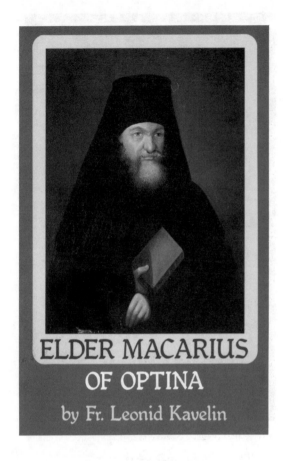

ELDER MACARIUS
OF OPTINA
by Fr. Leonid Kavelin

Volume III in the Optina Elders Series:

Elder Macarius of Optina

by Fr. Leonid Kavelin

A disciple and co-laborer of Elder Leonid, Elder Macarius
(†1860) further established the Optina spiritual tradition by
publishing major Patristic texts. He himself was an embodiment
of Patristic wisdom, an ancient Church Father come forth in
modern times. Meek, gentle, loving and noble, he was imbued
with the power of humility that exorcises evil spirits, chastens the
proud-minded, and strengthens the infirm.

390 pages, paperback, illustrated, $14.00

ISBN 0-938635-58-1

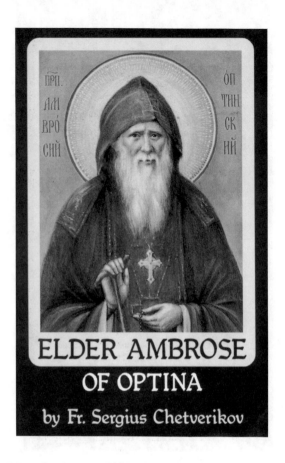

Volume IV in the Optina Elders Series:

Elder Ambrose of Optina

by Fr. Sergius Chetverikov

Considered the pinnacle of eldership in Optina, Elder Ambrose embodied the virtues of all the Elders in the highest degree: humility, purity of mind and heart, overflowing love, and total self-sacrifice for the salvation of others. So great were his gifts that hundreds of people from all over Russia flocked daily to his humble cabin. He was an angel in the flesh, who beheld the mysteries of the future age: the perfect love and silent oneness of immortal spirits.

472 pages, paperback, illustrated, $17.00

ISBN 0-938635-60-3

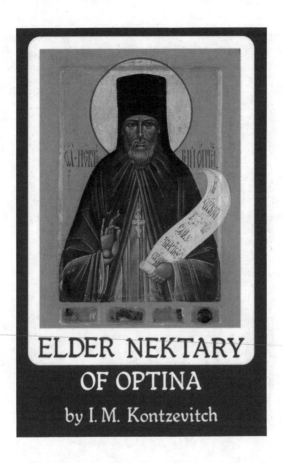

ELDER NEKTARY
OF OPTINA
by I. M. Kontzevitch

Volume V in the Optina Elders Series:

Elder Nektary of Optina

by I. M. Kontzevitch

Elder Nektary, a disciple of Elders Ambrose and Anatole I, was the last elder to function as such at Optina, being exiled from it by the communists when they closed it in 1923. At this time of immeasurable sorrow for Christian believers, God gave Elder Nektary to Russia as both a consoler of souls and a voice of prophecy. Marked by simplicity, childlikeness, spontaneity and creativity, he radiated joy to the thousands of suffering souls who came to him and, through his disciples, passed the Optina heritage on to believers in America.

520 pages, paperback, illustrated, $19.00

ISBN 0-938635-59-X

ST. HERMAN OF ALASKA BROTHERHOOD

For three decades, the St. Herman Brotherhood has been publishing works of traditional spirituality.

Write for our free 96-page catalogue, featuring sixty titles of published and forthcoming books and magazines.

St. Herman Press
10 Beegum Gorge Road
P. O. Box 70
Platina, CA 96076